W9-AMP-243

REFERENCE
DOES NOT CIRCULATE

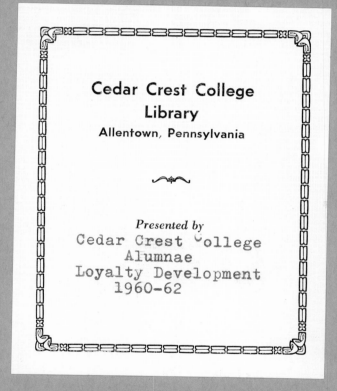

Cedar Crest College
Library
Allentown, Pennsylvania

Presented by
Cedar Crest College
Alumnae
Loyalty Development
1960-62

THE CONCISE ENCYCLOPEDIA OF MODERN DRAMA

TRANSLATED BY GEORGE WELLWARTH   **EDITED BY HENRY POPKIN**

HORIZON PRESS NEW YORK

THE
CONCISE
ENCYCLOPEDIA
OF
MODERN
DRAMA

FOREWORD BY ERIC BENTLEY

by SIEGFRIED MELCHINGER

643083

© 1964 by Horizon Press

Library of Congress Catalog Card Number: 64-8297

Manufactured in the United States of America

CONTENTS

ILLUSTRATIONS

ACKNOWLEDGMENTS

Sources: American National Theater and Academy, Culver Pictures, Grove Press, Alfred A. Knopf, Inc., Museum of the City of New York, Museum of Modern Art, New York Public Library, Theatre Arts Books.

Photographers: Zinn Arthur (136), Richard Avedon (181), Jerry Bauer (177, 180), Cecil Beaton (36), John Bennewitz (133), Bernand (37, 180), Brassai—Rapho-Guillomette (139), Henri Cartier-Bresson (96), Arthur Cantor (182), Culver Pictures (38, 41, 45), Jerry Dantzic (132), Ellen Darby—Graphic House (89, 130, 140), J. W. Denbenham (89), Eberstadt (185), John Seymour Erwin (137, 138), Franklin Photos (129), Fred Fehl (141), French Press and Information Service (92), Henry Grossman (40, 187), Squire Haskins (133), B. Herbold (144), Alix Jeffry (191), Karger Pix (71, 137), Angus McBean (89), Photo Pic (177), Ledino Pozzetti (48), Ed Rooney (42), Peter Rossiter (38), Sam Siegel (191), Talbot (144), Vandamm Studio (35, 39, 45, 48, 81, 82, 85, 86, 90, 91, 138, 140), John Vickers (131), White Studio (34), Wide World Photos (132), Ruth Wilhelmi (82, 143), Avery Willard (45, 47), Van Williams (39, 138).

DRAMA FROM IBSEN TO BECKETT

by Eric Bentley

Perspective I: Following the week to week theater news, one gets the impression that, so far as dramatic art is concerned, nothing of real note is happening or ever will. Perspective II: Looking back upon fifth-century Athens, Elizabethan England, the Spain and France of the "great" seventeenth century, one reaches the conclusion that *we* do not live in one of the supremely great periods of drama.

Both these perspectives are unfair to our playwrights, since real dramatic history cannot proceed at the pace of journalism, nor can any but a few centuries yield their Sophocleses, their Shakespeares, and Molières. The record of the modern drama is better than average and better than honorable. That "criticism of life" which Matthew Arnold put down as the function of all poetry has been conducted by many dramatic "poets" with more than competence and more than brilliance.

Ernst Robert Curtius has written that "the drama is the only form which can show human existence in its relation to the universe." I cannot see any truth in this remark, but I find significance in the fact that a great scholar could make it and in the enthusiasm of the moment forget so many of the great poets and novelists. The drama, we can certainly believe, has been pre-eminently the form in which human existence has been shown in its relation to the universe; in which, indeed, all the grandest "relations" of human life have been mirrored, especially in their ultimate significance, especially, one could put it, in terms of final principle. That is why the phrase Drama of Ideas should mean so infinitely more than it usually does: big ideas, urgent ideas, ideas "of life and death" have been the stuff of drama since Aeschylus, the first dramatist. Aeschylus handled ideas of the order of Revenge and Justice; so did Shakespeare. And although many modern dramatists have tended to be known for smaller ideas—ideas of limited application and duration—some of them, and those the best, have deserved a better fate. Ibsen had one master idea, and it was not an idea about women's suffrage or hereditary disease, it was the idea of integrity or healthy conscience. He had observed that the age of more and more individualism was an age of less and less individuality.

The drama shows human existence in its relation to an age. At its best it provides, not an account of fads and fashions, or even programs and policies, but an interpretation of an epoch, of a culture, of what Brecht calls a mode of "living together." Ibsen's image of the middle-class family, shut in among the antimacassars and the guilt, is in itself enough to stamp him a major playwright: for it was the image, in dramatic form, of his era. After Ibsen, the walls of the family living-room come down. Thornton Wilder even has them do so literally—to make the point. It is a double point, too, for, with the walls of that drawing-room and that civilization, the walls of the box-set in the theatre also came down. Ibsenic man was surrounded; his drama is claustrophobic; he is asphyxiated. Twentieth-century man is exposed, stripped; his drama is agoraphobic; he is lost.

This is felt first in Strindberg, then, to a lesser degree, in the Expressionists. To pass from Ibsen's *Ghosts* to Strindberg's *Ghost Sonata* is both literally and figuratively to pass from the nineteenth to the twentieth century. The Ibsenite walls have dissolved. Life is not only dream: it is phantasmagoric mist. Ibsen's people fail, but by standards by which failure can be measured. The Stranger in Strindberg's *To Damascus* seems, in comparison, merely disoriented. He has yet to find the standards by which he could even fail.

Wylie Sypher has written profoundly of "the loss of self" in modern literature. It was a progressive loss, and the stages can be marked in successive dramatists. After Strindberg, Pirandello. Strindberg's Stranger was at least searching. The Father in *Six Characters in Search of an Author* is only lamenting an absence, and surely the unfound Author is, among other things, God—who used to be called the Author, incidentally, in that distinctly Pirandellian dramatist, Calderón.

Waiting for God. This phrase, or something very close to it, has been found, not only in the title of Samuel Beckett's play but also in the work of Martin Heidegger and Simone Weil. After Pirandello, Samuel Beckett, who may be said to show human existence in its relation to the universe, and in a new sense: that it no longer has anything else to be related to. But this is to exaggerate. An intra-human relation there perforce must be, even in a Beckett play. The point is that it is unbelievably attenuated, and I use the word unbelievably on purpose: our grandparents would not have believed in it. Since self is not made up of self, but of response to other things, the "loss of self" means, paradoxically but literally, the loss of the non-self, of culture, of the world: *there is nothing left but God, and we do not believe He exists.*

André Malraux has said that the nineteenth century banished all the gods, and that the twentieth has the task of bringing them back again. Or, one might optimistically add, of bringing back other gods. Or even of discovering that the gods are within us and so had never really gone away. For perhaps the "banishment of the gods" and the "loss of self" are one and the same thing, and what we should be deploring is the decline, not of theology, but of imagination and personality.

There is wide agreement that the inner life is not going to be renewed without a renewal of the outer life, and that the individual will not be rediscovered and remade without a renewal of the non-individual matrix, the collectivity. In other words, modern persons of vision, one after another, join Churches and/or take up some form of Socialism. Hence there is nothing more ridiculous than to lavish ridicule (or ridicule only) upon the various Returns to Religion or Calls to Social Action. What would be truly appalling is the absence of such things, for it would indicate that conscience and hope were dead among those whose professional business it is to keep them alive.

The Return to Religion and the Call to Socialism are the rallying cries of modern dramatists from Shaw to Brecht, from Claudel to Adamov, from Strindberg to Arthur Miller. That is what we would expect; it is also what we ought to want. And yet, from Ibsen to Beckett, these two missions have been subordinate to a third one that is both more simple and more complex. This is the mission of courage, the ultimate virtue, and truth, the ultimate value.

There has been a great song and dance about the failure of modern drama—and indeed modern literature—to portray heroes. The decline of tragedy is a theme that every student nowadays can at once connect with the decline of aristocracy and the rise of the little man. In all the sermonizing on this subject, the positive side of modern writing gets overlooked. Unheroic literature, as heralded by works like Dostoevsky's *Notes from the Underground* and Tolstoy's *The Death of Ivan Ilyitch*, has a candor, a passion for honesty, all its own—as if *homo sapiens* had suddenly decided to "come clean." What a pity people decided to assume nothing more was involved in the truth-seeking of the modern movement than a little muck-raking! The modern honesty is the positive side of all the negative features which made headlines from syphilis in Ibsen to scurrility in Henry Miller. And it is only certain minor authors whose vision came out miniature and monochrome, muted and pianissimo. The vision of the modern masters is a harsh vision of horror: Dante's Inferno transposed to Times Square and Piccadilly.

Now, since what poets long for is bound to seem insubstantial beside that which they see, this vision of horror is stronger and more convincing than all the pleas for Religion or Community. That much is very clear from the work of writers who *have* pleaded for Religion or Community. Shaw is not at his best in *Back to Methuselah,* nor Brecht in *The Mother.* On the other hand, the "unemotional" Shaw writes movingly when his priest (in *John Bull's Other Island*) gives the classic Shavian presentation of the Inferno theme, and when Brecht writes this theme out at full length in *Mahagonny* he achieves one of the great dramatic images of this century. . . .

Well, these are nothing more than a few random thoughts and quick generalizations produced by looking back at a book I have consulted many times since it came out in German. This book presents itself as an encyclopedia: a book in which you can find when A was born and B died and C "flourished." Its main usefulness, parallel to that of dictionary and telephone directory, will rightly be of this kind. But we at once notice, with surprise and pleasure, that Siegfried Melchinger has attempted more. He is rash enough to bring thought to the thoughtless world of theater and theater writing. This means we shall all wish, at one point or another, to take issue with him. One can even take issue, and I think in the end one should, with the general scheme of thought upon which the book is hung. But only "in the end." To begin with, one must rejoice that a drama encyclopedia is hung on a scheme of thought at all, and concede that any scheme one might oneself propose would also be questionable. All our categories, as Bernard Berenson put it, are but a compromise with chaos. If there are readers today who find it odd that theory and opinion should enter into an encyclopedia, let them point to an encyclopedia of any scope into which theory and opinion have not entered. No: the choice is between good and bad theory and opinion. And there is a great tradition going back to Diderot that encyclopedias should be rich in lore (authentic and spurious), controversial, unorthodox, ingenious, ultra-modern, and occasionally wrong-headed.

AUTHOR'S PREFACE

The author's purpose in this book has been to provide friends of the theater with some sort of introduction to the confusing scene of the contemporary drama. Among the friends of the theater, I, of course, include professional people—actors, directors, producers. These may, perhaps, have a clearer view than others, but they may find it useful to know what a critic has to say about a particular playwright or play.

Nothing could be further from the author's intention than to try to force an opinion of his own on someone else. He has attempted to be as objective as possible, but the analysis of contemporary events, events which remain incomplete, often reaches the limits of established fact. A guide that invariably leads in the right direction is inconceivable. Nonetheless, anyone who reads this book will get a perspective on the modern drama which he will be able to compare with his own experiences and theories: perspectives can be clarified only by comparison.

In planning the second part of the book the author has put himself in the position of the theater-goer who wishes to know the most important facts about the authors whose plays he sees. The alphabetical list of modern playwrights has been compiled for this purpose. The author is particularly indebted to the artistic director of the Deutsches Theater in Göttingen, Hans-Geert Falkenberg, for checking the facts and dates in this section. Difficulties occur even in the purely statistical listing of authors, sometimes for quite obvious reasons (for instance, in the case of works by Communist authors), sometimes for entirely unexpected reasons, such as the personal peculiarities of certain writers. Thus it has at times been possible to attain only an approximate accuracy.

The choice of the names does not necessarily imply judgment of the author's worth—the compiler has not expressly chosen those who seem to him to be true dramatists, nor has he mentioned only those plays which seem to him to be particularly important. The basis of choice has been the prominence of the authors and the plays in the repertory of the world theater. Some readers may miss certain names which seem important to them. It is true that a certain amount of personal preference had to influence selection of the younger writers, but in general only those writers who have achieved some success with at least two plays are included.

The most important authors appear also in the section entitled "Documents on the Theory of the Contemporary Theater," with a selection of important passages from pertinent publications. These have not been chosen to disseminate the compiler's personal prejudices, even though the basis of his own theories may be found in them.

The theatergoer may have difficulty in understanding certain frequently used expressions—in program notes, critical articles and essays, and also in the first section of this book. Indeed, it must be admitted that even theater people often do not agree about the exact meanings of certain of these expressions. The Glossary is designed to provide the reader with explanations of such terms as "Epic theater" or "Topical play." Expressions left undefined in the first section in order not to impede the flow of the exposition are interpreted here.

The "Chronology of First Performances" lists events which have had international significance in theatrical history since 1900. Consequently certain premières have been included which were not the actual first performances but which stimulated subsequent international success.

Finally, the compiler would like to say a word in explanation of the point of view which the reader will find in this book. He does not consider drama a subdivision of literature, but rather a part of the living theater. His method is that of the critic who goes to see a play prepared for all possible eventualities, for all surprises. He does not count himself one of those who put ideological, moralistic or other puritanical principles above the play itself and who cover their sight with a vizor of predetermined and unchangeable views because they are of the opinion that things must be only thus and so, in accordance with their prejudices.

The basis of the author's point of view is to be found in Hofmannsthal's remark that the more "incomplete" a drama is, the greater it is. In other words, it is great in direct proportion to the degree in which it relies upon the stage and upon its effect on the public to get its truth across. It is only by this standard that we can gauge the dramatist's contact with the public for which he writes and with the times in which he lives. Communication has always been the central problem of the theater— not communication of ideas or ideologies, but communication between men.

PREFACE TO THE THIRD EDITION

Several sections of the third edition (in the original German) have been entirely revised. When the subject changes the explanation must change with it; and in the two years since the appearance of the first edition the world theater has not been standing still. New authors, new plays, and new theories as well, had to be examined. The author is satisfied that the theses put forward in the first chapter have not required any revision. Nevertheless, the first chapter has been revised, expanded, and to some extent re-written. The "Documents" now include Shaw, the omission of whose remarks was rightly objected to in view of the book's title. The Glossary needed relatively little revision. On the other hand, the list of authors has not only been augmented by many names, but has also been re-examined, revised, and expanded sentence by sentence. The difficulties of documenting contemporary facts can only be fully understood by one who has tried to do the same. The present material is the result of a labor of Sisyphus, for the compiler is aware that much has been left undone despite the fact that the work has been enormously expanded since the second edition, which had itself been much enlarged. The compiler is thankful for all help that he has received. For the third edition particular attention has been paid to the Scandinavian, Dutch-Flemish, Slavic, and Spanish dramatists. Special acknowledgment is due to Dr. Bertil Nydahl, B. Stroman, P. Jaarsma, Dr. Danuta Zmij, Oswald Kostrba-Skalicky, Siegmund von Schremovitz, Dr. Ilse Müller-Sontheimer, and Dr. Anton Dieterich. No less thanks go to the many readers who have sent in letters of advice.

INTRODUCTION
TO THE
MODERN DRAMA

The scene is confusing. It seems impossible to discover any order in this chaos. Furthermore, we no longer have any standards. The old axioms have become questionable. In the attempt to obtain an overall picture, the critic runs into few problems as puzzling as the public.

Nonetheless, quality persists, a paradox of which there are many examples. But the things which achieve acclaim are often so different from each other that one can only clutch one's head in despair and ask how all this can possibly take place simultaneously. For, after all, in any particular period in the history of the theatre there have always been labels, all or almost all of them associated with some movement. Realism, Naturalism, Symbolism, Expressionism—these have their place in the history of literature, each neatly placed in its niche. Nowadays, however, there is no talk of labels, and it seems utterly impossible to define anything like a movement.

CLASSIFICATION BY GENERATIONS

Let us make the attempt first with the all-inclusive classification more or less commonly made in all ages: the old generation vs. the young generation. After all, the father-son conflict is as old as mankind itself. But it soon becomes clear that not even that can get us anywhere. Nevertheless, the attempt is instructive. Let us therefore make a survey of the younger generation of successful writers —those who are today roughly between thirty and fifty-five years old.

In Paris, for example, we have Anouilh,

born in 1910, and Ionesco, born in 1912. Two more contrasting figures could hardly be imagined. On the one hand the ironic sceptic using conservative forms for his plays of conflict between appearance and reality; on the other, the proponent of the "anti-play," which impales the banality of the real and transforms it into grotesque absurdity. Here the virtuoso of conversational dialogue, there the destroyer of speech as a means of communication who would like nothing better than to conclude with babble.

What is the situation in London? Here we have the amazing stage success—particularly surprising in England—of two serious writers. Dylan Thomas (1914-1954) was a genius with the visions of Hölderlin and a poet with a diction whose imaginative metaphors were more reminiscent of the Baroque period than of the present. *Under Milk Wood,* a play for voices actually written for the radio, was shown on all the leading stages of the world after its success in London and Edinburgh and was as thoughtfully received by the critics as it was enthusiastically accepted by the public. The other writer is John Osborne, born in 1929, the "angry young man," as he has been called since he threw a bomb into the London entertainment world with his *Look Back in Anger.* An individualistic revolutionary, a moralist of the Tennessee Williams type, and as good a craftsman as Anouilh (he is himself an actor), he is, even if only his language is considered, poles apart from Dylan Thomas.

Let us take a look at America. Two world famous authors: Tennessee Williams, born in 1914, and Arthur Miller, born in 1915. In Williams' *The Glass Menagerie* and Miller's *Death of a Salesman* one can observe some common characteristics but such later plays as *A Streetcar Named Desire* and *The Crucible,* resemble each other at most only in the ruthlessness with which they present unpleasant truths. Today Williams and Miller follow widely divergent paths. Williams continues in the path of sexual-pathological revelations, while Miller proclaims a new social drama based on the form of ancient Greek tragedy.

What is the situation in the German-speaking drama? We have the Swiss Dürrenmatt, born in 1921, a capricious and self-willed personality who has created a personal style of his own: a mixture of the mysterious, the grotesque, the learned, and the unexpected. Does he have any forerunners? Or any followers? Hardly. The only other member of his generation who can lay any claim to world-wide recognition is Fritz Hochwälder, whose *The Holy Experiment* is written in a conservative style. There is little that is similar here. Differences are foremost. What else could one expect in a divided land? Zuckmayer has become an American, Brecht lies buried in East Berlin. Hubalek, one of the young authors of the post World War II generation, has made the switch from East to West, while his almost exact contemporary, Peter Hacks, has gone the opposite way. How supreme political considerations, how secondary the act of creation, must have been in the minds of these two men!

And now let us place the twenty-to-fifty-five-year-old dramatists together without regard to differences of language as they appear on the stage of today: Anouilh and Dürrenmatt, Williams and Dylan Thomas, Ionesco and Miller, Osborne and Hochwälder: there is no Movement here. Let us go back to the previous generation for a moment —to those in their fifties and sixties. Montherlant and Zuckmayer (born 1896), Thornton Wilder (born 1897), Brecht (born 1898), Lorca (born 1899), Sartre (born 1905), Samuel Beckett (born 1906), Christopher Fry (born 1907). The picture only becomes more confusing. So many names, so many styles. *Queen After Death* and *The Captain from Köpenick, Our Town* and *The Caucasian Chalk Circle, Blood Wedding* and *Dirty Hands, Waiting for Godot* and *The Dark Is Light Enough*. Each title opens up a different world, each world poles apart from the next.

WEIGHING THE RESULTS OF THE LAST REVOLUTION

And yet within the time-span of the present generation we have had an avant-garde movement and a literary revolution. They existed in many countries, and in many places they conquered the stage. Mostly they were associated with revolutionary directors—with Meyerhold, Taïrov, and Vachtangov in Russia, in Paris with Copeau, Dullin and Artaud. In Italy the theatre of Pirandello grew out of the Futurism of Marinetti and Ungaretti. In America O'Neill and others upset the conventional methods of stage production with their daring experiments. From Scandinavia Strindberg's influence spread over the whole world. Yet the conflict between old and new is nowhere as basic and explosive as in Germany. If we can speak at all of a general and international revolution in all the arts, with the year 1910 as its point of origin, we find that only in German literature did this revolution produce a unified movement. This movement, Expressionism, is now generally considered to have been an essentially German phenomenon.

In the legendary twenties sensations rained from the heaven of the theater with such plays as Fritz von Unruh's *Ein Geschlecht* and *Platz,* Georg Kaiser's *Gas,* Toller's *Transfiguration,* Hasenclever's *Der Sohn,* Werfel's *Spiegelmensch,* Sternheim's *Bürger Schippel,* Goering's *Seeschlacht.* Where have they all gone? Where can we find today one single play from that moving and turbulent time of the revolutionary theatre? Sensation and scandal, yes—but practically nothing that has survived the sensation and the scandal.

Some people are filled with regret for those days. "There was still some life in the theater back in those days," they say. The impulse toward contradiction was matched by the impulse toward enthusiasm. The public actually took part in the battles created for them by the revolutionary authors, followed by the critics with their banners and slogans. Today, whatever is shown on the stage is received with the same more or less lukewarm applause. *Mother Courage, A Streetcar Named Desire,* and *The Teahouse of the August Moon* are applauded on alternate evenings.

We shall not concern ourselves here with the public, which of course, has changed, just as the authors and the critics have changed. But we can perhaps find a starting point for our examination of the change that has taken place in the authors if we compare our present writers with the Expressionists.

Such a comparison must start with an examination of conditions in Germany. In no other country did the literary revolution of 1910 set tradition aside so forcibly. Germans have always had a predilection for throwing out the baby with the bathwater. In this way Germany progressed from Rococo to *Sturm und Drang,* from the Classic to the Romantic, from the Romantic to Realism and Naturalism. The cry was always *"tabula rasa!"* Elsewhere, of course, it was "Burn the Louvre!" —but only the Germans tried to put it into practice. And so, unlike the French and English, the Germans were never able to develop a national style as a result of their literary upheavals. The German theater's love of extremes may, however, supply us with points of view from which to examine the remarkable lack of direction displayed by the modern drama. In this hope let us proceed to our comparison.

We have said that today there are neither slogans nor movements. Certain premières of the twenties were illuminated by the blaze of flaming slogans. The forces both of Pro and Con concentrated their attention on these. One cheered plays not because they were good, but because one agreed with their slogans.

I can still see the white-haired Gerhart Hauptmann standing on the stage of the Munich Schauspielhaus while the audience whistled and hooted at him after the opening of *Dorothea Angermann* in 1926. He was already sixty-three years old then. I remember him smiling indulgently, and I have to admit I was one of the hooters. We were simply opposed to the play. Why? Because *Dorothea Angermann* was a bad play? Not at all. Because it was a naturalistic play. We saw in it a step backwards, a step toward reaction. We were for what was young and new, and we considered anything old to be finished, no matter how many times overlaid with the glitter of a Nobel Prize. We saw ourselves at the crest of a movement which was constantly driving the theatre to greater progress.

Decades have passed. The theater has gone on and on, but it has hardly advanced. *Dorothea Angermann* has proved surprisingly durable. It was revived and will be revived again because it is a good play. But the plays of the banner-bearers and the catchword-coiners are no longer performed: they wrote bad plays.

A POINT OF DEPARTURE: THE END OF THE SLOGANS

Is, then, one of the attributes of a good play that it does not follow a slogan? The question answers itself. Hauptmann himself followed a single slogan in his youth, and several of his plays of that period are still performed. Ibsen followed a slogan, and his plays are to be found in the repertoires of theaters all over the world. And of course Schiller, too, had his slogan. So did Victor Hugo. So did Büchner. That has nothing to do with it. Our modern writers do not write better plays because they lack slogans. We can blame slogans for the failure of Expressionism, but not slogans as such—only the particular slogans of

Expressionism. This would perhaps be a point of departure: the first opportunity to examine the complicated and confused state of the modern drama with a precisely formulated question. The question would have to be phrased somewhat like this: Why were the plays written in accordance with the slogans of Expressionism so ephemeral? And why were the slogans which Ibsen and Hauptmann followed less fatal to the durability of their plays?

The slogans of Expressionism were "Theater as Pulpit," "Theater as Forum," "Theater as Platform." The style was proclamatory. Whatever the essence of the poet's thought was—whether it was rebellion, anger, love of mankind, hate, prophecy, or blessing—it had to be brought to life on the stage as directly as possible, that is, expressionistically. One of the slogans mentioned, was "Burn the Louvre!" In other words, "Down with models and tradition!" "To the devil with the classics!" There are no problems of form anymore: plays write themselves by being hurled out. The talk was all of striving upwards and clenching the fist. A play, they said, has to be like a scream.

The slogans of the preceding period, which are classified in the history of literature under the inexact labels of Naturalism and Impressionism, were "A play must be like reality, like nature, like life!" "Life"—that was the great watchword. Zola proclaimed, "Everything that is alive is good and true and beautiful; everything that no longer lives must be cut off, no matter how noble and sublime it may seem." We can trace the influence of Nietzsche and of the biology of the Haeckel school in that remark, and even a little Marx (but really remarkably little of the latter). One of the leaders of the "modern" revolution of those days, Hermann Bahr, wrote in the nineties, "You know, we must have a mixture of brutality and cunning—wild and sudden . . ." Hofmannsthal, who, it is often overlooked, belonged to the movement also, and was as sensible of belonging to it as Schnitzler, Maeterlinck, and d'Annunzio, called this a "mixture of the animal-soul and the Hamlet-soul."

These revolutionaries, like the Expressionists later, protested specifically against the classics. Zola made it quite clear: the Good, the True, and the Beautiful—those were the watchwords of the idealism against which they were fighting. If, however, everything that lives is good and true and beautiful because it lives, then the classics were already destroyed. One must keep this viewpoint in mind in order to understand what Alfred Kerr, one of the prominent critics of his day, wrote about *Hamlet* in 1909:

> Let us be frank: the work has nothing to say to us today. Not only because Hamlet dies as a result of a mix-up of rapiers and the queen dies as a result of a mix-up of drinking glasses, but also because Hamlet's soliloquies nowadays border on the obvious. They have nothing to say about the questions which concern us today. We must recognize that it would be utterly idiotic for us to take ourselves back out of the problems of the present, out of this most familiar of all periods in history. Whoever understands the world of today is not greater than Shakespeare; but he is more advanced. O great but superannuated William!

We laugh at such sentiments. In Kerr's Germany the "most familiar of all periods in history" ended in the biggest mess ever known in human history, and the "fatherland" is still trying to rid itself of its results. Shakespeare, like the Louvre, has outlasted it. And there is no longer any real belief in progress *per se,* the belief on which the slogans both of Naturalism and Expressionism were based. That which is new, that which is to come, that which is modern *now*—that was the yardstick by which everything was measured. In contrast, one of the clearest characteristics of the present age is that *the New, as such, plays a far less important role in our thinking than it did in the twenties or the nineties.* Not only do we not possess any slogans, which were so important to the belief in progress—we actually mistrust slogans. For we have reason enough to be sceptical of anything that concerns the future.

BEYOND SLOGANS: FORM

At the same time that we have become more reserved, more sceptical, more careful, and more modest, we have also become more generous and broad-minded in our attitude to tradition. The battles that have been fought over slogans in the last century and a half! In Goethe's day one had to decide either for Shakespeare or for the Greeks—we shake our heads and ask, "Why not for both?" We are even prepared to place Chekhov and Hauptmann beside them. And we hold this same attitude toward contemporary authors: who would dream nowadays of refusing to consider Brecht merely because one is for Lorca, or *vice versa?* Such considerations are mere trifles in view of the obvious fact that all of these—Shakespeare and the Greeks, Schiller and Ibsen, presumably Brecht and Lorca as well—possess some quality which enabled them to write good plays.

From all this we can form one thesis which practically transforms our point of departure into a permanent position: there must be something in Shakespeare, in the Greeks, in Schiller, in Ibsen, in Lorca and in Brecht which is common to all and which rises above slogans and considerations of time; and it is there, in that something, that we must seek the power which enables their works to endure. And the reason that the Expressionists came to grief and that among the Naturalists those who paid the greatest attention to slogans did not survive must be either that they did not possess this power or that they possessed it but ruined it by adhering to their slogans. This power is opposed to the slogans to which it is subjected, in a manner of which the author is often unaware. It becomes greater than the slogans, either transforming them or destroying them.

Of course, one might say, this power is talent, it is genius. But I do not think it is that obvious. Even the failures among the Expressionists undoubtedly had talent. Some of them proved that very simply by writing plays of lasting value once they had gotten rid of their slogans. Closer examination reveals that dramatic talent is not found in explosive outbursts of mystical trances, but in a mysterious union between the writer, who is often hardly aware of it, and tradition. This union is found in form; or perhaps it would be better to say *in forms,* for a great number of variations, all of which we recognize as equally valid, have developed from the one specific form which we accept as common to the theater in general—unless, of course, like Zola or Kerr or the Expressionists, we insist on the "latest" slogans.

The heart of the matter is that both the theater of the past and the theater of the present have shown us that there are many ways in which a play may be written, but that this number is limited by the fact that there is only *one* basic form for the theater, one specific, basic form through which the theater is distinguished not only from the novel and the painting but also from the film and the circus. This form I shall call the "elementary" form, which may serve to indicate that I consider it no less primary and no less real than content. The old form-content conception becomes empty and inadequate as soon as one attempts to analyze the creative work in accordance with this distinction. Form is primary, and what we group under the heading "Content" (plot, idea, emotion) is to a great measure dependent upon formal processes.

Nonetheless, the distinction between form and content can be used *as a method* to the degree that we seize upon one or the other as a point from which to launch our investigation. We must only keep in mind the fact that everything we discover this way is provisional, and subject to alteration. If, then, we deal here with the problem of form in all its aspects, neither that approach, nor the insights inevitably resulting from the simultaneous examination of content, can prevent us from later beginning the investigation all over again using an entirely different method and starting point.

THE DECLINE OF ELEMENTARY FORM

During the last two centuries the elementary theatrical form has been decaying progressively, above all in the German-speaking theater. This happened as a result of the constantly greater and greater ascendancy of slogans. Tradition, which had handed down the idea of elementary form with its variations from generation to generation, grew ever weaker.

At the turn of the century there was a fairly rigidly prescribed method of writing plays. Without doubt this was *one* of the basic methods of writing plays. But this particular method had been raised to the status of an axiom. As a model it had become lifeless and conventionalized; it came to have an absurdly limiting effect on the imitative, threadbare plays written in accordance with it. This model (the analogue of the equilateral triangle, the act-divided play) became the conventional, orthodox form of the Illusionistic theater, a form based on the axiom that audience and stage must be separated from each other so that the action can become a picture-framed, self-contained reality. There can be no question that the Illusionistic theater had to have a destructive effect on the form which helped to bring it into being. The slate *had* to be wiped clean so that *other basic methods* of writing plays could become apparent.

At this point we can connect the results of our arrangement of German theatrical periods with theatrical development on an international scale. Until around 1910 theater men all over the world had held it right and proper to make use of only a relatively small part of the theatrical keyboard. The whole keyboard with all its scales and combinations of scales could become free once again only when these oppressive restrictions had been eliminated. In the German theater Expressionism ran amok in protest against the conventional theatrical form; and this revolt finally resulted in the self-destruction of the slogans. Form as such could come back with challenging strength as a basic necessity only when everything else had been razed to the ground. And yet as early as 1910 the problem of form itself was posed anew in theaters all over the world. Everywhere this question was forcefully asked: How can we create something like a non-subjective form in the presentation of a transformed world?

THE COMPETITION OF THE MACHINES

Form as such. Elementary form returning to take the place of the conventional form. The instant in which the breakup of the latter had to occur was dramatically forced forward from an entirely unexpected source. Just about the time, around 1910, that the great upheavals were taking place in the arts, the film started its mighty triumphal march. Soon radio joined it as well, and finally television. Many people thought that the end of the theater had come. They thought that the Technical Age would require the replacement of the age-old plays by various productions—or, rather, reproductions—of the machines. These prophecies have turned out to be wrong. More people go to the theater today than ever before. The theater, however, was obliged to cope with competition. It became increasingly necessary for the theater to rediscover elementary form, which became the prerequisite for the successful revival of the institution. New insights had to be achieved. If the theater wanted to go on living it had to concentrate its attention on those of its characteristics which distinguished it from film, radio, and television and which constituted and possibly might continue to constitute its superiority to the machines.

It is clear that the sphere of the stage had to be marked out anew, and a further reason for doubting the conventional dramatic form appeared. Was it not the peep-show stage of the Illusionistic theater that most closely resembled the machines with their windows and screens? It was recognized that the picture-frame stage was a relatively new form in the history of theatrical construction. Great eras of the drama had taken place in entirely different surroundings. Surely it was possible to bring back those conditions—the orchestra of the antique theater, the projecting stage of the Spaniards and the Elizabethans, the flower way of the Far East.

The essence of the stage is, indeed, *to build the platform for play*. "Play" here means that whatever takes place on the platform *does not pretend to be reality*. In this sense the axiom on which the Illusionistic theater was based was actually a demand that one believe in a lie. But why lie? Does anyone really believe that an actor is dead when he collapses from a dagger-thrust on the stage? Here, too, this consideration was forced on the theater by the films. The illusion of death can be given with distinctly greater realism on the screen, where a blood-covered body can be made to look so much like a real corpse that the two can hardly be told apart. But in the theater the truth of the age-old maxim that deception is neither desirable nor necessary suddenly became evident. Great realms of the imagination, long sealed, were opened up again. The public's ability to suspend disbelief was re-awakened by new devices. The decrease in the methods of illusion—in comparison with those of the camera—was balanced by the increase in the methods of fantasy, which were not so easily at the disposal of the camera.

In addition, the theater had a very basic advantage: the directness of contact between actor and public. The laughter of the public cannot reach the film comedian. The television star can never perceive the tears of his audience. We hear voices from the radio, but they are without echo and without modulation. The decisive moment for a work of art is the moment of contact—of contact with those for whom it was created. The final object of all art is communication. Even the esoteric poem, as Arnold Gehlen pointed out, contains words used by other people; even the esoteric novel is not written to be burnt. Nowhere is the moment of communication so actual and spontaneous as in the theater. In the art of the stage the moment of contact coincides with the moment of creation. A symphony or a picture is created in advance, but whenever an actor of quality dies the death of Lear it is always happening for the first and only time. Nothing speaks more for the immortality of the theater than this characteristic—this present moment which is more than any actuality.

CONSIDERATION OF THE ESSENCE OF THE THEATER

We have cleared up in a general way the essence of the basic differences between the productions of the theater and the productions of the machines. On the one hand, one had to rely on mechanical reproduction; on the other, one had the age-old and indestructible possibility of spontaneous presentation. Presentation is not only reproduction; it is at the same time expression and interpretation. It is the same as that which impelled Stone-Age cave-dwellers as they carved their walls. The anthropologist Gehlen, whom I have already cited, has called it "the human wish for stability" and the "attempt of a world which could not be represented by any other means to represent itself." In fact we recognize in this uprooting of time, in this transformation of the fleeting moment into an entity which has a beginning and an end and can be repeated, in this breaking through ordinary, everyday, passing reality to a different, momentarily stronger and truer, created *Contra-reality,* the basic impulse which underlies all drama. The works of the theater are created in opposition to time, which has neither beginning nor end, nor any structure which spans and orders and intensifies the minutes between beginning and end.

That is what is meant when elementary form is spoken of here. It is this form which transforms the material of reality into "appearance," i.e., into perspective so that everything can be crystalized into a picture which differs from reality in that it endures.

Today, the theater has been brought back to its proper time and place; to that festive island where people assemble of an evening in order to play and be played to. There they can see what they have seen for thousands of years wherever performances take place: transforma-

An Enemy of the People, by Henrik Ibsen. Florence Eldridge, Fredric March. 1950, New York

Rosmersholm, by Henrik Ibsen. Leona Roberts, Eva Le Gallienne. 1935, New York

The Master Builder, by Henrik Ibsen. Joan Tetzel, Oscar Homolka. 1953, New York

A Doll's House, by Henrik Ibsen. Sam Jaffe, Ruth Gordon. 1938, New York

The Sea Gull, by Anton Chekhov. Uta Hagen, Sydney Greenstreet, Lynn Fontanne. 1938, New York

The Sea Gull, by Anton Chekhov. Judith Evelyn, Sam Jaffe. 1954, New York

The Cherry Orchard, by Anton Chekhov. Athene Seyler, Charles Laughton. 1933, London

The Cherry Orchard, by Anton Chekhov. Eve Le Gallienne, Sayre Crawley, Alla Nazimova. 1928, New York

Liliom, by Ferenc Molnar. Burgess Meredith, Joan Tetzel, Ingrid Bergman. 1940, New York

Miss Julie, by August Strindberg. Viveca Lindfors, Morgan Sterne. 1963, Westport, Conn.

Left: *Lady Windermere's Fan,* by Oscar Wilde. Sets and costumes by Cecil Beaton. 1946, New York

Ubu Roi, by Alfred Jarry. Rosy Varte, Georges Wilson. 1958, Paris

Pygmalion, by George Bernard Shaw. Raymond
Massey, Gertrude Lawrence. 1946, New York

Major Barbara, by George Bernard Shaw. Eliot Cabot,
Percy Waram, Winifred Lenihan. 1928, New York

Saint Joan, by George Bernard Shaw.
Foreground: Ian Keith, Siobhan Mc-
Kenna, Dick Moore. 1956, New York

Heartbreak House, by George Bernard Shaw. Diana
Wynyard, Sam Levene, Alan Webb. 1959, New York

Caesar and Cleopatra, by George Bernard Shaw.
Cedric Hardwicke, Lilli Palmer. 1949, New York

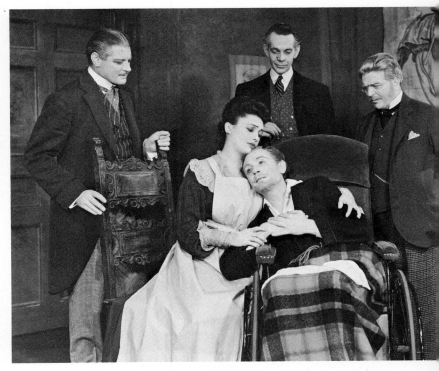

The Doctor's Dilemma, by George Bernard Shaw. Ralph
Forbes, Katharine Cornell, Bramwell Fletcher, Raymond
Massey, Whitford Kane. 1941, New York

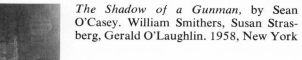

The Shadow of a Gunman, by Sean O'Casey. William Smithers, Susan Strasberg, Gerald O'Laughlin. 1958, New York

Juno and the Paycock, by Sean O'Casey. Sara Allgood, Barry Fitzgerald, Aideen O'Connor, Harry Young. 1940, New York

The Plough and the Stars, by Sean O'Casey. Bette Henritze, Jenny Egan. 1960, New York

Luigi Pirandello

Right You Are If You Think You Are, by Luigi Pirandello. Nancy Marchand, Joanna Roos, Jan Farrand. 1964, New York

The Hairy Ape, by Eugene O'Neill. Louis Wolheim. 1922, New York

Desire Under the Elms, by
Eugene O'Neill. Mary Morris,
Walter Huston. 1924

Desire Under the Elms, by Eugene O'Neill. Foreground: George C. Scott, Colleen Dewhurst. 1963, New York

Goat Song, by Franz Werfel. 1925, New York

R.U.R., by Karel Capek. Staged by Philip Moeller and Agnes Moran. 1922, New York

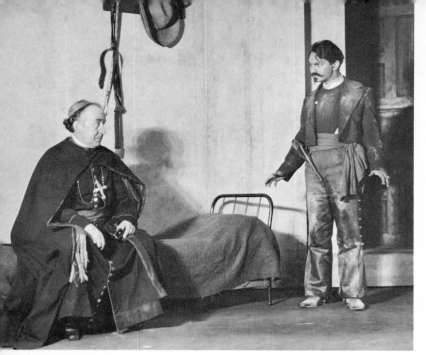

Juarez and Maximilian, by Franz Werfel. Dudley Digges and Edward G. Robinson. 1926, New York

Right: *What Price Glory?,* by Maxwell Anderson and Laurence Stallings. Louis Wolheim (2nd from left), William Boyd (4th from left). 1924, New York

Roar, China, by Sergei Tretyakov. Set by Lee Simonson. 1930, New York

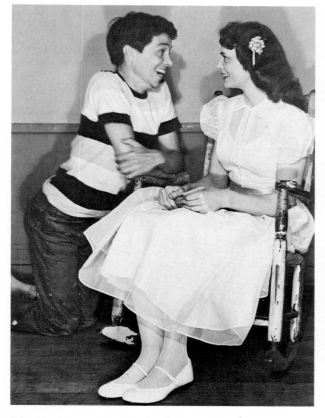

The No 'Count Boy, by Paul Green. Bettye
Ackerman, Wright King. 1954, New York

The Front Page, by Charles MacArthur and Ben Hecht.
Lee Tracy, Osgood Perkins. 1928, New York

Journey's End, by R. C. Sherriff. Henry Wenman, Colin
Keith-Johnston, Jack Hawkins. 1928, New York

The Constant Wife, by
Somerset Maugham. Grace
George, John Emery,
Katharine Cornell. 1951,
New York

Strange Interlude, by Eugene O'Neill. Glenn Anders,
Earle Larrimore, Lynn Fontanne. 1928, New York

Strange Interlude, by Eugene O'Neill. Glenn Anders,
Earle Larrimore, Lynn Fontanne. 1928, New York

A Man's A Man, by Bertolt Brecht.
John Heffernan, Olympia Dukakis.
1963, New York

The Threepenny Opera, by Bertolt Brecht, with music by Kurt Weill. Josephine Huston, Robert Chrisholm, Steffi Duna. 1933, New York

Bertolt Brecht and Eric Bentley

The Threepenny Opera, by Bertolt Brecht, with music by Kurt Weill. Tino Buazzelli, Checco Rissone. 1958, Piccolo Teatro, Milan

tion. How suspect that word became in the fact of the slogans of progress! Eros and Mask—what significance did these two most basic play-impulses have in the thesis plays? We lost the floor beneath our feet. The drama became almost totally rationalized. And now, after our experience with Expressionism, we see that those pieces which survived the era of slogans were based on at least one of the ancient impulses; and that the plays of Ibsen, Shaw, Pirandello, Hauptmann, Strindberg, O'Neill, drew their strength from one of those impulses which were so vital that they indicated the lifelessness of everything else. The course of history has vanquished the slogans. It has passed over the Sphinx which introduces the drama of Oedipus; over the kings and peers that people Shakespeare's stage world; finally, it has destroyed the society which Ibsen sought to unmask and to reform. And yet the plays still live: Oedipus lives, Henry V lives, Nora lives. Now we know why: because the form which the writers gave them was divorced from the influence of idols and slogans. When writers employ a *prescribed* method, they compose plays in order to give life to slogans or to pay homage to idols.

What could be more natural than that the theater, now that it has retired from its old prominence in society, should re-examine the essence of its nature—the essence peculiar to it, its basic impulses? There have always been times when recovery was more important than constant forward motion. In any case, "Progress" has become suspect for us; our path is toward revision. We are looking for what existed yesterday, exists today, and will exist tomorrow; what Shakespeare and the Greeks and Ibsen and perhaps Brecht had and which enabled their works to survive. Whatever purpose the theater has, whatever its place in our existence and today's society may be, the most important thing about it is that it is alive.

Bertolt Brecht, whose contributions to the theater are today perhaps discussed even more in London, Paris and New York than in Germany, understood the problem of form in all its depth, even though he spent the last part of his life writing pieces in accordance with a political, revolutionary slogan. Brooks Atkinson, then America's most influential drama critic, wrote on the occasion of the New York première of *The Good Woman of Setzuan* that he found nothing new in this manner of playwriting—that it was very much like the medieval Morality plays, which continued to flourish in the theater for a long time after the Middle Ages (as a matter of fact, they were not abandoned until the slogans of the last two centuries came along). We can cite Brecht himself in this connection with his "Song of the Playwright," which begins:

> I am a writer of plays. I show
> What I have seen. In the market places where men go about
> I have seen how a man deals with men.
> That is what I show, I, the writer of plays.

And the end:

> So that I can show what I see
> I read the plays of other times and other people.
> A few of my plays are copied from them, minutely
> Testing their technique to find out
> What of theirs I can employ.
> I studied the plays of the feudal
> Englishmen, giant figures
> For whom the world existed that they might shine.
> I studied the moralizing Spaniards,
> The Indians, masters of the beautiful sentiment,
> And the Chinese, who show us families
> And the colorful lives of the cities.

All this becomes evident in our present phase. If we are looking for the essence of theater, we must examine every possibility that has ever come about all over the world. It is still almost an underground movement, as Albert Camus said: "At the end of this darkness there will be a light, which we have already conceived and for which we must fight in order to bring it into existence. In the middle of the ruins on the other side of Nihilism we are all preparing a *Renaissance*. But few know it."

This concept of another Renaissance is unpleasant to many. But things are not so simple that one can equate a Renaissance with Reaction; from the point of view of the theater, the true Reaction nowadays is the perseverance in the *idée fixe* that the theater of the future can consist of the "new-at-any-price" and the "never-seen-before." We recognize that there have always been periods in the history of the arts in which the material of the past has been used in order to break off a phase of development which has become stagnant or in order to get out of a dead end. The phase of development which has become stagnant we have called *Illusionism*. This movement generally proclaimed that everything produced by Art must serve the progress of Mankind or the realization of a better world. The realization of a better world in the near future was actually thought possible. Nowadays when we talk of changing the world the goals are far more modest, even in the Marxist-Communist camp. Only the immediately necessary steps for the change of a particular social condition are considered and it is admitted that the next attainable dialectical position is still far away. Even those who believe in the possibility of an ideal world adopt the intellectual methods of the opposing sceptics: the struggle against evil will never cease because Man is good as well as evil, and therefore society can only be good as well as evil. It seems irrefutable that the last phase of dramatic development which has now ended was identical with the end of the pathetic slogans.

If it is true that we are now in the process of forming a classless society, then we may speak of the end of the age of the middle class as well as of its dramatic ideals. It is now possible to see the actual situation in the perspective of centuries; we will take advantage of our present perspective without, of course, concealing the fact that contradictions which often seem violent when looked at closely, appear insignificant from a distance.

History does not run in a straight, logical line. Even if we draw an all-encompassing arc over two or three hundred years, we must realize that inside the arc crises and revolutions occur in a rhythmic order which, like Toynbee, we can think of as "challenge" and "response," but which in the field of theatrical history is more conveniently classified as an order of organic reactions: Rise—Decay. The new—dearly loved and hotly espoused—does not remain as new as it was on the very first day: there comes a time when it becomes old, or one has simply had enough of it. One may continue with it for a bit, but finally the weariness becomes burdensome, irritating, like a contagious disease. It has to be shaken off, a new start has to be made, something new must be brought into play again, again it must be dearly loved and hotly espoused—the more extreme the previous weariness, the more enthusiastic the present state of mind. Let us, then, try to draw this great arc and examine the rhythmic waves within it.

THE HISTORICAL PERSPECTIVE

The great arc: the beginning assumes an end; the beginning of the middle-class drama assumes the end of the baroque drama. The grandiose ornamented form, the irrational sublimity of the tragedy and the irrational raciness of the comedy, the mask, the buskin, and the anti-realism of the stage were abandoned. The Baroque stage had been either bare or almost bare or filled with lavish decorations. Now scenery began to be "real" and to come closer to reality. In the framework of our great arc the new possibilities of illusion were opened up by the change from gas to electric light; total illusion was attained finally around the beginning of the twentieth century. The art of acting dispensed with broad gestures, poses, rhetoric, prosody, and choreographic groups; it paid homage to the ideal of naturalness, according to which there was to be as little difference as possible between the manners of the people on the stage and the people in the audience. At the same time the basic *vis comica* of the theater was destroyed with the elimination of Harlequin and the Vice. Laughter, also, became rationalized: it had to be sensible and proper in order to be tolerated. The educated middle-class public developed a horror of the coarse jokes and the erratic pranks with which the clowns of the improvisations tried to get the public to escape with them from reality. In comparison with the boldness—madness even—of the Baroque theater plays, the plays of the middle-class theater were of a puritan temperance. Here, too, we can see the development which led finally to Naturalism, to Reinhardt's atmospheric, Impressionistic productions, and to the discovery of understatement, into which the principle of naturalness of course was transformed. The author became more and more the dictator of the stage: not only did he take command of the actors (with the prohibition of extemporaneous playing), but he also eliminated the interlude music (even in Schiller's and Goethe's time there had been no plays without an overture and orchestral accompaniment) and pared away all mimic elements which did not bear on the causal interrelation of the situation. The arc led all the way to Stanislavski's scientific technique, which, in contradistinction to the mimic-musical autocracy of the baroque actor, stood for the complete subjection of actor to author.

The formal possibilities of playwriting became even narrower. In Ibsen's time we had in practice only the play divided into acts; in addition there was the episodic play, which was tolerated rather than permitted (*Peer Gynt* and Goethe's *Götz von Berlichingen* belong to this genre, which was wrongly supposed to be Shakespearean). In the act-divided play reality was most closely imitated: stage time was equated with real time, and the stage depicted a real room, as if the audience were looking through a great peep-hole of which the actors were unaware. In the final phase, in the twentieth century, impressionistic and symbolic effects were used by the authors. This did not yet involve a rejection of reality, but rather an intensification of it through the use of the inner eye, the world of dreams, and psychoanalysis. The concept of reality began to change, but the opinion that the function of the stage was to represent reality continued to be held.

Naturally every dramatic work had to serve humanity as a whole. Rousseau proclaimed a return to a truer, i.e., more natural, world. Schiller believed in the aesthetic education of mankind; the Romantics dreamed of a Universal Theater as a concrete ideal world in little. The period of idealistic and romantic programs for transformation of the world was followed by the industrial revolution and the advance of science, which resulted in a period of search for direct, practical applications. When Friedrich Engels, in a letter to an English author in 1888, defined realism as "faithful reproduction of typical characters in typical situations," it seemed obvious to him that "typical" meant "that which will be typical" after the Revolution. Realism had granted the poetic element a place in the theater (neither Marx nor Engels, possibly not even Lenin, held Realism to be the only permissible literary style), but Naturalism openly declared itself anti-poetic and in favor of the drama solely as a medium for the improvement of the world. As an old man, Ibsen acknowledged with pride that his plays could become obsolete in the course of time as the social criticisms on which they were based ceased to be valid. So clearly did one see oneself as a fighter for a better and not too distant world! What optimism! And what a fall was there! Wars, crises, catastrophes, together with their terror and their ruins, gradually brought these heaven-stormers to their senses.

They began to realize that Paradise was farther away than ever, and that the struggle against evil would never end. Once more, in Expressionism, the cry for world brotherhood rose up from the dramatists; and then the illusions exploded—and Illusionism exploded with them. Seen in this light, Brecht's subjection of himself to the political demands of Communism takes on a double meaning: first, as a last attempt to save the theater for the Illusionistic thesis which held it to be a means for world betterment; second, as a renunciation of the author's absolute power, which Zola, Ibsen, and the young Hauptmann had claimed in this same battle. But Brecht employed the *Lehrstück,* the didactic play, which is the end-point of the great arc, in only a relatively short phase of his career. Before and after that he was a writer of a very different type.

The development which saw the beginning of the new arc and the end of the old had already begun before the turn of the century. Let us take a look at the chief dramatists of the first half of the century. We see in each one of them an overlapping of both arcs. Even Ibsen can be taken as an example for the new arc. He had, after all, revived an age-old theatrical motif: the unmasking process. He tore the mask from the faces of his gentlemen and consuls in order to bring the truth to light: this was the first step on the way to the disintegration of the positivistic picture of man on the stage, which would be brought to its conclusion by Strindberg and Pirandello. And even Shaw, who was so fond of making pronouncements about the theater as a means to world betterment, was forced to broaden the scope of the stage world as in *Back to Methuselah* and *Man and Superman,* by bringing metaphysics to the stage, or, as in *Saint Joan,* by writing an epilogue which violates the realism of the rest of the play and which, for its form, might just as well have been written by one of the later writers—Thornton Wilder, for example. Strindberg frankly removed reality from the stage; a drama like *Advent* is closer to the medieval mystery play than to the middle-class Illusionistic play. O'Neill restored two ancient theater devices in his search for truth without illusion: the soliloquy, in *Strange Interlude,* in which play the characters impart their true thoughts in asides; and the mask, in *The Great God Brown,* in which the characters do not understand one another when they are without their masks. The form of the Illusionistic theater had already been attacked by Gorki in his

Lower Depths when he brought to the stage a type of *danse macabre* of human misery. In the middle twenties, Gorki associated himself with the great Russian theater revolutionaries (who were later liquidated by Stalin: Taïrov, Meyerhold; also with Stanislavski and the genial, short-lived Vachtangov) in order to revive the Commedia dell'Arte, the improvisation of Harlequin and his Russian cousin, Petrouchka. Stanislavski opened a special studio for this purpose, and Vachtangov's legendary production of Gozzi's *Turandot* appears to have been the high point of this movement. In Germany, Hauptmann's development, with its constant wavering between realistic and romantic milieus, between Illusionistic and Classical style, is typical of the transitional period. Hofmannsthal's program for a reunion of poetry and the stage led not unpredictably to the opera and, quite consciously, back to the Baroque (Calderón). Schnitzler's *La Ronde* showed another pre-Illusionistic way of writing plays. Wedekind, committed to Illusionism as a moralist of puritanical severity, substituted a panorama of already unmasked characters for Ibsen's unmasking process. German Expressionism, whose form was anti-Illusionistic, but whose slogans led it to Illusionism and eventual destruction, clearly stands within the perspective of this arc as well.

Among the dramatists of the first half of the twentieth century, Pirandello may be related more to the beginning arc than to the ending one. A later writer, Anouilh, has stated that Pirandello was the one who took the decisive step, and T. S. Eliot has recently attested his own debt to him. Beckett and Ionesco are absolutely inconceivable without Pirandello. He turned the unmasking of the various layers which compose a personality into a method: man was no longer a unified being, but rather a multi-faceted one. Pirandello's drama consists of the constant change back and forth between mask and face (each of them capable of standing for the other), and the transition, never precisely determinable, from appearance to reality and back again. Pirandello demonstrated in *Six Characters in Search of an Author* that an eminent theatrical device, the change of personality achieved in full view of the audience, had once more been made stageworthy. Naturally, the revival of the device on the modern stage did not include the elementary theatrical (Dionysiac) element of gaiety, which we usually tend in retrospect to associate with the style of the Commedia dell'Arte. It was hemmed in on all sides, shadowed by scepticism and twisted by anxiety. Yet, the revival of the device could take place only because the ground on which his predecessors had so confidently stormed forward before was shaken. But of that more later.

The Renaissance of Forms, which we have used as our point of departure in clarifying the confusing scene of the contemporary drama, now appears as the consequence and continuation of an historical process. If we add to this Renaissance the idea of the rhythmic alternation between rise and decay, challenge and response, then there can no longer be any doubt that authors, theatermen, and public had become tired of Illusionism—of the precisely realistic scenery and of the average people who expressed themselves therein in painfully guarded understatements. The rise of the next cycle led first to the error of the Expressionistic scream, in which, however, a class of elementary theatrical phenomena did reappear: rhetoric, the tirade, the great outburst, the monologue (which had, of course, been forbidden). Certainly the decay of the old social order and the disintegration of what had been the world of the stage were more than merely theatrical occurrences (and we will have to deal with that thoroughly later), but these merely theatrical occurrences mirrored the younger generation's irresistibly outbreaking scepticism with regard to the conditions of the real world and the possibility of making a realistic attack on their basic problems (which would then dissolve as soon as touched). When everything that was considered natural and taken for granted revealed itself to be doubtful, then what was previously held to be doubtful had to be granted an entirely new reality.

If the concept "Realism" had not taken on such a narrow meaning in popular usage, we could re-introduce the word in its old, scholastic sense: in the early Middle Ages those who believed in the reality of the ideal were called Realists.

In this sense of the word we could speak of a new Realism of the theater, insofar as the seeming-world on the stage and the people playing in it would be considered real, i.e., without asserting that they are mirroring "genuine" reality or being "natural," or requiring them to serve the cause of world betterment. The action that takes place on the stage is no longer bound up with factual reality; it depicts a life of its own and pretends to be nothing but what it is: play and players. This concept, this "anti-reality," will bring to light old, forgotten, and new techniques of creating drama—techniques still undiscovered.

THE RENAISSANCE OF FORMS

The first exit from the dead-end of Illusionism was the Renaissance of Forms. Let us list some of its elements one after the other in the manner of the Brechtian "Song of the Playwright":

THE CHINESE: Brecht's great parable plays, *The Caucasian Chalk Circle* and *The Good Woman of Setzuan,* are adaptions of the Chinese Theater's method of using the stage for what it is: a wooden podium onto which a man steps and says to the audience "I am the water-seller here in the town of Setzuan." What awkward expositions have been invented to support the fiction that those on the stage know nothing of those in the stalls! The much-discussed "alienation effect" is, as Brecht himself has stated, essentially derived from the Chinese theater. But the Chinese theater offered other possibilities as well. When Thornton Wilder's *Our Town* was first produced we thought we were seeing something entirely new and experimental in this pantomimic playing without properties. Wilder himself has told us where he got it, and when the Peking Opera made its triumphal tour through the cities of Europe its derivation was confirmed. *Our Town* had used an age-old theatrical device, which had been brought to its highest development in China. Paul Claudel, formerly a French diplomat in Peking, had adapted Chinese theatrical devices even before Brecht and Wilder, and soon afterwards the renaissance of pantomime took place in Paris. We need only mention Jean-Louis Barrault (in the film *Les Enfants du paradis* and in the performances of his troupe) and Marcel Marceau. The Parisian avant-gardists make more and more use of this device in their pieces. In Ionesco's fantasy play, *The Chairs,* we see two old people on the stage occupying themselves with nothing but chairs; the other people, who do not appear, are "seen" only in speeches and gestures with which the two old people invite them to sit. Age-old, elementary (and modern) theater.

THE INDIANS. The amazing success of Rabindranath Tagore (Nobel Prize, 1913) had its origins at a time when the lyrical, the subjective, and the dream-world still had their place on the stage. His *The Post Office* was played all over the world. But Tagore directed his attention to the old Indian drama, which had also aroused Goethe's interest. The Russian theater revolutionary Taïrov opened his Emancipated Theater in Moscow in 1914 with Kalidasa's *Shakuntala* (c. 400 A.D.). Taïrov did not use the word "emancipated" to mean emancipation from form, as some of the Expressionists did, but rather, as he himself put it, to mean the "theatricalization of the theater" through the re-introduction of the old anti-realistic elements—mimicry, pantomime, acrobatics, song and dance. Like the antique theater, the Indian theater was "opera" in that it combined words and music. It was composed in accordance with strict rules laid down in the instruction book of Natya Sastra. This instruction book is once again being studied today. Lion Feuchtwanger, who had a great success with his adaptation of the old Indian drama, *Vasantasena,* was Brecht's collaborator in the early *Life of Edward II* and in the posthumous *Die Gesichte der Simone Machard.* Ferdinand Bruckner based his last play *The Little Clay Cart,* on the old *Vasantasena.*

THE SPANIARDS. Since the time of Calderón the Christian drama has experienced a revival. Claudel, for example, has written a series of plays modeled on the Illusionistic pattern, but in *The Satin Slipper* and in the oratorios which he wrote for Honegger and Milhaud he revived Calderón's metaphysical theater. We must not overlook the anti-realistic basis of Calderón's drama, which Kommerell calls "an elevated ceremony of demonstration" ("demonstration"—direct communication with the audience—is, after all, also the object of the Brechtian drama). Calderón's stage sets up a world of its own—the world of "Contra-reality"—in opposition to the world of reality; it speaks directly to the public, not indirectly through the medium of illusion. In Calderón the *theatrum* becomes *theatrum mundi:* the world becomes stage and the stage becomes world.

THE ITALIANS were, strangely, not mentioned by Brecht. He did not feel sympathetic to the Commedia dell'arte. The spirit of Harlequin was opposed to his own, but it was not opposed to the theater of the time. The return of Harlequin is significant. Ever since rationalism drove him from the stage, he had been underground; he had preserved himself in the figure of the clown. Suddenly, after 1910, Harlequin appeared again everywhere: in the pictures of Picasso, in the costume of the classical ballet, in the grotesqueries of Charlie Chaplin. As has been mentioned already, this Renaissance was first proclaimed in the programs of the Russian theatrical revolution. Stalin's systematic liquidation of this revolution was due, among other things, to the Fool's traditional freedom of extemporization which Harlequin claimed for himself. Meyerhold put him on the stage in the guise of the old Russian Harlequin, Petrouchka (the equivalent of Pierrot), who had the right to tell the truth even to the Czar himself. (For the truth which he dared to tell Stalin Meyerhold paid with his life.) The improvisational art of the Commedia dell'arte also played a decisive role in the productions of the short-lived Vachtangov. Not without reason did Taïrov, at the opening of his aforementioned Emancipated Theater, place *The Fan* by the Italian Goldoni next to the Indian *Shakuntala*. Writers like Blok, Mayakovski, and Gorki also discovered the Commedia.

Since 1932 the effects of this movement on the drama have been throttled by the terror of Socialist Realism. But by 1932 the reborn figure of Harlequin had conquered other positions for himself. People were already talking of Pirandello's improvisation-comedies, and the great Irishman, Yeats, had written plays for dancers. Soon Ionesco would begin to turn out his *guignols* in Paris. And in Beckett's *Waiting for Godot* the clowns stepped on stage in order to expose the idiocy of the world.

The significant thing about all these symptoms is that nowhere do they petrify into slogans. How easy it would have been for Brecht to have said, "I will revive the Chinese theater." But no: he made use of the Indians and the English at the same time. There could be no greater contrast than that between Marlowe, the contemporary of Shakespeare, and the Chinese. The early English and Elizabethan theaters with their Moralities and Chronicle plays were in evidence not only in Brecht's *Life of Edward II* and *Threepenny Opera,* but also in an eruption which surprised many, in the verse dramas of Christopher Fry. The Mystery play, too, was revived in many forms—from Strindberg's *Dream Play* to Tennessee Williams' *Camino Real.* And the classics—if there were no other distinguishing mark of this Renaissance, this alone would be sufficient: that modern dramatists were attracted both by the subject-matter and the forms of the classics. Hardly one prominent author failed to make use of classical material or material derived from the classics: Giraudoux, O'Neill, Eliot, Hofmannsthal, the later Hauptmann, Wilder, Maxwell Anderson, Jeffers, Pound, Sartre, Anouilh, Brecht, Zuckmayer, Dürrenmatt, Miller, Tennessee Williams.

Other symptoms of the Renaissance of Forms: the Parable play came under discussion. This is one of the oldest and most universal models of the theater; Illusionism pushed it aside because it wanted to pretend that stage plays were Life. Brecht's didactic play is a type of parable, although narrow in scope because bound to an ideology. Brecht wrote true parable plays as well, however: *The Good Woman of Setzuan* and *The Caucasian Chalk Circle.* As we have suggested, he found his models in India and China, in the German popular theater, and in the English Morality play, which itself had influenced Shakespeare's theater. Hofmannsthal brought the English play *Everyman* to the Salzburg Festival (where it proved itself astonishingly alive).

The kind of allegory so popular in the Baroque period has found modern admirers in Max Frisch and Arthur Adamov. The *Moritat* comes from the popular fairground theater; our younger authors, especially, like to tell their stories in a strongly simplified, hard, proclamatory style, which they favor partly because it seems primitive. Next to this form is *Farce:* in Sartre's controversial satire, *Nekrassov,* we have an example of a genre which reached a peak in 15th century France. Anouilh's comedy, *Pauvre Bitos,* which caused a scandal in Paris because of its exposure of a resistance hero, also contains some of the elements of farce. And shortly before that Anouilh had discovered in the rococo comedies of Marivaux another form which he (and others) "found useful."

These examples should suffice. If we perceive them as symptoms of a tendency, then the confusing picture of the modern drama may become clearer. *In this aimlessness is to be seen a conscious disregard of aims and slogans.* This disregard goes so far that the realism which was fought so violently in the twenties has remained alive. Realism survives as one of the many methods of writing plays which the tradition of centuries and the world-wide repertoire place at our disposal—to be employed when wanted.

II

But, it will be asked, which path is the drama really steering through this archipelago of forms, styles, and models which appear simultaneously in the Renaissance? Is the question of form really the only compass? What is actually to be expressed by the new abundance of methods?

WHAT HAS THE MODERN DRAMA TO SAY TO US?

It has already been stated that form is in a profound sense both essence and expression, that it is as basic as what is commonly called content. In this sense, the Renaissance of Forms is not a formalistic process—if we understand by Formalism what the artistic theory of Stalinism understood by it. The fact that form or forms seem once more at all worth striving for points toward an existential solution. The period in which formlessness was identified with originality and freedom identified with innovation has ended. If this view is correct, the condition of the drama mirrors the condition of the times precisely. Our modern, more or less classless society, according to a widely held view, urgently needed new agreements on opinions after the destruction of the previous opinions.

What is the theater's position in our society? What function does it perform? This question must now be posed so that we can begin to attack our problem from the other point of view—that of content—in accordance with our previously characterized method of procedure. Such a discussion belongs to a consideration of the essence of the drama.

The return to forms in the drama has been revealed. Consequently the question which stands before all modern dramatists achieves even greater gravity and importance: What is the *purpose* of the theater in contemporary society?

Obviously the answer to this question cannot be given as conclusively as in the question of form and forms. Whenever the question of purpose is put, subjective elements enter: ethical philosophies, articles of faith, and ideologies appear in the background. We will attempt to avoid these matters here, that is, we will leave them to be disposed of by each after his fashion; and, consequently, although we will try to arrive at a reasonably convincing answer, it must be granted that absolutely conclusive proofs cannot be produced.

WHY DO WE STILL HAVE THEATERS, ANYWAY?

The question of the purpose of the theater in our time has two aspects: that of the stage and that of the public. And here we are halted at once. In some very early phase of human development the two aspects must have been identical. Of course, the separation of players and spectators must have taken place very early, for no other reason than that a player must have talent. Not everyone is a good football-player. Not everyone is a good stage-player. If we can imagine, then, the people of a tribe, in some far distant time when the drama was still very young, sitting around in a circle out of which one or another of them stepped now and then to show himself off while the others joined in the dancing and singing, we must also remember that this type of thing soon changed. One of the oldest forms of theater is the animal pantomime: whoever could give the best imitation of a lion or an ostrich was always called on, applauded, and rewarded. The division between spectator and performer which this primitive play soon assumed belongs today as much to the essence of the theater as the even older impulse which drives people to perform at all. Is there any child who does not like to play? On the contrary; for a child, play is life. It is no coincidence that we speak of the urge of the child in man to play. So we must assume that, although once the theater became divided and some played while others watched, only the audience's impulse to imagine itself joining in the play made theater possible in the first place. Even today the public joins in at every performance. One only has to ask the actors; they could sing songs about the feeling they get when coldness, indolence, and impatience are uppermost in the stalls. That is why performances differ. Each one is governed by the age-old suspense: Will it be possible to move those down there to sympathy, feeling, emotion? The extent of a particular performance's success is measured by the extent of communication between players and audience.

Play-acting, which we all perform either actually or in pretense, is preceded by an existential act. The existential element, as Huizinga has shown and modern anthropology has corroborated, lies in the impulse to crash through commonplace everyday events—the banality, the transience, and the restraints of our lives, all forced upon us under the shadow of nature, forces, machines, organizations, or ruling systems— to a short span of time which has a beginning and an end and in which rules, arrangements, and laws other than those of the real, matter-of-fact world are valid. This emphasis on the fictive element—the doing of something which is not so in actuality—belongs to play acting now as in our earliest days. For example, it was thought for a long time that only in modern times could a true popular theater be created because the age of feudalism is past and today the privileges of class and rank have finally been done away with. This is absolute nonsense. Only the slaves were barred from the ancient theater (and that is a matter concerned with an entirely different social problem); the government subsidized plays, just as governments do nowadays; Pericles paid the entrance fee for those who could not afford it (in the form of coins which we can still inspect in museums today); and as a matter of course there was no discrimination in the seating arrangements, apart from the practice of seating members of the government in the front row. The Spanish theater was equally democratic; it was actually controlled by the "Mosqueteros," a sort of playgoers' organization composed of "lower-class people" whose leaders tyrannized the authors and managers of the theaters. To what extent the theater of Shakespeare was a popular theater can be judged from the fact that more Londoners, in proportion to the city's total population, attended the theater then than now. The feudal period of the court theater and the period of bourgeois theater which followed it turn out to be interludes in the whole two-thousand year history of the European theater. It follows from this that the wish to experience a fictive world during the hours in which a play is performed and to identify oneself wherever possible with it and its characters is one of the basic impulses of humanity. It has maintained itself intact to this day even against the oft-repeated bans of church and state. There is no reason to suppose that it will cease to do so in the future.

THE SECOND PERSPECTIVE: OPPOSITION

As a result of all this we can now put forward a new thesis: *The Theater would not exist at all if, besides its involvement in social criticism and class struggles, this basic impulse to break through reality were not implicit in it.* This element of protest and opposition belongs to the essence of the theater.

The impulse to break through reality and create a "contra-reality" is, I believe, common to the play and to art generally. Two misapprehensions must be corrected here, however. First, scholarship has shown that *the Theater did not originate in religion.* Of course, Religion is a variety of social institution, and Theater is a variety of social institution. The theater was used since earliest times by the priests for their purposes, just as the magicians and medicine men used its techniques of disguise and transformation in order to strengthen their own authority. On the other hand, when the play dealt with the greatest problems of mankind, gods were called upon: the theater also used religion for its purposes. The Greek theater was religious in the sense that two separate institutions merged in it in the performance of a single, isolated act of art. At the same time, both institutions naturally continued to exist in themselves: cult and mime. It should be stressed that the historical act of the beginning of the Drama, which we can date precisely, broke through the religious character of performance by giving to the people the place which had previously belonged to the priests. This began when the legendary Thespis became an actor in order to provide a contrast with the chorus. Another great advance was made when Aeschylus provided a second actor as contrast to the first so that the dialogue between actor and chorus became a dialogue between actor and actor. A completely irreligious view was the basis of this exchange, namely, that the gods made use of men in order to punish them. Thus the priest was set aside, and individual man was directly confronted by fate and the gods.

This fact casts some light on a second misapprehension: namely, that the theater as such is or ought to be a cultural institution. It is one, certainly, every now and again when particularly distinguished plays are performed, but it does not have to be one. If a theater visit becomes a cultural duty, the performance will become a lecture. Huizinga defined a basic characteristic of play, including theatrical play, in this sentence: "Prescribed play is not play anymore." People should never feel obligated to go to the theater. Why else should they go? Naturally, because they want to! It is the desire to get away from everyday life, to be entertained and moved which leads people to go to the play.

THE BASIC FUNCTION OF THE THEATER: ENTERTAINMENT

The function of the theater in society is, was, and ever will be entertainment. Everyone is becoming conscious of this now. Eliot has always presented this point of view; Brecht, Dürrenmatt, Fry, Osborne, Anouilh, Ionesco agree. Even the greatest and most sublime poetry can live on the stage only if it is primarily entertainment. If we desire to remove fantasy and suspense from the drama, then all that is left is what was finally left in the Expressionistic plays: propaganda, election speeches, lectures.

Since a play uses words, it is always in danger of becoming, like the word, trite, arid, and abstract. This loss of clarity, of pertinence, of (let us speak frankly) *meaning* has a fatal effect on the performers and their actions. The performers become parrots, the actions become automatic. An apt remark by Arthur Miller is worth quoting here: a man can be dramatic on stage only when he possesses the "gift of surprise." With the parrot-actor we can predict every answer and every reaction in advance. There is no suspense in an action which does not have at least two possible solutions: in the case of the automatic action the one single solution that comes in question is decreed by an official ideology. That is the death of drama.

And so we have once more reached the thesis proposed above, this time from another direction: *Theater is contradiction because only the unexpected can make it entertaining.*

In this sense, *Faust* and *Hamlet* are, of course, also entertainments: two or three suspense-filled hours, and then they should cease to be played and should be relegated to the museum and to the classroom. Of course, a popular song is written with the same notes as Figaro's song; Van Gogh's "Sunflowers" are to be seen on millions of badly printed colored picture postcards; millions of pictures hanging in golden frames are far from being art even though they are painted with the same colors as the "Mona Lisa." It is the same way with the theater's entertainment function. Both grasses and flower buds grow out of the loam.

The theater's intellectual content is only one of the possible elements with which it performs its function of entertainment. The first sentence of Brecht's *Little Organon for the Theater* is pertinent here:

Theater consists of the living representations of historical or invented encounters between men—for the purpose of entertainment.

Drama as invented by the Greeks and as it still exists in the guise of idea and form in Sartre and Ibsen, built up on analytical dialogue, is only *one* of the many ways in which theater can be entertainment.

Today we can see the theater being forced to grow roots in the soft earth of entertainment and drawing new vitality from this source. Simultaneously with the international triumphs of classical ballet, with the already mentioned rebirth of pantomime, we can observe a loosening of the conventional divisions within the genres. Elements of the legitimate play are entering the opera, and the legitimate play uses elements of the opera, the ballet, and the pantomime. Nobody is surprised nowadays to hear songs or choruses sung during a play. Nobody is surprised when the mime becomes pantomime. Productions like Jean Vilar's at the Théâtre National Populaire have an élan imparted by great choreography. Choreography is generally being used more and more by the great international directors. The musical, which is spreading from America to all parts of the world, is no longer thought of as a variation of operetta with elements of the revue. A serious American critic (Brooks Atkinson) considers the text of the musical version of Shaw's *Pygmalion* (*My Fair Lady*) as intelligent as Shaw's own. *West Side Story* is a notable adaptation of the *Romeo and Juliet* motif to modern life, thanks to Jerome Robbins and Leonard Bernstein. Several authorities on the American theater are of the opinion that the musical is *the* theatrical form of the future. (At this point, incidentally, we have reached one of the specific formal definitions of our subject, moving from the direction of content and purpose. Such overlappings must always remind us that the form-content distinction is only being used as a method.)

A NEW STEP TOWARD TRUTH: THE PARABLE

All this proves that the modern drama has departed in its essentials from the axioms of rationality (for example, as presented in the Thesis play) as well as from those of naturalness. The act of playing does not become frivolous as a consequence of this, nor does watching a play become a flight from truth. This may often happen, but, nonetheless, truth is identical neither with rationality nor with naturalness. Even Realism is considered by its proponents to be no more than a method of extracting relevance from reality.

It is, as we have seen, the specific truth of the theater that it presents a fictive world, a "Contra-reality." There is an ineluctable drive towards truth in Contra-reality. The specific lie of the theater consists in its wishing to pretend that its world is the world of reality. Shaw once put it this way: the greatest joke on the stage is the truth. Since the time of Aristophanes, comedy has, in fact, been one of the most important means of bringing the element of opposition into the theater. Nothing is deadlier than to be ridiculous, Molière once pointed out to the Sun-king.

The trend toward truth has led to the rediscovery of a basic method of writing plays (in the case of those authors who write plays for the sake of truth): *the play becomes Bei-Spiel* (i.e., *by-play;* hence, *parable*). Here, too, "truth" disguises itself with Contra-reality. The action no longer deals merely with *some* slice of life; it is a slice of *exemplary* life. It contains elements which transcend themselves and become part of a higher, universal meaning. It is enough that sometimes it warns Man—Everyman, the beggar as well as the emperor—of his pride and presumptuousness or reminds him of his frailty and helplessness. Yet it can also rouse him from his unconcern, his indifference, his insensitivity, and shock him with the realization of the misery around him.

Although the action of the parable *may* have a moral purpose, it *need* not have one because the theater is not a moralistic institution; on the other hand, would it be possible to keep appeals to decency and horror at injustice from the boards?

The parable always concerns itself with the individual. The protest against injustice, against evil, against lies, against the complacency and torpor of the world can only be voiced with a strict insistence on freedom. And so the drama makes the actor the representative of Man. It may surround him with types that threaten his freedom or with other individual figures who are exposed to the same danger from evil, injustice, and lies as he, but who have perhaps already been conquered by them—while, he, the hero, may still have the power to live or to die for freedom.

In an age in which Man has been estranged from himself and reduced in significance, in a world which threatens the individual, the strengthening of the element of opposition is a necessity. If it is true that Man is an anti-conformist being, we may characterize the theater as an institution of protest. In society this institution can be defined by an analogy to an English parliamentary formula: "Their Majesties' opposition, the People." Now we can place next to the first general trend of modern dramaturgy—the Renaissance of Forms—a second, equally important: *the ascent to the symbolic*. People and events are no longer created in order to serve as personifications and allegorizations of theses; they are above all themes and figures in a play (Contra-reality) which is itself so enriched with life, truth—yes, even reality—that it has validity for the times—not abstractly, but on the basis of its common center—as a parable.

A few words about Brecht, the leading writer of the modern parable-drama, are in order here. The pieces which will (presumably) survive are the ones he wrote in exile. Once he had made up his mind to take over a theater in East Berlin, he ceased to be heard from as a serious writer. He had left the Opposition. His opposition to all authority, to all force, to all enforced obligations was condemned to silence. The pieces which he wrote in exile will survive him not as propaganda plays or *lehrstücke,* but as plays of opposition. There will always be people like the maid Grusha who will sacrifice everything and defy those in power out of love for a human child, even in East Berlin. Brecht's favorite subjects for heroes and heroines were young girls like this Grusha— not intellectuals and not functionaries, not even heroes of the class struggle, but rather beings still touched with the innocence of a belief in the good. The heroine of his posthumous drama, *Die Gesichte der Simone Machard,* an immature young girl, is a Joan of Arc of the year

1940; and she resembles the "St. Joan of the Stockyards" of 1930. She is a child to whom an angel appears in order to call upon her to combat injustice, evil and lies. She is the human in revolt, to use the words of Albert Camus. "Art and Rebellion will not die until the last man dies" said Camus, a brother of Brecht's, of whom Brecht did not want to know anything, perhaps because at the end he did not want to know anything at all anymore.

Let us call the Contra-reality, which is created in revolt and stands in opposition to the actual world, the second existence, which is set against the first. Another example from the modern drama can show us how deeply we can reach back from the second into the first existence and thus into the very center of all existence. The American Arthur Miller has published an essay on the "social drama" in which the concept of the social is extended much further than has up to now been the custom. For him it includes all aspects of the problem that men face in living with each other. The interpretation on the level of social criticism seems to him far too narrow. Drama is social drama wherever the question, "How shall we live?" is asked. The Greek drama was the most social of all drama. And so will the drama of the future be. For human history has entered a phase in which the problem is simply whether or not, in the face of machines, mechanism, officials, ideologies, and bombs, Man can still consider himself a man among men. Miller says, "Both sides have the bomb and both sides have the machine. . . . The only force that will keep them from destructive use will be a force strange to machine psychology, a force born of will—the will of man to survive." Miller continues, "Hard as it is for most people, the sheer struggle to exist and to prosper affords a haven from thought. Complain as they may that they have no time to think, to cultivate themselves, to ask the big questions, most men are terrified at the thought of not having to spend most of their days fighting for existence." According to Miller, it is the modern drama's responsibility to step in at this point. Its business is to remind us that there are hundreds of reasons why the ultimate questions should be examined once again: "The new social drama will be Greek in that it will face man as a social animal and yet without the petty partisanship of so much of past drama. It will be Greek in that the men dealt with in its scenes . . . will be more than ends in themselves and once again parts of a whole, a whole that is social, a whole that is Man."

Two phrases of Miller's are important for us: "will be Greek" and "the ultimate questions should be examined."

"The ultimate questions"—in the drama that does not mean the questions of Martin Heidegger, of atomic physics, or of Near Eastern politics. They are the questions of the concrete, unsubdued, unadapted man, of the individual who attains for himself the freedom of opposition, because he represents what Miller calls "a whole"—mankind. (In place of the thesis play we have, to make a rather fine point of it, the anti-thesis play.)

I do not wish by any means to imply by all this that the portrayal of the subdued man should be barred from the stage; quite the contrary—such a portrayal is, for the purposes of that mirror in which we all recognize ourselves, a modern day obligation. To be precise, it is the obligation to unmask. But neither Beckett nor Ionesco is satisfied with the mere mirroring of life; the former has brought on to the stage his sadness at the subjugation of man and his feeling of hopelessness; the latter has often asserted that absurdity is a basic characteristic of his plays and his people. Both dramatists stress protest and opposition. The subjugated man is depicted, in other words, because the writer finds him unsatisfactory.

It is, however, asserted in some quarters that this is the only true way of showing man on the stage nowadays. That would be true if the concrete, unsubjugated and unadapted man no longer existed. But he does exist; he is everywhere among us; in the midst of the dangers which threaten us we witness his drama, today as yesterday and always, in the cry of the threatened creature, in horror at injustice. It is Abel killed by his brother; it is Antigone breaking the laws for the sake of her brother; it is Romeo and Juliet loving each other today no less than in Shakespeare's Verona. And it is all of these—viewed in the light of the world in which we are forced to live, of that first existence which seems to contain only force and suppression, the powerful and the powerless, and inescapable destiny. If we wish to survive that first, and inescapable existence, we must set up against it the second existence, not only to escape it and to avoid being overwhelmed by it, but also to combat it. The more complex and fateful our situation threatens to become, the simpler are the essential questions, the questions of the man who will not adapt and content himself.

That is one side of the element of Opposition, the direct side.

The other is the indirect, yet elementary side. The drama "will be Greek," says Miller. Let us add that it will become Greek or Spanish or English or Chinese or German, in the sense of the Renaissance of Forms (as explained in the first part of this analysis). The simpler the truth becomes, the richer must the forms become—the forms of Contra-reality, created out of the specific and basic essence of the theater, born, in other words, of the opposition to the world, as the theater itself is.

III

We have traced two lines in the confusing scene of the modern drama. The two names with which we have labelled these two lines—Contra-reality and Opposition—do not have the character of slogans. Slogans are carried ahead like flags: one follows them. Our two concepts have been traced from the historical lines of development after the event: they are for purposes of interpretation, not of production. If most modern dramatists follow them, they do so without conscious intent. Each reflects a harmonious, more or less unavoidable, reaction (in the sense of the previously mentioned rhythmic cycles) to which each one of the modern dramatists saw himself forced if, acting for himself and without becoming committed to any party or movement, he was to try to find his way out of the dead end into which modern drama has strayed.

THE REAL REVOLUTION OF 1910

If we once more pass in review the principal authors of the modern drama, now that we are armed with these perspectives, we can see what the central problem underlined by the artistic revolution of 1910 was: How can we escape being subjective without succumbing to the spirit of the age of industry and the masses? Or: How can we remain non-conforming individuals without shutting ourselves up in catacombs or ivory towers? The central problem is man's own decision in the face of the forces which seem to leave him only two alternatives: adaptation or isolation. This problem has abandoned the realm of the subjective; from a subjective point of view it can neither be understood nor solved. Consequently, in the drama, the first reaction is the re-creation of form. Form is a means of communication, and the element of opposition can be made a truly protesting, contradictory power only on the widest possible basis of communication.

The *Musée imaginaire* of forms appeared to be one way of achieving this many-sided solution suited to the historical sense of the time, which had been radically altered by the liquidation of the optimistic faith in progress. *The Renaissance of Forms gave the dramatists the opportunity both to widen and to deepen the revolt based on opposition:* to widen it in the sense that dramatists could begin to rely on forms on which general agreement had already been reached (forms which had survived and had proved themselves to be lasting; that is the new definition of "classic"); to deepen it in the sense that the forgotten basic methods of writing plays were once more put into use by means of these surviving forms. Thus something of the elementary essence of the theater was won back piece by piece. The appeal to the unchangeable —that is to say, to man's basic impulse to play—became combined with the fusion between the performed Contra-reality and the impulse of Opposition, to form action itself, which in turn marks the genesis of Drama, as it does that of Art generally. For the category of freedom stands over them both.

APPLICATION OF BOTH PERSPECTIVES

Here I provide some notes for the interpretation of the modern drama in the light of the perspective given by the lines of Opposition and Contra-reality.

AMERICA. Dominant realism, of which "Everyman's realism" is the most typically characteristic form. "People like you and me." Strongly pessimistic social criticism from Elmer Rice, Clifford Odets, Robert Sherwood. Esoteric attempts at anti-realism: Gertrude Stein, Conrad Aiken, Ezra Pound. Poetic theater: Maxwell Anderson, Robinson Jeffers, Archibald MacLeish.

The great O'Neill died in 1953. He experimented in creating new forms and destroying old ones (*The Great God Brown, Strange Inter-*

lude). Also the outcry of a man caught and twisted by powers outside himself in *The Emperor Jones.* Finally, after the onset of his serious illness, his last works, in which the Ibsen-Strindberg form is brought back but completely transcended, and only the theme of reality and appearance is treated. In Ibsen the world of appearance (the "life-lie") had to be destroyed so that truth and good could come to power; now, in O'Neill, men hold despairingly on to the world of appearance (their "life-lie") and are tragically annihilated when it is taken away from them. Pessimistic realism: they are always annihilated. Reality conquers in *The Iceman Cometh, A Moon for the Misbegotten, Long Day's Journey into Night, A Touch of the Poet.*

William Faulkner's *Requiem for a Nun,* in which a basic dramatic motif, the trial, has, so to speak, involuntarily forced a novelist into writing drama. Contra-reality of the heightened trial before the judgment of conscience. Unmasking, revelation.

Tennessee Williams: Adaptation of Ibsen's technique of disclosure to the subject of sex and its pathology. Considered by Williams himself to be a revolt in the name of an anti-puritan morality (*A Streetcar Named Desire, The Rose Tattoo, Cat on a Hot Tin Roof*); in between, a curious attempt at a synthetic Mystery play in *Camino Real.*

Arthur Miller: Followed *Death of a Salesman,* an example of realism raised to a universal level, with *The Crucible,* an example of direct Opposition in the name of freedom. Later, the model of a social drama heightened by use of the elements of Greek form in *A View from the Bridge.*

Thornton Wilder: Complete breakdown of realism with forms taken from the Chinese: *Our Town.* Allegory of the element of Opposition in the human race in *The Skin of Our Teeth.* Constant starting-point: "a man like you or me," Everyman. Finally the notably successful attempt to transform an antique form and theme into a modern and Christian play: *The Alcestiad.*

ENGLAND/IRELAND/SCOTLAND. A double tradition in the national style: Elizabethan-Shakespearean theater and with it the tenaciously surviving, only semi-realistic drawing-room comedy. Craft of entertainment practised by writers like Noel Coward, Terence Rattigan and Peter Ustinov. J. B. Priestley's use of contemporary problems and formal experiments (the time-machine in *Time and the Conways*).

The form of the drawing-room comedy as a device for bringing in elements of the Mystery play and the adaptation of antique tragic elements in T. S. Eliot (*The Family Reunion, The Cocktail Party, The Confidential Clerk, The Elder Statesman*).

Conscious return to the poetic drama by Christopher Fry (who was first followed by Eliot). *The Lady's Not for Burning, Venus Observed, The Dark Is Light Enough.* The "angry young man"—John Osborne. Extreme use of the element of Opposition in his first play, *Look Back in Anger;* definite influence of Tennessee Williams' callousness. His style is only seemingly realistic—actually vaudeville technique. More definitely anti-Illusionistic in *The Entertainer.*

Outsider: Dylan Thomas, the prototype of the man in revolt, came to grief through his nonconformity (death in America was possibly sought deliberately). Baroque speech fantasy breaking through reality and raising it to a modern mystical symbolism in *Under Milk Wood.* The play for voices as a border-line possibility of theater, made permissible by the admission on principle of all other methods as well. Formal parallel in W. H. Auden's *Age of Anxiety.*

J. M. Barrie: Scottish realism in transition to irrationalism. Contrareality, leading to the supernatural element in James Bridie.

O'Casey: the Irish Resistance in the form of a realism like Gerhart Hauptmann's. Strong human power. New Irish development: Brendan Behan's *The Quare Fellow, The Hostage.* The strong Irish influence in English drama of James Joyce, William Butler Yeats (who consciously re-introduced the medieval legend play) and J. M. Synge. Later: Samuel Beckett (cf. France).

FRANCE. Strong, sustained trend to anti-realism bound up with the revolution in production (Copeau, Dullin, Artaud, Jouvet, Vilar). Claudel's impressive renewal of the Christian drama from three sides: in the strict form of the act-divided play (for example, *The Hostage*); in the form of a universal theater, partly based on the Peking Opera (*Joan at the Stake, Christopher Columbus*); and in the form of the Mystery play, with the added influence of Calderón (*The Satin Slipper*). Further attempts at a Christian theater: François Mauriac, Gabriel Marcel.

Giraudoux's impressionistic psychology with a strong tendency toward the renewal of forms and themes (Romantic and Classical). Colors comedies with poetry and tragedies with irony.

Montherlant's aristocratic ideals presented in the form of plays conforming to a rigid style (*Queen after Death, Malatesta, Port Royal*).

Pagnol's realistic plays of Southern France, tending toward the folk play and the folk comedy (*Marius* trilogy, *The Well-digger's Daughter*).

Sartre: Constant attempts to present his own philosophy and ideology in a great variety of forms. Classical: *The Flies.* Ibsenian: *No Exit.* Popular play: *Dirty Hands.* Romantic heroic drama: *The Devil and the Good Lord.* Dumas-drama: *Kean.* Farce: *Nekrassov.* Thesis play in Ibsen style with surrealistic overtones: *The Condemned of Altona.*

Camus: Plays of Opposition with strong dialectic: *State of Siege, The Just Assassins.*

Anouilh: After starting with the methods of Giraudoux (modern problems in a classical setting or classical plots in a modern setting) and the theme of Pirandello (appearance and reality), began to form an ever more individualistic comic style in a strict form with an uncompromising, sceptical element of Opposition. This was derived partly from the French tradition of Marivaux, partly from the Aristophanic heritage of Shaw. Examples of the translation of classic material into his own comedic form: *The Lark* (Joan of Arc) and *Ornifle* (Don Juan). Example of the use of Aristophanic material: *Pauvre Bitos.* Progress toward tragedy: *Becket.*

A break with logic and the extension of contra-reality into absurdity with Ionesco (the "anti-play" with strong, elementary-mimic impulses such as the pantomime in *The Chairs*), Audiberti, Adamov. New legend and parable style with Schehadé. The fascinating theater of Jean Genet: exaltation of the subconscious world of desire in the tirades of *The Maids;* Mystery play in the monstrous metaphor of *The Balcony.*

Samuel Beckett: the most daring attempt to depict the unreality of existence and of the stage: *Waiting for Godot,* the play in which the clowns philosophize and the philosophers become clowns. Existence as clowning, clowning as existence—the modern variation of the age-old formula: Life is play, the play is life; based on the central syllogism, Play = Nonsense = Absurdity, therefore Life = Absurdity. Because of its strict adherence to form, *Godot* designated as the modern *Bérénice*

(Racine) by the French. Still more radical decomposition of man in *Endgame, Krapp's Last Tape,* and *Happy Days.*

SPAIN. The Renaissance phenomenon, Lorca. Revival of the Spanish Romantic tradition. Inclusion of music in the form of song, ballad, spoken aria, chorus. Basic theme: the conflict of man with the world in which he lives. Protest of the younger Spanish generation in Alfonso Sastre.

SCANDINAVIA. The heritage of Ibsen still alive. Strindberg restored to fashion after a period of eclipse: his chamber plays taken as models of the "step beyond reality"; abandonment of social criticism for metaphysical speculation. Present-day production in the shadow of these greats of the recent past.

HOLLAND–BELGIUM. Frank anti-Realism in Ghelderode. The "step beyond reality" in Defresne. Poetic folk theater in Willems.

ITALY. Revival of Pirandello. Together with Strindberg's chamber plays, his comedies are the great patterns for the disintegration of reality. His comedies elevate the real character into the apparent world of the play (*Six Characters In Search of an Author, Tonight We Improvise*). In his later works he moves towards surrealistic myth.

Rosso di San Secondo's marionette comedies.

Ugo Betti's attempt to bring the world of Kafka onto the stage—Paolo Levi's use of religious themes in a modern realistic setting (*Gli dei di pietra*). Spontaneous folk theater (with influences from the national Commedia dell'arte) in the Neapolitan Eduardo De Filippo.

HUNGARY: The last followers of Molnar in exile: Lengyel, Bush-Fekete. In Hungary itself: resistance of the writer to the regime: Julius Hay.

GREECE: The eruptive personality of Nikos Kazantzakis. His attempt to bring back great subjects in the grand manner. Lively modern productions.

POLAND. A great deal of theatrical activity from the turn of the century. Since the end of Stalinism this activity has been revived. Close contact with theatrical movements all over the world. After the Impressionism of Thaddeus Rittner, the realistic satire of Zapolska (*Mrs. Dulska*), and the poetic theater of Wyspianski; the avant-gardism of Witkiewicz and the breakdown of reality by Szaniawski.

CZECHOSLOVAKIA. The success of Hašek's *Good Soldier*

Schweik. František Langer's realistic folk comedy, *Periphery*. In Communist Prague: E. F. Burian's *Fair Opera* and *Ragged Ballads* by Voskovec and Werich.

RUSSIA. Tolstoy's and Chekhov's dramas in the repertory of theaters all over the world, in spite of their contrasting character. Chekhov's impressionism widely copied as a means of veiling reality; Tolstoy keeps the outright nonconformism in the foreground. Gorki's *The Lower Depths* used as a model for the presentation of an unorganized group of individuals (e.g., O'Neill's *The Iceman Cometh*). Strong influences of the theatrical revolution which began before 1910 (principally Meyerhold, Taïrov, and later Vachtangov): Symbolism and anti-Realism in Andreyev (*The Life of Man*); Mayakovski (*Mystery Bouffe, The Bedbug, The Bathhouse*); Blok (*The Puppet Show*).

Revolutionary theater (experiments, satire) together with the Party drama until 1932. After 1932, liquidation of the revolutionaries, proclamation of Socialist Realism. Since then, mainly historical plays about the Russian Revolution (on the pattern of Vishnevski's *Optimistic Tragedy* or Pogodin's *The Chimes of The Kremlin*) and propaganda plays of "social reconstruction." Since the transitory "thaw," several revolutionaries such as Mayakovski have been performed again, but Socialist Realism is still the official policy.

GERMANY/AUSTRIA/SWITZERLAND. Difficult situation in post-war Germany and Austria. Painful efforts to re-establish contact with the rest of world theatre. Confusion caused by the desire to catch up after twelve years of repression. Practically all of the once leading Expressionists dead: Barlach, Hasenclever, Kaiser, Kornfeld, Toller, Sternheim, Werfel. The return of the refugees to a divided Germany. To the West: Zuckmayer, Bruckner, Plievier, Rehfisch. To the East: Brecht, Becher, Wolf, Arnold Zweig. (Examples of internal emigration: Jahnn, Weisenborn). Differences with the past essentially of a moral nature. The only valid artistic expression of the feelings of 1945: the post-Expressionistic, deeply pessimistic *The Man Outside* by Wolfgang Borchert, who did not live to see the first performance.

A cross-section of the repertory of half a century: Gerhart Hauptmann: his work representative of his whole period's lack of reliance on the elementary form. Disregard of structure because of lack of confidence in its efficacy, although he does attempt to imitate forms of all types. Survival assured because of the basic strength of the element of opposition in his poetic compassion with his fellow-man. His naturalistic pieces revived after the close of the dispute over slogans: *The Rats, Rosa Bernd, Drayman Henschel, Dorothea Angermann.*

Schnitzler's melancholy, poetic treatments of the death of the old middle-class way of life (*Light o' Love, The Lonely Way, The Vast Domain*), mostly written in the worn out form of the five-act play. Advance to a new form in the panoramic style of *Anatol* and *La Ronde,* the latter a masterpiece of elementary form.

Wedekind's forceful and systematic destruction of form. Points the way to Expressionistic abstraction. Moral philosophy. Very strong element of opposition, somewhat weakened in effect by his contempt for form. Those of his pieces written in conventional form have the best chance for survival: *The Marquis of Keith.* Wedekind introduced a surrealistic *Grand Guignol* element into the modern theater with the Lulu dramas.

The surrealistic element on the stage: the dramatization of Kafka's novels (*The Trial:* Barrault-Gide; *The Castle* and *Amerika:* Brod) exemplifying the breadth of the stage's panorama of life. Piercing through reality on principle: the transcendental element breaks through in the form of the incomprehensible, the demonic, the uncanny. Demonic elements also appear on the stage in Barlach (Expressionistic mysticism), and, to a somewhat lesser extent, in H. H. Jahnn and the early Billinger.

Hofmannsthal's extraordinary attempt to synthesize the Expressionistic trend toward allegorical abstraction with the Spanish Baroque form, i.e., poetry and theater. The culmination of this attempt was reached in the symbolism of *The Tower.* Also the comedies, which were likewise attempts to combine the Spanish and Austrian Baroque style with contemporary conversational style (*Der Schwierige, Cristina's Journey Home*). Contra-reality in the opera librettos he wrote for Richard Strauss (*Rosenkavalier, Ariadne, The Woman without a Shadow, Arabella*). A similar contrast between strict adherence to form and flippant comedy is to be found in Lernet-Holenia.

Max Mell's re-discovery of the medieval parable and Mystery play (previously classified erroneously in Germany as amateur theater) in *The Apostle Play* and *The Play of the Imitation of Christ*. Attempted synthesis of Christian testimony with classical strictness of form in *Jeanne d'Arc*. Fritz Hochwälder's path from the formal conservative tragedy (world-wide success of *The Holy Experiment*) to the parable play (*Die Herberge*) and the Mystery play (*Donnerstag*). The anti-realistic "thought plays" of Georg Kaiser and the satires of Carl Stern-heim with their rigidly compressed dialogue style rise out of the "O Mankind!" drama of Expressionism. Three authors left the ruins of Expressionism simultaneously, after having written their first pieces in accordance with its slogans: Ferdinand Bruckner, Carl Zuckmayer, Bertolt Brecht. Bruckner's large-scale, elaborately framed designs: *Die Verbrecher* and *Elizabeth of England*.

Zuckmayer, a disciple of Gerhart Hauptmann in his power to create human beings on the stage; romantic and satiric leanings. Masterpiece: *The Captain from Köpenick*. Introduces sharp element of satire into the panoramic style; unconscious revival of forms, probably under the stimulation of the post-Expressionistic living-newspaper style of the epic theater. Later made three attempts to capture contemporary events in the drama: a conventional act-divided play (*The Devil's General*); a broadly poetic baroque tragedy (*Der Gesang in Feuerofen*); and a con-temporary chronicle play (*Das kalte Licht*).

Brecht: most powerful influence in the modern theater, though he was somewhat hampered by his predilection for systematic theory and by his personal subjection to the ideology of Communism. His early (nihilistic and definitely anti-bourgeois) experiments: *The Threepenny Opera, Aufstieg und Fall der Stadt Mahagonny, St. Joan of the Stock-yards*. His didactic pieces, based on theory and leading into sterility (*The Measures Taken* is typical). The Renaissance of Forms in the great plays of his exile: *Mother Courage* (German Baroque), *The Good Woman of Setzuan* (Chinese theater), *The Caucasian Chalk Circle* (Parable play), *Herr Puntila und sein Knecht Matti* (Parable in the form of folk play), *Galileo* (panoramic history), *Die Gesichte der Simone Machard* (strict realism overlaid with tragedy), *Der aufhaltsame Aufstieg des Arturo Ui* (Gangster story in the blank verse of the Eliza-bethan theater). Went from the didactic piece to the Parable. His poetic instinct conquered his own orthodoxy; this can be observed finally even in his purely theoretical remarks. "Dialectic theater" or "Directive theater" would be better terms than "Epic theater."

The post World War II generation is without a definite movement. Contemporary themes are dealt with in realistic style with trends in the direction of the Parable. Few sustained successes. Most worthy of notice are Ahlsen, Hacks, Hubalek, Oelschlegel, Weymann, Wittlinger, Walser, Hochhuth.

Socialist Realism in East Germany: Hedda Zinner (*Teufelskreis, General Landt*), Strittmatter (*Katzgraben*). The Swiss writers, Max Frisch and Friedrich Dürrenmatt, are far more important.

Frisch's progress from the romance (*Santa Cruz*) to the contemporary allegory (*The Chinese Wall*), ironic intellectual comedy (*Don Juan*), and Parables (*The Firebugs, Andorra*).

Dürrenmatt is the most powerful writer in the German-speaking drama since the death of Brecht. Extraordinary scenic and mimic inventive powers. Uses variegated form elements, the grotesque as a means of revelation. Uses a cabaret style (*Romulus der Grosse*) and a dangerously rapid abstract style (*Die Ehe des Herrn Mississippi*) which he has controlled in the grand plan of *The Visit*. World-wide success.

THE LAST PROBLEM

It was, of course, impossible to prevent value judgments and personal opinions from creeping into these notes on the modern drama. The characteristic developments or aspects of the drama which we have found in our analysis are often difficult to recognize in practice. Yet, only the strict application of critical yardsticks makes possible a survey of present theatrical phenomena.

We have been able to discover two yardsticks for criticism by applying our newly-formed perspectives:

1. No one any longer calls for the destruction of forms as a matter of principle; instead, those forms of the classical repertory and of the international theater tradition which have been proved worthy of survival are being revived. This Renaissance is many-sided. The revival of the continuously valid forms automatically indicates a revival of the elementary form of the theater as it has appeared and re-appeared on all continents during thousands of years—in the form of Contra-reality. At the same time this

Mourning Becomes Electra, by Eugene O'Neill. Alla Nazimova, Alice Brady (seated). 1931, New York

Mourning Becomes Electra, by Eugene O'Neill. Anne-marie Düringer, Hans Putz. 1955, Berlin

Reunion in Vienna, by Philip Barry. Center: Alfred Lunt, Lynn Fontanne. 1931, New York

Of Thee I Sing, by George S. Kaufman and Morrie Ryskind. Lois Moran, William Gaxton. 1931, New York

Green Grow the Lilacs, by Lynn Riggs. Tex Cooper, Helen Westley, Franchot Tone. 1931, New York

The Green Pastures, by Marc Connelly. 1938, New York

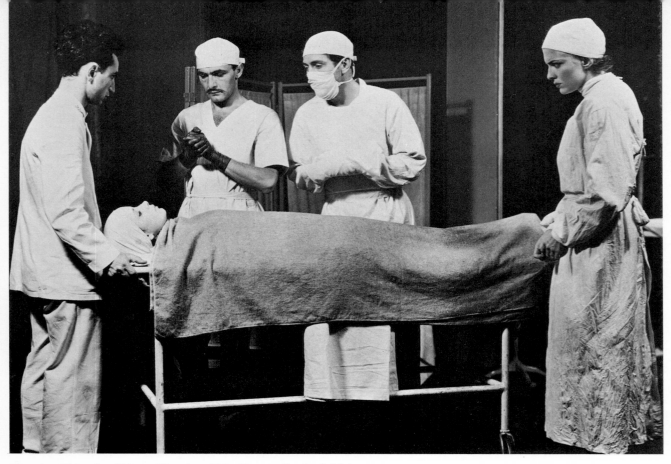

Men in White, by Sidney Kingsley. Elia Kazan, Sanford Meisner, Alexander Kirkland, Margaret Barker. 1933, New York

The Children's Hour, by Lillian Hellman. Robert Keith, Anne Revere, Florence McGee, Katherine Emery, Katherine Emmet. 1934, New York

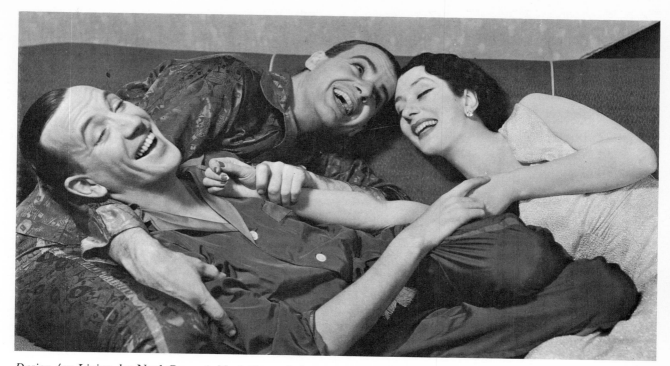

Design for Living, by Noel Coward. Noel Coward, Lynn Fontanne, Alfred Lunt. 1944, New York

Blood Wedding, by Federico Garcia Lorca. Inge Adams, Jay Barney, Alexander Scourby. 1948, New York

Four Saints in Three Acts, by Gertrude Stein and Virgil Thomson. Bruce Howard, Beatrice Robinson-Wayne, Edward Matthews. 1934, New York

Valley Forge, by Maxwell Anderson, Margalo Gillmore, Philip Merivale. 1934, New York

Murder in the Cathedral, by T. S. Eliot. Guy Spaull, G. R. Schjelder-up, Robert Speaight, Michael Lane, Norman Chidgey. 1935, London

The Family Reunion, by T. S. Eliot. Lillian Gish, Florence Reed, Fritz Weaver. 1958, New York

The Family Reunion, by T. S. Eliot. Michael Redgrave. 1939, London

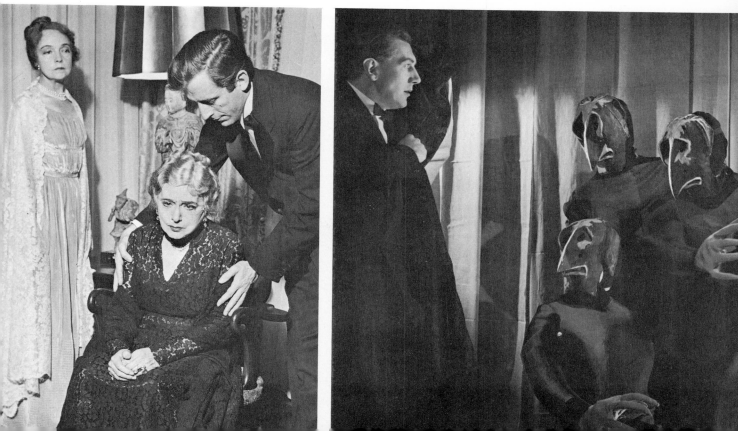

The Time of Your Life, by William Saroyan. Julie Haydon, Edward Andrews, Eddie Dowling. 1939, New York

The Male Animal, by James Thurber and Elliot Nugent. Elliot Nugent, Leon
Ames, Ruth Matteson, Amanda Randolph, Gene Tierney. 1940, New York

The Little Foxes, by Lillian Hellman. Tallulah Bankhead, Frank Conroy, Dan Duryea, Charles Dingle, Carl Benton Reid. 1939, New York

Thunder Rock, by Robert Ardrey. Morris Carnovsky, Ruth Nelson, Mary Fowler, Frances Farmer, Lee J. Cobb, Art Smith, Luther Adler. 1939, New York

Thieves' Carnival, by Jean
Anouilh. 1955, New York

Jean Anouilh

Time Remembered, by Jean Anouilh. Susan Strasberg, Helen Hayes. 1957, New York

Mother Courage, by Bertolt Brecht. Anne Bancroft, Barbara Harris. 1963, New York

The Good Woman of Setzuan, by Bertolt Brecht. Valentina Fortunato. 1958, Milan

The Good Woman of Setzuan, by Bertolt Brecht. Albert Salmi, Zero Mostel, Uta Hagen, Nancy Marchand. 1956, New York

Clash by Night, by Clifford Odets. Tallulah
Bankhead, Lee J. Cobb. 1942, New York

Jacobowsky and the Colonel, by Franz Werfel and S. N. Behrman.
Oscar Karlweis, J. Edward Bromberg, Louis Calhern. 1944, New York

The Skin of Our Teeth, by Thornton Wilder. Mary
Martin, George Abbott, Helen Hayes. 1955, New York

The Skin of Our Teeth, by Thornton Wilder. Fredric March, Florence Eldridge. 1942, New York

Antigone, by Jean Anouilh. Katharine Cornell, Cedric Hardwicke, George Matthews. 1946, New York

Albert Camus

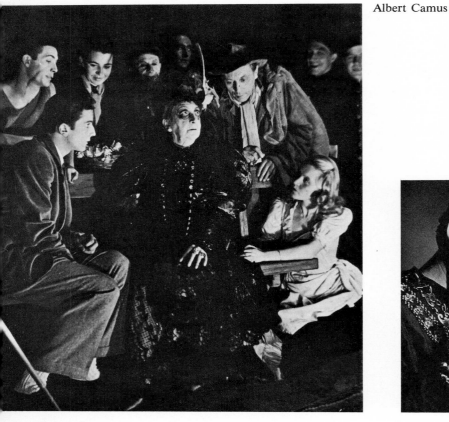

The Madwoman of Chaillot, by Jean Giraudoux.
Louis Jouvet, Marguerite Moréno. 1945, Paris

Caligula, by Albert Camus. Gérard Philipe, 1945, New York

indicates that extreme subjectivism of form has almost completely disappeared from the modern drama. The Renaissance of Form—or the re-employment of historical forms—will create a new understanding between author and public: communication.

2. Opposition is still a powerful basic impulse of Art, even though it may be originally derived from the desire to conform to ideologies and slogans which characterized earlier theatrical epochs. Thus the basic opposition of men to the world as it is has replaced social criticism. This protest of men against the world breaks through in the drama even when it is covered by the cloak of ideology. It is additionally provoked to reveal itself by the dangers of the time. Faced with a choice between conformity and isolation offered him by power and machines, Man is obliged to uphold *what is common to all men*. The dramatic expression of this opposition is the play which is staged as a parable of the protest against the everyday world.

As an historical process this development of the modern drama requires no qualification. It is what it is without any possibility of argument. The fact that it was not a consciously formed and agreed upon development only gives a greater appearance of necessity. The only way open after the complete disintegration of form was the way back to the old forms. Communicating Man's opposition to the world in the name of freedom was the only way to make him intelligible on stage after the collapse of belief in progress and the onset of a constantly increasing scepticism with regard to the current ideologies.

And what has been the effect of this process? Or, rather, how good are the plays which it has produced? We have no other yardstick than comparison. The amazing staying power of the classical repertory makes the comparison easy and at the same time induces new doubts. Hardly one of the new plays belongs in the same category with *Antigone, Hamlet, Tartuffe, Maria Stuart, Faust, The Prince of Homburg, Woyzeck, A Doll's House, Pygmalion, The Ghost Sonata*, or *Rosa Bernd*. Wherever compactness of form has been attained, as in Anouilh, it is usually on a small scale. Wherever the power of the oppositional element is strong enough to raise the play to greatness, as in Brecht, it becomes snared in other obstacles. Naturally, the level of greatness is more likely to be reached when one of the basic methods of writing plays is, so to speak, reborn in the writer. The revival of various forms makes the presentation of individuals easier, but this advantage is nullified by the apparent loss in creative energy.

Has creative energy, then, been used up altogether? Will the Renaissance in which we live take on the characteristics of a period of decadence (which, as historical parallels show, it need not be)? To bring the question still closer to the center of the contemporary problem, has the element of Opposition, both in the institution of the Theater and in the language of the playwright, any chance at all of still prevailing? Must it not take on some of the distorted aspect of impotent rage, as in Dürrenmatt, or some of the monotony of hopelessness, as in Beckett?

Who could answer these questions, with easy optimism, in the affirmative? A good many things strengthen the scepticism to which we have inclined. But as soon as we change the question from "What will happen?" to "What shall we do?" the answer becomes simple. Our own freedom is at stake, here as everywhere else. Perhaps we defend it best by declaring ourselves for Opposition wherever it exists.

From the Preface to Three Plays for Puritans, *1900:*

It does not follow, however, that the right to criticize Shakespear involves the power of writing better plays. And in fact—do not be surprised at my modesty—I do not profess to write better plays. The writing of practicable stage plays does not present an infinite scope to human talent; and the playwrights who magnify its difficulties are humbugs. The summit of their art has been attained again and again. No man will ever write a better tragedy than Lear, a better comedy than Le Festin de Pierre or Peer Gynt, a better opera than Don Giovanni, a better music drama than The Nibelung's Ring or, for the matter of that, better fashionable plays and melodramas than are now being turned out by writers whom nobody dreams of mocking with the word immortal. It is the philosophy, the outlook on life, that changes, not the craft of the playwright. A generation that is thoroughly moralized and patriotized, that conceives virtuous indignation as spiritually nutritious, that murders the murderer and robs the thief, that grovels before all sorts of ideals, social, military, ecclesiastical, royal and divine, may be, from my point of view, steeped in error; but it need not want for as good plays as the hand of man can produce. Only, those plays will be neither written nor relished by men in whose philosophy guilt and innocence, and consequently revenge and idolatry,

---

DOCUMENTS
ON CONTEMPORARY
PLAYWRITING

have no meaning. Such men must rewrite all the old plays in terms of their own philosophy; and that is why, as Stuart-Glennie has pointed out, there can be no new drama without a new philosophy. To which I may add that there can be no Shakespear or Goethe without one either, nor two Shakespears in one philosophic epoch, since, as I have said, the first great comer in that epoch reaps the whole harvest and reduces those who come after to the rank of mere gleaners, or, worse than that, fools who go laboriously through all the motions of the reaper and binder in an empty field. What is the use of writing plays and painting frescoes if you have nothing more to say or shew than was said and shewn by Shakespear, Michael Angelo, and Raphael? If these had not seen things differently, for better or worse, from the dramatic poets of the Townley mysteries, or from Giotto, they could not have produced their works: no, not though their skill of pen and hand had been double what it was. After them there was no need (and *need* alone nerves men to face the persecution in the teeth of which new art is brought to birth) to redo the already done, until in due time, when their philosophy wore itself out, a new race of nineteenth century poets and critics, from Byron to William Morris, began, first to speak coldly of Shakespear and Raphael, and then to rediscover, in the medieval art which these Renascence masters had superseded, certain forgotten elements which were germinating again for the new harvest. What is more, they began to discover that the technical skill of the masters was by no means superlative. Indeed, I defy anyone to prove that the great epoch makers in fine art have owed their position to their technical skill. It is true that when we search for examples of a prodigious command of language and of graphic line, we can think of nobody better than Shakespear and Michael Angelo. But both of them laid their arts waste for centuries by leading later artists to seek greatness in copying their technique. The technique was acquired, refined on, and elaborated over and over again; but the supremacy of the two great exemplars remained undisputed. As a matter of easily observable fact, every generation produces men of extraordinary special faculty, artistic, mathematical and linguistic, who for lack of new ideas, or indeed of any ideas worth mentioning, achieve no distinction outside music halls and class rooms, although they can do things easily that the great epoch makers did clumsily or not at all. . . . But the humblest author, and much more a rather arrogant one like myself, may profess to have something to say by this time that neither Homer nor Shakespear said. And the playgoer may reasonably ask to have historical events and persons presented to him in the light of his own time, even though Homer and Shakespear have already shewn them in the light of their time. For example, Homer presented Achilles and Ajax as heroes to the world in the Iliads. In due time came Shakespear, who said, virtually: I really cannot accept this spoilt child and this brawny fool as great men merely because Homer flattered them in playing to the Greek gallery. Consequently we have, in Troilus and Cressida, the verdict of Shakespear's epoch (our own) on the pair. This did not in the least involve any pretence on Shakespear's part to be a greater poet than Homer.

BERTOLT BRECHT

From "Notes to The Threepenny Opera" *(1931):*

The Epic drama inclines to materialism, is not much interested in involving the audience's emotions, recognizes an ending rather than a goal, and uses a different method of construction—one in which progress is not in a straight line, but in curves and even in leaps. The dynamic dramaturgy concerned with ideals and dealing with the human individual was far more radical in all its essential points when it began (with the Elizabethans) than German pseudo-classicism, which, coming 200 years later, exchanged the dynamics of the subject for the dynamics of form and had already "regulated" its concept of the individual. (The present-day imitators of the imitators have already disappeared: the dynamics of form have meanwhile become transformed into an empirically based, artful arrangement of many effects, and the individual, which is in the process of disintegration, is coming to be put together only for the sake of particular roles . . . just as if the individual had not simply fallen apart long ago). . . . Nowadays, when human character must be looked at as "the ensemble of all social conditions," only the Epic form is capable of grasping those processes which serve as dramatic material for a comprehensive view of the world.

Even Man—Man in the flesh—can only be understood in terms of the processes in which and through which he exists.

From "Dramaturgischen Blätter des Landestheatters Oldenburg" (1928/29):

The great modern dramatic subjects must be seen in a mimic perspective; they must be defined by gesture. They must be arranged with respect to human beings or groups of human beings.

From "Versuche" 4-7 (1930):

Dramatic Form of the Theater:	Epic Form of the Theater:
acting out	narrating
involves the spectator in the action on the stage	makes the spectator an observer, but
uses up his will to act	spurs him to activity
makes feelings possible for him	forces him to make decisions
individual experiences	universal picture
the spectator is placed inside something	he is placed opposite something
suggestion	argument
sensations are kept reined in	they are brought out until a verdict is reached

the spectator stands within the action, he shares in the experiences	the spectator stands outside the action and studies it
human character is assumed in advance to be known	human character is the subject examined
Man is unchangeable	Man is changeable and changed
suspense concerning the ending	suspense concerning the story line
each scene leading to the next	each scene for itself
growth	assembly
straight line action	action in a curve
evolutionary construction	leaps and bounds
Man as a fixed quantity	Man as a progression
thought governs being	social being governs thought
feeling	reason

From "Little Organon for the Theater" (1948):

It has always been the business of the theater—as it has been the business of the other arts as well—to entertain. It is this that invests the theater with its peculiar dignity; it requires nothing but humor, the one thing that is essential. One could not raise the theater by making it a market for morals, for example; it would then rather have to take care that it were not lowered, something that would happen instantly if it did not make the moral element conform to the general temper—

from which, to be sure, the moral element can only gain. We should not look to it to teach us anything more useful than how to exist pleasantly, either in a bodily or a spiritual sense. In other words, the theater must always be permitted to remain somewhat superfluous—which, naturally, will then indicate that one lives only for superfluity. Pleasures need to be defended less than all other things.

If we look to our theater for entertainment of a direct nature, for enjoyment that is all-encompassing and lasting, something that could be provided by representations of human social life, then we must think of ourselves as the children of a scientific age. Our social life as human beings—and that means *our* life—has been placed in an entirely different sphere by the sciences.

What is the productive attitude towards Nature and Society which we, as children of a scientific age, should willingly accept in our theater?

The attitude is a critical one.

Criticism (i.e., the chief method for producing pleasure) has nothing which it *must* do for the theater in the sphere of morals, and much that it *can* do. Society can even draw pleasure from what is anti-social, provided it is vital and important: it often displays intellectual significance and various other valuable qualities even though these are, of course, put in for destructive purposes. Society is able to take advantage even of a catastrophic flood, if it can assert its mastery; then the flood is ours.

In order to undertake such a project we will naturally be unable to leave the theater as we found it. Let us enter one of these houses and observe the effect on the spectator. Looking around, we see more or less motionless forms in a rather peculiar state: wherever they are not limp with exhaustion, they appear to have tensed all their muscles as if under great strain. They hardly seem to be aware of each other, and they look like an assembly of somnambulists.

All that the spectators in such a house care for is that they can exchange an inconsistent world for a harmonious one, a world that they do not understand very well for a dreamlike one.

The theater, as we find it, shows the structure of Society (portrayed on the stage) as independent of the influence of Society (in the auditorium).

Concerning the "Alienation effect":

An alienated representation is one which makes an object appear strange at the same time as it permits us to recognize it.

Since:

What has remained unchanged for a long time seems to be unchangeable. *The new theater, however,* must produce marvels for its public, and this will occur by means of a technique of alienating the familiar.

The great undertaking of the theater is the "fable," the sum total of all previous mimic proceedings, including communication and impulse, which shall henceforth be arranged by the pleasure of the public.

Since the public has, after all, not been invited to throw itself into the fable as if into a torrent in order to be swept indiscriminately here and there, the individual events must be tied together in such a way as to make the knots noticeable. The events must not flow into each other imperceptibly, because the audience must be able to make decisions after each one . . .

Many types of narration are imaginable, some known and others still to be discovered.

The exposition of the fable and its transmission by proper and fit alienation are the chief business of the theater.

It is the theater's task to amuse the children of the scientific age in a sensuous and cheerful manner. This is something we Germans especially cannot repeat too often, for we are very liable to slip into the ethereal and abstract and thus begin to speak of philosophies for the world when the world has already disintegrated.

In his theater, *the spectator* is able to enjoy as entertainment (together with the shocks of his constant transformation) the frightful and never-ending labors which really ought to provide him with his sustenance. Here he can perform in the easiest way, for the easiest way to exist is through Art.

From Berliner Ensemble: Theaterarbeit (*1952*):

The theater is for "playing." We may expect the description of this "playing" to be somewhat serious, since it could be of importance for Society. Nonetheless, it should not be assumed that the subject is being taken too lightly if the great concepts are not constantly tossed around during the discussion and the analysis of the technique. If this "playing" is to be artistic it will require seriousness, ardor, brightness, love of truth, curiosity, and a feeling of responsibility. But does one always hear true seekers speak of the love of truth or true revolutionaries speak of love of justice? They consider things of that sort self-evident.

From "Gespräch auf der Probe" (Schriften zum Theater, *1956*):

P.: How is it that one so often reads descriptions of your theater—mostly with adverse criticisms—without being able to form any clear picture of it?

B.: My mistake. These descriptions, as well as many of the judgments, are not valid for my theater, but rather for the theater which the critics conceive to be mine after they have read my pamphlets. . . . If the critics would only take a look at my theater, as the spectators do, without paying attention only to my theories, they would simply see theater—theater, I hope, with fantasy, humor, and sense . . . I think the trouble began because my plays had to be properly produced in order to have any effect, and thus I had to prescribe an Epic theater—Oh, woe!—for a non-Aristotelian theory of drama—Oh, horror!

From "Die Dialektik auf dem Theater" in Versuche 15 ("Studium des 1. Auftritts in Shakespeares 'Coriolan,'" 1953):

B: Let us have the pleasure—and give others the pleasure—of examining a play about some well-known historical event and of dealing with dialectics.

P.: Is the latter not something very refined and reserved for connoisseurs?

B.: No. The simple people, who are so complicated, loved stories of the rise and fall of the great, of eternal change, of the tricks and stratagems of the suppressed, of the potentialities that Man possesses, even in the days of the market-place booth-theater and the folk ballad. And they seek the truth, "that which is behind it all."

From a letter to an actor (1951):

Of course live, well-rounded, and naturally inconsistent people must appear on the stage of a realistic theater, together with all of their emotions and their immediate remarks and actions. The stage is no herbarium or zoölogical museum full of stuffed animals. The actor must be capable of creating these people!

CARL ZUCKMAYER

From "Die Kunst lebt vom Überfluss" (Deutsche Zeitung, *1955*):

There can be neither any doubt nor any question that dramatic art is a necessity, and for an immediate effect from man to man in the living theater, it cannot be replaced by any technical substitute, no matter how close to life and art. If dramatic art were to cease or to become degenerate, Mankind would sink back into a prehistoric and pre-religious state which would inevitably lead to its most terrible crisis, to its downfall, and to its spiritual—and, therefore, also physical—death. For him who has experienced this, devotion to the theater and unrelenting effort to improve its methods of expression is a natural and by no means hopeless task, even in those times in which there is only the smallest opportunity for doing so—yes, even in periods in which one is driven out and banned from the theater of one's native tongue.

The present world tension, the daily tragedies of life on the border or in No-man's land, are not favorable to the development of a new dramaturgy of grand style: they suck the blood and the breath out of drama, so to speak, and force it into a vacuum. Drama has not experienced any great, potentially fruitful flowering since the first World War, but it is a worthwhile task to maintain its art during the period of transition, to guard its secretly flickering fire and ever and again to fan it with one's breath. The form and substance of art is, naturally, not determined by what we call the taste or desires of the public, for in reality no such thing exists. The public has no pre-determined opinion, no collective desire, and certainly no taste that is valid for all. Probably as early as Sophocles' day people went to the theater in order to amuse themselves, or perhaps, like the great majority of the church-going public, out of habit. Only the inner truth, the powers of persuasion, and the vital substance of what is offered to the spectator has the responsibility of awaking and cultivating an opinion, a desire, and a receptive attitude in him.

First of all, the public, the mass built up out of single individuals, must be completely overpowered by the stage, it must be mastered—there is a suggestion here of erotic force—so that it is truly able and willing to surrender itself, to sympathize and to empathize. We refuse to have anything to do with restricting the theater to a purely sermonizing, didactic lesson, with narrowing it down to a school-room or to an evening course. On the contrary, we desire and advocate a direct, forceful, and responsible participation in the basic events of our time, by which we do not at all intend to postulate the error that the theater is directly able either to change, improve, or reform conditions and human beings. Nevertheless, we believe in our power to influence or prepare the spiritual temper of an age through the high-frequency of artistic radiation. *"Tua res agitur"*—you are concerned in what is played here—that is the supposition on which every deep and wide-spread effect that the theater has is based. This by no means implies that the presentation must conform to some current fad, but that it must originate in human necessity, need, or urgency and that it must be filled with that deeper meaning which even the most primitive visual curiosity at bottom longs for.

Peep-show booth, ballad song, circus, puppet theater, clown farce, strolling players—our dramatic art grew out of these free root impulses, and it was ever and again awakened to a realization of its true nature by the spirit and the power of the poetic word. We who have sworn to work creatively for the stage must never hesitate to risk our lives with every new scene, every new plot, and every new form of scenery or character. Those who do not care to walk the tight-rope and risk breaking their necks will never succeed in moving the hearts of their audiences. To move the heart, however, is what we have been commanded to do—not in order to injure it, but in order to kindle its holiest flames as with an arrow of fire. We call it Beauty, Truth, and Humanity.

JEAN ANOUILH

In memoriam, Jean Giraudoux

Happy are the young men who can speak to their idol and receive his well-meant advice! I grew up without a master. Until 1928 I carried Claudel in my heart and Shaw and Pirandello dog-eared in my pockets, but, nonetheless, I was alone. Alone with my fear of being twenty years old very soon, alone with my love for the theater and with all my clumsiness. Who could have revealed the secret to me in those days of the well-made play? Musset or Marivaux, read again for the umpteenth time? They were too far away; they came from a time which was already legendary, from a time when spoken French still had periods and commas, from a time when sentences danced. And yet there was a secret; a secret that without doubt had been long lost and I was far too inexperienced to re-discover alone. Eighteen years! and my studies uncertain, my means of existence troublesome. And my anxieties and clumsy fingers. Without doubt Claudel must have re-discovered the secret, or perhaps rather found an entirely different one, but he was a great and distant statue, a holy picture in the mountains, who could not be approached.

And then there came a wonderful, incomparable, mild spring which decked the Avenue Montaigne with blossoms.

I will never again see such chestnut blossoms or feel such mildness in the air, no matter how long I live. For several evenings I was close to the gods in the blue haze reflected from the undersides of leaves, in the noise of the automobiles, in the sudden completeness which encompassed everything for me in that part of Paris.

Oh, the performances of *Siegfried* . . . Honored Giraudoux, who will tell you now, since I never had the courage to tell you, how you inspired despair and joy, pride and tender humbleness in that young man in the gallery of the Comédie des Champs-Élysées? . . .

I never told you that it was on the evening I saw your *Siegfried* that I suddenly understood. I spent a night after that which it took me a long time to get over, which I will perhaps never fully get over. But I thank that spring evening in 1928 when I was the only spectator to weep even at your comic lines for bringing me one little step out of the night.

From a letter to Hubert Gignoux (1946):

I have now occupied myself for some time with the theater and with such success that I appear to have attracted an uncomfortable amount of attention. Some have explained this by saying that I am a skillful technician of the well-made play. I take this as a compliment, for my father was a tailor's cutter, a simple and honorable man who was an expert at his work and took great pride in it. I have always wished that I would be as good a handicraftsman as my father if the practice of literature should escape me.

We are in the process of eliminating the concept of the "well-made play" now that it has reigned supreme in the theater until it has become mummified. Pirandello decided one day to eliminate it with a stroke of genius which has a significance for the theater can never be sufficiently emphasized: *Six Characters in Search of an Author*. But despite this summary execution, despite everything that we can do, each in accordance with his ability, despite all this acuteness and patience— where are we? We look like the eternal pupils who have to take their exams once again.

A comedy must be written and played better than real life. Life can be very nice, but it has no form. Art does nothing but give it this form and make it by all means at its disposal truer than reality.

T. S. ELIOT

From "A Dialogue on Dramatic Poetry" (1928):

. . . As for us, we know too much, and are convinced of too little. Our literature is a substitute for religion, and so is our religion. We should do better if, instead of worrying about the place of drama in society, we simply decided what amused us. What is the purpose of the theatre except to amuse?

If there is a future for drama, and particularly for poetic drama, will it not be in the direction indicated by the ballet? Is it not a question of form rather than ethics? And is not the question of verse drama versus prose drama a question of degree of form? . . . Has human feeling altered much from Aeschylus to ourselves? I maintain the contrary. I say that prose drama is merely a slight by-product of verse drama. The human soul, in intense emotion, strives to express itself in verse. It is not for me, but for the neurologists, to discover why this is so, and why and how feeling and rhythm are related. The tendency, at any rate, of prose drama is to emphasize the ephemeral and superficial; if we want to get at the permanent and universal we tend to express ourselves in verse.

. . . When it comes to the present age, we are not going to be deterred by a fatalistic philosophy of history from wanting a poetic drama, and from believing that there must be some way of getting it. Besides, the craving for poetic drama is permanent in human nature. . . I believe that if you want a thing you can get it, and hang the economic factors. . . . We should hire a barn or studio, and produce plays of our own, or even disjected scenes of plays and produce them by ourselves and only for ourselves, no friends to be admitted. We might learn at least by practice first whether we have anything in common, and second what forms of versification are possible.

From "The Three Voices of Poetry" (1954):

It may be that from the beginning I aspired unconsciously to the theatre ... I have, however, gradually come to the conclusion that in writing verse for the stage both the process and the outcome are very different from what they are in writing verse to be read or recited.

    ... In a verse play, you will probably have to find words for several characters differing widely from each other in background, temperament, education, and intelligence. You cannot afford to identify one of these characters with yourself, and give him (or her) all the "poetry" to speak. The poetry (I mean, the language at those dramatic moments when it reaches intensity) must be as widely distributed as characterization permits; and each of your characters, when he has words to speak which are poetry and not merely verse, must be given lines appropriate to himself. When the poetry comes, the personage on the stage must not give the impression of being merely a mouthpiece of the author. ... And if you have to listen to a verse play, take it first at face value, as entertainment, for each character speaking for himself with whatever degree of reality his author has been able to endow him. Perhaps, if it is a great play, and you do not try too hard to hear them, you may discern the other voices too [*that of the poet speaking to himself, and that of the poet speaking to his hearers*]. For the work of a great poetic dramatist, like Shakespeare, constitutes a world. Each character speaks for himself, but no other poet could have found those words for him to speak. If you seek for Shakespeare, you will find him only in the characters he created; for the one thing in common between the characters is that no one but Shakespeare could have created any of them. The world of a great poetic dramatist is a world in which the creator is everywhere present, and everywhere hidden.

CHRISTOPHER FRY

From "Poetry in the Theater" (1953):

For a very long time now, for 70 years at least, in healthy reaction to the romantic fustian of the early and middle years of the 19th century, the theater has pursued this—if I say "surface reality" perhaps I shall mislead you into thinking I mean "superficiality," but I don't mean that: I mean the reality we have made for ourselves by 2,000,000 years of getting used to it: the domestication of the enormous miracle: the reality in which we no longer see a moving, articulate, thinking shape, of quite extraordinary design and substance, across the breakfast-table, but something which by a long, long process of getting-used-to we have subdued into a gentler image—our wife. And in the theater of the 20th century, so far the search has been for this particular reality. We have put four walls round the stage and obliterated space; used familiar words for Time, such as dinner-time, early-the-same-evening, two-days-later, and obliterated eternity. And because speech (that strange, brilliant, mature achievement of the human animal) has become subdued to a limited game of hit-or-miss, stage dialogue, in its pursuit of surface reality, goes to the limit of imitation and tinkles in time with the breakfast cups. . . . But the truth, surely, the greater reality, is that we should be out of place, as in fact in life, if we stop to think, we always are. If we stop pretending for a moment that we were born fully-dressed in a service flat, and remember that we were born stark naked into a pandemonium of most unnatural phenomena, then we know how out-of-place, how lost, how amazed, how miraculous we are. And this reality is the province of poetry.

. . . we have gone . . . about as far as we can go. We have invaded every room in the house, except perhaps the water-closet, and our escape from that has been a pretty near thing. We have thumped out political tracts, and burrowed with Freud, and the thumping and burrowing have made, at times, a lively theater, but we cannot live by Freud alone; we are still left with the mystery; . . .

And so, as we have pursued this one kind of realism to a dead-end, or at least to an uncertain terminus, the natural thing to do is to pursue the other kind of realism, the kind I believe to be far more realistic.

. . . We know what the world looks like . . . in everyday newspaper terms. The knowledge makes for dismay and a suffocation of the spirit. If the theater can help us to see ourselves and the world freshly, as though we had just rounded the corner into life, it will be what entertainment should be, a holiday which sets us up to continue living at the top of our bent, and worth, I think, any amount of admonition and prophecy or the photographic likeness of how we appear by custom. This change of viewpoint would be no escapism or fantasy. Nothing could be so wildly, perilously, incomprehensibly fantastic as reality itself, and we may as well dare to look at it, and like it . . . This theater I speak of . . . has to make the exploration in its own way. We can do it no service by thinking of it as a return to an earlier manner, as a sudden reversal to the 17th century, for example. It will see, I hope, strongly with its own eyes, and discover its own tensions . . .

The last word on man is very far from being spoken. There is always something new under the sun, because a mystery never ages. Our difficulty is to be alive to the newness, to see through the windows which are so steamed over with our daily breath, to be able to be old and new at one and the same time . . . And the theater we should always be trying to achieve is one where the persons and events have the recognizable ring of an old truth, and yet seem to occur in a lightning spasm of discovery.

THORNTON WILDER

From a conversation with Robert Jungk (1955):

This is an age of spiritual passivity. The masses are supplied with more ideas, legends, myths, and fairy tales than ever before, but all of them have already been pre-cooked and pre-chewed . . . Movie directors, stage producers, radio and TV arrangers, picture reporters, political editors, advertising men have constructed a monopoly in the realm of fantasy and are forcing their concepts on millions . . . They are the tyrants of the life of fantasy, the occupiers of that wide and boundless land in which ideas, no matter how wild or lawless or unusual, were permitted to live freely. The poets, the novelists, the movie writers, and the authors of advertising jingles have become the assistants of these dictators. With their photographically exact representations of characters, clothes, and moods, with their ever more detailed stage directions, with their pointed slogans and their sharply sketched type characters they have helped to crush the well-springs of individual fantasy, folk fantasy—yes, even our children's powers of imagination.

We will never again see a public like the Greek public, which was so moved by the monologue in *Medea* that pregnant women delivered their babies in the theater. Our sense of fantasy is hemmed in by our memories, by our knowledge of the hundred thousand details of history, and by the confused mass of personal histories which psychoanalysis has brought out into the open. Decades, and possibly centuries, will pass before the creative artist and his audience, who ought really to be his creator, will be able to free themselves from the avalanche of characters and events which is constantly being fed by the news events of each day. Sometimes, when I reflect that the shadows of other, similar figures from political and literary history surround each one of my own figures and that both my public and myself make comparisons more often than we experience something itself, I feel like despairing. We would really have to make for new lands altogether. I often think back these days to a remark, which I grasped only imperfectly at the time, of Professor Freud's. He told me, "The poets have always sensed what psychoanalysis has discovered. Now that this sphere of knowledge, which used to belong to them almost exclusively, has been illuminated by Science and has become available to every normally endowed person, the poets ought to submerge themselves in new depths of darkness." We must indeed once more become seers and our listeners must once more discover the art of sensing—an art which cannot be learned with the aid of searchlights and other such optical clarifiers, but only through a deep contemplation of the widening circles on the dark waters of the mind, which can only be released by the cast of a true poetic spirit.

TENNESSEE WILLIAMS

From the Afterword to Camino Real *(1953):*

I have read the works of "thinking playwrights" as distinguished from us who are permitted only to feel, and probably read them earlier and appreciated them as much as those who invoke their names nowadays like the incantation of Aristophanes' frogs. But the incontinent blaze of a live theater, a theater meant for seeing and feeling, has never been and never will be extinguished by a bucket brigade of critics. . . . And in my dissident opinion a play in a book is only the shadow of a play and not even a clear shadow of it. . . . The printed script of a play is hardly more than an architect's blueprint of a house not yet built or built and destroyed.

The color, the grace and levitation, the structural pattern in motion, the quick interplay of live beings . . . these things are the play, not words on paper, nor thoughts and ideas of an author, those shabby things snatched off basement counters at Gimbel's.

. . . *Dynamic* is a word in disrepute at the moment and so, I suppose, is the word *organic,* but those terms still define the dramatic values that I value most and which I value more as they are more deprecated by the ones self-appointed to save what they have never known.

From the foreword to Sweet Bird of Youth *(1959):*

. . . Guilt is universal. I mean a strong sense of guilt. If there exists any area in which a man can rise above his moral condition, imposed upon him at birth and long before birth, by the nature of his breed, then I think it is only a willingness to know it, to face its existence in him, and I think that at least below the conscious level, we all face it. Hence guilty feelings, and hence defiant aggressions, and hence the deep dark of despair that haunts our dreams, our creative work, and makes us distrust each other.

Enough of these philosophical abstractions, for now. To get back to writing for the theatre, if there is any truth in the Aristotelian idea that violence is purged by its poetic representation on a stage, then it may be that my cycle of violent plays have had a moral justification after all. I know that I have felt it. I have always felt a release from the sense of meaninglessness and death when a work of tragic intention has seemed to me to have achieved that intention, even if only approximately, nearly.

I would say that there is something much bigger in life and death than we have become aware of (or adequately recorded) in our living and dying. And, further, to compound this shameless romanticism, I would say that our serious theater is a search for something that is not yet successful but is still going on.

EUGENE IONESCO

Excerpts from interviews (based on information from H. R. Stauffacher Verlag, Ionesco's German publishers, Zürich, 1957):

The play is a picture of my inner universe projected onto the stage. The resistances and contradictions of an inner world drawn with lines of abstract force—a dynamic drawing. But this individual world contains the universal being within it. If this essentially inner world can be brought out, we see that it is in the form of the outer universe. This real theater of the inner being may be richer, more far-reaching, more real, and at all events purer than the Epic, the historical, the social or some unclassified theater. The theater of outer reality expresses only private matters and knows no universality. It has no interest for anyone in another social milieu or in another age. If I, however, truly unveil myself I am on the way to the discovery of the universal human element: I can become universal. Even if I do not succeed in this, at least I have the opportunity to be less private than before. We are separated by the thickness of the social walls, and are brought together by loneliness.

The only critic from whom I have learned anything made me aware of the fact that *my characters* are personifications of the pitiless void, of silence, of loneliness, and of the dynamism of anti-spiritual forces—in short, of everything that we are attacking. But I shall not give up the struggle despite all the unpleasantness. And if I succeed in invoking humor despite anxiety, then humor—the happy symptom of our other consciousness—will be my deliverance and my salvation.

The unusual—the reality behind reality—can emerge only out of the drab colorlessness of everyday life and its prose. Ordinariness is overcome as soon as it is felt to be absurd and improbable. But first it has to be experienced; and finally we realize that there is nothing so strange as the banal. The astounding is ready at hand.

From "Avant-garde *theater does not exist" (in* Arts, *1958):*

We can very easily create a popular theater, a boulevard theater, a propagandistic and edifying theater using conventional speech—in short, a theater of the masses. We must not, however, sacrifice to it that other theater which consists of seeking and experiment—the theater of the *avant-garde.* . . . Perhaps we cannot always ask, "What good does it do?" but even if this theater draws only fifty spectators each night (and it does draw this much) it thereby proves its own necessity. Politics, spiritual apathy, ill will, and envy threaten the *avant-garde* theater from all sides: they dangerously threaten Beckett, Vauthier, Genet, Schehadé, Weingarten and others who support them.

From an answer to Kenneth Tynan (in The Observer, *1958):*

Mr. Tynan seems . . . to acknowledge only one plane of reality: what is called the "social" plane, which seems to me to be the most external, in other words the most superficial. That is why I think that writers like Sartre (Sartre the author of political melodramas), Osborne, Miller, Brecht, etc., are simply the new *auteurs du boulevard,* representatives of a left-wing conformism which is just as lamentable as the right-wing sort. These writers offer nothing that one does not know already, through books and political speeches. . . .

I believe that what separates us all from one another is simply society itself, or, if you like, politics. This is what raises barriers between men, this is what creates misunderstanding.

If I may be allowed to express myself paradoxically, I should say that the true society, the authentic human community, is extra-social—a wider, deeper society, that which is revealed by our common anxieties, our desires, our secret nostalgias. . . . No society has been able to abolish human sadness, no political system can deliver us from the pain of living, from our fear of death, our thirst for the absolute. . . .

This "reality" seems to me much vaster and more complex than the one to which Mr. Tynan and many others want to limit themselves. The problem is to get to the source of our malady, to find the non-conventional language of this anguish, perhaps by breaking down this "social" language. . . . A work of art is the expression of an incommunicable reality that ones tries to communicate—and which sometimes can be communicated. That is its paradox, and its truth.

(Translated by Donald Watson)

FRIEDRICH DÜRRENMATT

From Theaterprobleme (*1955*):

For me the stage is not a showcase for theories, cosmic philosophies, and declarations, but an instrument whose potentialities I am trying to discover by experimenting with it. Naturally, some of the characters in my plays profess a belief or a philosophy: I am not interested in creating a bunch of blockheads. The play itself, however, does not exist for the sake of the philosophical declarations which these characters make; the declarations exist rather because my plays deal with human beings—and it so happens that thinking, believing, philosophizing do belong to human nature in their own small way. The problems which I face as a dramatist are problems of practical technique which I encounter as I work rather than before I begin—or, to be more precise, I usually encounter them after I finish my work, as a result of a certain curiosity to discover what I have in fact really done. I would like to mention these problems also with reference to the danger that the general longing for profundity has not been gievn its due and that the impression might therefore arise that a clumsy novice is writing these words. I do not, of course, have any idea how one might undertake to speak expertly on the subject of Art, and consequently I can speak only to those who fall asleep when they read Heidegger.

*   *   *

A play comes about of itself. In dramatic writing everything has to be transformed into a direct, visible, and perceptible form, although it must be added that some things cannot be translated into a directly perceptible form—for example, Kafka, who, consequently, does not really belong on the stage.

In Goethe's time the classics were played less. Occasionally they played Schiller, but mostly they played Kotzebue and all the others like him. Let it be clearly stated here that the film has taken the Kotzebues out of the theater. The mind staggers at the thought of what we would have to play in our theaters to-day if the film had never been invented and the movie script-writers had to write for the theater.

*   *   *

Every great theatrical era was made possible by the discovery of a particular theatrical form or style in which and by means of which plays were composed. We can see examples of this in the English theater, the Spanish theater, or the Viennese folk theater, that most wonderful of all theatrical phenomena in the German language. This is the only way in which we can explain the enormous number of plays that a man like Lope de Vega could produce. Stylistically, playwriting presented no problem for him. Theatrical writing becomes more and more of a problem in direct ratio to the degree in which a uniform theatrical style no longer can or does exist. The present-day theater thus has a dual character: on the one hand it is a museum, but on the other it is a field for experimentation, so much so that each play presents the author with new problems and new questions of style. Style nowadays is no longer something universal, but rather something personal —something, indeed, that has to be created differently for each particular case. There is no longer a style—only styles. That sums up the present-day situation of the arts. . .

Now we have only styles and dramatic methods, but not *a* dramatic method . . . And yet a dramatic method, one that will fit all possibilities, just as there is a geometry which encompasses all possible dimensions, is perhaps feasible. The desire to represent on the stage the richness and abundance of the world is a compulsion of mine—not always a happy one. Thus my theater may often seem ambiguous and confusing. Misunderstandings may also tend to creep in through people who search my dramatic chicken-coop for the egg of exegesis, which I have always unyieldingly declined to lay.

The action is the crucible in which Man must become Word. This means that I am obliged to put my characters into situations which force them to speak. If I show two men sitting together, drinking coffee, discussing the weather, politics, or the current styles, I am neither showing a dramatic situation nor presenting dramatic dialogue, no matter how clever it may be. Something has to be added in order to give the talk a double meaning—to make it dramatic. If, for example, the spectator knows that there is poison in one of the coffee cups or, better still, in both, so that we have a conversation between two poisoners, the trick instantly turns the coffee-drinking into a dramatic situation which provides us with the basis for dramatic dialogue. Dramatic dialogue cannot exist without the help of an unusual tension or an unusual situation.

The true representatives of drama are missing nowadays; the tragic heroes have no names. The present-day world is characterized better in a small-time crook, a clerk, or a policeman than in a senator or a federal chancellor. Art nowadays aspires to show only victims if it aspires to show humans at all. It no longer aspires to show the mighty. The case of Antigone is handled by Creon's secretary. The State has lost its character, and, just as Physics has shown us that the world can be reproduced only in mathematical formulas, the State can be shown only in statistics. Greatness takes on stature nowadays only when it can actually be shown, when it explodes—as in the case of the atom bomb, in that wonderful mushroom which rises up and spreads out, immaculate as the sun, uniting beauty and mass murder. The atom bomb can no longer be represented, since it can be presented.

*   *   *

It is still possible to show the courageous man.

And this is one of my chief aims. . . . The lost order of things becomes established in his (*the courageous man's*) breast, but the universal eludes my grasp. I decline to find universal meaning in any doctrine. I can discover only chaos in doctrines. The world (and consequently, the stage, which represents the world) seems to me something monstrous, an evil riddle, which, although it must be accepted for what it is, must on no account be bowed down to. The world is bigger than Man and therefore automatically takes on a threatening aspect. Although it would look perfectly harmless if observed from a detached point of view, I have neither the ability nor the right to detach myself from the world. Consolation may be found all too cheaply in poetry, but it is at any rate more honorable to keep a human perspective. The Brechtian thesis . . . which postulates that the state of the world is disastrous and tries to show how it came to be that way, can produce superb theater—as Brecht has, indeed, proved—but there are many aspects of the disaster that he must suppress to prove his thesis. Brecht thinks pitilessly because there are many pitiless things of which he does not think at all.

From "Note" to The Visit (*1957*):

I describe people, not marionettes; an action, not an allegory. I create a world, not a morality, as I have occasionally been thought to do. I do not even seek to confront my play with the world because that naturally happens of itself as long as the public continues to visit the theater. As far as I am concerned, a play is performed according to the possibilities presented by the stage and not according to some particular style. . . . When I write I address myself to the player because of an inherent faith in the theater. This is my principal motive. The material fascinates me. The actor needs only a very little in order to present a man, only the outer design—in other words, the text, which, naturally, must be right. . . . If the outline which I provide is played correctly, the inner reality will come of itself. I do not count myself as one of today's avant-gardists. Naturally, I have my own theory of art (one has to amuse oneself somehow), but I consider it a private opinion and keep it to myself (otherwise I might have to alter my conduct to conform to it) and prefer to be looked on as a confused child of nature with a deficient desire for form. The best way to handle my plays is to treat them as a type of folk play written by a sort of self-conscious Nestroy. Stick to my ideas and let the deeper meaning go . . .

From the speech given in acceptance of the Radio Prize of the Society of Blind War Veterans, Berlin, 1957:

The decisive questions, which are not self-evident and which cannot be solved by all of us together, but which have to be solved by each one of us for himself, originate behind the scenes of what may reasonably be demanded of politics and the state and what they can well afford to give—namely, freedom and social justice. It is the task of today's writers, but not their task only, to press forward through the levels of politics and, deeper, through the levels of everyday life to those ends.

GLOSSARY OF
MODERN DRAMATIC
THEORY

ABSTRACTION. Abstract drama. A concept drawn from the field of painting, it is only relatively applicable in the theater. In painting, abstract means non-objective, i.e., unrelated to objects found in reality. In this sense, the word *Abstraction* can apply to scene design, although when used with reference to actors it begins to lose meaning. A theater without actors is unthinkable; even the marionette theater can carry abstraction only to the point of substituting puppets for real actors.

The concept has been used to describe the separation of scenery and acting from the coherence of causality and logic. In this sense, a play like Beckett's *Waiting for Godot* would be abstract theater. Even here, however, the lack of coherence is only relative: both the "waiting" and "Godot" are, in a manner of speaking, parts of our real existence. A sort of theatrical causality and logic (in Genet's term, *"clownerie"*) has replaced scientific causality and rational logic, but in its own way it pays as much attention to "coherence" as the latter does. Abstraction, in the sense of the analogy to painting, is clearly a necessary concept for the modern drama: it distinguishes one of the few methods used by the majority of modern authors. In contrast to the richness of words and nuances which we find in Illusionism, the modern theater appears to be generally "abstracted," i.e., concentrated on essentials.

Excessively abstract speech is ineffective on the stage; excessively abstract figures become robots who carry a phonograph record inside them instead of emotion. The danger of abstraction lies in a disregard of spontaneity, of the "gift of surprise," which Arthur Miller holds to be the most important characteristic of the dramatic figure. In critical terminology, "abstract" in its positive sense is better called "concentric." See Concentric theater. Compare Brecht, Zuckmayer, Dürrenmatt.

ABSURD, THEATER OF THE. The absurd (from *absurdus*—discordant, contradictory) has been brought to the stage mainly through the work of three modern dramatists: Sartre, Camus, and Beckett. The first two represented objective reality in such a way as to expose the absurdity of our lives—Sartre conveying his revulsion against the senselessness of what happens to us and within us, a process which leads to the idea of chaos and thereby to freedom —and Camus urging moral resistance in the face of this senselessness; but Beckett made absurdity a part of the form of his plays. His *Waiting for Godot,* even though it is, in the words of one French critic, constructed like Racine's *Bérénice,* with almost classical symmetry, permits the actors to play like clowns, without causality, without psychology, without will, from pure reflexes, moods, notions, which immediately cancel themselves out. The actors look like human beings, but they embody the chaos which results when we add the sum total of human behavior on this earth. In the end they try, again and again, with their last strength, to play the old game which represents life: "The end is in the beginning, and yet one goes on and on." That is the definition of the absurd, so far as it is translated into action in the theater.

From another angle, and without this radical consequence for all of existence, Ionesco develops his absurd theater. He looks for the absurd contradictions in certain aspects of reality, contradictions which do not occur to us because we have gotten used to them. Absurdity is present especially in the banality of daily activity, according to Ionesco, and one need only show it and expose its consequences in order to make it obvious and even shocking. This author, too, approaches *guignolade* (clownishness), but he shuns philosophical abstractions and ideological didacticism. The absurd is always reflected in the form of his plays, but it still maintains its direct connection with its starting point in daily life.

While Ionesco's plays move further and further away from reality, in order to expose by exaggeration the absurdity of reality, certain dramatists of the "new wave" in England (Pinter, Wesker, Mortimer) remain within the framework of reality in order to show its absurdity in the sadness of lower-middle-class life.

In the form of the farce and in the grotesque style of the Grand Guignol, the Theater of the Absurd continues old traditions.

ACT-DIVIDED PLAY. A late development of the European theater, culminating in the work of Ibsen. Ibsen derived it from Scribe (1791-1862) and Sardou (1831-1908), who in turn derived it from the classical tragedy and the middle-class French tragedy. The division into acts is clearly a late structural refinement imposed upon the basic division into scenes (without which theater can hardly be said to exist). Nevertheless, the old Indian drama, which was entirely different, knew the form.

The Greeks did not know it: it did not appear until late classical times (first mentioned in Horace's *Ars Poetica,* ca. 10 B.C.). Shakespeare knew it imperfectly; some early editions of his plays have no act divisions. But the Greeks and Shakespeare do provide evidence that the elementary dramatic form is immanent in act-divided drama and comedy.

In the theater tension is created by something which occurs *between* the beginning and the end; it is relieved by a climax. Only rarely (in the detective play, for example) does this climax come at the end of the piece. Most plays are constructed in a triangular form, although the equilateral symmetry which puts the climax at the middle act (the second or third, depending on the total number of acts) makes for a somewhat artificial structure. This artificial structure, which is derived from the elementary form, without a doubt presents us with *one* of the basic methods of writing plays.

Lessing was not the first to protest against the act-divided play when it was represented as the only method (by the theoreticians of the French classical drama and their German followers), but, in the further refinement which it underwent on the way through Scribe and Sardou to Ibsen, it reflected patterns of dramatic technique which cannot be permitted to disappear from the stage.

In contrast to the act-divided play we have the "station play" (See Epic theater and Mystery play). It was harshly set aside by the Expressionists and later by the theoreticians of Epic theater. Brecht, however, like Shakespeare, now and again uses the elementary dramatic form which underlies act division (for example in *Die Gesichte der Simone Machard*). The modern American dramatists stick closely to the act-divided form for the most part as do Eliot, Anouilh, and Beckett in *Godot.*

ALIENATION EFFECT (see Epic theater).

ALLEGORY. A character becomes the representation of an idea, a concept (personification), such as Joy, Death, Faith, and so on, or a fable is invented in order to illustrate a thesis. Originated in classical times, it was particularly widespread in the medieval morality play and the late medieval farce; also very much in favor during the Renaissance and in the Baroque period. More or less out of style in the age of middle-class drama (primary exception: Goethe's *Faust*). First revived in Hofmannsthal's

Everyman and *Grosse Welttheater*. Modern examples: Adamov's *L'Invasion* and Max Frisch's *The Chinese Wall*.

ARISTOTELIAN DRAMA. Much used as a negative definition in contemporary drama. Brecht and others argue the cause of the "non-Aristotelian drama." We have to differentiate, therefore, between the words Aristotle really used and the ones which are put in his mouth. In the eighteenth century Lessing had found it necessary to correct the generally accepted misapprehension that Aristotle had prescribed the three unities—unity of place, unity of time, and unity of action—on which the French classical drama was based. Lessing maintained that Aristotle had prescribed only unity of action. The form of the classic drama arose out of this adherence to unity of action, which is, as E. R. Curtius (*European Literature and the Latin Middle Ages*) has pointed out more clearly than anyone else, "anthropocentric": "It frees Man from the cosmos and from supernatural powers; it places him in the exalted solitude of morality. Goethe's and Racine's tragic figures are faced with decisions; the reality with which they are concerned is the interplay of human spiritual powers. The greatness of the classical tragedy—and, at the same time, its limitation—is its confinement to the region of human psychology: it never breaks through the boundaries of this prescribed area." In this form the Aristotelian theory of drama remained supreme until Ibsen. Even the three unities, despite clarifications by various authorities as to their real status, remained part of the regular technique of play construction until Ibsen.

As early as Herder we find the contrary category, which was to lead to the founding of the non-Aristotelian drama in the 20th century: the story. Herder (*Shakespeare Aufsatz*) said, "Nowhere drama, everywhere story! . . . History! Heroic actions and actions of state for the illusion of meaner times. . . An event containing all the requirements of greatness and dealing with something of worldwide significance, with human fate." Goethe's first version of *Götz von Berlichingen*, a prototype of the Epic theater, was thrust directly into the midst of these theories. Brecht built his theory of Epic theater on the thesis that Man is to be depicted as the result of history: "History itself provides the material for drama, and the individual comes out of the stream of history and is realized only in it. Since this process (the stream of history) manifests itself in the form of chronological succession and in contrasts, in evolutionary and in revolutionary stages, in smooth and gradual and sudden movement, the dramatic picture must show all these things. It cannot content itself with a structure alone: it must show the living processes themselves. And it is this that leads to the Epic form. Brecht said in this connection, 'This form is therefore anything but a revue-like succession of scenes.' " (Schumacher, *Die dramatische Versuche Brechts*, 1955, pp. 159ff.)

The formal element—the rejection of the three unities—is still most important here, but in his notes to his dramatization of Gorki's novel, *The Mother* (1932), Brecht founded the "antimetaphysical, materialistic, non-Aristotelian drama," which was against purgation through pity and terror. Instead of becoming emotionally involved, the spectator is asked to maintain an objective critical attitude resulting in a resolve to change his attitude to the world. The "actual, decisive operation of the understanding" is that it "controls men." Brecht rarely used this extreme theory in his actual writing after *The Mother*. Also, it is worth mentioning that the moralizing and philanthropic interpretation of Aristotle has been directly attacked by modern classical scholars. Wolfgang Schadewalt, the Tübingen classicist, has declared, in an article entitled "Pity and Terror?" (*Stuttgarter Zeitung*, February 26, 1955), that even the translation of the Greek words is wrong; they should read alarm and awe, or grief and pathos. Catharsis is not to be understood as being moral in the sense of improving us, but moral in the sense of purging us. Tragedy makes us feel awe and grief in order to free us from them. Psychotherapy speaks in the same sense of "cathartic measures."

ATMOSPHERIC THEATER (see Impressionism).

BAROQUE THEATER. Collective name for the theatrical movement which dominated Europe from the end of the 15th century until the beginning of the 17th: the theater of Spain with Lope de Vega, Calderón, Tirso de Molina, Moreto; the Elizabethan theater with Kyd, Marlowe, Jonson, and Shakespeare; the French theater with Corneille, Racine, and Molière; the Commedia dell'Arte of the Italians; and the lesser undertakings of the Germans with Bidermann, Ayrer, Gryphius, Lohenstein, Reuter, and Weise. There was the development of scene decoration with the discovery of the principle of perspective (Bramante, Palladio, Peruzzi, Serlio); other characteristics of the movement were the elaborate theaters built for the festivals and triumphs, the new technical effects made possible by the introduction of the curtain, the invention of opera, the first successes of ballet, the international character of the traveling companies. All the theatrical aspects of theater were splendidly presented by the courts and cheered by the people: the baroque theater was court theater and folk theater at the same time. It collapsed when the theater was invaded by the axioms of prudence and naturalness which were brought in with the rise of the middle classes.

CHINESE THEATER. Non-illusionistic theater. Nowadays found in the classical form of the "Peking Opera" (which exists under this name in all the larger cities of China); it is faithfully preserved in modern China (repeal of ban on several religious tragedies, 1957). Includes use of masks, costumes (with prescribed symbols), dance, pantomime, acrobatics—elements which are only vaguely included in our concept of "opera." Contains the totality of primitive theatrical phenomena, each developed in its own way from its origin to its highest refinement. Texts and productions have remained unchanged for a long time; the audience cares more about how the production is staged than about the subject matter. Performances, which may encompass as many as forty acts, often take several days. Has had connections with our theater since the twenties; its influence can be seen in the acting style of the Russian theatrical revolutionaries, in the dramaturgy of Claudel, Brecht, and Wilder (*Our Town*), and in Brecht's theory of alienation ("On Chinese Acting," *Tulane Drama Review*, 1961).

CHRISTIAN DRAMA (see Religious theater).

COMMEDIA DELL'ARTE (see Italian theater).

COMMUNICATION (see Identification, Religious theater).

CONCENTRIC THEATER. The author's proposed designation for the modern concentrated or compressed theatrical style to distinguish it from abstract theater. The two styles resemble each other in being based on rejection. The abstract theater rejects everything but the skeleton: it is aesthetic and puritan. The concentric theater uses various theatrical methods in order to attain a style as rich as possible, but at the same time cleansed of all coincidences and other things not strictly pertinent (including overt psychologizing). Directors who have specialized in concentric theater: Jouvet, Fehling, Gründgens, Brecht, Felsenstein, Rennert, Strehler, Guthrie, Brook, Kazan.

CONVERSATION PIECE (see Society drama).

ELIZABETHAN THEATER. The age of Queen Elizabeth (1558-1603) brought the Baroque theater in London to a sparkling and many-faceted development. Several streams of influence came together here: the Mystery play; the Morality play which was particularly well developed in England, the best example being *Everyman;* and the Renaissance emancipation of the theaters. The Renaissance also brought scholarly influences (Buchanan's Latin dramas and translations of the Greek tragedies) to bear, as well as the animating element of the rediscovered Plautine comedy and the typically Baroque style of "Euphuism," with its elaborately convoluted language patterns, its word-plays, metaphors, and rhetoric (best known representative: John Lyly, 1554?-1606).

Of great importance are the Chronicle plays, which are forerunners of the modern Epic theater. The age begins with Thomas Kyd (1558-1594), George Peele (1556-1596), Robert Greene (1560?-1592) and Christopher Marlowe (1564-1593), whose *Edward II* was adapted by Brecht in 1924. The universalism of the Baroque age is reflected in the subject matter of Marlowe's *Tamburlaine, Dr. Faustus,* and *Dido;* with *The Jew of Malta* he became the founder of the character drama of individual psychology on a grand scale.

Shakespeare (1564-1616) outgrew all this: only the essence of the Baroque remains in him. We should never forget that his dramas were played practically without scenery and in broad daylight (even *A Midsummer Night's Dream*). The great demands made on the spectators' powers of imagination stimulated their fantasy in many ways. Baroque scenery and machines were being used in

The Glass Menagerie, by Tennessee Williams. Julie Haydon, Laurette Taylor. 1945, New York

Tennessee Williams

Dream Girl, by Elmer Rice. Betty
Field, Wendell Corey. 1945, New York

The Respectful Prostitute, by Jean-Paul Sartre. Willard
Swire, William Brower, Martin Tarby, Meg Mundy. 1948

Purple Dust, by Sean O'Casey. Harry Bannister, Mary
Welch, Paul Shyre, Kathleen Murray. 1956, New York

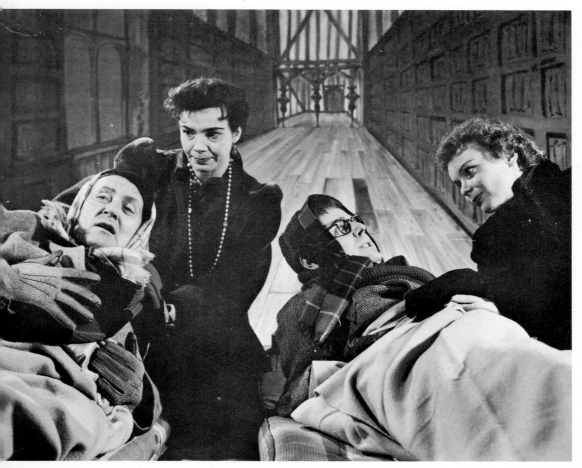

An Inspector Calls, by J. B. Priestley. Harry Andrews, Julien Mitchell, Marian Spencer, Alec Guinness, Margaret Leighton. 1947, London

Born Yesterday, by Garson Kanin. Frank Otto, Judy Holliday, Larry Oliver, Gary Merrill, Paul Douglas, Otto Hulett. 1946, New York

Rehearsing *The Iceman Cometh:* Eugene O'Neill, Ruth Gilbert, Dudley Digges, Marcella Markham. 1946, New York

The Iceman Cometh, by Eugene O'Neill. Farrell Pelly, Jason Robards, Jr., Albert Lewis, Phil Pheffer. 1956, New York

A Moon for the Misbegotten, by Eugene O'Neill. Cyril Cusack, Wendy Hiller, Franchot Tone. 1957, New York

The Country Girl, by Clifford Odets. Uta Hagen,
Paul Kelly, Steven Hill. 1950, New York

Cock-a-doodle Dandy, by Sean
O'Casey. John Denny, Bill Bray,
Peggy McCay. 1950, Dallas

The Lady's Not For Burning, by Christopher Fry.
Pamela Brown, Richard Burton, John Gielgud. 1950,
New York

Death of a Salesman, by Arthur Miller. Marcello
Mastroianni, Paolo Stoppa. 1951, Rome

The Member of the Wedding, by Carson McCullers. Brandon de Wilde (left),
Julie Harris (seated), Ethel Waters (2nd from right). 1950, New York

Summer and Smoke, by Tennessee Williams. Inge
Birkmann, Richard Bohne, Mila Kopp. 1953. Göttingen, Germany

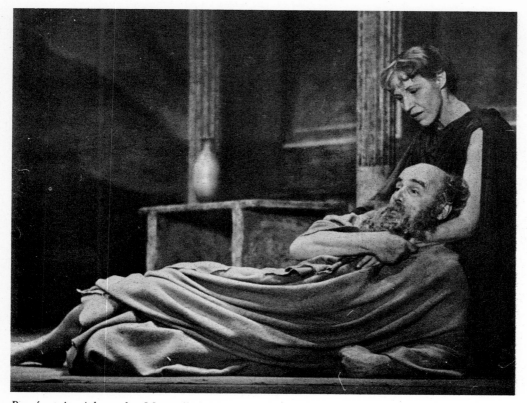

Barefoot in Athens, by Maxwell Anderson. Barry Jones, Lotte Lenya. 1951, New York

The Waltz of the Toreadors, by Jean Anouilh, Merial Forbes, Ralph Richardson. 1954

Come Back, Little Sheba, by William Inge. Paul Krauss, Sidney Blackmer, Wilson Brooks, Shirley Booth. 1950, New York

I Am a Camera, by John Van Druten. Martin Brooks, Julie Harris, William Prince. 1952, New York

The Rose Tattoo, by Tennessee Williams. Maureen Stapleton, Eli Wallach. 1951, New York

Quadrille, by Noel Coward. Lynn Fontanne, Alfred Lunt. 1952, New York

The Confidential Clerk, by T. S. Eliot. Ina Claire, Claude Rains. 1954, New York

The Crucible, by Arthur Miller. Ben Yaffee, Denholm Elliott, Osceola Archer, George Turner. 1964, New York

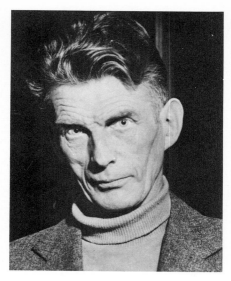

Samuel Beckett

Waiting for Godot, by Samuel Beckett. Alvin Epstein, Bert
Lahr, Kurt Kasznar, E. G. Marshall. 1956, New York

The Dark Is Light Enough, by Christopher Fry. Tyrone Power
(2nd from left), Katharine Cornell (4th from left, seated).
1955, New York

Requiem for a Nun, by William Faulkner. Ruth
Ford, Zachary Scott. 1959, New York

Duel of Angels, by Jean Giraudoux. Margaret Braidwood, Mary
Ure, Vivien Leigh, John Merivale. 1960, New York

141

The Lark, by Jean Anouilh. Boris Karloff, Julie Harris. 1955, New York

A View from the Bridge, by Arthur Miller. Eileen Heckart, Gloria Marlowe, Richard Davalos, Van Heflin. 1955, New York

Middle of the Night, by Paddy Chayefsky. Gena Rowlands, Edward
G. Robinson. 1956, New York

Look Back in Anger, by John Osborne. Alan
Bates, Vivienne Drummond. 1957, New York

143

The Matchmaker, by Thornton Wilder. Paul
Esser, Grete Mosheim. 1955, Berlin

Long Day's Journey Into Night, by Eugene O'Neill. Bradford Dillman,
Jason Robards, Fredric March, Florence Eldridge. 1956, New York

The Visit, by Friedrich Dürrenmatt. Lynn Fontanne, John Wyse, Eric Porter, Alfred Lunt. 1958, New York

Friedrich Dürrenmatt

The Chalk Garden, by Enid Bagnold. Set by Cecil Beaton. 1955, New York

plays in other parts of London at the same time, but Shakespeare never brought them into use at the Globe Theater. The projecting Elizabethan stage recalls the similarly shaped East Asian stage.

The great theatricality of the pre-illusionistic theater is one of the most important things which we must remember when we, in our present post-illusionistic phase, feel like quarreling with the Elizabethan theater. It then becomes clear to us also that the panoramic style which Goethe passed off as Shakespearean in his first version of *Götz* is a misunderstanding: Shakespeare's scene-changes do *not* mean changes of pictures; the inner structure of his plays is extremely exact and skillful, even though act division came into his plays only later. His comedies, besides, are influenced by the Commedia dell'Arte, which had conquered all the continent at that time and had a great deal of influence in England as well. His contemporary, Ben Jonson (1572-1637), was part of this movement also with his *Volpone* (which Stefan Zweig adapted in 1926) and *Epicoene* (which served as the source for Richard Strauss's opera *Die schweigsame Frau*, 1935). Besides the great romantic tragedy, the era of Elizabethan theater also included tragicomedy (Beaumont and Fletcher), bourgeois drama (Dekker and Heywood) and, in Webster (/-1634?) and Tourneur (1575-1626), the stronger and bloodier characteristics of the Baroque style. The Elizabethan theater was liquidated in 1642 by the Puritans, who ordered the closing of all theaters. In actual point of fact the Puritan influence continued for centuries. Even when the theaters were opened again the Puritan influence was still felt—and not only in England. The extreme antithesis of the Puritan attitude is the theatrical attitude—the attitude of the Elizabethan theater. In this connection, Brecht has said (Notes to *The Threepenny Opera):* "The dynamic dramaturgy, directed toward the imagination and dealing with the individual, which the Elizabethans originated, was far more radical, in all important points, than the dramaturgy of German pseudo-classicism which came 200 years later and confused the dynamics of performance with the dynamics of what is to be performed." Peter Brook's Stratford production of *Titus Andronicus* is an example of the significance this scenic-mimic dynamism can have for the modern theater.

EPIC THEATER. Formulated and promoted by Brecht (non-Aristotelian drama, cf. Aristotelian drama. References: Above, pp. 101-107; Schumacher, *Die dramatischen Versuche Bertolt Brechts*, pp. 125ff., 211ff., 290ff.—stays close to the Communist line; Jürgen Rühle, *Das gefesselte Theater*, pp. 220ff.—critical; Peter Szondi, *Theorie des modernen Dramas*, pp. 98ff.—academic; Eric Bentley, "The Stagecraft of Brecht," *In Search of Theater*. Worth mentioning: George Lukács' strong adverse criticism of Brecht's theories).

"Epic" in the sense that Brecht uses it, is to be understood as the negation of "dramatic" in the sense in which that word is used to describe the last phase of the middle-class illusionistic drama. It incorporates two types of attack: 1. against the act-divided play and 2. against the dramatization (usual meaning: filling with excitement) of events and dialogue.

The belief that the actors had to behave as if they knew nothing of the spectators went out with the elimination of the act-divided form. At the same time, the awkward "exposition" with which the middle-class drama had to concern itself so much (if possible it was to be introduced surreptitiously into the first act) was set aside, as was the drive toward the greatest possible "naturalness" of dialogue.

The illusionistic "dramatization," according to Brecht, took place both on the stage and in the audience: on the stage by having the actors identify themselves completely with their roles so that they became immersed in them, thus playing in a trance through which the action could be completely resolved in an ostensible truth. In the audience this dramatization was achieved by means of sympathy, suggestion, enchantment, intoxication—in other words, also by means of a trance. The Epic theater, on the other hand, put ahead of everything the assertion that the theater is theater and nothing else. The actor "is not Lear, Harpagon, Schweik— he depicts these people." (This is the Alienation effect.) The attitude of the audience in the modern scientific age is a critical one. This method also implies a cutting down of the individualistic element and of differentiating psychology. If the play and the audience are to be brought nearer to each other, then the psychology must be generalized, and the characters must be made more typical.

From the standpoint of theatrical history, this is

all part of a return to the pre-illusionistic theater, in which the theatrical element had not yet been made suspect by the axiom of naturalness. Epic theater, as Brecht defined it, was the Chinese, the Indian, and partly also the Elizabethan theater. From the standpoint of human history, the Epic theater is the most conscious attempt to bring the public into communication with the stage by showing them as far as is possible, supra-individual themes which move them directly in the form of the parable: *"tua res agitur:* your affairs are being dealt with."* Obviously, the "dramatic element," in the sense of dynamic tension, is in no way neglected here. Brecht often made the point in his last years that, as a descriptive term, "Epic theater" is inadequate. (Cf. particularly "Die Dialektik auf dem Theater" in *Versuche 15* and "Gespräch auf der Probe" in *Schriften zum Theater.*)

EXISTENTIALISM. The French variation of existentialist philosophy became significant for the drama not only through the union of thinker and dramatist in Jean-Paul Sartre, but also through the school of dramatists which the philosophy created with its concept of Man and its view of the world. It contains the roots of the very important category of self-alienation, which Pirandello took to its ultimate extreme with his "stratification" of the character. ("Man is always outside himself.") In Sartre, whose technique is more conservative than anything else, this stratification has been confined to the sphere of the will (as in *The Devil and the Good Lord*): it does not matter whether man wills good or evil, because whatever he does the result is always evil, i.e., meaningless. For the Existentialist this "absurdity" is the most distinctive characteristic of life. And in his analysis of the power of imagination, Sartre has also provided the basis for the activity of someone like Ionesco: only the imaginary, he has said, is real. Consequently, the apparent reality of the world in which we live has to be denied: "Man is only what he makes of himself." He exists only insofar as "he frees himself from himself." Sartre has brought this denial of the real, i.e., everyday, world to the point of justifying immorality and crime.

Saint Genet, Comédien et Martyr is Sartre's apologia for an actual convict who began to write plays after the publication of his sensational memoirs; it is printed as the first volume of the Galli-

mard edition of the works of Jean Genet. This problem of morality was the basis of the quarrel between Sartre and Albert Camus, who is often also classified as an Existentialist because he too subscribed to Nietzsche's dictum, "God is dead" and replaced God with Man (a substitution which is the basis of Sartre's "Humanism"). For Camus, the Good is a category which is at the same time unconditional and unattainable: Man is always in "revolt" against meaninglessness and evil. It is precisely the hopelessness of his revolt that gives Man dignity. An excellent analysis of Sartre's Existentialism appears in Fritz Heinemann, *Existenzphilosophie lebendig oder tot?* 1954, pp. 112ff.

EXPRESSIONISM. Everything that must be said about Expressionism and the slogans has been said already. The beginning of Expressionism in the drama is usually fixed historically as 1912 with Reinhard Johannes Sorge's *The Beggar.* Strindberg and Wedekind are the forerunners of the movement. That Expressionism represents a special and peripheral German variation of the dramatic revolution of 1910 is shown by its exaggerated subjectivism, which the true revolutionaries, as well as Kafka, who came somewhat later, were trying to overcome. Examples of this subjective drama: Kokoschka's *Der brennende Dornbusch* (1910), Barlach's *Der tote Tag* (1912), Hasenclever's *Der Sohn* (1913), von Unruh's *Ein Geschlecht* (1916) and *Platz* (1920), Johst's *Der junge Mensch* (1916) and *Der Einsame* (1917), Toller's *Die Wandlung* (*Transfiguration*) (1919), Lauckner's *Wahnschaffe* (1919), Werfel's *Spiegelmensch* (1920), Zuckmayer's *Kreuzweg* (1921). There were also Kaiser's compressions of form and Sternheim's compressions of speech, and Sternheim was an exponent also of Wedekind's cabaret style. Social aggressiveness became stronger in the twenties: Toller's *Man and The Masses* (1921) and *The Machine-Wreckers* (1922). The turnabout in the young Brecht is very curious: he himself designated his first play, *Baal* (1921) as "a glorification of the naked ego-search," but as early as 1922, with *Trommeln in der Nacht,* he wrote a play which can be interpreted as a satiric declaration of war against Expressionism.

FARCE. The free play of mimic tomfoolery. Impudence's elementary love of mockery: touching upon a wide range of human traits (especially the erotic) and political actualities. Earliest farce characteristics to be found in classical comedy. A high point of the genre came in 15th and 16th century France, whence it spread to Spain, England, and Italy. Continues in vaudeville, revue skits, and Offenbach-style operetta. Modern adaptations: Sartre's *Nekrassov* (1955); "tragic farce" (with ironic implications) in Ionesco's *The Chairs* (1952).

FORMALISM. According to the Stalinist doctrine of art, which has been loosened only a little, any type of artistic activity which does not fall under the heading of "Socialist Realism" (see Realism, Social drama). To put it more exactly, any type of drama which does not serve to influence the masses, i.e., toward "party-loyalty" and the "aims of socialist construction." In contrast, we have Brecht's definition of Formalism (in *Berliner Ensemble, Theaterarbeit*, p. 432): "Creating a rigid external form without regard to the subject matter; a way of looking at and forming a thing which is concerned solely with formal obligations and does not pay attention to the contents or to historical considerations." This definition is similar to that of Georg Lukács, for whom Formalism is a separation of theme from subject matter and a false conception of art.

FRENCH THEATER. The renewal and consummation during the Renaissance of the classical drama, based on the (supposed) rules of Aristotle, particularly the three unities (see Aristotelian drama). Masters of the French theater in the grand style: Corneille (1602-1684), Racine (1639-1699), Voltaire (1694-1778). Molière (1622-1673), the Aristophanes of modern comedy, transcended the style and his time. All of these were still in the pre-illusionistic manner. First appearance of illusionism with Marivaux (1689-1733), though he wrote mainly in the Commedia dell'Arte style; greater illusionism came in with Diderot (1713-1784: middle-class tragedy). The French theater adheres to strictness of form even in illusionistic dramas. The act-divided play was perfected in the 19th century by Sardou, Scribe, and Dumas, fils, and this perfection is retained by Sartre. The grand style of the pre-illusionistic theater (preserved in unbroken continuity by the stage traditions of the Comédie Française) was re-discovered after the fall of Illusionism. The theater of grand gesture, choreography, prosody, rhetoric, and rhythm is specifically advocated in Jean Vilar's *De la Tradition théâtrale:* "The theater is not an analytical display of our circumstances; it is the dithyrambic song of our deepest wishes or of our jests." We can find classicist tendencies in this sense in many dramas of Claudel, Montherlant (above all, *Queen After Death*), Cocteau, Giraudoux, Salacrou, Sartre (*The Flies*), Anouilh, Camus, and even Genet.

GERMAN THEATER. The German theater, in contrast to the Spanish, English (Elizabethan), French, and Italian (Commedia dell'arte) theaters, which have tradition-building and still vital forms, is completely without any traditional forms. The closest approach to a traditional form was in the brief period of the classic Weimar style which later degenerated into the court theater style and was finally destroyed by Naturalism. The theatrical history of the Germans is characterized by revolutions, which always proposed the complete elimination of everything that had gone before. Even today the self-criticism as well as the practice of the German theater has this tendency to be doctrinaire. The first doctrinaire critic was Gottsched; Gottsched was followed by Lessing, who destroyed him; a few years later came the *Sturm und Drang* movement, which destroyed Lessing. And so on until we come to Expressionism, which is often considered, not unreasonably, a typically and exclusively German art concept.

Today, when the desire for revolutions has become rather limited, the nature of the German theater is determined by the various persons who help create it. Outside Germany Brecht is taken as the representative of modern German theater. Most of the younger authors, however, used the radio as their medium while Brecht put the greatest emphasis on the visual element. (The majority of the most interesting premières of the last few years have been adapted radio plays.) Contact with the theaters of other countries, which was interrupted during the Hitler era, is being re-established with difficulty. The only person besides Brecht who can assume a position of international rank as a representative of the German-speaking theater is Dürrenmatt. This poverty of representation applies only to writers, however. The situation on the stage itself is quite different: in the last few years German producers, directors, and scene designers have successfully broken the isolation and presented theater of world-wide significance. Nonetheless, a German national style, similar to the English, French, or American styles, is, in view of the meager sense of tradition in Germany, still unthinkable.

GREEK THEATER (see Aristotelian Drama, Act-divided play).

HARLEQUIN. Merry Andrew, Punch, Hanswurst, Pierrot, Petrouchka, Vice, Clown—and whatever other names the immortal "comic character" assumes. A character, originating in the elementary desire for play, who has appeared in every age and among all peoples, wherever the non-illusionistic theater is to be found. The classical mime, the folk-devil of the Mystery plays, the *vidushaka* of the Indians, the fools of Shakespeare, Goethe's Mephisto —all of them are Harlequin. Illusionism drove him from the stage: Gottsched in Leipzig, Sonnenfels in Vienna, Goldoni in Venice (the last, of course, confined himself to depriving Harlequin of his mask, which up to then he had worn like all the characters of the Commedia dell'arte). After the end of Illusionism he appeared again everywhere: in Chaplin, in Karl Valentin, in Max Pallenberg, in Danny Kaye, in the pantomimes of Marcel Marceau, in Stravinsky's Pulcinella, in Picasso's paintings, in the revolutionary theater of the Russians, Meyerhold, Taïrov, and Vachtangov, in Giorgio Strehler's Milan production of Goldoni's *Servant of Two Masters.* Cf. Thelma Niklaus, *Harlequin,* New York, 1957; Melchinger, "Harlekins Wiederkehr" in *Merkur,* XI, 1957; Melchinger and Jäggi, *Harlekin—Das Bilderbuch der Spassmacher,* Basel, 1959. (Also see Italian Theater).

HOMO LUDENS. A term introduced by the cultural historian, Huizinga (1872-1945) to indicate "Man as player," thus providing a term to stand with *Homo faber* ("Man as doer"). A basic concept for the phenomenology of the theater.

IDENTIFICATION. Refers both to the immersion of a player in his role and the audience's mental participation in the action of the play. While the illusionistic theater sought to bring about identification by presenting apparent reality (imitation, "naturalness"), the non-illusionistic theater seeks to bring it about by delving into deeper, more elementary

spheres: by appealing, for example, to the critical faculties of the audience (Brecht). In this method author and actor aim at identification by awakening the audience to *their* views of the action. Identification represents the consummation of the theater's purpose: great theater can exist only where the most direct and intensive communication between stage and audience has been achieved.

ILLUSIONISM. The present writer's proposed name for the theatrical style which flourished in the age of the middle-classes, ca. 1750-1910. Illusionism means a belief in the ability to create illusions (or ideas or Utopias)—in a double sense: 1. a belief in the possibility of producing the illusion of reality on the stage; 2. a belief in the possibility of inserting illusion (i.e., what does not exist) into reality and thus changing it. The first sense is based on the axiom of naturalness as a basic principle of stage production. The second sense is based on a belief in progress. The negative sense implied in the word "Illusionism" is deliberate, because I consider the twentieth-century destruction of the belief in progress to be the direct result of the artistic revolution of 1910. This revolution occurred at the same time in all the arts and in many countries. The end of Illusionism in the theater means the renaissance of the pre-illusionistic and non-illusionistic theater, as it still exists in living tradition or in the *Musée imaginaire* of our fantasy. This renaissance brought about the return of such non-illusionistic procedures as the strengthening of the theatrical side of character, the use of operatic, choreographic, and pantomimic techniques, the revival of the grand gesture; it brought back as well the parable style, in which the play regains the actuality which is its source. (Cf. Melchinger, *Theater der Gegenwart,* 1956).

IMPRESSIONISM. A term derived from art history and applied to the trend toward atmospheric or mood theater after 1900. Chief representative: Max Reinhardt. It involves the abandonment of strict form and of direct communication; aims at greater "naturalness" through "understatement." In Reinhardt's hands it became more subtle and closely approached the method of alienation: the actor speaks on a level other than the one on which he feels; true emotion lies *behind* the spoken word and breaks through its surface.

INDIAN THEATER. The importance of the Indian theater for the modern Occidental theater begins with Goethe. In 1791, when Georg Forster showed him Kalidasa's *Shakuntala* (c. 400 A.D.), he wrote:

> *Will ich die Blumen des frühen, die Früchte*
> *des späteren Jahres,*
> *Will ich, was reizt und entzückt, will ich, was*
> *sättigt und nährt,*
> *Will ich den Himmel, die Erde, mit einen*
> *Namen begreifen,*
> *Nenn ich Sakuntala, dich, und so ist alles gesagt.*

> [*When I would speak of the flowers of spring,*
> *of the ripe fruits in fall,*
> *Of what charms and delights, of what nourishes*
> *and fills,*
> *Of the sky and the earth—then, Shakúntala,*
> *I speak your name, and all is said.*]

We know that the idea for the "Prologue in the Theater" came from *Shakuntala*. Every Indian drama is opened by such a prologue in which the director comes on in order to discuss the piece with the actors or with the stage manager. It is no coincidence that Gustaf Gründgens developed the production plan of his 1957/58 *Faust* production in Hamburg on the basis of this prologue, which he, like the Indians, connects directly with the body of the play (by means of costume changes onstage).

The Indian theater is non-illusionistic. It uses no scenery, only costumes which have a definite symbolic significance. It clearly appears to be derived from shadow and puppet plays, and consequently has a great deal of mimicry and gesture, elements which are as strictly regulated and familiar to the audience as in the Chinese drama. The pantomimic element has the greatest significance; it figures in the theory of the feelings applied to practical production in the manuals of *Natya-Sastra:* the feelings are as varied as they are artificial. Naturalness is intended only nominally. Brecht refers to this when he speaks of the Indian "Masters of delicate feelings." (In his play *A Man's a Man*, which is set in India, Brecht has shown us another characteristic trait of this theater: playing with toys; an elephant is represented by means of toys.) Music and dance are not dispensed with; the connection with mime is strong, particularly with reference to the *vidushaka* and other characters who resemble the types of the Commedia dell'arte.

Unlike the Greek drama, the Indian drama is not tragic. All the productions of the Indian theater (basic authority: Silvain Lévi, *Théâtre indien*, 1890) show the incredible artificiality, refinement, subtlety, and sublimation for which this non-illusionistic theater strives in its great creations, particularly in those of Kalidasa. The connection between Strindberg's *Dream Play* and Indian drama goes beyond the similarities of subject matter. There was an Indian renaissance in the Russian theater revolution: Taïrov opened his theater in Moscow in 1914 with *Shakuntala*. Note also Feuchtwanger's and Bruckner's adaptations of *The Little Clay Cart* of Sudraka.

ITALIAN THEATER. *Théâtre italien, Comédie italienne,* Commedia dell'arte. A distinctive element of the modern European theater, international in concept: practically the whole comedy production of the Renaissance was "Italian." In England, for example, some plays were written in the "Italian style" (Ben Jonson, the early Shakespeare). Italian comedy was supreme in Paris when Molière came on the scene, and although he fought and conquered it, he could not silence it: the *Théâtre italien* in Paris was not finally liquidated until the French Revolution. Its origin as a genre coincided with the freeing of *Homo ludens*—parallel with the rise of the third estate—in the Renaissance. Humanistic elements (Plautus, Terence) mixed with elementary folk theater; and to this was added the rise of the professional actor ("dell'arte"). We can see how rapidly the movement swept over Italy— and soon afterwards over all national boundaries— by studying the origin of the types, the "masks," in the various towns of Italy: from Bergamo we have Harlequin, who began as a booby and ended as a philosopher, and Brighella, the schemer, the type of the servant who betrays his master. From Venice came Pantalone, the rich and usually deceived merchant; from Bologna, the Dottore, in whom the boastful bourgeois intellectual is mocked; and from Naples we have the Capitano, who is the same as Plautus' old *Miles gloriosus*. New types were constantly added to these: Pulcinella from Naples, Bajazzo from Sicily, Truffaldino, Scaramouche, and so on. We can judge the vitality of the Commedia dell'arte by the great variety of types it produced.

Gradually, however, these types grew rigid. As

the taste of the time changed, they changed, too: by the time the middle-class reformers wanted to chase Harlequin from the stage, he had become so refined that he was reciting fables by La Fontaine and making his points with thoughts culled from the philosophers. The movement which sought to get rid of the Italian genre also proclaimed the illusionistic drama, the theater of naturalness, restraint, and taste. This new movement made the charge of "barbarism" against the eccentric behavior of the mime, who knew no prudery and shied away from no foolery, "barbaric." The older tradition was merely theater for the sake of theater, and nothing else. For a long time there had been no authors. Only scenarios were used—the text was improvised, although there were the *lazzi* (we could call them "gags") which were passed down from player to player. A Harlequin would be judged, among other things, on the basis of how many such *lazzi* he knew. His other skills were acrobatic and pantomimic. Significantly, only the comic figures wore masks. The noble lovers and ladies represented the better people, so to speak, and were mocked less than the middle-class upstarts. Goldoni's famous "reform" caused a refinement of the types and an "unmasking" for the sake of naturalness.

Although Goldoni was very cautious in his reforms (and in many of his comedies the old masked types appear again), he earned the bitter enmity of the old style mask-players. These latter gathered in Venice around Count Carlo Gozzi, who actually succeeded in driving Goldoni out of the city (1761) with his Commedia dell'arte pieces. Goldoni must be given the posthumous victory, however. With the exception of the wonderful but short rebirth of the genre in the Viennese folk comedy of Raimund and Nestroy, the theatrical basis of the Commedia, the mimic-pantomimic-acrobatic improvisation, disappeared for over a hundred years from the serious European stage.

At the beginning of the 20th century a variety of attempts to revive it were made: by Hofmannsthal and Reinhardt; by Maxim Gorki and the Russian theatrical revolutionaries, Meyerhold, Taïrov, and Vachtangov; by Stanislavski, Alexander Blok, Yeats, Pirandello, Rosso di San Secondo, and Chiarelli, With the disintegration of Illusionism the Italian genre *had* to come into evidence again. Traces of it are to be seen in production (Copeau, Dullin, Strehler, Peter Brook, Jacques Fabbri) as well as

in writing (Beckett, Ionesco, Audiberti, Eduardo De Filippo) (see Harlequin, Improvisation).

JAPANESE THEATER. Like the Chinese theater, by which it is influenced up to a point, strictly non-illusionistic. All theatrical elements (music, song, dance, mime, gesture, masks, elaborate costumes) combined to produce a strict stylization. This stylization still exists and is still influential through the Nō-play (since the 14th/15th century) and the Kabuki (17th/18th century). The modern Occidental theater in its post-illusionistic phase has similarly made a great deal of use of the runway projecting into the auditorium. "The Japanese theater originated the trapdoor, used first chiefly for ghosts and finally for all aspects of the scenery, and the revolving stage. This technical apparatus seems to have been perfected as early as the 18th century." (Gregor). The Japanese trapdoor was, in fact, anticipated by the Elizabethans. See A. C. Scott, *The Kabuki Theatre of Japan,* London, 1955.

LEHRSTÜCK. A special form of Epic theater, used by Brecht in his middle period (*Der Jasager, Die Massnahme*), but later absorbed into the all-encompassing parable form (see Parable Play). Andrzej Wirth has written of its undeniable relationship to the mediaeval Morality play (e.g., *Everyman*) in the second Brecht issue of *Sinn und Form,* 1957, p. 377: "With this form Brecht modernized the Morality play and made it capable of dealing with the complicated problems of his time. The traditional form of the mediaeval Morality with its allegorical characters which personify the struggle between good and evil is related to the modern Brechtian *Lehrstück* somewhat as a philosophical tale is related to the great society novels of the 19th century."

MIME. Mimic theater. The antique form of the non-literary, elementary, mostly comic, improvisatory play (*mimos* = buffoon, actor = later, buffoonery) with a prescribed plot and definite number of roles, the nature of the characters being also rigidly prescribed. This antique art form, which always exists underground, emerging for air every now and again, and which later became folk theater, dominated the late classical stage. It was first definitively described by Hermann Reich in his book, *Der Mimus* (1903). This book is the source of the concept of mime as a category of theatrical history. Mime in this loose sense may refer to the Indian "cursing-plays," as well as to the buffooneries of the Japanese theater or the Italian Commedia dell'arte.

Mimic production is an essential characteristic of the post-illusionistic era (Brecht, Wilder, Taïrov, Chaplin, Marceau), which has rejected the aesthetic of physical production based on the axiom of naturalness. The mimic element originates in reality and then develops equally into the clowning of Harlequin and serious symbolism. It is both anti-realistic and supra-realistic (as the French often put it: a concentration of truth). Example of a mimic drama: Ionesco's *The Chairs*.

MORITAT. Ballad sung with barrel-organ accompaniment and illustrated with a series of pictures (Example: "Und der Haifisch, der hat Zähne," prologue to *The Threepenny Opera*). Derived, in a strongly simplified and grotesque form, from the spontaneous, non-professional folk entertainment of medieval fairs: the marketplace theater.

MUSÉE IMAGINAIRE. A classification introduced by André Malraux in his *Psychology of Art* to describe the simultaneous presence of historical forms and characters in the imaginary world of art. As applied to the theater: 1. The simultaneous presence of characters such as Oedipus, Antigone, Caesar, Don Juan, Faust, Romeo and Juliet, Hamlet, Tartuffe, Mary Stuart, Gretchen, Tell, Figaro, Salome, Hannele, Joan of Arc, Peer Gynt, the Captain from Köpenick, Mother Courage, etc. 2. The simultaneous presence of invented dramatic themes (e.g., the riddle, the bet, the trial; according to Schiller, there are only a very few basic dramatic themes, which are used again and again). 3. The simultaneous presence in drama of the characteristic forms of modern dramaturgy described in this book.

MUSICAL THEATER. Modern music's appropriation of the forms of opera (Verdi) and music drama (Wagner) by means of "Epicizing" (scenic oratorio and scenic concert) and literary adaptation (the use of plots from theatrical literature). Examples: Stravinsky's *Oedipus Rex* (Sophocles), Honegger's *Joan of Arc at the Stake* (Claudel), Milhaud's *Columbus* (Claudel), Britten's *Rape of Lucrece* (Obey), *A Midsummer Night's Dream* (Shakespeare), Orff's *Antigonae* [sic] and *Oedipus Rex*

(Sophocles-Hölderlin), Egk's *Irish Legend* (Yeats) and *The Inspector-General* (Gogol), von Einem's *Danton* (Büchner), Liebermann's *School for Wives* (Molière), Henze's *König Hirsch* (Gozzi), Fortner's *Blood Wedding* (Lorca), Klebe's *Die Räuber* (Schiller).

MYSTERY PLAY. A form of Christian theater which spread over all Europe in the Middle Ages (see Religious theater). The relation of the form to ancient sources is significant: the ancient mysteries were rites or representations of a transformation having to do with "initiation" (consecration), which is common to most religions. This is, of course, a theatrical process (transformation). The mediaeval passion plays, invariably climaxing in the scene of Christ on the Cross, were considered to be Mystery plays. The station stage of the Passion Play (several stages, or "stations," in a large clearing) provides us with one of the basic methods of writing plays and has been much used in the modern drama (see Epic theater). When we call such plays as Strindberg's *The Road to Damascus* modern Mystery plays, we use the term in its philosophical sense, but Shaw's designation of *Candida* as a Mystery play is ironic.

NATURALISM. Identical neither with naturalness, nor with the historical-literary era classified under that title. Naturalness is the axiom of the era of Illusionism, which lasted from the Enlightenment to Impressionism, c. 1750-1910; it also includes Idealism, through which Nature was equated (according to Rousseau, re-equated) with the Good, the True, and the Beautiful. Naturalism proclaimed itself basically by aggression; it was opposed to Idealism. Its basic thesis was that everything alive was necessarily good, true, and beautiful. This belief manifested itself in dramatic practice by bringing on the stage everything that was ugly, sick, oppressed and exploited—the victims of an unjust society or its representatives. The "milieu" of drama was understood to be the milieu of the exploiters, who persisted in their warped view of life, or the milieu of the exploited, the proletariat, which had not previously been considered proper for the "high-class" stage. If we extract everything from the historical-literary era of Naturalism that came on the stage only because it was previously considered "taboo," we are left with practically nothing. The difference between Naturalism and Realism is purely historical; that is, it involves the specific forms of aggression to which they were dedicated. The dramatic principle of Naturalism—the photographic reproduction of reality—has really been applied only by authors of ephemeral fame; all the great writers have always been aware that the stage can only simulate reality. They have used the naturalistic principle only in the aggressive form of a method of unmasking, and from this they learned that Naturalism's great illusionistic "No!" to the subterfuges of life in order to bring about a better world founded on a purer truth is itself closer to Idealism than to Realism. As a method of writing plays, Naturalism seems definitely to be outdated, something that cannot be said of Realism.

PARABLE PLAY. A medieval drama form, related to the Morality play and the *Lehrstück*. Originally derived from the Biblical parables and then extended to cover anything capable of being allegorized. The Parable is one of the basic methods of writing plays.

PEEP-HOLE STAGE (see Illusionism).

PLURALISM. The simultaneous use and validity of several historical or actual styles (see *Musée imaginaire*).

PSYCHOLOGICAL DRAMA. Strictly speaking, psychological drama dates from the spread of Freud's teaching. The drama of illusionism tried to make its characters as "true to life" as possible and emphasized knowledge of human nature. The basis of human behavior on the stage is, of course, the supposition that people *must* act in a certain way in a certain situation (later, when Historicism came in, this was extended to mean in a certain epoch). Attempts to ignore this supposition—and several modern *avant-garde* writers did attempt it—had to fail because they ran counter to the basic principle of Identification.

Thus Freudian psychoanalysis—and the no less influential Adlerian psychology of the individual and the Jungian doctrine of the collective unconscious —turn out to be merely extensions of the "psychology" previously used to reproduce human affairs on the stage. This "psychology" began with the discovery of the diseased side of life by Naturalism and finally led to the literary discovery of dreams (Kafka et al.), repressions, and sexual pathology (*Streetcar:* Tennessee Williams). The psychological drama, as it was practiced exclusively in the last phase of Illusionism, tried to direct the audience's interest *solely* to the presentation of psychology.

The non-illusionistic drama nowhere (not even in Beckett's *Waiting for Godot* or in Ionesco) ignores the newly-drawn boundaries of the "truth" of human behavior discovered by depth psychology. The farcical clowning in *Godot* and the surrealistic excesses in Ionesco have a specifically psychological basis: they are supposed to show the self-alienation, indeed, the schizophrenia, of modern man. As long as men act on a stage before other men, human affairs can be shown only within the boundaries (far-flung though they may be) of psychological credibility.

REALISM. One of the most difficult and disputed concepts in modern dramaturgy. Doubtless it would be easiest to define it as the Anglo-American critic, Eric Bentley, suggests in "The Stagecraft of Brecht," *In Search of Theater,* as "midway between the two extreme methods of the modern theater . . . naturalism and symbolism." But even if Bentley explains that Symbolism not only includes hanging up a disk to depict the sun, but also the method of playing pantomimically, without properties (as in Thornton Wilder's *Our Town* and *The Happy Journey*); and that Naturalism consists of presenting a room with the fourth wall missing, there are still difficulties. According to Bentley, Realism would, for example, select real objects which represent a room (instead of presenting it), but then, these selected objects would regain their symbolic meaning because they *stand for* a room. After all, the floor of the stage is no more the floor of the room than its doors, walls, and chandelier are actually those objects. At this point Bentley suggests another interpretation: "Why not accept the reality of the theater, accept the stage as a stage, admit that *this* is a wooden floor and not a stone highway, admit that *that* is the back of the theater and not the sky." Realism would then consist of *not* simulating reality, not even by means of a carefully considered selection.*

* Footnote by Eric Bentley: No, realism would not "consist" of not simulating reality, it would *entail* not simulating reality *in certain ways* (which I describe). Besides, my subject was realism in stagecraft, not in literature.

This Realism would, of course, be the extreme opposite of *Socialist Realism,* as defined and demanded by Communist art theory (official definition: "a true, historical-concrete presentation of reality from the point of view of its revolutionary development"). Socialist Realism requires the presentation of a realistically created world, seen as changeable by the application of Communism; the apparent reality of scene and action must be so convincing that the greatest possible number of people accept it as real and are spurred on by it to "realistic" (i.e., socialistic) behavior. This requires a simplification (often derided by Brecht and others) which explains the Communist drama's inclination toward banality. The demand for a positive hero, which was not given up even after the de-Stalinization, shows to what extent Realism is merely a point of departure in this theory. Practical morality and the special pleader (see Religious theater) are indispensable factors in this dramaturgy which really only pretends to be realistic. Brecht, who refused to let Mother Courage point out the moral of her experiences on the stage, was sharply attacked for this (and superbly defended by Hans Mayer in *Deutsche Literatur und Weltliteratur,* 1956). Critics like Lukács, Alfred Kurella, and other Communists, have charged Brecht's *Lehrstück, The Measures Taken,* with ideological inadequacy—even with "Idealism." They trace Brecht's constantly propounded "critical attitude of the spectator" back to the "idealistic and bourgeois thesis of the superiority of understanding over emotion." Emotional appeal, i.e., the indirect persuasion of the public by shocking and delighting, is of course of the greatest importance in Socialist Realism; and it is precisely this means which Brecht, true realist, ignored. As early as 1938 he was obliged to defend himself against the accusations of the dogmatists in his essay, "Weite und Vielfalt der realistischen Schreibweise": "Literary form should not be based on any aesthetic theory, not even on the aesthetics of realism; it should be based solely on the demands of reality itself. Truth can be suppressed in many ways, and it can also be expressed in many ways. Our aesthetic, like our morality, is determined by the demands of our struggle." But was not Stalin moved by "the demands of the struggle" when he banned "Formalism" and called the authors "Engineers of the Soul"? According to Socialist Realism, drama is a means of influencing the masses; it must align the masses in manageable platoons. In all of his plays, Brecht addressed himself to the individual; he tried to convince him by means of examples: only by this roundabout way could the individual become part of the platoon. In his best plays, the individual in question is able to draw a moral from the example, and this moral does in fact not lead him to the platoon, but rather strengthens him in opposition to all uniforms and platoons. It is in *this* realism that Brecht proves his stature as a writer.

The debate over the category "Realism" can only be carried on with concrete examples. Let us, therefore, once more call on Brecht: in *Berliner Ensemble, Theaterarbeit,* Realism is defined with reference to the draft of a letter from Engels to Margaret Harkness as the "reproduction of typical people in typical surroundings." Without a doubt Realism's use of the typical aspects of the world as it is, of existence, and of human affairs is the most important difference between its point of view and the idealistic and naturalistic attitudes. Naturalism uses reality, no matter where found, for an aggressive purpose. Idealism uses reality through a systematic selection designed to show how it may be elevated by ideals. Both of these attitudes toward reality are illusionistic; they have as their basis a vision (illusion) of a truer, better, and more beautiful world which they are trying to realize. (This vision is also the basis of Socialist Realism.)

The distinguishing characteristic of Realism is referred to in Engels' definition: the *objective* attitude to reality. Accordingly, the task of artistic presentation would be *to show the real world in its typical form.* The spectator's attitude to this aim remains, as far as possible, an open one (naturally, objectivity can only be approached, never attained). The author does not speak on the stage in his own person. The world which he presents is the same world which the spectator, for the most part, recognizes as his own. The people who go through the actions on the stage are people like us. This world and these people have always been the same in all times and in all places. The *status quo* has always stimulated resistance; Man recognizes himself, again and again, in desire and pain and in despairing effort.

Where does the category of Contra-reality, established in the introduction to this book, fit in here? Every attempt to present the world and make it permanent and capable of being repeated involves a contra-reality. Making things typical requires concentration; it never involves mirroring reality as it is, but rather a presentation of a "contra-picture" of reality, somewhat in the manner of a concentrate which brings out only the essential, i.e., typical, traits. Not even the most daring unreality on the stage can survive, in fact, without the objects and material of reality, no matter how much it believes it is annihilating these with the help of fantasy. The anti-realistic form is perfectly in accord with the sort of Realism which shows typical people in typical circumstances—so long as this Realism aims to communicate through Identification, resisting the subjective element. Brecht, to call upon this great realist for the last time, rejected Realism whenever he brought in satire (the three gods in *The Good Woman of Setzuan*), preaching (the last scene of *Galileo*), or instruction (the prologue to *The Caucasian Chalk Circle*). The objectivity of showing the world as it is and Man as he is can also lead to the spirit of Opposition by way of the desire for change, but only in the sense in which Brecht himself defended Mother Courage: on the stage she learns nothing, but "the spectator can learn something by observing her." Thus the art of the Realist is "the art of digging out the truth from the rubble of the obvious, of strikingly connecting the particular with the general and of arresting the singular event in a broad framework." (*Berliner Ensemble, Theaterarbeit*, p. 264.)

RELIGIOUS THEATER. The widely held theory of the religious origin of drama is of significance for the contemporary theater because it attributes the modern drama's problems to its secularization, from which it also draws inferences and consequent challenges. Without a doubt the central problem of the modern theater is communication, the building of a bridge between stage and auditorium. The new audience of the classless society (in the days of middle-class predominance far fewer people went to the theater—but they went more often: the same people always attended the premières; nowadays more people go to the theater—but not so often: one hardly knows anyone in the audience) presents the drama with new challenges. One of the consequences is the strict rejection—so characteristic of the contemporary drama—of subjectivism. We cannot even answer affirmatively whether or not Identification, which aims at communication between the stage and the audience, creates a "community" as intended by the theory of religious theater. After all, the public would already have formed this community (which consists in a unity of thought) by means of unconscious identification beforehand.

The difference between the religious act and the dramatic act is that in the former, the process of communication is fortified by the anticipated or presumed concurrence of the audience. (The Mystery play is a border-line case.) The community in the church finds itself in agreement outside the church. Christian drama, which is a form that *must* be taken into consideration when we speak of the modern Western theater, supposes—insofar as it does not have a *purely* religious character—the existence of a faithless or doubting public which has to be convinced, either by being appealed to or by being moved. Its character of "appeal" (for example, the *Memento mori* in the "Dance of Death" or in *Everyman*) suggests that the outcome of the drama is problematical—at least, as far as the agreement, or identification, is concerned. With this submission to the basic principle of all drama, the religious element becomes secondary.

Once we grant that the theater really originated in religious rites, we see that drama could not really have been created until the theater had cast off religion. This process seems to have taken place in the Greek theater in two steps: first, when Thespis added the actor to the chorus, which until then had been alone, and thereby invented dialogue; secondly, when Aeschylus added a second actor to the first in order to depict the dialectic tension between men, tension created by the knowledge that the Gods use men in order to afflict them. This signified the substitution of poetry for the worshipping or preaching voice of the priest, and poetry used the ritual only as much as the priestly ritual had previously used poetry.

The Greek religion is distinguished by an intimacy between Gods and men which has always inspired admiration. There was a god for each human impulse. Thus Dionysus was the god of that impulse in which (as Plato, clearly referring to the theater, tells us) the basic human desire to leap (act like a goat) is expressed (goats = *tragoi*, goat-song = *tragoedia*). To ask what came first, the impulse or the god, is like asking whether the egg came before the chicken. The fact that the tragedies followed the satyr-plays at the Dionysian revels indicates that the era in which the poet (and not the priest) wrote for the theater must have been a later period which incorporated both very old and completely new elements. An example of one of these old elements is the form of the mime, or mimic play, which continued as an independent type of theater together with tragedy and Aristophanic comedy, and survived them both well into Roman times to such an extent that an Emperor was able to raise a popular mime player to the throne (Justinian, who made Theodora Empress of Byzantium). The mimic impulse to disguise and transform oneself, to play a role, belongs, as modern anthropology has shown us, to the most elementary of human impulses.

If theater did not originate in religion, there is at least an affinity between them: this affinity lies in the elements of magic, conjuring, and symbolism common to both. But it also lies in the fact that both strive for "the highest human ideals," for deepest knowledge and purest sublimation. Thus the divine had to be appealed to and represented in the Attic tragedy, as well as in the Spanish "World-theater," because in both cases the writers were dealing with the highest and most final things. On the other hand, this affinity can imply an equally deep enmity. In the Middle Ages, the Christian Church banned the theater: 1210, 1227, 1293, and 1316. (The fact that it had to be banned four times speaks for the unconquerable power of the mimic impulse in men.) The London theaters were closed by the Puritans who, of course, held play-acting to be a sin and do so to this day.

When we speak of the religious theater, therefore, we should keep in mind that only by means of a two-fold effort can such a concept be realized: the religious element must turn toward the theatrical, and the theatrical must become religious, as in Wagner's *Parsifal*. But the theater will hardly become a substitute for religion, any more than the religious motive will countermand and replace the elementary impulse to play theater. Both have always stood in a polar relationship in which both are contained. Communication with an audience is and always will be different from communication with a community. The latter is everlasting and presumed; the former is a single event which has to be newly achieved on each evening of performance.

ROMANTICISM. Romantic theater is one of the types of theater regarded as contrasting with realistic theater. The explanation of the concept involves several different approaches. Outside Germany the word "romantic" is applied to elements of the world of pure fantasy: fables, legends, fairy tales, myths. Thus everything irrational and metaphysical on the stage is classified as "romantic." In this sense, Goethe's *Faust* is romantic; among contemporary dramas, Giraudoux's *Ondine* and Sartre's *The Devil and the Good Lord* would qualify as romantic.

SOCIAL DRAMA. Social drama has been spoken of since the rise of the workers' movements whose aims were used as slogans by the revolutionaries of Naturalism in the eighties and nineties of the last century. It expressed itself first of all in an opening up of the lower-class milieu, which had not been considered stageworthy before; the proletariat appeared on the boards. Naturally, the theater was on their side. Their side was not only the side of progress, which one had to serve in an age of technical and scientific advances, but also the side of justice. The social drama was typified by Zola's "J'accuse." It was moralistic and also illusionistic insofar as its authors believed themselves able to bring about a better future by their fight against lies and injustice. The opinion that their pieces would be outdated in a few decades, when the conditions which they attacked would be gone, was held both by Ibsen (who need not necessarily be classified as a social dramatist, although his unmasking of middle-class society comments on social issues) and by Brecht. Middle-class society is, in fact, more or less disintegrating today. Nonetheless, Ibsen's pieces are still played, and Brecht's pieces will still be played fifty years from now, for as long as men are powerless against force and oppression the struggle against injustice will go on. Thus, Hauptmann's *The Weavers* still has the power to shock, although social progress has long ago destroyed the injustices which Hauptmann scourged in that play: we use this injustice as an analogy for another one done to us or to others. These survivals show that the true value of the social drama does not lie in its usefulness for a particular class struggle. Arthur Miller is right when he directs his attention to a general and not class-bound "sociality" of men, which expresses itself in the question, now more than ever valid: "How shall we live?" Or more exactly: How shall we live together?

Miller is of the opinion that this was the question which occupied the Attic tragedians as members of their society and that therefore the Greek drama is the real social drama, which we should strive to emulate. Examples of the social drama in this sense: Büchner's *Woyzeck,* Hauptmann's *The Weavers,* Gorki's *The Lower Depths,* O'Neill's *The Iceman Cometh,* Miller's *Death of a Salesman,* Brecht's *St. Joan of the Stockyards.*

Socialist Realism either removes the social problem into the past or into whatever stage of its transformation the Communist regime has reached; in both cases optimism is strictly prescribed: the Communist must always conquer. An example: Erwin Strittmatter's *Katzgraben* (1953).

SOCIALIST REALISM (see Realism, Social drama).

SOCIETY DRAMA. Identical with the conversation piece. Reflects the conversation of (middle-class) society in the salons: the *causerie,* with wit, humor, charm, points and paradoxes. On the other hand, society reflects the society drama. In 19th century Vienna adolescents were sent to the comedies at the Burgtheater in order to learn the correct conversation of society. Society drama appears to grow out of the dialogue drama of the grand style. Thus the comedy of Menander in the second half of the 4th century B.C. may be considered a sort of society drama because of its natural and psychologically true dialogue. Illusionism saw in the society drama the pattern of a "natural" dramaturgy.

Wherever non-illusionistic theater is in favor, dialogue cannot occupy the dominant position it holds when the mimic presentation is narrowed down to an imitation of reality. Faithfulness to nature has its limits, indeed, in the necessity for producing witty speech: the more amusing a society comedy, the better constructed a society drama, the more unnatural is its dialogue, and the more unnatural is its plan of action. We can trace a direct path from the society dramas of Scribe, Sardou, and Dumas to the wit-plays of Oscar Wilde and the love-triangle comedies of Verneuil, Guitry, Molnar and Coward.

It would be right to say that the end of the society drama came with the end of middle-class society only if the end of the dialogue play were in sight also. Since, however, the play with words and sentences in dialogue is not ending even in the classless society, a renaissance of the society drama is possible at any time. At all events, it still has its home nowadays in London (Eliot, Fry, and Osborne use the form of the society drama in order to express their ideas and purposes), on Broadway, and in the Paris Boulevard theaters. For the most part society drama's purpose is diversion—a not at all outmoded form of entertainment. Naturally the cast of characters changes as society changes. Even the Soviet theater has produced a new socialist society comedy (cf. Akimov in the magazine *Oktjabr,* 1959).

SPANISH THEATER. Like the French, English, and Italian theaters, this institution is more than merely a term for a national literature: it is an entity which transcended national boundaries from the beginning. The Spanish theater lives in the modern world theater not only in the unsurpassable works of the classic writers of the "Golden Century"—Lope de Vega (1562-1635; 468 plays), Tirso de Molina (1584?-1648; 82 plays, creator of the Don Juan figure), and Calderón (1600-1681; 120 plays); to whom we may add as writers of the second rank, though still playable, Fernando de Rojas (d. 1541, author of *Celestina*), Ruiz de Alarcon (1580-1639), Rojas Zorrilla (1607-1648), Moreto (1618-1669), Leandro Moratín (1760-1828) and others—but also it lives in the modern Renaissance, which brought back the term "Spanish" as a concept of modern theatrical form. Three names are particularly important in this respect: Claudel, Hofmannsthal, and Lorca. What does this term "Spanish" mean? E. R. Curtius (in *European Literature and the Later Middle Ages*) refers it back to a classic metaphor: the World as Play, the *theatrum mundi,* which is brought to the boards: "The play metaphor, fed by classical and medieval tradition, returns to a live theater and becomes the form of expression for a theocentric conception of humanity, a conception known neither to the English nor to the French drama." Curtius continues:

The drama is the only form which can show human existence in its relation to the universe . . . The greatness and at the same time the limitation of neo-classical tragedy is its confinement to psychology. It never breaks through the circle of its strict set of rules. The tragic hero can only be crushed by these rules. He cannot even resign himself to his fate. But this tragedy is an artificial creation on the general field of European tradition: it grew out of a misunderstood philosophical theory of the Humanists. It was its impossible ambition to bridge the thousands of years between Pericles and Louis XIV: Goethe himself had to destroy this form in creating his universal poem, Faust.

Curtius then praises the attempts to revive the form by Hofmannstahl in his *Jedermann,* the *Salzburger Grosse Welttheater, Der Turm* and *Semiramis* (a fragment), as well as in his adaptation of Calderón's *The Phantom Lady.* He goes on to say:

The poetry of the Spanish Golden Age certified the truth of Christian philosophy. It saw an "archive of ages" (ed. note, cf. Musée imaginaire) *in which the people of all times and places had recorded their thoughts. The kings and the heroes, like the martyrs and the peasants, are players on the great stage of the world. Supernatural powers affect human history. Everything is encompassed by the dispensation of God's Mercy and Wisdom.*

Hofmannsthal wished to recombine theater with poetry, as Curtius mentions elsewhere; he wanted to create "metaphysical theater." This universal theater, in which the world was to be universalized directly by means of the stage, has been revived most skilfully, as well as most happily, by Claudel in his *The Satin Slipper,* which is subtitled "in the Spanish style." The fact that Lope de Vega's theater lives today may be attributed also to the unconscious dramatic impulses which the poet put into it rather than to its contents and his intentions. The contents of Lope de Vega's plays were so realistic that modern literary historians are able to speak of them as "society dramas." His intentions were to contact the people directly—so much so that his works appear in historical perspective to be folk theater. The effect on the modern stage outside Spain is different: there the Spanish element—in the most immediate sense—is only a charming nuance of the theatrical element. Lope's "comedias" have the same effect as the Commedia dell'Arte—but this too belongs to the Renaissance inheritance

of modern dramaturgy (see Italian theater). Thus Lorca's completely Spanish character has far less of a "Spanish" effect (in the world theater) on the stage than Claudel's or Hofmannsthal's. The sources of his lyric theater lie in ballads and romances, folk poetry—in the "elemental Spanish," so to speak. This "elemental Spanish" becomes a new and very modern elemental theater in him. In his "The Authority of the Theatre" (*Theatre Arts,* 1950), Lorca says, "The theater is . . . a free rostrum on which men can clearly expose old or ambiguous moral standards and on which they can express the eternal rules of human hearts and emotions by means of live examples." This suggests Lorca's significance for the modern Parable drama.

STATION PLAY (see Mystery play).

SUBTEXT. A method of presentation favored by Stanislavski and Reinhardt, based upon the theory that the behavior of men rarely reflects the experiences they are undergoing. The technique of understatement requires the actors to be occupied with actions that have nothing to do with what they are saying or what they are supposed to be feeling.

TECHNIQUE THEATER. The whole complex of nonnatural body movements, only attainable through training, as they were used in pre-illusionistic plays —especially in the form of acrobatics. In the productions of the Peking Opera one could see a mob of actors performing double somersaults, triple somersaults—even somersaults over the tops of walls. We are told that when the great Harlequin, Thomassin, appeared in Paris in 1720 as Don Juan's servant he turned a complete somersault when the Commandant entered—without spilling a single drop from the filled wine-glass he was holding in his hand. The Russian theatrical revolutionaries, Meyerhold, Taïrov, and Vachtangov, attempted to revive such elements of technique with the help of Gorki between 1920 and 1930.

We also use the term "technique theater" to refer to productions in which the actors conform to a particular style of behavior as opposed to those productions in which they try to imitate reality as closely as possible. It is opposed to the axiom of naturalness, which controlled the bourgeois theater.

THEATRICALIZATION. Alexander Taïrov's term for the theatrical revolution which he and the other great Russian directors introduced: "Theatricalization of the Theater." Favoring the analytical and dialectical elements in the bourgeois drama had led to a dictatorship of the authors. The scenic-theatrical elements, particularly the elements of mime and gesture, became cramped. In order to restore them, the Russian theatrical revolutionaries studied the non-illusionistic theaters of China, India, and Italy. The "emancipation" of the actor, of which Taïrov also spoke, is to be understood as meaning an emancipation from the author's dictatorship. This dictatorship is by no means to be replaced by a director's or an actor's: the author is simply accepted as an equal partner in the teamwork of the theater. Brecht, who wrote his plays as scenic artist and theatricalist, also emphasized this teamwork. Jean Vilar has also come out for the theatricalization of the theater (in *De la Tradition théâtrale,* Paris, 1955). Cf. John Gassner, *Form and Idea in the Modern Theater,* New York, 1956, pp. 133ff.

THESIS PLAY. A contemporary dramatic form in which conversation replaces action or in which the action serves only to put across an argument for some ideological thesis. The one-dimensional character, who represents a particular point of view without possibility of being changed, belongs to the thesis play, either as the personification of a type (e.g., the country gentleman, the capitalist) or as allegorical representatives of some quality (e.g., helplessness).

TIME MACHINE. A term adapted from H. G. Wells to indicate suspension of chronological order in the drama, mixing past and future in order to show action in a double light. For example: in Priestley's *Time and the Conways* the last act is set in time previous to the second act; we know when we see the last act that one of the characters will not live much longer because she was already dead in the second act.

TOPICAL PLAY. A play whose action takes place in the present and which deals with contemporary problems or presents some case which is symptomatic of the times. The topical play is vigorously advocated by some critics, who consider the choice of historical plots or plots not obviously applicable to the times a "flight from reality."

In the following biographical section, the titles of plays written in French, German, Italian, and Spanish are given in their original form. When such plays have been translated and the translations are accessible, the titles are given in English as well. For plays written in foreign tongues other than those named, only English titles are provided; if these plays have been translated, this information is added. We are indebted to Professor Seymour Flaxman and to Mrs. David Boroff for translating the Dutch and Czech titles respectively.

The dates given for plays have been, whenever possible, the dates of first productions. When the dates of authorship and publication have seemed especially important, they have also been given. In verifying dates we have relied upon correspondence and personal observation but most of all upon a great number of published works, including Arthur Hobson Quinn, A History of American Drama from the Civil War to the Present Day; *Barrett H. Clark and George Freedley,* A History of Modern Drama; *Martin Esslin,* The Theatre of the Absurd; *David I. Grossvogel,* 20th Century French Drama; *Wallace Fowlie,* Dionysus in Paris; *Jean-Paul Borel,* Théâtre de l'impossible, *and many others.*

BIOGRAPHIES OF PLAYWRIGHTS

The choice of the names does not necessarily imply judgment of the author's worth—the compiler has not expressly chosen those who seem to him to be true dramatists, nor has he mentioned only those plays which seem to him to be particularly important. The basis of choice has been the prominence of the authors and the plays in the repertory of the world theater. Some readers may miss certain names which seem important to them. It is true that a certain amount of personal preference had to influence selection of the younger writers, but in general only those writers who have achieved some success with at least two plays are included. (From the author's preface)

In adding new entries for the English language edition, with the approval of the author, the translator and the editor have been guided by the same principles of selection.

ABBOTT, George, b. 1889, American director and author of comedies and musicals. World-wide success with *Three Men on a Horse* (1935, with John Cecil Holm). Also wrote *Broadway* (1926, with Philip Dunning); *Coquette* (1927, with Ann Preston Bridgers); *Sweet River* (1936, adaptation of *Uncle Tom's Cabin*); *The Boys from Syracuse* (1938, musical based on Shakespeare's *The Comedy of Errors*); *Where's Charley?* (1948, musical based on Brandon Thomas' *Charley's Aunt*); *A Tree Grows in Brooklyn* (1951, with Betty Smith); *The Pajama Game* (1954, with Richard Bissell); *Damn Yankees* (1956, with Douglass Wallop); *New Girl in Town* (1957, musical based on O'Neill's *Anna Christie*); *Fiorello!* (1959, with Jerome Weidman); *Tenderloin* (1960, with Jerome Weidman); and others.

ABEL, Lionel, b. 1910, American playwright and poet. Translator of Sartre, Pissarro, Apollinaire, Ghelderode. *The Bow and the Gun* (1947, verse play); *The Death of Odysseus* (1953); *Absalom* (1956); *The Pretender* (1960).

ABELL, Kjeld, 1901-1961, Danish dramatist. Social critic noted for technical experiments (pantomime, cabaret style). *The Melody That Got Lost* (1935, translated); *Anna Sophie Hedwig* (1939); *Judith* (1940); *Silkeborg* (1945); *Days on a Cloud* (1947); *Vetsera Does not Bloom for Everyone* (1950); *The Blue Pekinese* (1954); *Camellia Ladies* (1958); and others.

ACHARD, Marcel, b. 1900, French dramatist. Parisian comedies with tragic undertones, poetic theater. *Voulez-vous jouer avec moâ?* (1923); *Jean de la lune* (1929); *La belle Marinière* (1930); *Domino* (1931); *Le Corsaire* (1938); *Auprès de ma blonde* (1946, adapted by S. N. Behrman as *I Know My Love*); *Nous irons à Valparaiso* (1948); *Le Moulin de la galette* (1951); *Patate* (1957, translated); *Bagatelle* (1958); *L'Idiote* (1961, adapted by Harry Kurnitz as *A Shot in the Dark*); *Turlututu* (1962); *La Polka des lampions* (1962); *Dance du feu* (1963); and others.

ADAMOV, Arthur, b. 1908, French dramatist of Russian birth. Post World War II avant-gardist; has translated Büchner, Gorki, and others and has adapted Gogol's *Dead Souls* (1960). His early work strongly influenced by Kafka. His plays are comic parables which hold everyday reality up to ridicule. *La grande et la petite Manoeuvre* (1950); *L'Invasion* (1950. Adamov: "By 'Invasion' I mean the creeping conquest of a man by his own pressing affairs, by the presence of other men who on their part are also oppressed with their own troubles, and finally by the pressure of external events, which can be brought into harmony with the inner life only with difficulty." In this play we have a writer who has devoted his whole life to the obviously senseless Sisyphus-task of editing the posthumous works of his late friend. In the first act the whole room is in disorder because the friend's manuscripts are lying all over the place, including the floor. As this disorder diminishes the inner confusion of the hero grows in direct proportion. At the end all the papers are neatly tucked away in a chest, and the room looks the model of respectability; but before the hero leaves the stage for the last time he childishly tears all the papers into bits and pieces.); *La Parodie* 1952); *Le Professeur Taranne* (1953, *Professor Taranne*); *Tous contre tous* (1953. A radio, which makes official announcements at the end of each scene, informs us of the sharply pressed pursuit of the "fugitives," an imaginary group of people who may be identified with the persecuted peoples of the world—the Jews or displaced persons or anyone else. The play tells of the fate of these fugitives and of their various attempts to save themselves.); *Ping-Pong* (1953, translated. A play about pinball machines, which represent the pointlessness of human affairs and ambitions. Two friends have decided to try to improve the machines, but learn, when they present their plans to the syndicate, that somebody else has forestalled them. One of the friends now finishes his studies, while the other, constantly absorbed with new ideas, degenerates more and more. At the end the two friends, old gentlemen now, "discover" a way of eliminating machines and occupy themselves with playing ping-pong. From Adamov's directions: "Take particular care not to let the piece seem symbolic. Naturally the ping-pong game stands for something universal, but the metaphysical character of things must in no way be indicated. None of the characters, for example, may represent a prototype. Each one has his personal characteristics . . . In order not to stray into symbolism, a new style—the style of a new realism—must be discovered. All the gestures used by the actors must be related to everyday life, and despite their resemblance to types, none of them should give a marionette-like effect. All properties and furniture should be realistic. Finally, stylization of gesture should be avoided . . . True symbolism is always the opposite of apparent symbolism."); *Comme nous avons été* (one act, published in 1953, *As We Were*). Undertook writing epic drama in the manner of Brecht: *Paolo Paoli* (1957, translated, takes place in pre-1914 Paris).

Adamov: "I am amazed to see that certain elementary laws of the stage remain completely disregarded in the modern theater. The theater cannot maintain itself in the long run with intellectual statements and abstractions. Practically all dramatists forget that the function of the theater is to present the world, not to observe it. The leaning towards long speeches is contrary to the nature of theater. In almost all modern plays chatter comes first. . . . True theatrical poetry does not arise through words only—the scene itself brings it out, the gestures of fear, of tenderness, of shame, the gestures which suddenly reveal hidden meanings. In a real theater piece the visible world impinges on the invisible; the invisible is expressed through gestures, the bearing and the body—things which speech cannot express by itself. A speech pattern based on bodily expression, however, attains a power which we may well call poetry. . . . What is the purpose of Art, and particularly theatrical art? To transform the invisible into the visible. . . . Good plays are not the only things that are full of symbols; the stage itself, this heightened forum, is a symbol." Hubert von Ranke: "I asked Adamov what had brought him to the basic concept of his theatrical writing, namely, the loneliness of the individual, and he told me this anecdote: During the occupation he saw a solitary blind beggar. Two young girls, humming the hit song, 'J'ai fermé les yeux, c'était merveilleux,' came along and almost knocked him over." *Les Ames mortes* (1960, dramatization of Gogol's *Dead Souls*); *Printemps 71* (published 1960, performed Leipzig 1961, London 1962, about the Paris Commune); *La Politique des restes* (one act, published 1962, performed London, 1963).

AFINOGENOV, Alexander Nikolayevitch, 1904-1941, Russian dramatist, killed in an air raid on Moscow. Early works under the influence of the theory of proletarian art: *Robert Tim* (1923); *South of the Slot* (1926, based on a story by Jack London); *At the Breaking Point* (1926); *Keep Your Eyes Open* (1927); *Raspberry Jam* (1927). Reaction from proletarian art, return to a socialist romanticism: *The Trail of the Wolf* (1927); *The Eccentric* (1929, the intelligentsia's reconciliation with the Russian Revolution); *Fear* (1931, translated, change in the old Russian intelligentsia and the formation of a new intelligentsia); *Far Taiga* (1935, translated); *Salute, Spain!* (1936); *The Second Track* (1939, sequel to *Far Taiga*); *Mashenka* (1940, comedy, adapted as *Listen Professor!*), *On the Eve* (1942, posthumous war play), and others.

AHLSEN, Leopold, b. 1927, German playwright of the post-World War II generation, Realism with leaning toward parable style. *Pflicht zur Sünde* (1952); *Zwischen den Ufern* (1952); *Wolfszeit* (1954); *Philemon und Baukis* (1955, greatest success of the younger German drama. Topical play about the partisan fighters in the Greek mountains. Two old people perish because, out of humanity, they hide first a partisan and then a wounded German.); *Raskolnikoff* (1960; free dramatization of Dostoevski's *Crime and Punishment*).

AIKEN, Conrad, b. 1889, American lyric poet and novelist. Pulitzer Prize for poetry, 1929. *Mr. Arcularis* (1949).

AKINS, Zoë, 1886-1958, American woman dramatist. Plays examining women's problems. *The Magical City* (1916); *Papa* (1919); *Declassee* (1919); *The Varying Shore* (1921); *The Texas Nightingale* (1922, also called *Greatness*); *The Greeks Had a Word For It* (1930); *The Old Maid* (1935, Pulitzer Prize; adapted from Edith Wharton's story).

ALBEE, Edward, b. 1927, American experimental dramatist. One-act plays: *The Zoo Story* (1959); *The Sandbox* (1960); *The Death of Bessie Smith* (1960); *The American Dream* (1961). *Who's Afraid of Virginia Woolf?* (1962); *The Ballad of the Sad Café* (1963, from the story by Carson McCullers).

ALBERTI, Rafael, b. 1902, Spanish lyric poet and dramatist. Friend of Lorca, lives in Buenos Aires.

El adefesio (1944, tragedy set in the mountains of Spain); *El trebel florido* (1955, tragi-comedy); and others.

ALTENDORF, Wolfgang, b. 1921, German dramatist of the post-World War II generation. Realistic parables. *Der arme Mensch* (1952); *Die Mücke und der Elefant* (1953); *Die Feuer verlöschen* (1954); *Das Dunkel* (1956); *Partisanen* (1956); *Thomas Adamsohn* (1956); *Die Wettermaschine* (1956); *Schleuse* (1957; the East-West problem); *Weg durch den Sumpf* (1958; a play about Hungary); *Die Stunde der Mutter* (one act).

ALYOSHIN, Samuil, b. 1913, Russian dramatist, originally an engineer. Plays about the lives of workers and of the intelligentsia of technicians, and also on historical subjects. *The Director* (1950); *Gogol* (1952); *The Strict Girl* (1953); *The Man from Stratford* (1954); *Alone* (1956, translated. About adultery, a new subject characteristic of the Thaw.); *Everything Abides* (1959); *The Fulcrum* (1960).

AMBESSER, Axel von, b. 1910, German actor and author of the post-World War II generation. *Das Abgründige in Herrn Gerstenberg* (1946, popular topical satire influenced by surrealism). Has also written the comedies, *Wie führe ich eine Ehe?* (1940); *Lebensmut mit hohen Preisen* (1943); *Die Witwe von Ephesus* (1950); *Mirakel in Müll* (1960).

ANDERSON, Maxwell, 1888-1959, American dramatist. Every genre, from social criticism to verse tragedy. Championed the cause of the theater as a moral institution in *The Essence of Tragedy* (1939, reprinted in *Off Broadway*, 1947). *White Desert* (1923); *What Price Glory?* (1924, with Laurence Stallings); *Saturday's Children* (1927); *Gods of the Lightning* (1928, with Harold Hickerson); *Night over Taos* (1932); *Both your Houses* (1933); *Valley Forge* (1934); *Winterset* (1935. An attempt, largely in verse, to interpret the Sacco-Vanzetti Case by means of symbolic figures.); *The Wingless Victory* (1936); *High Tor* (1937); *Knickerbocker Holiday* (1938, musical; score by Kurt Weill); *Key Largo* (1939); *The Eve of St. Mark* (1942); *Lost in the Stars* (1950, musical; score by Weill); *Bad Seed* (1954); *The Day the Money Stopped* (1957, with Brendan Gill). Historical plays: *Elizabeth the Queen* (1930); *Mary of Scotland* (1933); *The Masque of Kings* (1936, Mayerling tragedy); *Journey to Jerusalem* (1940. Play about Jesus); *Joan of Lorraine* (1946); *Anne of the Thousand Days* (1947, Anne Boleyn); *Barefoot in Athens* (1951, Socrates); *The Golden Six* (1958, the six grandchildren of Augustus).

ANDERSON, Robert, b. 1917, American dramatist of the younger generation. World-wide success with *Tea and Sympathy* (1953. Treats the fate of a boy in boarding school whose classmates make him a scapegoat because he is different, more sensitive than they are; he is suspected of homosexuality but is accepted as a lover by a motherly woman, more out of pity than love.); *All Summer Long* (1954); *Silent Night, Holy Night* (1959).

ANDRES, Stefan, b. 1906, German novelist, achieved one of the greatest theatrical successes of the postwar period with the dramatization of his novelette, *Wir sind Utopia,* as *Gottes Utopia* (1950). Other plays: *Schwarze Strahlen* (1938); *Ein Herz, wie man's braucht* (1946); *Tanz durchs Labyrinth* (1946, topical drama preaching Christianity); *Und Zeus lächelt* (1957); *Sperrzonen* (1958, political tragedy); *Wann kommen die Götter?* (1961).

ANDREYEV, Leonid Nikolayevitch, 1871-1919, Russian modernist and symbolist. Revolutionary leanings in *To the Stars* (1905, translated) and *Savva* (1906, translated). Plays produced by the Moscow Art Theatre: *The Life of Man* (1907, translated); *Anathema* (1909, translated); *King Hunger* (1908, translated); *The Black Maskers* (1909), translated); *The Ocean* (1909, translated). Later abandoned symbolism and wrote comedies of student life, *The Days of Our Life* (1910) and *Gaudeamus* (1910). Other plays: *Anfisa* (1910); *The Sabine Women* (1912, translated); *Professor Storytsyn* (1912, translated); *Katerina* (1913); *He Who Gets Slapped* (1915, translated); *The Waltz of the Dogs* (1914, published 1922, translated).

ANOUILH, Jean, b. 1910, most popular of contemporary French dramatists, one of the representative authors of the modern theater. Wrote his first theatrical works while secretary to Louis Jouvet. Jouvet's production of Giraudoux' *Siegfried* in 1928

was a decisive experience for him. Early works: *Humulus le muet* (1929, a ten-minute sketch); *Mandarine* (1929); *Y'avait un prisonnier* (1934).

"Pièces noires": *L'Hermine* (1931, *The Ermine*); *Jézabel* (1932); *La Sauvage* (1934, *Restless Heart*); *Le Voyageur sans bagage* (1936, *Traveller Without Luggage;* prodigal's return); *Eurydice* (1941, *Legend of Lovers.* Modern adaptation of the classical legend with Orpheus as a musician in a touring band and Eurydice as an actress in a provincial company.); *Antigone* (1942, translated, with the same title; one-acter with narrator and chorus, Creon in tuxedo, Antigone in pullover); *Roméo et Jeannette* (1945, *Romeo and Jeannette;* modern version of *Romeo and Juliet*); *Médée* (1946, *Medea;* one-acter, another example of classical material brought from the sphere of myth into that of timeless reality).

"Pièces Roses"; *Le Bal des voleurs* (1932; *Thieves' Carnival;* ballet for actors); *Le Rendez-vous de Senlis* (1937, *Dinner With the Family*); *Léocadia* (1939; *Time Remembered.* Typical of the plays written as attacks on the already completely collapsed world of aristocracy. The protagonist always lives wrapped in his illusions and meets a young girl who possesses the fresh innocence of nature and sensuality. She is then made unhappy by becoming involved in the illusionary world. Chief role: the Baroness.).

"Pièces Brilliantes": *L'Invitation au château,* (1947, The old motif of identical twins played by one actor; also, a young girl, a ballet dancer, who becomes involved in corruption and swindling; adapted by Christopher Fry as *Ring 'Round the Moon,* and made into one of the representative productions of the modern world theater through the direction of Peter Brook.); *La Répétition ou L'Amour puni* (1950, *The Rehearsal.* Collision between the young girl, this time governess in a castle, and a hypocritical and demoralized society at the performance of a play of Marivaux's; the lord of the castle falls in love with the girl, who protests in vain.); *Colombe* (1950, *Mademoiselle Colombe.* The young girl in theatrical society; the son of a great actress demands of his mother, whom he hates, that she support his young wife, Colombe, while he is away in the army; Colombe becomes involved in the hodgepodge of the theater world and loses herself. When her husband comes home on furlough and visits her backstage, he finds her playing a Marquise and unwilling to cancel a rendez-vous that she has made. After the bitter ending, the stage is darkened and we see again the prologue to the first act; we see how everything began, a moving love song—but now we know how it is to end.); *Cécile ou l'École des pères* (1949, *Cecile or The School for Fathers*. A wedding present for the author's daughter in the form of a rococo masque-comedy dealing with a clever and pretty governess who gets the better in every respect of the Count, who is wandering in forbidden paths; against his will he is forced to bless his daughter's engagement. The high point is a *quid pro quo* scene, as in the last act of *Figaro*).

"Pièces grinçantes": *Ardèle ou la Marguerite* (1948, *Ardele*. Anouilh's bitterest and most unpleasant play. Two lovers perish at the hands of a brutal and rotting society); *La Valse des Toréadors* (1951, *The Waltz of the Toreadors*. Comedy of disillusionment. A retired general with a Don Juan streak and his bedridden wife, who tyrannizes over him. The illusions are exploded by the revelation of a fanciful epistolary love affair that the general is conducting.); *Ornifle ou le Courant d'air* (1955. Don Juan in modern dress; he is now a Count who supports himself in comfort by grinding out hit songs. The women around him consist of his charming wife, of whom he takes no notice; his secretary, who worships him with self-torturing hysteria; and a chambermaid, who was once one of his numerous mistresses. There is also a friend who finances his business and is as faithful as he is stupid and uneducated. Fate approaches in the form of a young man, who is the son of a woman Don Juan-Ornifle abandoned in a particularly brutal manner, and who wishes to kill his father. The revolver does not fire because the young man's girl friend has taken the bullets out in order to prevent his becoming a murderer. However, Don Juan-Ornifle has a stroke. The young man, who is a medical student, makes a correct diagnosis and renders first aid. Two famous physicians are called in and make themselves ridiculous by joking at the patient's expense. But Ornifle manages to commit one last transgression even on his sickbed: he seduces his son's fiancée. Filled with elation at his victory and convinced that he is cured, he gets up after the girl has left and goes across the street to a hotel where another mistress is waiting for him. There he suffers his final stroke as the thunder and lightning of a very peculiar thunder-storm—the time is December—fill the room.); *Pauvre Bitos ou le Dîner de têtes* (1956. Sensation and scandal; banned outside France by the author. The hero is a resistance fighter who looks upon himself as a second Robespierre—"l'incorruptible"—and exercises a moral tyranny over his comrades. His former schoolfriends decide to teach him a lesson. They invite him to a Dinner of Heads: each guest is to appear wearing the mask of a prominent figure of the French Revolution. Bitos is now mercilessly stripped bare of the role of Robespierre. At the end he is truly only "poor Bitos," a creature who has lost belief in himself: "You trapped me." It is the author's intention that we pity him.).

In 1953, two very French pieces appeared: *L'Alouette* (Adapted by Fry, and more freely by Lillian Hellman, as *The Lark*. An almost joyous version of Joan of Arc, ending with the coronation. The trial is handled so that Joan may show the judges by means of witnesses how everything happened, a very modern trick. The dialogue is brilliant; cheerfulness reigns. Joan herself is the transfiguration of all of Anouilh's previously created young girls. When he was asked what he was trying to say with his version of the Joan mystery, he answered that he considered such attempts at clarification would put him in the position of the child that has taken his toy apart and now knows what is inside but no longer has a toy: "I avoid telling children how things work, even when I happen to know; and in the case of Joan, I confess I did not know.... We protect the right of children, and older people too, to make bouquets of daisies and to pretend to imitate the songs of birds in play, even if they have not the slightest knowledge of botany and ornithology. That is approximately what I have done."); *L'Hurluberlu ou le Réactionnaire amoureux* (1959, *The Fighting Cock*, comedy); *La petite Molière* (1959; Molière's wife; adapted from a film version); *Madame de . . .* (1959; dramatization of a novel by Louise de Vilmorin); *Becket ou l'Honneur de Dieu* (1959, *Becket*. Same subject as T. S. Eliot's *Murder in the Cathedral* and Christopher Fry's *Curtmantle*. A tragedy of friendship. King Henry II, wishing to raise his crony, Thomas Becket, to the highest possible honor, appoints him Archbishop of Canterbury. But Becket, as soon as he has taken on his new position, sees himself as the servant of a greater master and considers himself obligated to fight the crowned wastrel, his former friend. The latter cannot understand this. The struggle goes on for a long time, but finally the king, exasperated by a new attack of Becket's, cries out, "Will no one free me from this man?" At this four of his barons go to the cathedral to kill the Archbishop. In the last scene the king scourges himself, mixing his lamentations for his dead friend with his cries of pain. Here we see the basic motifs of Anouilh's theater: the ineluctability of everything that happens in this world, in which we have to live with each other, and the hopelessness of saving the really human elements—love, friendship, decency—from this fate.); *La Grotto* (1961, violence among the servants); *La Foire d'empoigne* (1962, Louis XVIII favored over Napoleon); *L'Orchestre* (1962, farcical curtain-raiser).

ANSKY, S. (Salomon Rappaport), 1863-1920, Russian-Jewish dramatist. Wrote *The Dybbuk, or Between Two Worlds* (translated, a dramatic legend from the world of the Chassidim) which became world famous through Vachtangov's 1922 Habimah production in Hebrew after Vilna performance in Yiddish, 1920.

APOLLINAIRE, Guillaume, 1880-1918, one of the revolutionaries of modern lyric poetry ("Poetry of the Unconscious"), wrote the first surrealistic drama: *Les Mamelles de Tirésias* (allegedly written 1903, first produced 1917, a wife changes her sex, whereupon her husband follows suit and bears several thousand children, thereby raising the failing birth rate of Zanzibar); *Couleur du temps* (written 1917, performed 1918, fantastic expedition to the South Pole); *Casanova* (written 1918; published 1952, *"comédie parodique"*); also some unpublished works.

ARBUSOV, Alexey Nikolayevitch, b. 1908, Russian dramatist, actor, and director. Became known as the "poet of youth" because the heroes of his plays are mostly young people. School of Chekhov in his psychological approach. *The Class* (1930); *The Six Darlings* (1934); *The Far Way* (1936); *Tania* (1938); *City in the Dawn* (1941); *The Cottage in the Suburbs* (1943, revision 1954); *Encounter with Youth* (1947); *European Chronicle* (1953); *Travel Year* (1954); *The Twelfth Hour* (1959); *It Happened in Irkutsk* (1959, translated, his most successful play; erection of a factory in Siberia; jealousy between young workers over a flirtatious girl; withdrawal of the positive hero; characters individualized; less programmatical).

ARCHER, William, 1856-1924. Influential British critic, helped to introduce Ibsen to the English-speaking world. *The Green Goddess* (1921, popular exotic melodrama); and other plays.

ARDEN, John, 1930, English dramatist. *The Waters of Babylon* (1957); *Live Like Pigs* (1958, the disintegration of moral values in the Welfare State); *Serjeant Musgrave's Dance* (1959, anti-militaristic didactic play in style of Brecht); *The Happy Haven* (1960; Kenneth Tynan: "An elephantine comedy of humours about an old people's home."); *The Business of Good Government* (1962, Christmas play, written for a church in Somerset); *The Workhouse Donkey* (1963; political and personal rivalries in a Northern industrial town); *Ironhand* (1963; free adaptation of Goethe's *Götz von Berlichingen*).

ARDREY, Robert, b. 1908, American dramatist. Symbolic fantasies. *Star-Spangled* (1936); *Casey Jones* (1938); *How To Get Tough About It* (1938); *Thunder Rock* (1939); *Jeb* (1946); *Sing Me No Lullaby* (1955); *Shadow of Heroes* (1958; Hungarian rebellion).

ARENT, Arthur, b. 1905, American dramatist. Wrote for the WPA Federal theater and helped to develop the Living Newspaper style. Editor and co-author of *Ethiopia* (1936). Wrote *Triple-A Plowed Under* (1936); *Injunction Granted* (1936); *Power* (1937); *"1935"* (1937); *. . one-third of a nation . . .* (1938).

ARNICHES, Carlos, 1866-1943, Spanish dramatist, wrote about 200 comedies, among them *Casa editorial, El fuego de San Telmo, El probre Valbuena, El amigo Melquiades, El padre Pitillo*.

ARRABAL, Fernando, b. 1932. Dramatist born in Spain, living in France, writing in French. *Théâtre*, published 1958, contains: *Oraison; Les Deux Bourreaux (The Executioners); Fando et Lis (Fando and Lis); Le Cimitiere des Voitures (The Automobile Graveyard)*. Also published 1958: *Pique-nique en Campagne (Picnic on the Battlefield)*. Also: *Le Tricycle; Guernica; Orchestration théatrale* (performed 1959). Combines love, cruelty, innocence, childishness in bizarre settings.

ARTSYBASHEV, Mikhail Petrovich, 1878-1927. *Jealousy* (1913); *Enemies* (1913, also translated as *Lovers and Enemies*); *The Law of the Savage* (1913); *War* (1914). Cynicism, egoism, misogyny. Popular before the Russian Revolution; in exile afterwards.

ASCH, Sholem, 1880-1957, Polish-Jewish novelist, wrote for the Yiddish theater: *The God of Vengeance* (1907, translated, produced by Reinhardt); *Sabbatai Zevi* (1909, translated); *The League of the Weak* (1910); and others.

ASMODI, Herbert, b. 1923, German dramatist of the post-World War II generation, Gerhart Hauptmann Prize. *Jenseits vom Paradies* (1954); *Pardon wird nicht gegeben* (1958, satire); *Nachsaison* (1959, comedy).

AUDEN, Wystan Hugh, b. 1907, one of the leading English poets, now an American citizen. Verse dramas with songs, odes, choruses: *The Dance of Death* (1933); *The Dog beneath the Skin* (1935, with Christopher Isherwood); *The Ascent of F 6* (1936, with Isherwood); *On the Frontier* (1938, with Isherwood); *The Rake's Progress* (1951, with Chester Kallman; opera libretto for Stravinsky). Most important work: *The Age of Anxiety* (1947. Pulitzer Prize, 1948. Three men and a woman, seated on bar stools and bowed over their glasses, think and talk and dream in prose and verse. All of them find themselves opposed to their ordinary existences. The play gives a Christian answer: "These people feel that the washed out, the boiled out, the hollow and the empty dominate their existence, but, on the other hand, they are still convinced that something universal lives in them and that they know all." [Benn] Also wrote libretto for Benjamin Britten's *Paul Bunyan* and Hans Werner Henze's *Elegie für junge Liebende*.

AUDIBERTI, Jacques, b. 1899, one of the leading Parisian avant-gardists. Basic theme: the impossibility of love. His plays leap out, the rationality and naturalness of their dialogue completely flooded by cascades of words, the scenes driven forward only by a stupendous *élan* and a theatrical logic.

Quoat-Quoat (1946. The captain of a ship bound for Mexico captures a secret agent whom the French Government has sent, disguised as an archaeologist, to search for the hidden treasure of the Emperor Maximilian. According to an old law of the sea, all secret agents who try to seduce a woman must be shot. The captain's daughter sets the trap, and the secret agent falls into it. The captain surprises them together and arrests the agent. The agent is visited in his cabin by a mad Mexican woman who possesses a stone belonging to the Mexican God Quoat-Quoat, which has the power to destroy everything; she wants to learn the secret of the treasure from the agent and then to help him escape. The agent, however, turns her and her stone over to the captain. Finally an old hag shows up and tells the captain that the man he arrested is only a stooge and that she is the real secret agent. The "agent," hearing he can no longer be executed goes mad, locks the captain in his cabin, and rushes on deck to be shot by the watch. The captain, in despair, stretches out his hand, which holds the destroying stone. The curtain falls.); *L'Ampelour* (actually *L'Empereur;* one act); *Les Femmes du Boeuf* (1949, one act); *Le mal Court* (1947. A dramatic fairy tale, set in a poetical landscape between East and West in an imaginary, somewhat rococo time. The daughter of an impoverished king is to be married to a rich king from the West, but during the journey to his territory the political situation has altered. Those who are really in power intrigue against the marriage with all their strength —among other things, they send a Monsieur F. to seduce the princess by pretending to be the king. The princess, fruitlessly revolting against the path of evil ("le mal court"), sets herself at the head of a revolution of evil against evil: "Until now my life, my innocent, upright conduct, was nothing but camouflage for the approaching thunder of my sudden anger. My fury breaks out! All the evil that I have not done, I do now at one stroke. The steppes lie open! Let the black mountain streams flood them. . . ."); *La Fête noire* (1948. A country doctor searches for love and fights a monster who is laying waste the country and who finally devours him and his wife, whom he loves.); *Pucelle* (1950, Joan of Arc story); *Les Naturels du Bordelais* (1954, Don Juan story); *La Logeuse* (1954); *Opéra parlé* (1956); *Le Quallou* (One-acter in thieves' slang directed against corruption); *Al-*

tanima (1956, lyrical theme, a sort of opera libretto); *La Mégère apprivoisée* (1957, based on Shakespeare's *The Taming of the Shrew*); *La hoberaute* (1958, A tragedy with elves and knights, "spoken opera."); *L'Effet Glapion* (1959, Comedy about the "mechanism of illusion." Professor Glapion invents an "effect" which enables people to experience their dreams and wishes as reality.); *La Fourmi dans le corps* (1962, historical drama with a touch of the grotesque); *Pomme, pomme, pomme* (1962); *La Brigitta* (1962).

AXELROD, George, b. 1922, American dramatist. Contributed to *Small Wonder* (a revue, 1948). *The Seven Year Itch* (1953, comedy); *Will Success Spoil Rock Hunter?* (1955, comedy); *Goodbye Charlie* (1959, comedy).

AYMÉ, Marcel, b. 1902, French novelist and dramatist. Ironic and erotic writer, with leanings toward surrealism: "The unfathomable" (Anouilh). Successful plays: *Lucienne et le Boucher* (1948); *Clérambard* (1950, translated with the same title. Satirical comedy about the return of St. Francis); *La Tête des autres* (1952, satire on the law); *Les quatre Vérités* (1954, jealousy and truth serum); *Les Oiseaux de lune,* (1956, *Moonbirds*); *La Mouche bleue* (1957, anti-American); *Patron* (1959, musical about thieves); *Louisiana* (1961, the race problem in America); *Les Maxibules* (1961, farce). French version of Miller's *The Crucible: Les Sorcières de Salem; Le Minotaure* (1963).

BABEL, Isaak, 1894-ca. 1935, Russian story writer, disappeared during the purges. *Sunset* (1928, translated, Jewish life in Odessa); *Maria* (1930).

BACCHELLI, Ricardo, b. 1891, Italian dramatist and novelist. *Bellamonte* (1928); *La smorfia* (1928); *L'alba dell'ultima sera* (1949); *Amleto* (1956); *Il figlio di Ettore e Nostos* (1957, three tragic acts and a farcical epilogue on the fall of Troy); *La famiglia del caffetiere* (1957, fantasy on a motif of Goldoni); and others.

BAGNOLD, Enid, b. 1889, English novelist. *Lottie Dundass* (1943); *National Velvet* (1946, from her novel); *Poor Judas* (1946); *Gertie* (1952); *The Chalk Garden* (1954); *The Last Joke* (1960); *The Chinese Prime Minister* (1964).

BAHR, Hermann, 1863-1934, Austrian author. Leader of the Viennese moderns from 1890 on; later commented on most of the fashionable literary movements in his excellent essays. As dramatist he gradually descended from elevated literature to society comedy. Several pieces from the latter genre are still in the repertory of German-speaking, especially Austrian, stages: *Wienerinnen* (1900); *Der Krampus* (1901); *Ringelspiel* (1907); *Die gelbe Nachtigall* (1907); *Das Prinzip* (1912); above all, *Das Konzert* (1909, *The Concert*. Society comedy with witty and still vital figures: the famous pianist who neglects his wife and is discovered by her and by his friend—a wonderful part—in a mountain hut with the friend's wife and is subsequently cured). Many other plays, now forgotten.

BALDERSTON, John, 1889-1954, American dramatist. *The Genius of the Marne* (1919); *A Morality Play for the Leisure Class* (1924); *Berkeley Square* (1926, with J. C. Squire; from Henry James's novel *The Sense of the Past*); *Dracula* (1927, with Hamilton Deane; from Bram Stoker); *Red Planet* (1932, with J. E. Hoare); and others.

BARLACH, Ernst, 1870-1938, famous German expressionistic sculptor and graphic artist—as a dramatist worked in the same style. North German Protestant mysticism, archaic themes with Christian salvation. Began influenced by Strindberg and anticipating Kafka: *Der tote Tag* (1912. One of the earliest purely expressionistic dramas. Place: "the great plain," always in a half light; archaic figures: the mother, the old blind woman, gnomes, elves and, the only clearly seen figure, the son.); *Der arme Vetter* (1918. Easter in an imaginary resort on the Upper Elbe, ten scenes in Strindberg style; direct transition from the real to the spiritual.); *Die echten Sedemunds* (1920. The first of his dramas of "exposure." North German small town during a religious festival; collapse of the characters' conceit and self-righteousness. The real Sedemunds: "Yes, that's how they are—you can't make them any better! The Sedemunds stink to high Heaven like a pile of excrement. A lion's jaws gape open and howl furiously at us, and you call me a real Sedemund. At this moment any name in the world is considered more honorable than ours. The color on a soap smear, the gleam of a soap bubble is more solid than our position at the moment."); *Der Findling* (1922. A transitional piece, leading to the later plays which break through the last vestige of reality. The stone-breaker and the red Emperor, the prophet Pentecost with his servant Vesper; the Pope, Death and the Devil—all as Punch and Judy figures. Verse and Prose.); *Der blaue Boll* (1926. The last piece written around small town life, whose representative, Boll, receives a call, breaks the chains of bourgeois life, and prepares "to bring forth a new Boll." Barlach's idea of the eternal evolutions of Man and the world, of the transfiguration which occurs in all of us.).

Even before *Der blaue Boll*, *Die Sündflut* appeared; it is the first of a series of visionary dramas which belong to the school of Claudel, Hofmannsthal, Eliot, and Wilder, though they are sketched with increasing individuality, and show a highly personal mysticism (Barlach was branded as "degenerate" by the Nazis). *Die Sündflut* (1924. Noah, the poor man, and Calan, the rich man; God as a travelling salesman and as a beggar: "I regret it, I regret it, let them rot, I will cry out against them and drown them, sink them, forget them." The angels and Awah, who washes their feet; the call to Noah as the only servant of God in this world of force, blasphemy, and murder. While Noah builds the ark, the great Calan becomes "poor and wet and cold," for the flood is rising, but at the end, as "the rats tear the eyes out of his sockets," even Galan sees: "God grows even in me and transforms himself in me to something new."); *Die gute Zeit* (1929. A ten-act mystery play. The poor and the rich again, the purified and those who have remained as they were. Atlas has created a sort of refuge of "absolute insurance" for the rebirth of the good times on a southern coast. It is only for the rich, and ladies and gentlemen come from all over in order to be released from the cares of life in it: "Life as an absolute club armchair—that's how far we have progressed!" There is even a queen incognito among Atlas' disciples. The queen, Celestine, clashes with the king, the father of the age-old world, the ragged village bailiff Syros, just as the court ambassador, whose task it is to bring her back, arrives. She refuses to go back and flees into the wilderness. The others pursue her. In the wilderness she meets Syros again, this time together with his sons, and she has her first version of a "word that is like a cross." Thus, while the flight and pursuit move ever higher into the mountains, her transformation begins. At dawn members of the tribe of Rifeh prepare a cross on an open mountainside for one who is to be executed, a member of Syros's family. Celestine, the guilty one, takes the sin of this man, who is guiltless, on her shoulders. That is the salvation. In the face of crucifixion, Celestine says: "Judge me according to the heaviness of my sin. The numberless clusters of the stars receive me in their beauty. . . . The guilt that the earth gave me is extinguished. The evil reality will yield to the good reality.").

In 1951, one of Barlach's posthumous works appeared, *Der Graf von Ratzeburg* (Middle Ages, time of the Crusades—again one who has received the call and has begun a pilgrimage designed to free him from the riches of this world. The character is Offerus, who is to be transformed into Christopher. The "Power in Red," the fallen angel, and the Lord of the World, the tempter, also appear. Hilarion, the Christian ascetic, meets the ghost of Moses, who must wander and seek eternally, on Sinai. The scene at the river follows; in a transformation Christopher is created. He meets the captured Count Henry, condemned to torture and death, on a street-corner in Mölln, where the sinners' bell rings; he wants to save him, but the Count cannot praise God: "I have no God—but glory to him, that it is as it is: I have no God, but God has me." As "sufferer of endless humility" he must suffer his death: "I drank my pleasure at her source, limitless as you, my obedience serves yours and disappears and swims as yours in the ocean of its limitless certainty." Furious troops with spears stream on to the stage. They are those who "befoul the holy ones" and know only revenge: "their spears are seen pointing against Henry from all sides; he is surrounded by them as if by a stream of rays. He falls.").

BARNES, Djuna, b. 1892, American novelist. *Antiphon* (Published 1958. Blank verse. An English family in 1939.); and some short plays.

BARRIE, James Matthew, 1860-1937, one of the most popular of modern English dramatists, son of a Scottish weaver, rose to become a baronet. Like

Shaw, he began with witty social satires but soon manifested an irrepressible preference for the fantastic and romantic with which he departed from the illusionistic form and entered new territory. *The Admirable Crichton* (1902. Lord Loam, Barrie's favorite character, wishing to be considered a modern thinker, invites his domestic staff to tea once a month. All the servants and chambermaids are bored, especially the admirable Crichton. This particular party is a farewell gathering: the next day Lord Loam is to depart on a spartan world cruise on his yacht accompanied only by Crichton and the kitchenmaid as servants. They are shipwrecked on a lonely island and cast into a completely different way of life. Here, the butler becomes king and the master becomes servant. They are rescued by a ship, taken back home, and there everything is as it was before.); *Peter Pan* (1904. Barrie's most famous play—subtitle, *The Boy Who Never Grew Up*. Peter Pan, who has been taught to fly by fairies in Kensington Gardens, has gone to Never-Never Land, where he commands the troop of lost children, the children whom careless nursemaids let drop out of their perambulators. Looking for his shadow, which he has lost, Peter meets Wendy and her younger brothers. He takes all three to Never-Never Land, where they live like Robinson Crusoe. The Redskins, with whom they are allied against the Pirates, watch over them, but they are surprised and dragged onto the pirate ship. Peter, however, frees the children and brings them back home. Although he loves Wendy, he cannot make up his mind to stay and flies back to Fairy Land.); *Dear Brutus* (1917. A small, crazy, gnome-like man named Lob puts a spell on his guests and lets them re-live their lives the way they would wish to have lived them. But when the magic goes away they are unchanged: they will eternally repeat the same mistakes, even if they could begin over again a hundred times. Ancient Celtic themes woven into a social satire which can hardly be said to favor any particular class.); *Mary Rose* (1920. The story of a girl who has been enchanted by the "Island" and comes home again, but she is never again able to cast off her longing for the dream world she has known. She persuades her young husband to help her try to find the island again. Suddenly she is taken back. She returns again 25 years later, completely unchanged, not a day older, as if she had been away an hour. She is disturbed by the meeting with her aged husband; only her son, who has just returned from the war, is able to release her from the spell.

Other plays: *Walker, London* (1892); *The Professor's Love Story* (1894); *The Little Minister* (1897); *Quality Street* (1902); *Little Mary* (1903); *Alice Sit-by-the-fire* (1905); *Josephine* (1906); *What Every Woman Knows* (1908); *Rosalind* (1912); *Rosy Rapture* (1915); *A Kiss for Cinderella* (1916); *The Old Lady Shows Her Medals* (1917); *A Well Remembered Voice* (1918); *The Truth About the Russian Dancers* (1920); *Shall We Join the Ladies?* (1922); *The Boy David* (1936, for Elizabeth Bergner).

BARRY, Philip, 1896-1949, American dramatist. Popular in the late twenties and early thirties. Wrote fashionable problem plays. *A Punch for Judy* (1921); *You and I* (1923); *The Youngest* (1924); *In a Garden* (1925); *Poor Richard* (1926); *White Wings* (1926); *John* (1927); *Paris Bound* (1927); *Cock Robin* (1928, with Elmer Rice); *Holiday* (1928); *Hotel Universe* (1930); *Tomorrow and Tomorrow* (1931); *The Animal Kingdom* (1932); *The Joyous Season* (1934); *Bright Star* (1935); *Spring Dance* (1936); *Here Come the Clowns* (1938); *The Philadelphia Story* (1939); *Liberty Jones* (1941); *Without Love* (1942); *Foolish Notion* (1951, completed by Robert E. Sherwood); and others.

BASSHE, Emjo, c. 1899-1939, American dramatist. Social protest drama. *The Centuries* (1927, tenement housing); *Earth* (1927); *Doomsday Circus* (1938); and others.

BATAILLE, Henry, 1872-1922, French dramatist. Pre-eminent in French theater before World War I. Abandoned early writing of verse plays for dramas of passion. *La Chambre blanche* (1895); *Résurrection* (1902, from Tolstoy's novel, translated as *Resurrection*); *Maman Colibri* (1904, a mature woman's disappointment in love); *La Femme nue* (1908); *La Scandale* (1909, *The Scandal*); *L'Enfant de l'amour* (1911, *The Love Child*); *Les Flambeaux* (1912, *The Torches*); *La Tendresse* (1921, translated under its own name); and others.

BAYR, Rudolf, b. 1919, Austrian lyric poet, dramatist, and essayist. New version of Sophocles' *Oedi-*

pus at Colonnus (1952); *Sappho und Alkaios* (1953); *Die Liebe der Andrea* (1954); *Agamemnon muss sterben* (1955); *Lass wehen die Zeit* (1957); *Teestunde* (1962, one act).

BECHER, Johannes R., 1891-1958, German author of the post-World War I generation; Minister of Culture in East Germany, National Literature Prize, Stalin Peace Prize. Went from Expressionism to Communism. *Arbeiter, Bauern, Soldaten* (1924); *Der grosse Plan* (1931, hymn to Soviet man and the five-year plan); *Winterschlacht* (1942. The battle for Moscow, 1941, the defeated Germans in the Russian winter. One of them is ordered to bury captured Russians alive, refuses, and is shot. Final speech of the Soviet general: "For the enemy there is no way to Moscow." Prose and verse.); *Das Führerbild* (1945); *Der Weg nach Füssen* (1956. Story of the years 1933-1942, told in the fate of a worker's family. Oratorio in verse.).

BECHER, Ulrich, b. 1910, German dramatist, returned to Europe from exile in Brazil and America. Atmospheric realism, has a predilection for the anti-social, the vagabonds, the disinherited, the wrecks and drunkards. According to Becher, the theater is the battle-ground against the devil in today's world: "A telescope through which the observer sees a piece of the world transformed by art; or a microscope; or a skylight, through which he looks down into a ballroom in which a party of fools is dancing; or a barred gate through which he looks into a prison cell or a death cell; or a window, covered with frost and ice, as long as the glass does not burst asunder through a last, irreparable crack." *Niemand* (1936, modern Mystery play); *Der Bockerer* (1948, with Peter Preses. "Tragic farce" —better called a folk-play of 1938 Vienna); *Der Pfeifer von Wien* (1950, with Peter Preses. "Tragic farce" dealing with "lieber Augustin" in the time of the plague.); *Samba* (1951, emigrants in Brazil); *Feuerwasser* (1952, German-American tragedy); *Mme. Löwenzorn* (1953, comedy); *Die Grossen und die Kleinen* (1956); *Der Herr Kommt aus Bahia* (1957); *Biene, gib mir Honig* (1960).

BECKETT, Samuel, b. 1906, Irishman living in Paris and writing in French. The most important avant-garde writer. Radical destruction of reality. Dialogue of the absurd distinctly directed against Ex-istentialism. Spiritual clowning leads to a peculiar regularity of form in which the clowns settle their senseless affairs. This regularity led French critics to compare *Waiting for Godot* (1953) with Racine's *Bérénice*. The alienation of the human being and the destruction of reality appear necessarily to be the way to a denial of reality on the stage—a total anti-reality. The denial remains a sad one, however —it is the denial of the lost and the hopeless. They do not know the identity of this Godot, for whom they are waiting; they pass away the time with absurd actions and "playing around." Anouilh called *Waiting for Godot* one of the three or four key plays of the contemporary theater. The world-wide success of the play, which began in Paris and went on to Germany, England, and finally Broadway, proves that contemporary man recognizes himself here in the senselessness of his world—but also in the unquenchable desire to free himself from it. Thus the four characters—the two vagabonds and the animal tamer with the slave he has turned into an animal—have almost become representative figures of the modern theater. Beckett's second play, *Endgame* (1957), continues the "clownerie." Again we have four characters and again the manner in which they conduct their lives is totally senseless. Two of them are in ashcans, which are opened now and again so that their heads can appear. Hamm, the master, is hunched, lame and blind, in an armchair, while Clov, the servant, is unable to sit down. Clov: "I love order. It's my dream. A world where all would be silent and still and each thing in its last place, under the last dust." The play is so designed that the clowns, who represent the human race, always attempt with all their strength to revive "their old games," i.e, the games of life. Always they have to break off the attempt after a short time because it exhausts them. Thus we have a succession of purposely monotonous scenes.); *All that Fall* (1957, radio script); *Krapp's Last Tape* (1958, one-act play for one actor); *Embers* (1959, radio script); *Happy Days* (1961); *Play* (1963, one act. Three ghosts recall the past).

BECQUE, Henry, 1837-1899, French dramatist. Important innovator, exponent of bitter, ironic, selective realism. *Sardanapale* (1867, a libretto based on Byron); *L'Enfant prodigue* (1868); *Michael Pauper* (1870); *L'Enlèvement* (1871); *La Navette* (1878, *The Merry-Go-Round*); *Les honnêtes*

Femmes (1880); *Les Corbeaux* (1882, *The Vultures*, a bourgeois family facing sudden disaster; first done by the Comédie Française); *La Parisienne* (1885, *The Woman of Paris*, pleasures and crises of a *ménage à trois*, staged by Antoine at the Théâtre Libre); *Madeleine* (published 1896, one act, part of *Les Polichinelles*); *Veuve* (published 1897, one-act sequel to *La Parisienne*); *Le Domino à quatre* (published 1897, one act, *A Quiet Game*); *Le Depart* (published 1897, one act); *Une Exécution* (published 1897, one act); *Les Polichinelles* (incomplete, published 1910, finished by Henri de Noussanne).

BEERBOHM, Max, 1872-1955, English essayist, humorist, drama critic, caricaturist, and, incidentally, dramatist. Drama critic of the *Saturday Review* of London, 1898-1910, succeeding Bernard Shaw and succeeded by John Palmer. *The Happy Hypocrite* (1900, one act; expanded into 3 acts by Clemence Dane, 1936); *The Fly on the Wheel* (1902, with Murray Carson); *A Social Success* (1913).

BEER-HOFMANN, Richard, 1866-1945, Austrian dramatist of the circle of Hofmannsthal and Schnitzler. Biblical and Jewish motifs. Elevated speech. Won attention with *Der Graf von Charolais* (1904, based on *The Fatal Dowry*, by Massinger and Field); *Jaakobs Traum* (1918, *Jacob's Dream*, "a prelude," first part of contemplated trilogy about David); *Der junge David* (1933, second part of the David trilogy); *Verspiel auf dem Theater zu König* (1941, fragment of the last part of the trilogy).

BEHAN, Brendan, 1925-1964, Irish dramatist of the younger generation. Spent eight years in prison for I.R.A. activities. *The Quare Fellow* (1957. In an Irish prison, on the eve of an execution); *The Hostage* (1958. "A completely Irish story. With murdered hostage, music, dance, love, a lot of drinking, easy women. . . . The inimitable Irish blarney with pungent swearwords, full of sarcasm, self-mockery, impudent jabs at God and the world, including the Queen. . . ." [Friedenthal]. "It is Commedia dell'arte." [Tynan]); *The Big House* (1958, radio play).

BEHRMAN, S. N., b. 1893, American dramatist. Fashionable drawing-room comedies. *Bedside Manner* (1923, with J. Kenyon Nicholson); *The Man Who Forgot* (1926, with Owen Davis); *Serena Blandish* (1929); *Meteor* (1929); *Brief Moment* (1931); *Biography* (1932); *A Love Story* (1933); *Rain from Heaven* (1934); *End of Summer* (1936); *Amphitryon 38* (1937, adapted from Giraudoux); *Wine of Choice* (1938); *No Time for Comedy* (1939, about a dramatist who is in danger of responding to the wrong, i.e., non-escapist, impulse); *The Talley Method* (1941); *The Pirate* (1942); *Jacobowsky and the Colonel* (1944, adapted from Werfel); *Dunnigan's Daughter* (1945); *Jane* (1947); *I Know My Love* (1949, adapted from Marcel Achard); *Let Me Hear the Melody* (1951); *Fanny* (1954, musical, with Joshua Logan); *The Cold Wind and the Warm* (1959, dramatization of his autobiography); *Lord Pengo* (1962); *But for Whom Charlie* (1964); and others.

BEIN, Albert, b. 1902, American dramatist. Plays of social protest. *Little Ol' Boy* (1933); *Let Freedom Ring* (1935. Play about North Carolina mill workers; based on Grace Lumpkin's novel, *To Make My Bread.*); *The Heavenly Express* (1940, poetic drama); *Land of Fame* (1943, with Mary Bein. Greece's struggle to regain her position.).

BENAVENTE, Jacinto, 1866-1954, Spanish dramatist, Nobel Prize, 1922. Wrote more than 300 plays of all types, particularly society comedies. Began as a pioneer of realism, finally a practitioner of every dramatic type. Examples: *El nido ajeno* (1894); *La gobernadora* (1901, *The Governor's Wife*, politics in the provinces); *La noche del sábado* (1903, *Saturday Night*); *La princesa Bebe* (1904, *Princess Bebe*); *Rosas de otoño* (1905, *Autumnal Roses*); *Los Malechores del bien* (1905, *The Evil Doers of Good*, comic treatment of some busybodies); *Los intereses creados* (1907, *The Bonds of Interest*, Commedia dell'arte); its sequel, *La ciudad alegre y confiada* (1916); *La malquerida* (1913, *The Passion Flower*); *La verdad* (1915, *The Truth*); *Campo de armiño* (1916, *Field of Ermine*); *Una señora* (1920, *A Lady*).

BENELLI, Sem, 1877-1949, Italian dramatist. World fame with *La cena delle beffe* (1909, *The Jest*). Also wrote *La maschera di bruto* (1908); *tignola* 1908); *L'amore dei tre re* (1910, *The Love of the Three Kings*); *Il mantellaccio* (1911); *Rosmunda* (1911), *La gorgona* (1913); *Le nozze dei centauri* (1915); *Ali* (1921); *L'arzigogolo* (1922); *La* *sagra della Santa Primavera* (1923); *L'amorosa tragedia* (1925); *Il vezzo di perle* (1926); *Con le stelle* (1927); *Orfeo e Proserpina* (1928); *Fiorenza* (1930); *Eroi* (1931); *Madre Regina* (1931); *Adamo e Eva* (1932); *Caterina Sforza* (1934); *Il ragno* (1935); *L'elefante* (1937); *L'orchidea* (1938); *La festa* (1940); *Paura* (1947).

BENNETT, Arnold, 1867-1931, English novelist who wrote successful plays, mostly based on his novels. *What the Public Wants* (1909, satire on the press); *Milestones* (1912, with Edward Knoblock); *The Great Adventure* (1913); and others.

BERGMAN, Hjalmar, 1883-1931, Swedish story teller and dramatist. Mostly character plays and comedies; has peculiar characters, but usually they exist in a realistic milieu. *The Weavers of Bagdad* (1923, a blind man quarrels with the rich Hassan. The Caliph settles the dispute.); *The Nobel Prize* (1925, the honorable character of a Nobel Prize winner who insists on the principle of honor.); *The Swedenhielms* (1925, translated). Other plays: *Dollar* (comedy); *The Rabble* (comedy); *En Saga* (poetic play with dream qualities); *Marionette Plays* (1917): *Death's Harlequin, A Shadow, Mr. Sleeman Is Coming* (translated); *His Grace's Last Testament* (1931).

BERNANOS, Georges, 1888-1948, French poet of Catholic realism. Shortly before his death he wrote *Les Dialogues des Carmélites* (1947-48), a film script produced in 1952 in a stage version by Albert Béguin and Marcelle Tassencourt, set to music by Francis Poulenc. Based on a novelette by Gertrud von le Fort. Deals with the execution of the Carmelites of Compiègne during the French Revolution in a series of dialogues which become more and more heightened as death approaches. At the end the nuns ascend the scaffold one after the other. Translated as *The Carmelites.*

BERNARD, Jean-Jacques, b. 1888, French dramatist. *Le Feu qui reprend mal* (1921, *The Sulky Fire*); *Martine* (1922, translated with the same title); *L'Invitation au voyage* (1924, *Invitation to a Voyage*); *Le Printemps des autres* (1924, *The Springtime of Others*); *Denise Marette* (1925), *Le Secret d' Arcers* (1926); *L'Ame en peine* (1926, *The Unquiet Spirit*); *Jeanne de Pantin* (1933);

Nationale 6 (1935); *Le Jardinier d'Ispahan* (1939); *Marie Stuart, Reine d'Ecosse* (1942); *Louise de Lavallière* (1943); *La Librairie Jalin* (1945); *Notre-Dame d'en haut* (1950).

BERNARD, Tristan, 1866-1947, French comedy writer of the boulevard theater. *Triplepatte* (1905; *Toddles*).

BERNSTEIN, Henry, 1876-1953, French dramatist. Wrote many dramas in the tradition of Sardou and Dumas fils, most of them rather sensational. His interest shifted from sensation to psychology. *La Rafale* (1905, translated as *Baccarat* and *The Whirlwind*); *La Griffe* (1906, *The Claw,* about an unscrupulous woman); *Le Voleur* (1906, *The Thief,* much ado about a theft in society); *Israël* (1908, translated under its own name; anti-Semitism and an affair of honor); and many others.

BERTIN, Charles, b. 1919, Belgian dramatist. *Les Prétendents* (1947); *Don Juan* (1948); *Cristoforo Colombo* (1953).

BESCH, Lutz, b. 1918, German dramatist. *Aller Tage Abend* (1951); *Rast vor Hamchang* (1953); *Die Leute aus Saggad* (1956).

BETTI, Ugo, 1892-1953. Most important Italian dramatist since Pirandello, whose work he continues, although distinctly under the influence of Kafka. For many years he was a judge in Rome, and his experience is reflected in his most successful play, *Corruzione al Palazzo di giustizia* (1949, *Corruption in the Palace of Justice*): a judge who has been nominated to the position of President of the Court becomes conscious of his own guilt and offers himself for trial. The ever growing abstraction which Betti employs here alienates his themes from reality without weakening them. Other plays: *La patrona* (1927); *La donna sullo scudo* (1927); *La casa sull'acqua* (1929); *L'isola meravigliosa* (1930); *Il diluvio* (1931); *Un albergo sul porto* (1933); *Frana allo scalo Nord* (1935); *Una bella domenica di settembre* (1937); *Il cacciatore di Anitre* (1940); *I Nostri Sogni* (1941); *Il paese delle vacanz* (1942, *Summertime*); *Notte in Casa del Ricco* (1942); *Il vento notturno* (1945); *Ispezione* (1947); *Moglie* (1947); *Favola di Natale* (1948); *Lotta fino all'Alba* (1949); *Irene innocente*

(1950); *Spiritismo nella antica casa* (1950); *Delitto all'Isola delle Capre* (1950, *Crime on Goat Island*); *La regina e gli insorti* (1951, *The Queen and the Rebels*); *Il giocatore* (1951, *The Gambler*); *L'aiula brucciata* (1953, *The Burnt Flower-Bed*); *La fuggitiva* (1953).

BILL-BJELOZERKOWSKI, Vladimir, b. 1884, Soviet dramatist. *Storm* (1925); *Life Goes on* (1934).

BILLETDOUX, François, b. 1927, French dramatist. *À la nuit la nuit* (1955); *Tchin-Tchin* (1959, translated); *Le Comportement des époux Bredburry* (1961); *Va donc chez Törpe* (1961, *Chez Torpe*); contributed to *Chemises de nuit* (1962).

BILLINGER, Richard, b. 1893, Austrian dramatist. Began with apprentice pieces of forceful natural power: *Rauhnacht* (1931); *Rosse* (1931); *Stille Gäste* (1933). These pieces are set in a ludicrous and often demonic peasant milieu. In 1937 he treated the clash of town and country in his most successful play, *Der Gigant* (the rich farmer's daughter's dream of the golden city, i.e., Prague; and her maddened father's judgment upon her). After this his plays became gradually flatter and finally became mere clichés. *Gabriele Dambrone* (1938, also known as *Am hohen Meer*); *Melusine* (1940); *Die Fuchsfalle* (1941); *Der Galgenvogel* (1948); *Der Plumpsack* (1953); *Das Augsburger Jahrtausendspiel* (1955); *Der Zentaur* (1959); *Bauernpassion* (1960); *Die Schafschur* (1963); and others.

BIRABEAU, André, b. 1890, French comedy writer. *Déjeuner de soleil* (1925, adapted as an American musical, *Lovely Lady*); *Dame nature* (1936); *Fiston* (1936, political comedy); *Pamplemousse* (1937, adapted as *Little Dark Horse*); and many others.

BJORNSON, Bjornsterne, 1832-1910, Norwegian dramatist. Historical plays, followed by social dramas. *Between the Battles* (1857); *The Bankrupt* (1875, translated, social drama); *Beyond Human Power* (first part, 1883; second part, 1895, translated—two separate plays, the first examining faith, healing, and miracles, the second offering a Christian nostrum to modern society); *When the New Wine Blooms* (1909, translated) and many others. Regarded in his time as a serious rival to Ibsen.

BLAGA, Lucian, 1895-1961, Rumanian author, uses psychoanalytic, historical, and folklore material. *Troubling the Water* (1923); *Master Manole* (human sacrifice during the construction of a bridge); *Children's Crusades* (1930); *Avram Iancu* (1934; historical drama).

BLITZSTEIN, Marc, 1905-1964, American composer and librettist. *The Cradle Will Rock* (1937); *No For An Answer* (1941, opera); *Regina* (1953, musical based on Lillian Hellman's *The Little Foxes*); English version of Brecht's *Threepenny Opera* (1955).

BLOK, Alexander, 1880-1921, Russian revolutionary lyric poet. First appearance on the stage with the symbolic drama, *The Puppet Show* (1906, translated). Begins with a meeting of "mystics" who are awaiting a vision. But the woman who appears is Columbine, and Pierrot, the melancholy dreamer, is the one waiting for her. Harlequin carries her off. Masks, clowns, knights, and ladies enter. At dawn Death appears. Pierrot meets him with outstretched arms, but everything dissolves and Pierrot is left alone. He takes his flute out of his pocket and plays the song of his painful life and his bride, Columbine. So ends this airily gracious, romantically ironic play, woven out of pain. [Account based on Wanda Berg-Papendiek's unpublished monograph on Blok.]) Also, lyric dramas such as *The King in the Square* (1906); *The Unknown Woman* (1906); *The Song of Fate* (1908); *The Rose and the Cross* (1913, historical verse drama); *Rameses* (1919).

BLUME, Bernhard, b. 1901, German dramatist of the post-World War I generation, now Professor of German at Harvard University. *Fahrt nach der Südsee* (1924); *Bonaparte* (1926, Epic style); *Treibjagd* (1927); *Im Namen des Volkes* (1929, the Sacco-Vanzetti Case). Comedies: *Feurio* (1928); *Gelegenheit macht Diebe* (1930).

BOMPIANI, Valentino, b. 1898, Italian dramatist. *L'amante virtuosa* (1931); *Delirio del personaggio* (1937); *La conchiglia all'orecchio* (1941); *Albertina* (1948); *Anche i grassi hanno l'onore* (1950); *Paura di me* (1953); *Angelica* (1954).

BONTEMPELLI, Massimo, 1878-1960, Italian journalist and dramatist. *Nostra Dea* (1925, the heroine changes her character as she changes her clothes); *La guardia alla luna* (1916); *Siepe a nordovest* (1923); *Valoria* (1931); *L'innocenza di Camillo* 1948); *Venezia salva* (1949); *La fame* (1949); *Nembo* (1958).

BORBERG, Svend, 1889-1947, Danish dramatist. Philosophic-psychological plays with technical experimentation: *No One* (1920); *Saints and Sinners* (1942).

BORCHERT, Wolfgang, 1921-1947, German dramatist of the post-World War II generation. *Draussen vor der Tür* (1947, *The Man Outside*. The fate of a returning soldier who no longer belongs anywhere; in the form of outcry and accusation with symbolic figures and expressionistic technique. Moving because of its truth and inevitability. First performed in Hamburg on the day after the author's death.).

BORGEN, Johan, b. 1902, Norwegian dramatist. *The Family Andersson* (1935); *While We Wait* (1937).

BOSPER, Albert, b. 1913, German dramatist of the post-World War II generation. *Brot, Honig und Sarafan* (1953); *Die Fischfabrik* (1954, comedy); also *Der Bruderkuss; Noch nicht der Jüngste Tag.*

BOUBER, Herman, b. 1880, Dutch man of the theater and author of folk plays such as *Peach and Plum* (1918); *The Ruffian* (1919); *The Sailor* (1921 and 1923, two parts); *The Clown* (1922); *Sailor's Wives* (1928); *The Queer Duck* (1930); *The Jordan* (1931); *The Fellow Boarder* (1933); *Women for Everyone* (1936); *Kidnapping* (1945).

BOURDET, Edouard, 1887-1945, French popular dramatist. Comedies of manners, with social criticism. *Le Rubicon* (1910); *La Prisonnière* (1926, *The Captive*); *Vient de paraître* (1927, *Best Seller*); *Le Sexe faible* (1929, *The Sex Fable*); *Les Temps difficiles* (1934, *Times Have Changed*); and others.

BRANDSTATTER, Roman, b. 1906, Polish dramatist, known in the West for his play *Silence* (1956, criticism of Stalinist Poland). Also *The Way to Assisi* (1947), *The House of Stone* (1955); *The Weeping Odysseus* (1956); *Medea;* and others.

BRANNER, H. C., b. 1903, Danish novelist and dramatist. Realism rising to symbolism. *The Riding Master* (1950); *Sisters* (1952); *Thermopylae* (1958).

BRAUN, Felix, b. 1885, Austrian poet of the Hofmannsthal circle. Wrote the tragedies and dramas *Tantalos* (1917); *Aktion* (1921); *Esther* (1925); *Beatrice Cenci* (1936); *Kaiser Karl V* (1936); *Rudolf der Stifter* (1953); *Joseph und Maria* (1956); and others.

BRAUN, Mattias, b. 1933, German author of the post-World War II generation. *Ein Haus unter der Sonne* (1954); *Die Frau des Generals* (1954); *Die Troerinnen des Euripides* (1957); *Die Medea des Euripides* (1958); *Die Perser des Aischylos* (1960); *Der Gefangene* (1960); *Unkenpfuhl* (1962).

BRECHT, Bertolt, 1898-1956, most important modern German dramatist and man of the theater. Early pieces: *Baal* (1918, translated. Expressionistic "glorification of naked searching for the self."); *Trommeln in der Nacht* (1919, the Spartacus uprising. First use of epigrammatic placards, such as "Everyone looks best in his own skin" or "Don't stare so romantically."); *Leben Eduards des Zweiten* (1924, historical play based on Marlowe and written with Lion Feuchtwanger. Station play with *moritat* insertions, an "étude in classical realism," according to Schumacher. First attempt to write strictly Epic theater.); *Im Dickicht der Städte* (1923, *In the Jungle of the Cities,* subtitled "The Struggle of Two Men in the Giant City of Chicago"; also translated as *In the Swamp.* Prologue: "The time is 1912, the place, Chicago. You will observe the inexplicable struggle of two men and the destruction of a family that has come out of the plains into the jungle of the big cities. Don't rack your brain trying to figure out the motive for this struggle, but take an interest instead in the human aspects of the play, judge objectively the fighting form of the two opponents, and direct your interest to the outcome." Brecht: "The endless isolation of Man makes enmity impossible." Interestingly constructed. Prologue played as a boxing match.); *Mann ist Mann* (1926, *A Man's a Man.* Comedy. Subtitle: "The Transformation of the Porter Galy Gay in the Military Barracks of Kilkoa in the Year 1925." British soldiers in India lose one of their comrades during a plundering expedition and replace him with Porter Galy Gay, whom they attempt systematically to rob of his individuality. Gay becomes a tool of the collective spirit, in this case seen negatively as the army. Brecht: "The development of Gay is carefully divided into four parts, for which four masks should be used: The 'Porter-face'—to be used until the trial; the 'natural face'—to be used until he awakes after the shooting; the 'blank face'—to be used until after the funeral speech; at the end: the 'soldier's face.'" Distinct satire of anti-individualistic tendencies: the "Soldier's face" is that of the "human fiighting machine." First occurrence of strong Eastern, particularly Indian, influences: inserted songs, the stage-manager as chorus, soldiers turned into monsters by means of stilts and wire-hoops, scene-titles.)

Middle period: *Die Dreigroschenoper* (1928, *The Threepenny Opera*. Based on John Gay's *Beggar's Opera*, 1728. Music by Kurt Weill. Uses parts of K. L. Ammer's translation of Villon. Founding of the Epic theater in the "Notes" to the play, even though in the play itself the act-divided form is retained. Aggressiveness without any particular ideological ties: the middle-class respectability of the highwayman: wedding scene, the rapacity of the citizen combined with the corruption of authorities: Beggar-King Peachum: "Poverty as a Commodity." Epic form—nowadays no longer considered a parody of opera.); *Happy End* (1929, written with Elisabeth Hauptmann, set to music by Kurt Weill. Underworld detective story, forerunner of *St. Joan of the Stockyards;* not accepted by Brecht in the canon of his works.); *Aufstieg und Fall der Stadt Mahagonny* (1930, *Rise and Fall of the City of Mahagonny*. Opera in three acts, music by Kurt Weill. Four lumberjacks found a city: "But this whole Mahagonny / Only exists because things are bad / Because there is no peace / And no harmony / And because there is nothing / To hold on to." The discontented of all cities come "out to Mahagonny—where the air is cool and fresh." But "all those who truly seek are disappointed." "This Mahagonny is no good, after all"; peace, quiet, and harmony are ephemeral. Only under the pressure of an approaching hurricane, which "threatens to destroy the city," do the men find their true selves and the great "You may!": "We don't need any hurricane / We don't need any typhoon / Any shocks they can give us / We can

give to ourselves." The hurricane passes the city by, but now its inhabitants live as if there were always a hurricane approaching. Chief occupations in Mahagonny: Eating, Drinking, Sex, Boxing: "Above all, see to it / That everything is permitted here." Trial and execution of the hero, Paul Ackermann—for in Mahagonny the laws are "not worse than other laws." Parades with placards such as "Hooray for the high cost of living," "Hooray for the fight of all against all," "Hooray for the Golden Age." Conclusion is that no philosophy can "help you or us or anyone at all." Brecht called the opera a "tale of human morals." It is clearly intended as a satire on the capitalistic world. But Brecht's pessimism goes deeper: the four men who found the city are not workers for nothing. Marxist critics such as Schumacher have correctly observed that this fact has eliminated the possibility of using the work for ideological class propaganda. The man who is worse than a typhoon is not the middle-class, capitalistic man, but Man in general. In regard to form, Brecht was not trying to turn a play into an opera, as he did with *The Threepenny Opera;* he was trying to modernize the conventional opera.).

Lehrstücke, 1929-1930: *Der Flug des Lindberghs*, revised as *Das Badener Lehrstück vom Einverständnis; Der Jasager* (*The Man Who Says Yes*, from Japanese play, *Taniko*); *Der Neinsager* (*The Man Who Says No*); *Die Massnahme* (*The Measures Taken*, a Communist propaganda play with music by Hanns Eisler); *Die Mutter* (Written 1930-31, *The Mother;* dramatization in 14 scenes of a novel by Gorki. Model *Lehrstück:* "Antimetaphysical, materialistic, non-Aristotelian dramaturgy"; *Die Heilige Johanna der Schlachthöf* (*St. Joan of the Stockyards,* written in 1929-30 in observance of the 500th anniversary of the death of Joan of Arc; radio performance, 1932; first stage performance, 1959; Transforms St. Joan into a Salvation Army member and sets the scene in the meat-packing houses of Chicago, a much discussed area of exploitation in those days. The first of Brecht's women who dies fighting for a better world and retains her belief in goodness. Transitional piece between the *Lehrstück* and the parable.); *Die Ausnahme und die Regel* (1930; first performed, 1947; *The Exception and the Rule. Lehrstück.* Prologue: "We'll tell you right away / The story of a journey. An exploiter / And his two victims go on it. / Please observe their relationship closely: /

You'll find it estranging, even though not strange / Unexplainable, but not unusual / Incredible, but the rule. / Observe mistrustfully the smallest seemingly simple action / And examine its necessity—especially if society accepts it! / We request you most especially— / Don't look on that which happens all the time as natural! / For nothing is natural / In such a time of bloody confusion / Ordered disorder, planned despotism, / Dehumanized humanity—so that nothing / Is accepted as unchangeable."); *Die Rundköpfe und die Spitzköpfe* (1932-33, *The Roundheads and the Peakheads;* first performed 1936. "This play originated in discussions dealing with an adaptation of Shakespeare's *Measure for Measure*. The plan for a re-working of the Shakespeare play was dropped during the writing."); *Die sieben Todsünden* (1933, *The Seven Deadly Sins*. Ballet written with Weill for Lotte Lenya); *Die Horatier und die Kuratier* (1934, in the manner of the Chinese theater). Plays written in exile: *Die Gewehre der Frau Carrar* (1937, *Señora Carrar's Rifles*. One-act play suggested by J. M. Synge's *Riders to the Sea*). *Furcht und Elend des Dritten Reiches* (1935-38, performed 1938, *The Private Life of the Master Race*); *Der aufhaltsame Aufstieg des Arturo Ui* (1941, performed 1958. "An attempt to explain the rise of Hitler to the capitalistic world by transposing it into a familiar milieu." American gangster story told in the form of an Elizabethan chronicle play. "Double alienation." In the second part, Brecht uses the scene in Martha's garden from *Faust,* Banquo's ghost from *Macbeth,* and the wooing scene from *Richard III* for satirical purposes. Keeps the action close to reality by inserting announcements telling which events in the rise of Hitler to power are being allegorized by the action). Chief works of the exile period: *Das Leben des Galilei* (Written and rewritten 1938-39, 1945-46, 1955-56, first performed 1943, *Galileo*. 15 scenes. Galileo's fight for the truth, his trial and recantation, his subsequent life. Brecht's later explanation: Galileo's crime is the original sin of the modern scientists who have held themselves aloof from the class struggle; Gilileo is pictured as a great researcher, but socially a scoundrel.); *Das Verhör des Lukullus* (1939, first radio performance 1940, first stage performance 1951, *The Trial of Lucullus*. Opera with music by Paul Dessau. Anti-war parable set in ancient Rome, re-worked into *Die Verurteilung des Lukullus—The Sentencing of Lucullus*

—because of Party criticism.); *Der gute Mensch von Sezuan* (1938-1940, first performed 1943, *The Good Woman of Setzuan*. A parable about three gods who pass through the Chinese town of Setzuan during their search for a good person. Only Shen Te, a prostitute, offers them shelter. When Shen Te obtains money and buys a shop she discovers that those to whom she is good are not good to her in return. She disguises herself as her "cousin" and in this character acts harshly to her fellow beings. She tries in vain to win the love of her fiancé, a flier, and to save her baby from want: "For your great plans, O Gods / I, poor and alone, was too small." Purest form of the parable using Chinese models.); *Mutter Courage und ihre Kinder* (Written 1938-39, first performed 1941, *Mother Courage*. A chronicle of the Thirty Years' War based on themes of Grimmelshausen. Parable of the devastation caused by war and a peddler-woman who learns nothing from all the evil.); *Herr Puntila und sein Knecht Matti* (1940-41), performed 1948, parable based on a scenario, in the form of a Finnish folk-play, by the Finnish writer, Hella Wuolijoki.); *Der Kaukasische Kreidekreis* (probably written 1944-45, first performed 1948, *The Caucasian Chalk Circle*. Parable of the maid Gruscha who loves the child which has been entrusted to her more than its own mother does and who lets herself be persecuted for its sake. Azdak, the judge, decides in favor of Gruscha after giving her the chalk circle test: the child is put inside the circle and whoever pulls him out first, gets him. Gruscha lets go because she does not want to hurt the child: "I brought it up! Should I tear it apart? I can't do it." This shows who the real mother is. The lesson is, "Things should belong to those who are good to them, as children to the motherly." Two styles: Epic style in the first part, and parable style in the trial.); *Die Tage der Kommune* (1948-49, first performed 1956, the Paris Workers' Revolt of 1871 and its suppression. No final version.); *Die Gesichte der Simone Machard* (1941-43, first performed 1957, written with Lion Feuchtwanger. Strictly constructed drama in four parts; the story of Joan of Arc transposed into the German occupation of France, 1940. The heroine is a child, the model of innocence, who rises up against injustice in her dreams, in which she becomes Joan of Arc and experiences war, coronation, judgment, and execution. The figure of the angel is drawn without irony. Later remark of Brecht's: "I am the last of the Roman Catholic writers." A combination of topical play and Mystery); *Schweyk im zweiten Weltkrieg* (1941-44, first performed 1957. Continuation of Hasek's military satire, which Brecht had helped to adapt in 1918 for Piscator.). Unpublished unfinished works: *Dan Drew and the Erie Railroad;* fragment of a play about Einstein. *Salzburger Totentanz* (1949). Adaptations: *Antigone* (1948, stage version of Holderlin's translation of the Sophocles' play; with "Prologue, Berlin, 1945"); *Wassa Schelesnowa* (1949, from Gorki); *Der Hofmeister* (1950, from Lenz); *Biberpelz und roter Hahn* (1951, from Hauptmann); *Der Prozess der Jeanne d'Arc zu Rouen* (1952, from a radio script by Anna Seghers); *Don Juan* (1952, from Molière); *Coriolanus* (1952-53, lacking Scenes Four through Ten. Includes a commentary written in 1953 on the meaning of the first scene.); *Pauken und Trompeten* (1956, from Farquhar's *The Recruiting Sergeant*); *Turandot* (Posth., from Gozzi).

BRIDIE, James, (Osborne H. Mavor), 1888-1951, physician and important Scottish dramatish. Realism and topical satire. First spectacular success was *The Anatomist* (1931. Based on the Burke and Hare murders—the story of an anatomist who becomes involved with criminals through his need for cadavers. His students, who worship him, protect him from an enraged mob. Bridie lets his Nietzsche-like protagonist attain tragic stature.). Other plays: *The Sunlight Sonata* (1928); *The Switchback* (1929); *The Girl Who Did Not Want to Go to Kuala* (1930); *Tobias and the Angel* (1932); *Jonah and the Whale* (1932); *The Amazed Evangelist* (1932); *A Sleeping Clergyman* (1933); *Marriage is No Joke* (1934); *Colonel Witherspoon* (1934); *Mary Read* (1934); *The Black Eye* (1935); *Susannah and the Elders* (1937); *The King of Nowhere* (1938); *The Devil and Mr. Bolfry* (1943); *Daphne Laureola* (1949); and others. His *Storm in a Teacup* (1936, called *Storm over Patsy* in New York) is an adaptation of Bruno Frank's *Sturm im Wasserglas.*

BRIEUX, Eugène, 1858-1932, French social dramatist. Didactic, concerned with specific social problems. *Ménages d'artistes* (1890, *Artists' Families,* produced by Antoine); *Les trois Filles de M. Du-* pont (1897, *The Three Daughters of M. Dupont,* translated by St. John Hankin, the misery of enforced marriage); *La Robe rouge* (1900, *The Red Robe,* injustice in the law courts); *Les Avariés* (1902, *Damaged Goods,* syphilis); *Maternité* (1903, *Maternity,* translated by Mrs. Bernard Shaw); *La Foi* (1909, *False Gods,* religion); *La Femme seule* (1912, *Woman on Her Own,* translated by Mrs. Bernard Shaw, about an independent woman); and others.

BRIGHOUSE, Harold, 1882-1958, English dramatist. Regional author of the Manchester School. *The Price of Coal* (1909); *Hobson's Choice* (1915; staged at the National Theatre, 1964. A tyrannical father is tamed by his daughter); and others.

BRONNEN, Arnolt, 1895-1959, German dramatist of the post-World War I generation, began as Expressionist, changed to living newspaper style, then joined the Nazis; in 1945 became a Communist. Resided in East Berlin at his death. Sensational first play, *Vatermord* (1920), followed by *Geburt der Jugend* (1922); *Exzesse* (1923); *Anarchie in Sillian* (1924); *Katalaunische Schlicht* (1924); *Rheinische Rebellen* (1925); *Ostpolzug* (1926); *Reparationen* (1927); *Michael Kohlhaas* (1929); *Sonnenberg* (1934); *N* (1938; Napoleon); *Gloriana* (1941); *Kette Kolin* (1950); *Kaprun* (1955); *Die jüngste Nacht* (1958, Comedy about the coming of the Americans to the Salzkammergut).

BRUCKNER, Ferdinand (Theodor Tagger), 1891-1958, popular Austrian dramatist of the post-World War I period. Began writing, under his real name (Tagger), with expressionistic pieces (*Die Komödie vom Untergang der Welt,* a cycle, 1920); adopted the pseudonym of Bruckner upon becoming a theater director in Berlin. Became world famous with the plays written under his new name, first of all with *Krankheit der Jugend* (1926, Freudian sexual pathology), then with *Die Verbrecher* (1928, modern panorama on a three-level stage, critical of the reigning form of justice). After *Die Kreatur* (1930) came the world renowned *Elisabeth von England* (1930, *Elizabeth of England,* Historical chronicle play staged with two simultaneous scenes of action: Spain and England. Elizabeth's struggle with Essex and with Philip analyzed from a sexual-pathological viewpoint.).

The Blacks, by Jean Genet. Marlene Warfield, Billy Dee Williams, Louise Stubbs. 1960, New York

The Condemned of Altona, by Jean-Paul Sartre. Claire Bloom, Diane Cilento. 1961, London

Jean Genet

Jean-Paul Sartre

The Entertainer, by John Osborne. Joan Plowright, Laurence Olivier. 1958, New York

A Touch of the Poet, by Eugene O'Neill. Kim Stanley, Helen Hayes. 1958, New York

The Summer of the Seventeenth Doll, by Ray Lawler. Kenneth Warren, Ray Lawler, June Jago, Madge Ryan, Ethel Gabriel. 1958, New York

The Potting Shed, by Graham Greene. Sybil Thorndike, Lewis Casson. 1957, New York

Paolo Paoli, by Arthur Adamov. Directed
by Roger Planchon. 1958, Paris

Eugène Ionesco

Right: *Rhinoceros,* by Eugène Ionesco. Zero Mostel. 1960, New York

Two for the Seesaw, by William Gibson. Anne Bancroft, Henry Fonda. 1958, New York

Peppino and Eduardo de Filippo

The Hostage, by Brendan Behan, Glynn Edwards, Maxwell Shaw, Victor Spinetti. 1960, New York

A Taste of Honey, by Shelagh Delaney. Nigel Davenport, Angela Lansbury. 1961, New York

Shelagh Delaney

Tchin-Tchin, by François Billetdoux. Anthony
Quinn, Margaret Leighton. 1960, New York

The Miracle Worker, by William Gibson. Anne Bancroft, Patty Duke. 1959, New York

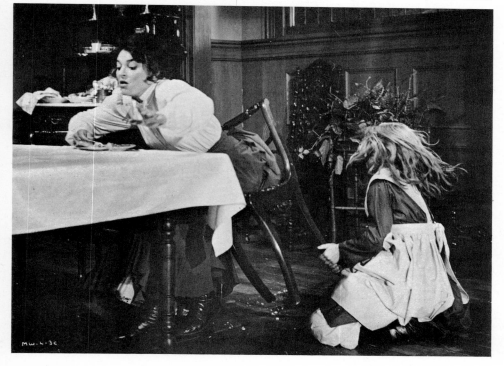

Edward Albee

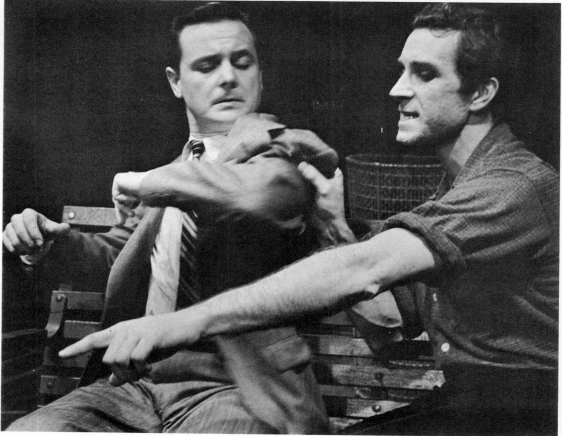

The Zoo Story, by Edward Albee. William Daniels, Mark Richman. 1959, New York

The Connection, by Jack Gelber. Warren Finnerty. 1959, New York

A Man for All Seasons, by Robert Bolt. Paul Scofield,
Olga Bellin, Carol Goodner. 1962, New York

Toys in the Attic, by Lillian Hellman. Irene Worth, Jason
Robards, Jr., Maureen Stapleton. 1960, New York

Oh Dad, Poor Dad, Mamma's Hung You in the Closet and I'm Feelin' So Sad, by Arthur Kopit. Austin Pendleton, Jo Van Fleet. 1962, New York

Who's Afraid of Virginia Woolf?, by Edward Albee. Ben Piazza, Uta Hagen, Arthur Hill. 1962, New York

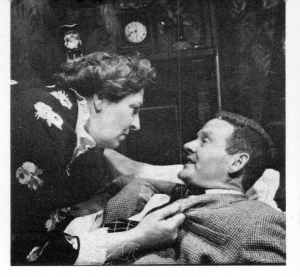

Say Nothing, by James Hanley. Margot Boyd, Denys Graham. 1962, London

Biedermann and the Firebugs, by Max Frisch. Ernst Shröder, Elsbeth von Lüdinghausen, Margot Trooger, Gustav Knuth, Boy Gobert. 1958, Zurich

Plays for Bleecker Street, by Thornton Wilder. Charlotte Jones, Mary Doyle, Richard Libertini, MacIntyre Dixon. 1962, New York

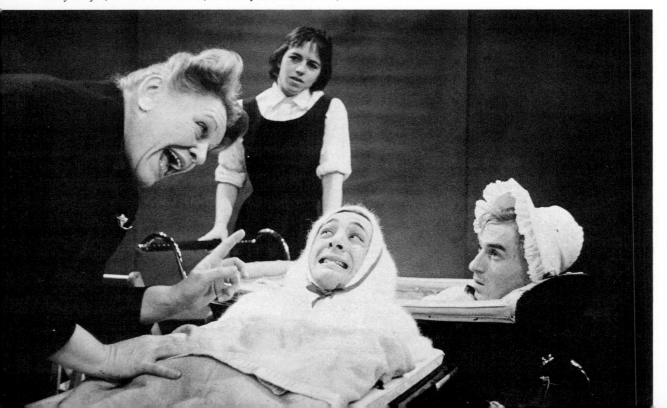

Dylan, by Sidney Michaels. Louisa Cabot, Alec
Guinness, James Ray. 1964, New York

Andorra, by Max Frisch. Right Foreground: Fritz Tillmann. 1962, Berlin

Chips with Everything, by Arnold Wesker. Michael Standing, John Noakes, 1963

The Deputy, by Rolf Hochhuth. Emlyn Williams. 1964, New York

Play, by Samuel Beckett. Marian Reardon, Michael
Lipton, Frances Sternhagen. 1964, New York

The Lover, by Harold Pinter. Hilda Brawner,
Michael Lipton. 1964, New York

Harold Pinter

The Physicists, by Friedrich Dürrenmatt. Theo Lingen, Hans Christian Blech, Gustav Knuth. 1962, Zurich

After the Fall, by Arthur Miller. Jason Robards, Jr., Barbara Loden. 1964, New York

Other plays: *Timon und das Gold* (1931, adapted from Shakespeare); *Die Marquise von O.* (1933, based on Kleist); *Die Rassen* (1933, *Races*); *Bolivar* (1943-45, two parts); *Napoleon I* (1936); *Heroische Komödie* (1939, set in the time of Napoleon); *Fährten* (1939, concerns the legitimacy of an unborn child); *Denn seine Zeit ist kurz* (1945); *Die Befreiten* (1945); *Früchte des Nichts* (1947); *Pyrrhus und Andromache* (1952); *Die Burlschwestern* (1954, adapted from Lenz); *Tod einer Puppe* (1956, topical play in verse with chorus); *Der Kampf mit dem Engel* (1956, in verse); *Das irdene Wägelchen* (1957, adaptation of *The Little Clay Cart* by the Indian king Sudraka). Bruckner's aim: modern tragedy.

BRÜES, Otto, b. 1897, German dramatist with Christian leanings. Wrote *Die Heilandsflur* (1921); *Die Füchse Gottes* (1922); *Stab und Stein* (1922); *Der Prophet von Lochau* (1923); *Der Spiegel der Helena* (1936); *Der alte Wrangel* (1936); *Menander bleibt in Athen* (1956); *Die kluge Anna* (1956); *Der Fisch an der Angel* (1957); *Johanna in den Zelten* (1956); *Nansen* (1958).

BULGAKOV, Mikhail, 1891-1940, Russian dramatist, banned by Stalin. Chief work: *Days of the Turbins* (1926, translated). Other plays: *The White Guard* (adapted from his novel); *The Purple Island* (1928); *Molière* (1936); *The Last Days* (1940; Pushkin's death). Dramatization of Gogol's *Dead Souls* (1928).

BUERO VALLEJO, Antonio, b. 1916, Spanish dramatist and social critic. *Historia de una escalera* (1949); *En la ardiente oscuridad* (1950); *La tejedora de sueños* (1952, *The Weaver of Dreams*); *Hoy es fiesta* (1956); *Un soñador para un pueblo* (1958); *Las meninas* (1960); *El Concierto de San Ovidio* (1962); and others.

BUSH-FEKETE, Ladislas, b. 1898, Hungarian dramatist, now living in Los Angeles. Has written *Jean; The Tight-Rope Dancer; Ladies and Gentlemen* (1938); and many other comedies.

BUZZATI, Dino, b. 1906, Italian writer of the Kafka school. Wrote *Un caso clinico* (1953. A healthy man is committed by his relatives to a clinic, where he is slowly and remorselessly destroyed.).

CAMUS, Albert, 1913-1960, French writer and philosopher. Nobel Prize, 1957. His philosophy has to do with the eternal revolt of Man against the world as it is. Dramas: *Caligula* (1943; character study of megalomania); *Le Malentendu* (1944, *The Misunderstanding,* also translated as *Cross Purposes.* An innkeeper and her daughter murder a guest, who turns out to be her son; she commits suicide.); *L'État de siège* (1948, *State of Siege.* New version of the theme of the famous novel *The Plague.* Here the pestilence falls on a 20th century Spanish town in the form of a dictatorship; it becomes a symbol of all force in our lives, against which one single man takes up the absurd battle.); *Les Justes* (1950, *The Just Assassins.* Tragedy of judicial murder based on the attempted assassination of the Grand Duke Sergius in 1905.). Camus favored strictness of form and was thus in the mainstream of the classical French drama. He used a chorus and near-stychomythic, pointed dialogue. Adaptations: *The Devotion to the Cross* from Calderon; *Un caso clinico* from Buzzati; *Requiem for a Nun* from Faulkner; *The Possessed* from Dostoevski. Camus: "True artists do not concern themselves with politics, for they cannot take the death of an opponent lightly. They are witnesses of the spirit, not of the law. Their profession damns them to experience, even to what is deadly to them. In our world of death-sentences we artists are the witnesses of man's protest against death. . . . Some men want to make us believe that the world of today needs men who conform completely to its doctrines. In the present state of the world, I consider this attitude extremely dangerous."

CANETTI, Elias, b. 1905, Austrian novelist and dramatist. *Hochzeit* (1932); *Komödie der Eitelkeit* (1950); *Die Befristeten* (1956), Canetti calls his characters "acoustic masks." Ideas stated in an essay, "Die Masse und die Macht" (1960).

CANKAR, Ivan, 1876-1918, important Slovenian dramatist. Realist. *For the Good of the People* (1901); *The King of Betajnovi* (1902); *Jernej Is Right* (1907). *Youths* (1910); *Scandal in St. Floren's Vale* (1910); *Beautiful Vida* (1912, based on a folk tale).

ČAPEK, Karel, 1890-1938, Czech dramatist and prose writer. Joined the revolutionary literary movement of 1910 with pieces which have a largely anti-illusionistic tendency. Drew attention in 1921 with his allegorical *The Insect Comedy* (also translated as *The World We Live In,* written in collaboration with his brother, Josef, 1887-1945); the robot drama, *R.U.R.,* came out almost at the same time (1921, translated). It concerns automatons who destroy their masters. Other plays: *The Makropoulos Secret* (1923, translated. Problem of longevity. Turned into an opera by Janacek.); *Adam the Creator* (1927, with Josef Čapek, translated); *Power and Glory* (1937, translated); *The Mother* (1938, translated).

CAPOTE, Truman, b. 1924, American novelist, known in the theater for *The Grass Harp* (1951, dramatized, romantic-lyric realism); also wrote *The House of Flowers* (1954, dramatized short story; takes place in a West Indies whorehouse).

CAPUS, Alfred, 1858-1922, French dramatist. Optimistic realist, champion of women. *Brignol et sa fille* (1894, *Brignol and His Daughter*); *La petite Fonctionnaire* (1901, a woman on her own); *Les deux Écoles* (1902, *The Two Schools*); and others.

CARAGIALE, Ion Luca, 1852-1912, Rumanian dramatist. Satiric comedies: *A Stormy Night* (1878, translated, Bucharest suburbia); *Mr. Leonida and the Reactionaries* (1879, translated, one-act farce); *The Lost Letter* (1884, translated. An election in a county seat in the Rumanian mountains. The leader of the Progressive Party obtains a love letter from the county chairman to the wife of the President of the Election Committee. The latter does everything to suppress the scandal, while the Progressive candidate attempts to win the election by means of the letter. Furious election campaign. Happy ending, with the victory of corruption.); *Carnival Scenes* (1885, translated); *Woe* (1890); some fragments while in exile in Berlin.

CARROLL, Paul Vincent, b. 1900, Irish dramatist. *Things That Are Caesar's* (1932, with Teresa Deevey); *The Wise Have Not Spoken* (1934); *Shadow and Substance* (written 1934, performed Dublin and New York 1937); *The White Steed* (1939); *The Coggerers* (1939. One act. Easter Rebellion);

Kindred (1939); *The Old Foolishness* (1940); *The Strings, My Lord, Are False* (1942); *The Wayward Saint* (1955); *The Devil Came from Dublin* (1957).

CASONA, Alejandro, b. 1903, Spanish dramatist, friend of Lorca, now living in Buenos Aires. Real name: Alejandro Rodríguez Álvarez. World fame for *Los arboles mueren de pie* (1949, comedy about artistic illusion). Also: *La sirena varada* (1934); *Otra vez la diablo* (1935); *La dama del alba* (1944, *The Lady of the Dawn*); *La barca sin pescador* (1944).

CAU, Jean, b. 1925, French journalist and dramatist. Goncourt Prize, 1961. *Les Parachutistes* (1961, controversial play about the Algerian war).

CÉSAIRE, Aimé, b. 1913, French dramatist from Martinique. *Et les Chiens se taisaient* (1946, the Negro's struggle for freedom in the Antilles).

CHAPIN, Harold, 1886-1915, English author of American birth. Middle-class English realistic dramas. *Art and Opportunity; The New Morality; Elaine; The Marriage of Columbine* (all published posthumously in 1921).

CHASE, Mary, b. 1907, American playwright. World success with *Harvey* (1944. Pulitzer Prize. Comedy about a psychopath who thinks he is constantly accompanied by his friend Harvey, a rabbit.). Other plays: *I've Done It* (1937); *Mrs. McThing* (1952).

CHAYEFSKY, Paddy, b. 1923, American dramatist, best-known for the film, *Marty. Middle of the Night* (1956), a grandfather marries a young girl); *The Tenth Man* (1959); *Gideon* (1961); *The Passion of Josef D.* (1964, about Stalin and Lenin).

CHEKHOV, Anton, 1860-1904, Russian short story writer and dramatist. Atmospheric realism, mood plays which proceed casually, declining to create the emphatic turns of an obvious plot. Unfulfilled expectations and strenuous efforts that fail expose the characters more strikingly than the more conventional sort of theatrical action. The characters often express themselves by soliloquies and asides which may or may not be addressed to others on the stage, and they thus reflect their isolation.

Critics often employ musical metaphors to describe the structure of these plays, speaking of such elements as "arias" and "symphonic patterns." A favorite subject of the plays is the isolation of the intellectual in the provinces. Chekhov's method has been extremely influential. Shaw imitates it—but adapts it to his own purposes—in *Heartbreak House.* John Van Druten finds the Chekhovian "play of mood" in Tennessee Williams' *The Glass Menagerie,* Carson McCullers' *The Member of the Wedding,* and, by implication, in his own *I Am a Camera.* In Soviet Russia, such visionaries as Astrov in *Uncle Vanya* and Trofimov in *The Cherry Orchard* are taken to be prophets of the Russian Revolution. Chekhov's plays are considered to be highly suitable to the realistic method of the Moscow Art Theater, which, under Stanislavski's guidance, gave them their first successful stage productions, but Chekhov complained that Stanislavski missed his comic intentions and made his characters "crybabies." His earliest surviving dramatic work is an untitled play of great length, variously translated as *That Worthless Fellow Platonov, Don Juan in the Russian Manner,* and *A Country Scandal* (Written approximately 1881, not performed in Chekhov's lifetime but recently staged in Milan, Paris, Moscow, New York, and London.) One-act farces, all of them translated, most of them based on his own short stories: *The Harmfulness of Tobacco* (Many versions, beginning with 1886); *Swan Song* (First version, 1887, later revisions. About an old actor.); *The Bear* (1888, also translated as *The Boor* and *The Brute.*); *The Proposal* (Written 1888, performed 1890, also known as *The Marriage Proposal*); *A Tragedian in Spite of Himself* (Written 1889, also known as *Summer in the Country*); *A Wedding* (Written 1889); *The Celebration* (Written 1891-92, also known as *The Jubilee* and *The Anniversary*). Early, relatively conventional realistic plays, all translated: *Ivanov* (Staged 1887, subsequently revised. A frustrated idealist in the provinces.); *The Wood Demon* (1889, later rewritten as *Uncle Vanya.* A provincial idealist dedicates himself to reforestation.). Plays reflecting Chekhov's mature, distinctive method, all available in various translations: *The Sea Gull* (Unsuccessfully performed in St. Petersburg, 1896; successfully done by the Moscow Art Theater, 1898. The frustrations of literary and theatrical people.); *Uncle Vanya* (Written 1896, performed 1899. A professor and his young wife visit their country estate and demoralize the good soul who has managed it for them.); *Three Sisters* (1901. A sensitive, intellectual family in the stultifying atmosphere of the provinces.); *The Cherry Orchard* (1904. An aristocratic family unable to face a financial crisis. Freely adapted by Joshua Logan as *The Wisteria Trees,* 1950.).

CHIARELLI, Luigi, 1886-1947, Italian dramatist, chief representative of the revolutionary "grotesque theater," a movement which paralleled Futurism. *La maschera e il volto* (1916, *The Mask and the Face*); *La lacrima e le stelle* (1918); *La scala di seta* (1917); *La morte degli amanti* (1921); *Fuochi d'artificio* (1923); *La Reginetta* (1934); *Un uomo da rifare* (1932); *Il cerchio magico* (1937); *Teatro in fiamme* (1945); *Essere* (1953); and others.

CHLUMBERG, Hans von, 1897-1930, Austrian dramatist. *Das Wunder um Verdun* (1930, *Miracle at Verdun,* powerful anti-war play).

CHODOROV, Edward, b. 1904, American dramatist. Light comedies. *Wonder Boy* (1931, with Arthur Barton); *Kind Lady* (1935, from Hugh Walpole); *Common Ground* (1945); *Oh, Men! Oh, Women!* (1953); *The Spa* (1956, from Ferenc Molnar); *Monsieur Lautrec* (1959); and others.

CLAUDEL, Paul, 1868-1955, important French writer. Revived the Roman Catholic drama. Several youthful dramas written before his conversion in 1886. First Christian dramas: *Tête d'or* (published 1890; second version 1891; performed 1924. Translated with the same title); *La Ville* (1890, *The City*); *L'echange* (published 1901, performed 1914. Early example of a method Claudel often employed later in his career—using criminal acts, in this case an exchange of husbands, to cause the collapse and subsequent repentance of protagonists); *Le Répos du septième jour* (1901. Early example of the use of unusual forms; a sort of Chinese Mystery play about an Emperor's penance for his people.); *Partage de midi* (1906, revised and performed 1948, *Break of Noon.* Set in an atmosphere which mixes up love and sex, drives the God-seeker to a woman, who betrays him but finally comes back to die with him. The play, which interprets the horrors of the Chinese Boxer Rebellion, has been compared to Wagner's *Tristan* because of its love dialogue.).

The Papal trilogy, spanning three generations: *L'Otage* (Published 1911, performed 1914, *The Hostage*. Time: The reign of Napoleon from the coronation to his fall. The last survivor of a noble family destroyed in the revolution gives herself to the murderer of her people, the imperial prefect and police chief, in order to save the Pope, whom she is hiding in her mansion. She marries the prefect and bears him an heir. In the last act the Bourbons come back, but the heroine prevents her former fiancé from killing her hated husband by throwing herself between them and being killed by the bullet herself.); *Le Pain dur* (Published 1918, performed 1949, *Crusts*. Time of the restoration of the Bourbons. The prefect of the previous play, now a minister, is shot by his own son because he attempts to seduce the latter's fiancée; the son, left by his fiancée, marries his father's mistress in order to eat "the bitter bread of damnation" with her.); *Le Père humilié* (Published 1920, performed 1953, *The Humiliation of the Father*. Rome, 1869-1871. The young Italian nation annulled after the freeing of the Holy City; great scene: the confession of "the humbled father." The French ambassador, grandchild of the heroine of *The Hostage,* appears as the defender of the Pope, together with his blind daughter; the latter, courted by the two nephews of the Pope, loves the older one, whose child she bears; but she contracts a nominal marriage with the younger one for the sake of the child after the father is killed fighting the Prussians. The dialectic between worldly and heavenly power corresponds to the dialectic between physical love, which disregards the sacraments, and heavenly, self-sacrificing love.).

The great Mystery drama, *L'Annonce faite à Marie* (1912, *The Tidings Brought to Mary*. Violaine, a rich young girl, renounces her fiancé out of pity for a leper who has tried to rape her and goes to the leper. This is her annunciation, her sanctification. Eight years later she is able to bring a dead child back to life. The child has become, through a sort of Immaculate Conception, her own: it has her eyes. The last of the "four events" of the play is the transfiguration of Violaine in death. Its language and its scenic effects establish the spiritual nature of the play.); *Protée* (1914, Farce. Menelaus lands on a lonely island on the way back from Troy with Helen). Claudel worked five years (1919-1924) on his great dramatic poem, *Le Soulier de Satin* (*The Satin Slipper,* first performed 1943 by the Comédie Française. This play renews the Spanish theocentric world theater; the action takes place at the time of the great discoveries and presents two lovers who wait in vain for each other their whole lives. Their unsatisfied longing sanctifies their love. A great many visions, symbolic figures, and Renaissance types, as well as a profuse abundance of settings—"The scene of this action is the World," —make up the play. The heroine says: "I want to become one with your inner self! I want to unite with the essence of your being! I want to learn, with God, to keep nothing for myself, to be this fully good, fully selfless being, to whom nothing is left, from whom everything is taken! This universal mysticism broke up all the realities of illusionism, to which Claudel had always, especially in the strongly classical Papal trilogy, been strictly faithful; it made possible the most powerful theatricalization of religious matter which the contemporary drama has seen. It uses the stage as the basis for a *theatrum mundi et dei,* in which nothing is without meaning, in which every playing technique is used and at the same time made sublime, in which everything that is, is seen in the mirror of non-being, of eternity, of the world beyond.).

Claudel's further projects in mystical theater: the texts of the oratorios, *Le Livre de Christoph Colomb* (performed 1930, published in English 1930, in French 1933, *The Book of Christopher Columbus,* music by Darius Milhaud); *Jeanne au bûcher* (1939, *Joan at the Stake,* music by Arthur Honegger); *L'Histoire de Tobie et de Sara* (published 1942, performed 1947, *Tobias and Sara,* written for Stravinsky, but set to music by Dugend).

CLAUS, Hugo, b. 1929, Flemish story teller and dramatist of the younger generation. *A Bride to the Morning* (1955); *The Murderer's Song* (1957); and others.

CLAUSEN, Svend, b. 1893, Danish dramatist. Social satires. *Our Own Mandarins* (1920); *Palace Revolution* (1923).

CLAVEL, Maurice, b. 1918, French dramatist. *Les Incendiaires* (1946); *La Terrasse de Midi* (1947); *Snap; Maguelone* (1951); *Canduela* (1953); *Leonor* (1954, based on Benavente's *Balmaseda*).

COCTEAU, Jean, 1889-1963, French writer, came to the stage by way of the ballet (most famous: *Parade*, 1917, with music by Satie, scenery by Picasso; *La Boeuf sur le toit*, 1920, with music by Milhaud, scenery by Dufy); later tried his hand at all forms: operettas, sketches, oratorios. *Antigone* (1922, opera by Honegger, 1942); *Romeo et Juliette* (1924); *Oedipe-roi* (written 1925 for Stravinsky, published 1927, performed 1927); *Orphée* (1926. Translated under its own name. Filmed by the author in 1950); *La Voix humaine* (1930. *The Human Voice*. Used as a libretto for an opera by Poulenc. An hour-long telephone conversation at the end of which the speaker commits suicide.); *La Machine infernale* (1934, *The Infernal Machine*); *L'Ecole des veuves* (1936); *Les Chevaliers de la table ronde* (1937; Arthurian theme); *Les Parents terribles* (1938, *Intimate Relations,* dramatized novel); *Les Monstres sacrés* (1940, *The Holy Terrors*); *La Machine à écrire* (1941, *The Typewriter*); *Renaud et Armide* (1943, verse drama); *L'Aigle à deux têtes* (1946, *The Eagle Has Two Heads*. Based on the murder of Elizabeth, Empress of Austria.); *Phèdre* (1950, ballet for Auric); *Bacchus* (1951. Scene is a Swiss wine-growing village, where, according to ancient custom, a young man is chosen each year to be Bacchus for eight days. This means that during that time he has absolute power of life and death over the inhabitants of the town. In the play a handsome peasant boy, who has been pretending to be feeble-minded ever since the more high-born youth of the town have rejected and insulted him, seizes the power of Bacchus in order to create a regiment which will fight for freedom and his revenge. Ideas of the Reformation and the Peasant's Revolts run through the play, but in a dialogue between Bacchus and a cardinal sent from Rome to inspect the district the former is shown to be a person of unbridled individualism, a Narcissus, who loses himself when he falls in love, and is headed for the stake. The cardinal tries in vain to call him back to the right path. He is finally killed by a bullet, which saves him from a worse fate. Cocteau: "*Bacchus* is a play about purity: the difficult purity which I oppose to the easy purity. That was also the real, underlying theme of my letter to Maritain, namely, to give back to God the cleverness usually ascribed to the Devil. . . . The piece is free of polemic intent throughout. It shows only the terrible loneliness in which those young men live who feel themselves obligated only to their own selves and refuse to follow any guiding principles whatsoever."). Also adaptation of Tennessee Williams' *A Streetcar Named Desire;* many short dramatic sketches in monologue form.

COHAN, George M., 1878-1942, American author noted for flamboyant showmanship. *Forty-five Minutes from Broadway* (1906); *Get Rich Quick Wallingford* (1910; from a story by G. R. Chester); *Broadway Jones* (1912); *Seven Keys to Baldpate* (1913; from a story by Earl Derr Biggers); *The Tavern* (with Cora D. Gannt, 1920); *The Song and Dance Man* (1923); *Baby Cyclone* (1927); *Pigeons and People* (1933); *Dear Old Darling* (1936); and others.

COLUM, Padraic, b. 1881, Irish playwright. *Broken Soil* (1903, at the Abbey Theatre; revised as *The Fiddler's House* 1907); *Thomas Muskberry* (1910); *Balloon* (1929); and others.

CONKLE, E. P., b. 1899, American dramatist. Associated with the WPA theater. *Two Hundred Were Chosen* (1936); *Prologue to Glory* (1938); many one-act plays.

CONNELLY, Marc, b. 1890, American dramatist. Wrote the following plays in collaboration with George S. Kaufman: *Dulcy* (1921); *To the Ladies* (1922); *The Forty-niners* (1922); *Merton of the Movies* (1922); *Helen of Troy, N.Y.* (1923); *The Deep Tangled Wildwood* (1923); *Beggar on Horseback* (1924); *Be Yourself* (1924). Also wrote *The Amber Empress* (1916); *The Wisdom Tooth* (1926); *The Wild Man of Borneo* (1927, with H. J. Mankiewicz); *The Green Pastures* (1930. Pulitzer Prize. Biblical scenes interpreted as a Negro fantasy.); *The Farmer Takes A Wife* (1934, with Frank Elser, from a novel by Walter D. Edmonds); *Everywhere I Roam* (1938, with Arnold Sundgaard); *The Flowers of Virtue* (1942); *A Story for Strangers* (1948), *Hunter's Moon* (1958).

CONRAD, Joseph, 1857-1924, English novelist of Polish birth. Three plays, adapted from his fiction. *One Day More* (performed 1905); *The Secret Agent* (performed 1922); *Laughing Anne* (published 1925).

COOK, George Cram, 1873-1924, American producer, dramatist. Founder in 1915 of the Province-town Players, which fostered the early work of Eugene O'Neill. *Suppressed Desires* (1915, with his wife, Susan Glaspell); *Change Your Style* (1915); *Tickless Time* (1918, with Susan Glaspell); *The Spring* (1921).

COPEAU, Jacques, 1878-1949, French director, critic, and dramatist. As director of the Theater of the Vieux-Colombier, he advocated "pure theater," staged classics and the plays of such non-commercial dramatists as Gide and Claudel, influenced the work of actors and directors, including Louis Jouvet, Charles Dullin, and Jean-Louis Barrault. *Les Frères Karamazov* (1911, with Jean Croué, from Dostoevski); *La Maison natale* (1928); *Le petit Pauvre* (1946, *The Little Poor Man*, St. Francis of Assisi).

COPPÉE, François, 1842-1908, French poet, dramatist. Influenced by Hugo in his historical dramas. *Le Passant* (1869, one-act play in which Sarah Bernhardt appeared); *Severo Torelli* (1883); *Pour la Coronne* (1895, *For the Crown*); and others.

CORDIER, Charles, b. 1911, Belgian writer and dramatist. *Le Fleuve* (1950); *Chant XXV* (1951, the Odysseus story); *Les Dés sont jetés* (1951); *Canossa* (1953); *Face à la nuit* (1954); *Un certain Monsieur Smorzick* (1956); *Celui qu'on n'attendait pas* (1953); *L'Heure du Pharaon* (1957). Also, adaptations of Plautus, Terence, and Menander.

COUBIER, Heinz, b. 1905, German dramatist. Greatest success achieved with *Aimée* (1938). Other plays: *Ivar Kreuger* (1939); *100,000,000 Dollars* (1940); *Piratenkomödie* (1941); *Francisquita* (1950); *Morgen ist auch ein Tag* (1951); *Der Kommandant* (1953); *Penelope oder die Lorbeermaske* (1957).

COURTELINE, Georges, 1858-1929, French comedy writer, wrote numerous farces and one-acters mostly in a middle-class milieu, e.g., *Boubourouche* (1893, translated); *Les Boulingrin* (1898; *These Cornfields*); *L'Article 330* (1900; *Article 330*); *La Paix chez soi* (1903, *Peace at Home*); *La Cruche* (1910), and many others. Real name, Georges Moineaux.

COWARD, Noel, b. 1899, English comedy writer, able Boulevard theater technician, plays characterized by witty conversation and delicate eroticism. *The Vortex* (1924); *Fallen Angels* (1925. Two married women are upset upon hearing that a man whom they have both loved is coming to visit); *Easy Virtue* (1925); *Hay Fever,* (1925. Each of the members of a slightly insane family invites a house guest for the weekend. The guests feel lost and insulted in the boundlessly individualistic milieu and at the end the family is left alone, reunited in a new harmony.); *The Queen Was in the Parlor* (1926); *Sirocco* (1927); *This Year of Grace* (1928); *Bitter Sweet* (1929, Musical); *Private Lives* (1930); *Cavalcade* (1931); *Post Mortem* (1931); *Design for Living* (1932); *Tonight at 8:30* (1935, 1936); *Blithe Spirit* (1941); *Present Laughter* (1943); *Relative Values* (1951); *Quadrille* (1952); *Nude with Violin* (1956). Also revues, musicals, the Utopian play *Peace in Our Time* (1947); *Waiting in the Wings* (1960); *Sail Away!* (1961, musical); and others. Wrote songs for *The Girl Who Came to Supper* (1963).

CROMMELYNCK, Fernand, b. 1885, Belgian dramatist. Farcical, savagely ironic comedies. *Nous n'irons plus au bois* (1906); *Le Sculpteur de Masques* (1908, performed in revised version 1911); *Le Marchand de regrets* (1913); *Le Cocu magnifique* (1920, about a self-made cuckold, a great popular success); *Les Amants puérils* (1921); *Tripes d'or* (1925, symbolic examination of avarice); *Carine, ou La jeune Fille folie de son âme* (1929); *Une Femme qu'a le coeur trop petit* (1934); *Chand et froid, ou L'Idée de Monsieur Dom* (1934); *Le Chevalier à la lune, ou Sir John Falstaff* (published 1954, based on Shakespeare).

CROTHERS, Rachel, 1878-1958, American dramatist. Leading American woman dramatist of the first three decades of the century. *Nora* (1903); *The Point of View* (1904); *The Three of Us* (1906); *The Coming of Mrs. Patrick* (1907); *Myself, Bettina* (1908); *A Man's World* (1910); *The Herfords* (1912, revived as *He and She*, 1920); *Ourselves* (1913); *Young Wisdom* (1914); *The Heart of Paddy Whack* (1914); *Old Lady 31* (1916); *Once Upon a Time* (1918); *A Little Journey* (1918); *39 East* (1919); *Nice People* (1921); *Everyday* (1921); *Mary the Third* (1923); *Expressing Willie*

(1924); *A Lady's Virtue* (1925); *Venus* (1927); *Let Us Be Gay* (1929); *As Husbands Go* (1931); *Caught Wet* (1931); *When Ladies Meet* (1932); *Susan and God* (1937); and others.

CSOKOR, Franz Theodor, b. 1885, Austrian dramatist. *Die rote Strasse* (1918, expressionistic); *Ballade von der Stadt* (1924); *Gesellschaft der Menschenrechte* (1929, about Büchner); *Besetztes Gebiet* (1930); *Gewesene Menschen* (1932); *Der dritte November, 1918* (1936, dissolution of the Austro-Hungarian Empire); *Gottes General* (1938, Ignatius Loyola); *Wenn sie zurückkommen* (1940); *Kalypso* (1942); *Der verlorene Sohn* (1945); *Caesars Witwe* (1948); *Hebt den Stein ab* (1956, "a comedy about ultimate matters"); *Treibholz* (1959); *Die Erweckung des Zosimir* (1960); *Das Zeichen an der Wand* (1963).

CUMMINGS, E. E., 1894-1962. American lyric poet, influenced by Gertrude Stein and Ezra Pound. Wrote the surrealistic play, *him* (1927); *Santa Claus* (1946, modern Morality play in one act).

CUREL, Francois de, 1854-1928, French dramatist. Plays of sentiment, then plays of ideas. His first plays produced by Antoine. *L'Envers d'une sainte* (1892, *A False Saint*); *Les Fossiles* (1892, *The Fossils,* a dying aristocracy); *L'Invitée* (1893, *The Guest Wife*); *Le Repas du Lion* (1897, *Lion's Meat*); *La nouvelle Idole* (1899, faith vs. science); *La Fille sauvage* (1902, *The Savage Girls,* primitivism vs. civilization); *L'Ame en folie* (1919, popular success); *Ivresse du sage* (1922); *Terre inhumaine* (1922; *No Man's Land;* war); and others.

DAGERMAN, Stig, 1923-1954, Swedish dramatist, follower of Kafka. *The Condemned* (1947, translated); *The Shadow of Mart* (1948. Existentialist play for four characters. The shadow of a son who has fallen fighting against the Germans hangs over a family. Mart's brother shoots his mother when she tries to destroy his love for Mart's wife.); *No One Is Free* (1949); *The Climber* (1949).

DANE, Clemence (Winifred Ashton), b. ?, English writer of popular stage pieces. *A Bill of Divorcement* (1921); *The Terror* (1921); *Will Shakespeare* (1921); *The Way Things Happen*

(1924); *Naboth's Vineyard* (1926); *Granite* (1926); *Mariners* (1927); *Adam's Opera* (1928); *Gooseberry Fool* (1930, with Helen Simpson); *Wild Decembers* (1932, about the Brontës); *Come of Age* (1934, about Thomas Chatterton); *Moonlight Is Silver* (1934); *Herod and Mariamne* (1938); *Cousin Muriel* (1940); *Call Home the Heart* (1947); *Eighty in the Shade* (1958); and others.

D'ANNUNZIO, Gabriele, Principe de Montenevoso, 1863-1938, Italian playwright. Representative of the Nietzschean drama as opposed to Naturalism flourishing at the same time. Writes of life as beauty and intoxication. Chief works: *La Città Morta* (1898); *La Gioconda* (1899, written for Duse); *Francesca da Rimini* (1902); *La Figlia di Iorio* (1904); *La Fiaccola sotto il moggio* (1905); *La Nave* (1908, the founding of Venice); *Le Martyre de Saint Sébastien* (1910; Mystery play); *Parisina* (1913).

DAVIS, Owen, 1874-1956, American dramatist. *The Detour* (1921); *Icebound* (1923, Pulitzer Prize); *The Good Earth* (1932, with Donald Davis, from Pearl Buck); *Ethan Frome* (1936, with Donald Davis, from Edith Wharton); and many others.

DE FILIPPO, Eduardo, b. 1900, reviver of the Neapolitan folk and dialect comedy, actor and director, adaptor of the Commedia dell'arte. International success with *Napoli Milionaria* (1946, governments change, but the Neapolitans go on—made into a film) and with *Filomena Marturano* (1946, Neapolitan family play, with a great mother figure—also filmed). Other plays: *Gennariello* (1932); *Uomo e galantuomo* (1933); *La speranza ha trovato un alloggio* (1936); *Uno dei capelli bianchi* (1938); *Non ti pago* (1941); *Natale in casa Cupiello* (1943); *Questi fantasmi* (1946, a deceived husband thinks his house is haunted); *S. Carlino 1947* (1947); *Le bugie con le gambe lunghe* (1948); *Le voci di dentro* (1948); *La grande magia* (1949, influence of Pirandello; a deceived husband entertains an illusion); *La paura numero uno* (1950); *Mia famiglia* (1955); *Bene mio, coro mio* (1955); *De pretore Vincenzo* (1957); *La fortune va in cerca di tasche* (1958); *Pulcinella in cerca sella sua fortuna per Napoli* (1958, adapted from Pasquale Altavilla). *Sabato, Domenica è Lunedi* (1960); *Sindaco del* *rione Sanità* (1960, tragedy, the transformation of a dying gangster into the wise arbiter of a private justice); *Il figlio die Pulcinella* (1962). De Filippo: "What I want to express is that I have changed nothing in the theater since Pulcinella first appeared as a sly clown in the chronicles of the 16th century. For our weaknesses remain exactly the same; we still overrate our unimportant selves and underrate our neighbor . . . Pulcinella must not die, for he embodies human conscience." De Filippo's brother, Peppino, has also written numerous plays.

DEFRESNE, August, b. 1893, Dutch dramatist and man of the theater; today among the most important dramatists of his country. Began with Expressionism. *Murder Romance* (1923); *The Lord Lister Legend* (1923); *Kings* (1923); *The Houseboat* (1924); *The Parasite* (1926); *The Comical Judge* (1927); *Other Leaders* (1928); *The Uninhabited Island* (1941, international success); *Free People* (1945, fifth act of a collaborative drama celebrating the liberation); *The Nameless Ones of 1942* (1945); *Anno Christi 1948* (1948, allegory celebrating the golden anniversary of the Queen of Holland's coronation); *The Eternal Chance* (1958. A comedy which begins as a play about criminals in an infamous section of Amsterdam and becomes more and more symbolic as it goes on.).

DE HARTOG, Jan, b. 1914, Dutch prose writer and dramatist. International success with *Skipper Next to God* (1942, performed in New York 1948). A ship carrying Jewish refugees, whom nobody wants, is scuttled by its captain, who thus saves his passengers by turning them into shipwreck survivors); *The Sinking of the "Freedom"* (1937); *Death of a Rat* (1939, translated as *This Time Tomorrow*. Experiment with a girl who is supposed to return from the dead in order to tell science what she has seen "over there"); *The Fourposter* (performed in New York, 1951, a two-character comedy running from the wedding night to old age); *Land in Sight* (1953).

DEKKER, Maurits, b. 1896, Dutch novelist and dramatist. Wrote the second act of the liberation drama, *Free People* in 1945. Also wrote *The World Has No Waiting Room* (1949); *The Other Law* (1951); *For Whom Are You Singing?* (1954, based

on his own novel, *Kabeljetje*); *Little Conflict* (1955).

DELANEY, Shelagh, b. 1940, young English dramatist, was usherette in a film theater. *A Taste of Honey* (1958, a girl neglected by her mother, loved by a Negro, befriended by a homosexual); *A Lion in Love* (1960).

DENNIS, Nigel, b. 1912, English dramatist, novelist, and critic. *Cards of Identity* (1956); *The Making of Moo* (1957, a satiric comedy subtitled, "The History of Religion"); *August for the People* (1961). Drama critic of *Encounter*.

DEVAL, Jacques, b. 1893, French dramatist. Became well known with *Tovaritch* (1933, adapted as *Tovarich* by Robert E. Sherwood). Also wrote *Beauté* (1924); *Dans sa Candeur naïve* (1926, *Her Cardboard Lover*); *Mademoiselle* (1932, trans. same title); *L'Age de Juliette* (1934); *Prière pour les vivants* (1933); *Corrida* (1957); *La Venus de Milo* (1962); and others.

DIETZENSCHMIDT, Anton, 1893-1955, German dramatist; expressionist. *Die Vertreibung der Hagar* (1916); *Verfolgung* (1924); later wrote Christian plays for amateurs.

DONLEAVY, J. P., b. 1926, American dramatist and novelist. Plays first performed in London. *The Ginger Man* (1959, based on his own novel); *Fairy Tales of New York* (1961; satirical examination of American life).

DONNAY, Maurice, 1859-1945, French dramatist. Comedies of love. *Amants* (1895, *Lovers,* history of a civilized love affair); *L'Affranchie* (1898, *The Free Woman*); *Le Torrent* (1899, unhappy ending to a love affair); *Le Retour de Jérusalem* (1903; *The Return from Jerusalem;* vs. romance between Jew and Gentile); *Oiseaux de passage* (1904, with Lucien Descaves, vs. revolutionaries); *Les Éclaireuses* (1913, vs. feminism); and others.

DOS PASSOS, John, b. 1896, American novelist. Wrote three experimental plays of social criticism: *The Moon Is a Gong* (1926, also called *The Garbage Man*); *Airways, Inc.* (1929); and *Fortune Heights* (1934).

DREISER, Theodore, 1871-1945, American novelist, leading American exponent of naturalism. One full-length play, *The Hand of the Potter* (Begun 1916, published 1919, performed without success. Study of sexual perversion). Short plays collected in *Plays of the Natural and the Supernatural* (1919). His novel *An American Tragedy* (1925) has been dramatized.

DRINKWATER, John, 1882-1937, English dramatist, known for his historical chronicle plays. *Rebellion* (1914, in verse); *X-O; A Night of the Trojan War* (1917, a peace play in verse); *Abraham Lincoln* (1919); *Oliver Cromwell* (1922); *Mary Stuart* (1922); *Robert E. Lee* (1923); *Bird in Hand* (1927, popular comedy); and others.

DUNCAN, Ronald, b. 1914, English dramatist and poet. *The Unburied Dead* (1938, one act); *Ora Pro Nobis* (1939, one act); *Pimp, Skunk and Profiteer* (1939, one act); *This Way to the Tomb* (1945, masque and anti-masque); *Stratton* (1949); *Our Lady's Tumbler* (1950); *Don Juan* (1956); *The Death of Satan* (1956); *The Catalyst* (1958); *Abélard and Heloise* (1960).

DUNNING, Philip, b. 1890, American dramatist. *Broadway* (1926, with George Abbott); *Get Me in The Movies* (1928, with Charlton Andrews); *Night Hostess* (1928); *Sweet Land of Liberty* (1929); *Lily Turner* (1932, with George Abbott); *Kill That Story* (1934, with Harry Madden); *Remember the Day* (1935, with Philo Higley).

DUNSANY, Lord (E. J. M. D. Plunkett), 1878-1957, Anglo-Irish dramatist. Wrote many one act plays dealing with exotic and supernatural subjects. *The Glittering Gate* (1909); *King Argimenes* (1911); *The Gods of the Mountain* (1911); *The Golden Doom* (1912); *A Night at an Inn* (1916); *The Queen's Enemies* (1916); *The Tents of the Arabs* (1917); *The Laughter of the Gods* (1919); *The Lost Silk Hat* (1921); *Fame and the Poet* (1921); *The Compromise of the King of the Golden Isles* (1921); *A Good Bargain* (1921); *The Prince of Stamboul* (1921); *If* (1921); *Mr. Faithful* (1927); *The Jest of Hahalaba* (1927); *Lord Adrian* (1937); *Alexander* (1938); *The Bureau de Change* (1939); *The Strange Lover* (1939); and others.

DURRELL, Lawrence, b. 1912, English novelist and poet. *Sappho* (1950, verse drama); *Acte* (1961, based on the life of Nero).

DÜRRENMATT, Friedrich, b. 1921, Swiss dramatist. Most important talent in the German-speaking theater since the death of Brecht. Extremely strong impulse to Opposition and a leaning toward cabaret-style satire in his habit of grotesque exaggeration and travesty of all bourgeois idols. Influenced by Aristophanes and Nestroy. Plays: *Es steht geschrieben* (1945-46, about the Anabaptists in Münster); *Der Blinde* (1948, parable); *Romulus der Grosse* (1949, adapted by Gore Vidal as *Romulus*. Contemporary satire in historical dress: the capture of Rome by the Ostrogoths.); *Die Ehe des Herrn Mississippi* (1952, adapted as *Fools Are Passing Through*. Political horror play and parody of old-time theater combined: poisoning, revolution, and confessions.); *Ein Engel kommt nach Babylon* (1953. Symbolic comedy: a beggar pitted against the mighty in biblical times; the misfortunes of an angel sent to Earth in the guise of a young girl.); *Der Besuch der alten Dame* (1956, adapted by Maurice Valency as *The Visit*. Fate comes to a small town in the form of the multimillionairess, Claire Zachanassian, a native of the town who was once betrayed there and cast out from it. She is prepared to give the town an enormous sum on one condition—that they kill the man who betrayed her. The coffin for the body is part of her luggage. At first the people are revolted, but gradually the thought of the money begins to corrupt them. The betrayer, a married man with a son and daughter, the model of a peaceful and law-abiding citizen, sees that he must sacrifice himself. He makes a last outing with his family in the new car bought by his son on the strength of his forthcoming death; and soon afterwards the old lady is able to take his body away with her. The citizens form a chorus similar to that of the classical tragedies.); *Herr Korbes empfängt* (1957; a crime comedy); *Frank V—Oper einer Privatbank* (1959, music by Paul Burkhard); *Die Physiker* (1961, *The Physicists*); *Hercules und der Stall des Augias* (1963). Has also written numerous radio scripts.

DYMOV, Ossip, 1878-1959. Russian-Jewish dramatist. Successful in the post World War I period on west European stages with *Nju* (1914, made into a film with Elisabeth Bergner, translated); *Bronx Express* (1919); *Human Dust* (1927); *Shadows over Harlem* (1930); *Juschik* (Fairy-tale play); and others.

ECHEGARAY, José, 1832-1916, Spanish dramatist. Nobel Prize, 1904. Wrote in the style of classical Spanish drama and the modern society play. *O locura o Santidad* (1876, *Madman or Saint*); *El gran Galeoto* (1881, *The Great Galeoto*); *El hijo de Don Juan* (1892, *The Son of Don Juan*); *Mariana* (1892, translated); *El loco Dios* (1900, *The Madman Divine*); and many others.

EGGE, Peter, b. 1869, Norwegian prose writer and dramatist. *Jacob and Christopher* (1900); *The Idyl* (1910); *The Rift* (1914); *The Fool* (1917); *The Last Act* (1954); and others.

ELIOT, Thomas Stearns, b. 1888, leading English poet. He was already world-famous through *The Waste Land* when he became interested in the theater, at first writing essays, then experimental dramas in verse. *Sweeney Agonistes* (published 1926-27, fragment of an Aristophanic drama); *The Rock* (1934, Christian festival play in the style of Yeats); *Murder in the Cathedral* (1935, Christian play on the martyrdom of Thomas Becket, who permits himself to be killed in the cathedral by the king's knights because this martyrdom is the intention of God.); *The Family Reunion* (1939. A Form of English society drama broken by anti-illusionistic devices. The members of the family reunite to celebrate the birthday of Lady Amy. The oldest son, Lord Harry, confesses that he has murdered his wife. While the normal lights go down, the Eumenides appear in their own light. There is a curse on the family: Harry's father has also entertained murderous thoughts. Harry recognizes that he must take the family curse upon himself.). *The Cocktail Party* (1949. Comedy, again a familiar society milieu. Ladies and gentlemen of society gather at a cocktail party; behind the social mask of well-being they are confusedly and sinfully connected with one another. A psychiatrist diagnoses inability to love, lack of contact, inner isolation. He soon becomes a mystical figure: accompanied by his two assistants, he becomes the teacher of mysteries and introduces the novices to the secrets of their existence. He gives each of them some task to per-

form. In the last act they gather again at another party. One of them has died in the tropics while serving there as a nurse. A broken marriage has been repaired. The way to salvation through expiation has been shown.); *The Confidential Clerk* (1953. A comedy in which the plot of Euripides' *Ion* is transposed to modern England. Exchanged illegitimate children bring more and more new relationships to light. Real and mystical figures and real and mystical dialogue constantly merge with each other, pointing out the transcendence of all being.); *The Elder Statesman* (1958. Society drama in verse. Classical parallel: the aged Oedipus. Lord Claverton, former minister and businessman, now retired and very sick, is being cared for by his daughter. His son's activities are a source of great worry to him, and in his sickness he is visited by personifications of his memories: a friend of his youth whom he was partly responsible for turning into a businessman of questionable honesty, and a a girl whom he once jilted. Both are now doing very well. The one wants nothing more than to meet him in society on equal terms; the other has become a rich widow. But these ghosts out of the past make the old man, now near his death, realize his own guilt. Now he recognizes himself in his son, who has tried to break away from him in order to lead a "life of sin": he learns to understand and to forgive. He has triumphed over himself. Now, at last, he can love his son—now that the concealing curtains have been ripped away and everything can be seen in the perspective of a cosmic light. God has entered the scene. Humility and resignation now enable him to give up his daughter to her lover. The young couple play the last scene—a paean to love.).

ERDMANN, Nikolai, 1902-1936 (?), Russian dramatist, involved in the liquidation of Meyerhold, at which time he disappeared. *The Warrant* (1925, satiric comedy); *The Suicide* (performance forbidden).

ERNST, Paul, 1866-1933, German dramatist, proponent of a neoclassicism of idealistic tendency, primarily moralistic. Imitated Renaissance literary motifs; his forms are mostly copies of other styles rather than actual, original creations. *Demetrios* (1905); *Das Gold* (1906); *Canossa* (1908); *Brunhild* (1909); *Ninon de Lenclos* (1910); *Ariadne* *auf Naxos* (1912); *Preussengeist* (1915); *Kassandra* (1915); *Yorck* (1917); *Chiemhild* (1918); *Pantalon und seine Söhne* (1916; Comedy in the Goldoni manner); and others.

ERVINE, St. John, b. 1883, Irish dramatist. *Mixed Marriage* (1911); *The Magnanimous Lover* (1912); *Jane Clegg* (1913); *The Critics* (1913); *The Orangeman* (1913); *John Ferguson* (1915, the second play and first success of the Theatre Guild); *The Island of Saints* (1920); *The Wonderful Visit* (1921, with H. G. Wells); *The Ship* (1922); *Mary, Mary, Quite Contrary* (1923); *The Lady of Belmont* (1925); *Anthony and Anna* (1926); *Old George Comes to Tea* (1927); *She Was No Lady* (1927); *The First Mrs. Fraser* (1929); *Boyd's Shop* (1936); *Robert's Wife* (1937); *People of Our Class* (1938); *The Christies* (1939); *William John Mawhinney* (1940); *Friends and Relations* (1941); *Private Enterprise* (1947); *My Brother Tom* (1952); *Esperanza* (1957).

ESSIG, Hermann, 1878-1918, German dramatist of the Expressionist movement. *Überteufel* (1912); *Napoleons Aufstieg* (1912); *Des Kaisers Soldaten* (1915). Other plays: *Der Schweinepriester* (1915); *Mariae Heimsuchung* (1909); *Die Glückskuh* (1918); *Die Weiber von Weinsberg* (1909); *Ihr stilles Glück* (1912); *Der Held von Wald* (1913).

EULENBERG, Herbert, 1876-1949, German dramatist of the transition period. Histories and society dramas. *Anna Walewska* (1899); *Kassandra* (1903); *Ritter Blaubart* (1905); *Der natürliche Vater* (1907); *Allies um Liebe* (1910); *Thomas Münzer* (1932); *Tilman Riemenschneider* (1934); and others.

EVREINOV, Nikolai, 1879-1953, Russian dramatist. Symbolic dramas depicting the projection of the inner ego. Many plays, among them *The Theater of the Soul* (1912, translated, a "monodrama") and *The Chief Thing* (1921, translated). In 1920 he staged a pageant called *The Storming of the Winter Palace* to celebrate the third anniversary of the October Revolution.

FABBRI, Diego, b. 1911, Italian dramatist. Became internationally known with his *Processo a Gesù* (1955, Trial of Jesus). Earlier plays: *Orbite* (1941); *Paludi* (1942); *La libreria del sole* (1943); *Inquisizione* (1950); *Rancore* (1950); *Il seduttore* (1951); *Processo di famiglia* (1953). Later plays: *La bugiarda* (1956); *Veglia d'armi* (1956); *I demoni* (1957, based on Dostoyevsky); *Delirio* (1958); *Figli d'arte* (1959); *Rituatto d'ignoto* (1962); *La scoiattolo* (1963).

FAESI, Robert, b. 1883, Swiss poet. Tragedies and comedies, among them *Odysseus und Nausikaa* (1911); *Fassade* (1918); *Opferspiel* (1925); *Leerlauf* (1929); *Der Magier* (1938).

FAULKNER, William, 1897-1962, leading American novelist. *Requiem for a Nun* (1952, with Ruth Ford. Originally appeared in novel form; the drama uses the basic dramatic form of the trial. Very modern in a theatrical sense in that it has a double field of action: the outer field—Negro woman accused of child murder—and inner field—self-deception and self-recognition of the real guilty party, the well-to-do mother with the horrible past. The mother's past is revealed in a dialogue in which the truth breaks through the many words of her self-deception. The opposed elements consist of the Negress-Nun, who, as the guiltless/accused, stands for her race, and the figures of the attorney and the governor.). Earlier (1935) *As I Lay Dying* had been dramatized by Jean-Louis Barrault.

FEILER, Max Christian, b. 1904, German critic and stage writer. Most successful play was *Die sechste Frau* (1939, about Henry VIII and Catherine Parr).

FERBER, Edna, b. 1887, American novelist. Has been connected with the stage since *Showboat* (1926, with music by Oscar Hammerstein II). Together with George S. Kaufman wrote *The Royal Family* (1927); *Dinner at Eight* (1932); *Stage Door* (1938); *The Land is Bright* (1941); *Bravo!* (1948).

FERDINAND, Roger, b. 1898, French author of comedies. Achieved success with his plays about young people, *Les J3 ou la nouvelle école* (1943) and *Trois garçons, une fille* (1947). Other plays: *La Machine à souvenir* (1925); *Irma* (1926); *Ils ont vingt ans* (1947); *Le Mari ne compte pas* (1949); and others.

FERRERO, Leo, 1903-1933, Italian dramatist. *La chioma di Berenice* (1924); *La campagna senza Madonna* (1927); *Angelica* (Published 1934, produced 1936 by Pitoëff in Paris. An anti-Fascist allegory of revolution and dictatorship in the manner of the Commedia dell'arte).

FEUCHTWANGER, Lion, 1884-1958, German novelist and dramatist. Brecht's collaborator on *Leben Eduards II* and *Die Gesichte von Simone Machard* (the latter based on his novel *Simone*). Stage journalism in *Warren Hastings* (1916, later turned into *Kalkutta, 4 Mai* with Brecht's help; revision published 1927 with *Die Petroleuminseln* and *Wird Hill amnestiert?* as "Anglo-Saxon plays"; revision translated as *Warren Hastings*); *Jud Süss* (1917, later a novel); *Die Kriegsgefangenen* (1919); *Thomas Wendt* (1920, "dramatic novel," influence on Brecht's epic drama); *Der holländische Kaufmann* (written 1923, acted 1928); *Die Petroleuminseln* (*The Oil Islands*); *Wird Hill amnestiert?*; *Wahn oder der Teufel in Boston* (1948); *Die Witwe Capet* (1957, Marie Antoinette). Adaptations: Aeschylus, *The Persians* (1915); Aristophanes, *Peace* (1916); Sudraka, *The Little Clay Cart* (1915); and *Der Konig und die Tänzerin,* from Kalidasa.

FEYDEAU, Georges, 1862-1921, French dramatist. Some of his farces in the repertory of the Comédie Française; some English translations performed but not published. *Un Fil à la patte* (1894; *The Lady from Lobster Square*); *L'Hôtel du libre échange* (with Maurice Desvallières, 1896, *Hotel Paradise,* translation published, performed in London by Alec Guinness and in New York by Bert Lahr); *Le Dindon* (1896); *La Dame de chez Maxim* (1899, *The Girl from Maxim's*); *Occupe-toi d'Amélie* (1908, *Keep an Eye on Amélie!,* more freely adapted by Noel Coward as *Look out for Lulu*—both versions published); *On purge Bébé* (1910, *Going to Pot*—published); *La Puce à l'oreille* (1910, *You Never Know, Y'Know*); *Mais ne promène pas toute nue* (1911); and many others.

FIELDS, Joseph, b. 1895, American dramatist. *My Sister Eileen* (1940, with Jerome Chodorov); *Junior Miss* (1941, with Chodorov); *The Doughgirls* (1942); *The French Touch* (1945, with Chodorov); *Gentlemen Prefer Blondes* (1949, musical, with Anita Loos); *Wonderful Town* (1953, music by Leonard Bernstein); *Anniversary Waltz* (1954, with Chodorov); *The Ponder Heart* (1956, with Chodorov); *The Tunnel of Love* (1957, with Peter de Vries); *Flower-Drum Song* (1958, musical, with Oscar Hammerstein, score by Richard Rodgers).

FISCHER, Leck, 1904-1956, Danish dramatist. *The Child* (1936); *Mother Love* (1943); *Fools of Love* (1950).

FITCH, Clyde, 1865-1909, American dramatist. Popular, prolific author of comedies, dramas, historical plays, probably at his best in such comedies as *Captain Jinks of the Horse Marines* (1901). Also *Beau Brummell* (1890); *Nathan Hale* (1899); *Barbara Frietchie* (1899); *The Girl with the Green Eyes* (1902); *The Truth* (1907); *The City* (1909); and many others.

FITZGERALD, F. Scott, 1896-1940, American novelist. Wrote one play, the satiric *The Vegetable* (1923).

FLAVIN, Martin, b. 1883, American dramatist. Some symbolic and expressionistic elements but, elsewhere, straight realistic technique. *Children of the Moon* (1923); *Lady of the Rose* (1925); *The Criminal Code* (1929); *Broken Dishes* (1929); *Amaco* (1933); *Achilles Had a Heel* (1935); *Tapestry in Gray* (1935); *Around the Corner* (1936); and others.

FLEISSER, Marielouise, b. 1901, German dramatist of the post-World War I generation. *Die Pioniere von Ingolstadt* (1928); *Fegefeuer* (1926); *Karl Stuart* (1946); *Der starke Stamm* (1946).

FODOR, Ladislaus, b. 1898, Hungarian dramatist living in Hollywood. Biggest success with the comedy, *A Church Mouse* (1928). Other plays: *Good Morning, Bill* (1928, adapted by P. G. Wodehouse); *I Love an Actress* (1931); *Jewel Robbery* (1931); *Love is not so Simple* (1935); and many others.

FORSSELL, Lars, b. 1924, Swedish lyric poet and dramatist. *The Fool* (1935, clown play in modern milieu); *The Coronation* (1956).

FORSTER, Friedrich, 1895-1958, German dramatist. Most successful play was *Robinson darf nicht sterben* (1932). Other plays: *Die Infanten* (1943); *Candide* (1948); *Die Gesteinigten* (1956); *Die*

Gänse des Kapitols (1958); *Die Insel der Frucht-bäume;* and others.

FORSYTH, James, b. 1913, English dramatist. *Héloïse* (1951, Héloïse and Abelard); *The Other Heart* (1952, Francois Villon); *Emmanuel* (1960); *Fifteen Strings of Money* (1961, after an old Chinese play).

FORZANO, Gioacchino, b. 1884, Italian dramatist. International success with his comedy, *Un colpo di vento* (1929). Also many historical plays, including two written with Mussolini: *Campo di Maggio* (1930, about Napoleon); *Giulio Cesare* (1930).

FRANK, Bruno, 1887-1945, German dramatist, began as an Expressionist. *Die Schwestern und der Fremde* (1918); *Das Weib auf dem Tiere* (1921, tragedy of prostitution). Later turned to the well-made play: *Zwölftausend* (1928, *Twelve Thousand*); *Perlenkomödie* (1928); *Sturm im Wasserglas* (1930; *Storm over Patsy*); *Nina* (1931); *Der General und das Gold* (1932, Johann Sutter).

FRANKEN, Rose, b. 1895, American novelist and playwright. Psychological plays about female sex involvement. *Another Language* (1932); *Mr. Dooley, Jr.* (1932); *Claudia* (1941); *Outrageous Fortune* (1943); *Doctors Disagree* (1943); *Soldier's Wife* (1943).

FRANK, Leonhard, 1882-1962, German writer. Dramatization of his novel *Karl und Anna* (1929, *Karl and Anna*. Also wrote *Die Ursache* (1929); *Der Aussenseiter* (1937, satiric comedy, revised as *Die Hutdynastie* in 1958); *Hufnägel* (1938, revised as *Die Kurve in* 1958); *Das Männerquartett* (1958, dramatization of parts of his novel, *Das Ochsenfurter Männerquartett*); *Ruth* (1958, dramatization of the novel, *Die Jünger Jesu*. Concerns the fate of a Jewish girl who cannot free herself from the suffering of the Hitler era.).

FRISCH, Max, b. 1911, Swiss architect and successful author of the post-World War II generation. *Santa Cruz* (Written 1944, performed 1946, romance, a dream play with flashback into the past. A woman's humdrum, everyday life is invaded by a mortally sick former lover. The great longing for *real* life: "Once more to be able to weep, once more to be able to love and to be thrilled by the breath of the night! To be able to sigh! Once more to be able to feel how wonderful it is to be able to live—to live in this one breath, before it escapes us forever." The scenes take place in a castle and on a ship.); *Nun singen sie wieder* (1945; attempt at a requiem for the dead of World War II); *Die chinesische Mauer* (1946, second version, 1955; *The Chinese Wall,* an allegory, designated as a "dramatic farce," with mythical, historical, and literary characters who appear in a timeless scene in order to talk about power and guilt.); *Als der Krieg zu Ende war* (1949). Scene is occupied Berlin. A German woman has hidden her husband, a German officer, and, to save him, has entered into a relationship with a Russian officer. Jealousy forces the husband to reveal himself, and he is arrested as a war criminal. Discussion with his wife about guilt, in which her relationship with the Russian plays a part. Suicide of the wife.). *Graf Öderland* (1951, revised, 1956, *Count Oederland.* Allegorical *moritat.* Theme: Power and helplessness.); *Don Juan oder die Liebe zur Geometrie* (1953. Comedy with witty variation on the old theme: Don Juan is not a seducer at all, but a victim. In reality he loves only geometry, but women will not leave him alone. Don Juan's journey to hell is represented as a trick of his to enable him to end his days in a monastery. In the last act, Don Juan, his plot unsuccessful, is seen retired from the world, a henpecked husband under the thumb of his wife, the Countess, a retired whore who is about to bear him a child.); *Biedermann und die Brandstifter* (1958, *The Firebugs,* "a didactic play without a lesson," but with obvious reference to the danger of indifference to the world crisis; based on a radio play. One-act epilogue, *Biedermann in der Hölle.*); *Die grosse Wut des Philipp Hotz* (1958, *Phillip Hotz's Rage,* one-act farce about an angry husband); *Andorra* (1961, translated same title. Parable drama about anti-Semitism).

FRY, Christoper, b. 1907, popular English dramatist, former actor and teacher; like Eliot, a reviver of the verse drama. Strongly romantic tendencies, a lyricism reminiscent of Lorca. His pieces are best characterized as "romances." Poetry in his theater a stimulus toward Contra-reality. Has revived various theatrical forms in addition to the Elizabethan, in which he attained his first world-wide success, *The Lady's not for Burning*.

Early attempts at plays of Christian legend in the manner of Yeats and Eliot: *The Firstborn* (written 1940-46, performed 1948, symbolic handling of the story of Moses and Pharaoh); *A Phoenix too Frequent* (1946. The first authentic Fry—a variation on the ancient theme of the Widow of Ephesus: love triumphing joyously and impudently over mourning.); *Thor, with Angels* (1948, Christians and Teutons); *The Lady's Not For Burning* (1948. Takes place in 1400, in a small English village. End-of-the-world hysteria, witch hunt, confused emotions. Self-accusation of a former soldier, who believes himself to be a devil who has murdered a number of people and wishes to be punished. The devil and the witch—the man who wants to be hanged and the woman who wants to be saved from the stake—fall in love. The self-accusation is found to be false and the lovers flee—to life.); *Venus Observed* (1950. This play is somewhat like the society drama in form, although there is a strong streak of poetry in it. The scene is the castle of a contemporary nobleman who invites three of his former mistresses so that his son can select his father's wife from among them. The nobleman, however, fall in love with the daughter of his business manager, who has just returned from America, and who in her turn loves his son. In order to bring the nobleman "back to earth," one of his former mistresses, the only one who had really loved him, sets fire to the castle while the nobleman is in his observatory with the girl. The last act clears up the difficulties. The nobleman decides to marry the arsonist as soon as she has expiated her crime); Revival of the form of the Mystery play in *A Sleep of Prisoners* (1951, written for the Religious Drama Society); *The Dark Is Light Enough* (1954. Takes place on a country estate near the Hungarian border during the rebellion of 1848-49. This is the home of the Countess Rosemarie, an old woman who has unearthly powers over men. She hides a deserter from the occupying revolutionary army and later, after the rebels have been beaten, she hides a Hungarian officer from the Austrians. A dim symbolism surrounds her relationship to the deserter, a radical egoist and Nietzschean non-conformist, though not free of cowardice: is he intended to represent the spirit of the male element and she the spirit of the female?) *Curtmantle* (1960. The tragedy of King Henry II of England, known as Curtmantle, and his friend, Archbishop Thomas à Becket. Cf. Eliot's *Murder in the Cathedral* and Anouilh's *Becket ou l'honneur de Dieu*).

Earlier plays worth mentioning: *Siege* (1933); *The Boy With a Cart* (1938); *The Tower* (1939); *Thursday's Child* (1939). Adaptations of Anouilh (*Ring 'Round the Moon* and *The Lark*) and Giraudoux (*Tiger at the Gates* and *Duel of Angels*).

FUKUDA, Tsuneari, Japanese dramatist. Intellectual comedies, such as *The Man Who Stroked the Dragon*. Translator of Shakespeare.

FÜRNBERG, Louis, 1909-1958, German dramatist, holder of the East German National Prize. *Spiel unter Bürgern* (1932); *Ein Mensch ist zu verkaufen* (1938); *Der Bruder Namenlos* (1947); *Spanische Hochzeit* (1947).

GALE, Zona, 1874-1938, American dramatist. *Miss Lulu Bett* (1920, dramatization of her own novel. Pulitzer Prize); *Mr. Pitt* (1924); *Grandma* (1932); *Papa La Fleur* (1933); *Faint Perfume* (1933).

GALSWORTHY, John, 1867-1933, English novelist. Wrote several successful plays. Nobel Prize, 1932. *The Silver Box* (1906, injustice of the law); *Joy* (1907); *Strife* (1909, a destructive, pointless strike); *Justice* (1910, attack on prison life); *The Little Dream* (1911); *The Eldest Son* (1912); *The Pigeon* (1912); *The Fugitive* (1913); *The Mob* (1914); *A Bit o'Love* (1915); *The Foundations* (1920); *The Skin Game* (1920); *Loyalties* (1922, anti-Semitism in an English club); *A Family Man* (1922); *Windows* (1922); *The Forest* (1924); *Old English* (1924); *The Show* (1925); *Escape* (1926); *Exiled* (1929); *The Roof* (1929). Realism, criticism of social abuses.

GARBORG, Arne, 1851-1924, Swedish poet. Social criticism with a religious bias. *Paulus* (1898); *The Lost Father* (1901); and others.

GELBER, Jack, b. 1926, American dramatist. *The Connection* (1959. Experimental play about drug addiction, with jazz accompaniment); *The Apple* (1961, experimental play in which a bigot denounces minorities).

GENET, Jean, b. 1910, French prose writer and dramatist, one of the most unusual and fascinating phenomena of modern literature. Born out of wed-lock, he grew up in foster homes, and spent many years in prisons. Prominent Parisian writers appealed to the President of the Republic for the commutation of his sentence of life imprisonment. Sartre wrote a long book about him with the blasphemous title, *Saint Genet, comédien et martyr*, in which he claimed that Genet was the prototype of the Existentialist man who no longer distinguishes between good and evil and who thus precisely fits this "worst of all possible worlds." He is the "chosen one of the black wonder"; the loneliness of modern man is raised into a passion in him: "Today we are concerned with showing the subject, the guilty subject, this barren and horrible beast, which can rear itself up in us at any time; Genet holds the mirror up to us; we must see ourselves in it." Others have called him a new Rimbaud.

No less a person than Jouvet staged his play *Les Bonnes* (1947, *The Maids*. Two maids, sisters, attempt to escape their surroundings and their obligation to be servile by going through a "ceremony" whenever their mistress is away: they alternate in playing the parts of servant and mistress. They become more and more ecstatic in their imitations, and the role of the mistress becomes mixed up with their own subconscious wishes. They take the first step back to reality: one of them sends an anonymous letter to the police which is designed to cause the arrest of their mistress' lover. Madame, when she returns from the police station, sees herself as inconsolably suffering, shut off from the joys of the world and faithful to the prisoner. Her tirades are theatrical and transparent. Meanwhile, however, the two maids have learned of the lover's release. Afraid that the origin of the anonymous letter will come to light, they determine to use poison. But the mistress, who, on hearing the news, has returned effortlessly to her previous, comfortable existence, capriciously decides not to drink the poisoned cup of tea which the maids repeatedly offer her. The maids' trepidation rises to hysteria as the mistress goes out to meet her lover. In a last powerful tirade, one of the maids sees herself as the "famous murderess, sentenced to death." The other drinks the poisoned tea.).

Haute Surveillance (1949, *Deathwatch*, set among convicts); *Le Balcon* (1956, *The Balcony*. Fifteen scenes in two acts, in the second of which the characters of the first act are assembled as in a medieval *danse macabre*. The scene is a brothel, which symbolizes a house of illusions, of perverted wishes, of fantastic escape from normal reality. Visitors to this house of pleasure dress up as bishop, judge, and general, and the perversion is raised to the highest level of imagination as they identify themselves with their roles. The Chief of Police is also a regular visitor: he conducts his campaigns from here. A rebellion breaks out, and the royal palace is attacked. The Chief of Police takes a hand. He forces the "bishop," the "judge," and the "general" to play these roles of their secret lives out in the open. At the end the "judge," the "bishop," and the "general" demand the powers and privileges of their "offices"; the Chief of Police forces them to bow to him.); *Les Nègres* (1957), *The Blacks;* Subtitled "Clownerie"); *Les Paravents* (1961, *The Screens*, civil war in Algeria).

Genet on his theatrical style: "What I have heard of the Japanese, Chinese, and Balinese theaters . . . convinces me that the basis of the Occidental theater is too coarse and clumsy. . . . The Occidental actor does not even try to be a symbol."

GÉRALDY, Paul, b. 1885, French poet and dramatist. Society dramas. *Aimer* (1921) and others.

GHELDERODE, Michel de, 1898-1962, Belgian dramatist. Started with puppet plays, combined the tradition of the Flemish Mystery play with brutal realism in the manner of Brueghel. Theater viewed as a "last, even if new, liturgy." *Le Cavalier bizarre* (written 1920, published 1938, *danse macabre* in an old people's home); *La Farce de la Mort qui faillit trépasser* (performed 1925); *La Mort du Docteur Faust* (published 1926, performed 1928, Faust and a modern actor playing Faust); *Trois Acteurs, un drame* (written 1926, published 1929, performed 1931, *Three Actors and Their Drama*); *Christophe Colomb* (published 1928, performed 1929, *Christopher Columbus*); *Escurial* (published 1928, performed 1929, translated); *Barabbas* (written 1928, performed 1929, translated) *Don-Juan* (performed 1928); *Les Femmes au tombeau* (written 1928, published 1934, *The Women at the Tomb*); *La Transfiguration dans le cirque* published 1928); *Pantagleize* (written 1929, performed 1930, translated, a burlesque); *Fastes d'Enfer* (written 1929, published 1943, successfully staged by Reybaz in Paris, 1949, *Chronicles of Hell*); *Magie rouge* (performed 1934); *Les Aveugles* (published 1936, *The Blind Men*); *Sire Halewyn* (performed 1938, *Lord Halewyn*); *Hop Signor!* (published 1938); *La Farce des ténébreux* (published 1942, a satire on the Puritans); and others.

GHÉON, Henri, 1875-1944, French dramatist. Wrote religious Mystery plays: *Le Pauvre sous l'escalier* (1920); *Sainte Thérèse de Lisieux* (1934); *Le Noël sur la place* (1935, Christmas in the Market Place); *Oedipe ou le crépuscule des Dieux* (1942); *Judith* (posth.). Other plays. *Le Pain* (1911); *L'Eau-de-vie* (1914); *Les Aventures de Gilles ou le saint malgré lui* (1922); *L'Histoire du jeune Bernard de Menthon* (1925, *The Marvellous History of St. Bernard*).

GHERARDI, Gherardo, 1890-1949, Italian writer of comedies. Wrote, among others, *Gran cinema* (1928); *Ombre cinesi* (1931); *Truccature* (1933); *Questi ragazzi* (1934); *I Figli del Marchese Lucera* (1935); *L'Arcidiavolo* (1935); *Le Stelle ridono* (1937); *Autumno* (1939); *Lettere d'amore* (1939); *Non fare come me* (1945); *Il nostro Viaggio* (1948); *Un tale che passa* (posth.); *Santa Caterina da Siena* (1957).

GIBSON, William, b. 1914, American dramatist. International success with *Two for the Seesaw* (1958. Two-character play). Also wrote *Dinny and the Witches* (1959, a fantasy, unsuccessful off Broadway); *The Miracle Worker* (1959, story of Helen Keller, successful on Broadway).

GIDE, Andre, 1869-1951, French novelist and man of letters, wrote several dramatic versions of ancient myths: "All ancient myths are forms of timeless rational truth." *Saül* (1896, *Saul*, staged by Copeau 1922); *Philoctète* (1899, *Philoctetes*); *Le Prométhée mal enchaîné* (1899); *Le roi Candaule* (written 1900, staged 1901 by Lugnée Poë; *King Candaules*); *Le Retour de l'enfant prodigue* (1907, *The Return of the Prodigal*); *Bethsabé* (1908, *Bathsheba*); *Oedipe* (written 1930, staged 1932 by Georges Pitoëff; *Oedipus*); *Perséphone* (1933, *Persephone*; set to music by Stravinsky). Dramatized his novel, *Les Caves du Vatican* (1949). Adapted Kafka's novel, *The Trial*, together with Barrault (1947, translated); translated Shakespeare's *Antony and Cleopatra* (1921) and *Hamlet* (1945). *The Immoralist* (1954), adapted from Gide's novel by Ruth and Augustus Goetz.

GIEROW, Karl Ragnar, b. 1904, Swedish lyric poet and dramatist. Symbolic verse dramas, e.g., *The Beast of Prey* (1941) and comedies, e.g., *At Heart's Desire* (1945); *Cembalo* (1962).

GIONO, Jean, b. 1895, French writer, has dramatized some of his novels about Provençe. *Le Lanceur des grains* (1936); *Le Bout de la route* (1942, a stranger in a mountain village). Has also written a play set in Napoleon's time, *Le Voyage en calèche*, which he calls a "romantic divertissement."

GIRAUDOUX, Jean, 1882-1944, most famous dramatist produced by France in the first half of the century. Known for his suspension of illusion and his unlocking of new theatrical worlds. Fruitful collaboration with the great actor-director, Louis Jouvet. Started writing for the stage when he was already 46 years old with *Siegfried*, the dramatization of his novel, *Siegfried et le limousin* (1928, translated. A French officer suffering from amnesia lives in Germany under the name of Siegfried—and becomes a government minister). *Amphitryon 38* (1929, adapted by S. N. Behrman, same title. The 38th version of the classical theme—gracious and ironic); *Judith* (1931, translated, same title. Characteristically ironic reversal in interpretation. Judith loves Holofernes and becomes a heroine of her people against her will after she has killed him in a paroxysm of love and hate.); *Intermezzo* (1933. Adapted as *The Enchanted*. A supernatural comedy partly in the world of reality and partly in the world of fantasy.); *Tessa* (1934, adapted from *The Constant Nymph*, by Margaret Kennedy and Basil Dean); *La Guerre de Troie n'aura pas lieu* (1935. Adapted by Christopher Fry as *Tiger at the Gates*.); *Électre* (1937, Electra. Humanization of the tragic myth. Electra's fanatical lust for revenge becomes an incurable complex, for absolute purity cannot have any other relationship with the world. Égisthe wants Electra to marry a gardener in order to be healed. A beggar appears as a mystical apparition. Orestes is a harmless young man who is forced to become a murderer because everything is inevitable); *Ondine* (1939, trans. same title. A pure nature spirit is broken upon contact with an inflexible human spirit, which alone can continue unchanged in the world as it is.); *Sodom et Gomorrhe* (1943. The battle of the sexes leads to the destruction of true love.); *La Folle de Chaillot* (1945, posthumously produced, *The Madwoman of Chaillot*. The mad "Countess" who is adored by all the people around her proves herself a true human being by thwarting the plans of the "pimps" who are out to destroy Paris and the world.); *Pour Lucrèce* (1953, *Duel of Angels*. The tragedy of purity. The wife of a state's attorney is unwilling to take part in the immoralities of small town society; her enemies trap her by faking a rape.). One-act plays: *Supplément au voyage de Cook* (1935, *The Virtuous Island*); *Cantique des cantiques* (1938, *The Song of Songs*); *L'Apollon de Bellac* (1942, one-act, *The Apollo of Bellac*.)

GLASPELL, Susan, 1882-1948, American novelist and dramatist. *Bernice* (1919); *The Inheritors* (1921); *The Verge* (1921); *Alison's House* (1930, Pulitzer Prize); *The Comic Artist* (1931, with Norman Matson). Other plays with her husband, George Cram Cook (q.v.). One of the founders of the original Provincetown Playhouse.

GOERING, Reinhard, 1887-1936, German dramatist, wrote the expressionistic anti-war play, *Seeschlacht* (1917. "Fatherland, Fatherland, dear Fatherland!/ We are swine/Waiting for the butcher,/We are calves, readied for the slaughterer./Our blood gives color to the fish./Fatherland, see, O see!"); *Der Erste* (1918); *Der Zweite* (1919); *Scapa Flow* (1919); *Die Retter* (1919); *Die Südpolexpedition des Kapitäns Scott* (1929. Factual report in verse with choruses). Posthumous: *Der Vagabund und das Mädchen* (1931, with R. Büschgens).

GOETZ, Curt, 1888-1960, popular German writer of comedies. Pointed dialogue, scenic originality, solid plot construction. Wrote a personal variant of the international boulevard style. *Der Lampenschirm* (1911, revised 1957); five one-act plays, 1918: *Nachtbeleuchtung, Lohengrin, Tobby, Maria Magdalena, Der fliegende Geheimrat;* four one-act plays under the collective title, *Menagerie* (1921. *Der Spatz vom Dache, Die Taube in der Hand, Der Hund im Hirn, Der Hahn im Korb*); *Ingeborg* (1921. Comedy); three one-act plays of 1923: *Der Mörder, Das Mädchen, Die tote Tante* (combined in 1953 in the comedy, *Das Haus von Montevideo*); *Hokuspokus* (1926, comedy of justice); *Der Lügner und die Nonne* (1928); *Dr. med.*

Hiob Prätorius (1932. A medical comedy, subtitled "an unpolitical story"; has a prologue involving Sherlock Holmes and Dr. Watson; filmed as *People Will Talk*); *Tovarich* (1936. Comedy of Russian emigrés in Paris, based on Deval's play); *Nichts Neues aus Hollywood* (1956); *Alte Möbel* (1958); *Miniaturen* (1958, consists of three one-act plays: *Rache, Herbst, Die Kommode*).

GOETZ, Wolfgang, 1885-1956, German dramatist. Success with *Neidhardt von Gneisenau* (1922). Other plays: *Robert Emmet* (1925); *Der Ministerpräsident* (1936); and others.

GOLD, Michael, b. 1894, American dramatist. Plays of Marxist social criticism. *Hoboken Blues* (1928); *Fiesta* (1929); *Battle Hymn* (1936, with Michael Blankfort, performed by WPA Theatre).

GOMBROWICZ, Witold, b. 1904, Polish dramatist, living in Argentina. Existentialist. *Iwona, Princess of Burgundy* (1938); *The Wedding*, 1953.

GORKI, Maxim, 1868-1936, (Alexei Maximovitch Pyeshkov), the leading Russian dramatist in the period after Chekhov and Tolstoy. Most famous play: *The Lower Depths* (1902, translated, drama of the damned, the lost. Scene: a flop-house run by a thieving couple for those who have nothing to lose anymore. The characters: the pilgrim Luka, the degenerate baron, the whore Nastya, the cardsharp Satine, the cobbler Alyosha, the thief Pepel, the capmaker Bubnov, the locksmith Klestsch and his mortally sick wife. They are all people who "have been," the forgotten of the earth, but still human.). *The Petty Bourgeois* (1902. Translated also as *The Courageous One* and *The Smug Citizens*. The strength of the proletariat as compared with the spiritual poverty of the bourgeoisie; the hero is the proletarian locomotive engineer, Nil). Other plays of the early period: *Summer Folk* (1903); *The Children of the Sun* (1905, translated. Theme: pogroms); *Barbarians* (1906, translated); *Enemies* (1906, translated); *The Last Ones* (1908); *Queer People* (1910, translated); *Vassa Zheleznova* (1910, revised 1936, translated. Chief characters, as described by Brecht: "Vassa, 42, owner of a Volga river-boat concern, refuses to let her daughter-in-law, the revolutionary worker Rachel Topas, have her son because she wants him as the heir to her business. Rachel tries to save her child from the unhealthy atmosphere of the house. Zheleznov, 60 years old, former captain, unprincipled and decayed, guilty of child rape; Vassa forces him to commit suicide in order to avoid the scandal of a public trial. Natalya, 18 years old, prevented from leaving the country by Vassa; embittered by the hopelessness of her position and filled with hate for her fellow human beings, she becomes a drunkard. Lyudmila: 16 years old, Vassa's favorite, infantile and spoiled; Vassa deliberately keeps her in the state of a simple-minded child. Prokhor: Vassa's brother, 57 years old, uncontrollable and alcoholic, leads Vassa's daughter into a similarly unbridled life; forces the housemaid, whom he has made pregnant, to kill herself." The character of the revolutionary, Rachel, becomes a sort of "positive heroine" only in the later version.); *The Zykovs* (Written 1912, acted 1918, translated); *The Judge* (1919, translated. Gorki: "I have tried to show how unpleasant it is when a man becomes totally absorbed in his troubles and gradually comes to the belief that he has the right to torture others because of it.").—Plays from the 'thirties: the cycle, . . . *and others:* according to Gorki, it is enough to present sharp delineations of character—the dramatic explosions occur automatically as a result. There is, consequently, a lack of action when real psychological truth is depicted—more picture than drama. *Somov and Others* (Written 1930-31, produced posthumously. Intellectuals who are not ripe for the revolution turn to sabotage: engineers, technicians, decadent aesthetes, bourgeois, vagabonds); *Yegor Bulychov and the Others* (1933, translated. The capitalist recognizes the signs of the times); *Dostigayev and Others* (1933. The merchant who fits into everything so well that he finally fits into the revolution too).

GRACQ, Julien, b. 1910, French prose writer in the surrealistic style; wrote the drama, *Le Roi pêcheur* (1949).

GRANVILLE-BARKER, Harley, 1877-1946, English dramatist, critic, actor, producer, director, and scholar. Produced the first performances of many of Shaw's plays. Wrote *Prefaces to Shakespeare.* Comedies with social comment, the best of them reminiscent of Shaw. *The Marrying of Ann Leete* (1901); *Prunella* (1904, with Laurence Housman);

The Voysey Inheritance (1905); *Waste* (1907); *The Madras House* (1910); *Rococo* (1911); *The Secret Life* (1923); *His Majesty* (1928); and others.

GRASS, Günter, b. 1928, German experimental dramatist of the post-World War II generation. *Hochwasser* (1957); *Onkel, Onkel* (1958); *Die bösen Köche* (1959); *Noch zehn Minuten bis Buffalo* (1959; one act); *Zweiunddreissig Zähne* (1961, farce).

GREEN, Julien, b. 1900, American novelist writing in French. *Sud* (1953. Takes place in a Southern mansion during the War Between the States; the hero is a homosexual officer); *L'Ennemi* (1954); *L'Ombre* (1956).

GREEN, Paul, b. 1894, American dramatist of Southern life. Specializes in folk plays and pageants. *The No 'Count Boy* (1924); *Fixin's* (1924, with Erma Green); *In Abraham's Bosom* (1926, Pulitzer Prize); *The Field God* (1927); *The Last of the Lowries* (1927); *The House of Connelly* (1931); *Roll, Sweet Chariot* (1934. Symphonic play of Negro life. Earlier version *Potter's Field*); *Shroud My Body Down* (1935); *Johnny Johnson* (1936, antiwar play set to music by Kurt Weill); *Hymn to the Rising Sun* (1936); *The Lost Colony* (1937); *Unto Such Glory* (1937); *The Enchanted Maze* (1939); *The Highland Call* (1939, American history play with music and dance); *Native Son* (1940, with Richard Wright); *The Common Glory* (1948); *The Founders* (1957, founding of Jamestown, Va.), and others.

GREENE, Graham, b. 1904, English novelist, whose novels, *The Power and the Glory* and *The End of the Affair,* have been adapted for the stage. His own plays have religious themes set forth in a form recalling Ibsen: *The Living Room* (1952. Tragedy of a girl among hypocrites and conformists, a person with the "power of despair."); *The Potting Shed* (1957. Another play about the way to belief, which the hero finds after a misspent life by realizing the mystical significance of a childhood experience—the "miracle" in the potting shed); *The Complaisant Lover* (1959, comedy of a lover who must tolerate his mistress's husband, a dentist).

GRESSIEKER, Hermann, b. 1903, German dramatist. *Baron Trenck* (1930); *Der Regenbogen* (1947, comedy); *Die goldenen Jahre* (1951, tragedy); *Heinrich VIII und seine Frauen* (1956).

GRIEG, Nordahl, 1902-1943, Norwegian dramatist. Dedicated anti-Fascist; shot down in a bombing plane over Berlin. *Barrabas* (1927); *A Young Man's Love* (1927); *The Atlantic Ocean* (1932); *Our Honor and Our Power* (1935, his first considerable success, about war-profiteering among Norwegian shipowners in World War I); *But Tomorrow—*(1936); *The Defeat* (1937, translated. The revolt of the Paris commune in 1871).

GRIESE, Friedrich, b. 1890, German novelist and dramatist. *Mensch aus Erde gemacht* (1932); *Wind im Luch* (1937); *Der heimliche König* (1940); *Wenn der Schein zerfällt* (1956).

GRÜNBERG, Karl, b. 1891, German story-writer and dramatist, active in East Germany. *Golden fliesst der Stahl* (1949); *Elektroden* (1953).

GUITRY, Sacha, 1885-1957, popular French comedy writer in the boulevard style (also made several attempts at historical drama). *La Jalousie* (1915); *Faisons un rêve* (1916, *Sleeping Partners*); *L'Illusioniste* (1917); *Deburau* (1918, translated by Harley Granville-Barker); *Pasteur* (1919, translated); *Mon Père avait raison; Le Grand Duc* (1921, *The Grand Duke*); *Mozart* (1925); *Le nouveau Testament* (1934, *Where There's a Will*); and others.

GUTKELCH, Walter, b. 1901, German dramatist of distinctly Christian tendency. *Roulette* (1928. Comedy); *Die Begnadigten* (1951. Trilogy); *Duell um Clementine* (1953); *Der grosse Mut des Hiskia* (1954); *Die Feuerprobe* (1955); *Der Herr von drüben* (1955).

HACKS, Peter, b. 1928, German dramatist of the post-World War II generation. Went from Munich to East Berlin. Dramaturge at Deutsche Theater until 1963. *Eröffnung des indischen Zeitalters* (1955, Columbus play in epic style); *Die Schlacht bei Lobositz* (1955, historical comedy); *Das Volksbuch vom Herzog Ernst* (1955); *Der Müller von Sans Souci* (1958, about Frederick the Great); *Die Uhr geht nach* (1958, one-act play about Frederick the Great); *Briketts* (1959); *Die Sorgen und die*

Macht (1962, banned soon after opening; adaptation of Aristophanes *The Peace*).

HAECKER, Hans Joachim, b. 1910, German dramatist. *Hiob* (1937); *Die Stadt* (1940); *Segler gegen Westen* (1941); *Der Tod des Odysseus* (1948); *David vor Saul* (1951); *Leopard und Taube* (1951); *Das Öl der Lampen* (1952); *Piavara* (1954); *Dreht euch nichtum* (1961, one-act); *Der Briefträger kommt* (1961).

HALBE, Max, 1865-1944, German naturalistic dramatist. Chief plays: *Freie Liebe* (1890); *Eisgang* (1892); *Jugend* (1893, *Youth*); *Mutter Erde* (1897, *Mother Earth*); *Haus Rosenhagen* (1901); *Der Strom* (1903); *Blaue Berge* (1909); *Der Ring des Gauklers* (1911); *Freiheit* (1913); *Die Friedensinsel* (1944).

HALL, Willis, b. 1929. Known for *The Long and the Short and the Tall* (1959, war play); *Last Day in Dreamland* (1959, one act); *A Glimpse of the Sea* (1959, one act); *Billy Liar* (1960, with Keith Waterhouse, from Waterhouse's novel); *Celebration* (1961, with Waterhouse); *England, Our England* (1962, revue, with Waterhouse); *All Things Bright and Beautiful* (1962, with Waterhouse); *Squat Betty* (1962, one act, with Waterhouse); *The Sponge Room* (1962, one act, with Waterhouse); adapted Billetdoux's *Tchin-Tchin* (as *Chin-Chin*, 1960).

HAMILTON, Patrick, b. 1904, English dramatist. *Rope* (1929); *The Procurator of Judea* (1930, from the French); *John Brown's Body* (1931); *Gaslight* (1938); *The Duke in Darkness* (1942); *Ethel Fry* (1945); *The Man Upstairs* (1953).

HAMSUN, Knut, 1859-1952, Norwegian epic poet. Six plays: the Kareno trilogy, *At the Gates of the Kingdom* (1895, translated), *The Play of Life,* and *Evening Glow* (1895-1898. The bitter tragedy of a man with Nietzschean ideals, the man "who would not bow down," first as a student of philosophy: "They won't get me down, no one will get me down."; then as tutor: "Then I will go to the ends of the world and be silent while the others talk, and I will listen to what they say and laugh at them."; finally as a tamed political candidate: "For 20 years I defied my common sense. I served my mistake faithfully and honestly—I served it stubbornly and knew nothing beside my belief, my truth, my triumph. Until the day came when Life itself raised its deep bass voice and called, 'Halt!' Then I obeyed this voice and reviewed my opinions. What was the result? My defiance began to weaken. . . . After a long and strife-ridden life I have found my peace, . . . the way to the peaceful sundown."); the verse drama, *Munken Vendt* (1902, Nordic folk ballad); *Queen Tamara* (1903, exotic love story); *In the Grip of Life* (1910, translated. Tragicomedy of an aging vaudeville singer; terrifying revelation of human drives).

HANKIN, St. John, 1869-1909, English dramatist. Witty, cynical comedies. *The Two Mr. Wetherbys* (1902); *The Return of the Prodigal* (1905. A ne'er-do-well blackmails his own family); *The Charity That Began at Home* (1905); *The Cassilis Engagement* (1907. Marriage between two different social classes is averted because of drawbacks on both sides.); *The Burglar Who Failed* (1908, one act); *The Constant Lover* (1908, one act); *The Last of the De Mullins* (1908), *Thompson* (posthumous, completed by George Calderon).

HARRIS, Frank, 1855-1931, Irish man of letters and editor, lived in England and America. *Mr. and Mrs. Daventry* (1900, from a scenario by Oscar Wilde); also: *Shakespeare and His Love; Joan La Romée; A New Commandment; The Bucket Shop.*

HART, Moss, 1904-1961, American dramatist and author of musicals. *The Hold-Up Man* (1923); *Jonica* (1930, with Dorothy Heyward); *Once in a Lifetime* (1930, with George S. Kaufman); *Face the Music* (1932, musical, with Irving Berlin); *As Thousands Cheer* (1933, musical, with Irving Berlin); *The Great Waltz* (1934, adaptation); *Merrily We Roll Along* (1934, with Kaufman); *Jubilee* (1935, musical, with Cole Porter); *You Can't Take It With You* (1936, musical, with Kaufman, Pulitzer Prize); *I'd Rather Be Right* (1937, with Kaufman); *The Fabulous Invalid* (1938, with Kaufman); *The American Way* (1939, with Kaufman); *The Man Who Came to Dinner* (1939, with Kaufman); *George Washington Slept Here* (1940, with Kaufman); *Lady in the Dark* (1941, musical, with lyrics by Ira Gershwin and score by Kurt Weill); *Winged Victory* (1943); *Christopher Blake* (1946); *Light Up the Sky* (1948); *The Climate of Eden* (1952,

from a novel by Edgar Mittelholzer). Autobiography, *Act One* (1959).

HASENCLEVER, Walter, 1890-1940, German dramatist, began as Expressionist with *Der Sohn* (1914, conflict between the generations); *Der Retter* (1915); *Antigone* (1917, adapted from Sophocles for Reinhardt); *Menschen* (1918, *Humanity*); *Die Entscheidung* (1920); *Jenseits* (1920, *Beyond*); *Gobseck* (1921, from Balzac); *Mord* (1926). Later changed to light comedy with *Ein besserer Herr* (1927. Satire in cabaret style on marriage announcements); *Ehen werden im Himmel geschlossen* (1928); *Bourgeois bleibt Bourgeois* (1929, with Ernst Toller); *Napoleon greift ein* (1930); *Kommt ein Vogel geflogen* (1931); *Kulissen* (1932); *Münchhausen* (1933); *Konflikt in Assyrien* (posth.).

HAUPTMANN, Carl, 1858-1921, Gerhart Hauptmann's older brother. Wrote a series of dramas, most important of which are *Die Bergschmiede* (1901); *Die lange Jule* (1912); *Die armseligen Besendiner* (1913, Silesian fairy tale); *Tobias Buntschuh* (1916); *Musik* (1918); *Der abtrünnige Zar* (1919).

HAUPTMANN, Gerhart, 1862-1946, most important German dramatist of the first half of the 20th century. Started with Naturalism, but became a writer who dealt with all aspects of human character, its heavens and hells, its helpless suffering. His use of historical, legendary, and finally classical material is not so much a change of style as an expansion of his basic dramatic impulses. To the end of his career he always returned periodically to the naturalistic milieu. His concentration on the spiritual side of human character forced him to pay less attention to theatrical form as such: the act-divided, well-made play, which usually formed the basis of his structure, often became only a vague framework. (Dates given are those of composition.)—Naturalistic period: *Vor Sonnenaufgang* (1899, *Before Sunrise*); *Das Friedensfest* (1889; *The Reconciliation*); *Einsame Menschen* (1890; *Lonely Lives*); *Die Weber* (1891-92. *The Weavers*. Chief example of the expansion of Ibsen's treatment of family problems—unmasking of the "life-lie"—approach to treatment of social problems); *Kollege Crampton* (1892, *Colleague Crampton*. First comedy); *Der*

Biberpelz (1892, *The Beaver Coat.* Second comedy); *Hanneles Himmelfahrt* (1893, *Hannele.* Poor, lower-class milieu combined with an irrational world of dreams).—Second period: *Florian Geyer* (1894, translated); *Elga* (1896, translated); *Die versunkene Glocke* (1896, *The Sunken Bell,* fairy tale in verse); *Fuhrmann Henschel* (1896-97, *Drayman Henschel*); *Der arme Heinrich* (1897-1902, *Henry of Auë*); *Schluck und Jau* (1899, *Schluck and Jau.* Picaresque comedy); *Michael Kramer* (1900, translated); *Der rote Hahn* (1902, *The Conflagration*); *Rose Bernd* (1903, translated); *Und Pippa tanzt!* (1905, *And Pippa Dances*); *Gabriel Schillings Flucht* (1905-6, *The Flight of Gabriel Schilling*); *Die Jungfern vom Bischofsberg* (1906, The Maidens of the Mount); *Das Hirtenlied* (1906, fragment); *Kaiser Karls Geissel* (1906, *Charlemagne's Hostage*); *Griselda* (1908, translated); *Peter Brauer* (1908-10); *Der Bogen des Odysseus* (1910-12, *The Bow of Ulysses*); *Die Ratten* (1910, *The Rats*); *Festspiel in deutschen Reimen* (1912-13, *The Commemoration Masque*); *Magnus Garbe* (1914-15); *Winterballade* (1914-16, *A Winter Ballad*); *Der weisse Heiland* (1912-15, *The White Savior*); *Indipohdi* (1913-19, translated); *Veland* (1898-1923, translated); *Herbert Engelmann* (1924, adapted by Zuckmayer in 1950); *Dorothea Angermann* (1924). Later works: *Vor Sonnenuntergang* (1928-31, *Before Sunset*); *Die goldene Harfe* (1933, *The Golden Harp*); *Hamlet in Wittenberg* (1930-35); *Ulrich von Lichtenstein* (1910-37); *Die Tochter der Kathedrale* (1935-38, *The Daughter of the Cathedral*); *Finsternisse* (1937), Requiem for Hauptmann's Jewish friend, Max Pinkus. Takes place in a Silesian town in 1934.); the Atrides tetralogy: *Iphigenie in Delphi* (1940); *Iphigenie in Aulis* (1940-43); *Agamemnons Tod* (1944); *Elektra* (1945).

HAUSER, Harald, b. 1912, East German journalist and dramatist. Lessing Prize, 1959. *Prozess Wedding* (1953); *Am Ende der Nacht* (1955); *Im himmlischen Garten* (1958, Tibet); *Weisses Blut* (1960); *Nitschewo* (1961).

HAUSMANN, Manfred, b. 1898, German writer, author of plays for Christian theaters, e.g., *Worpsweder Hirtenspiel* (1946); *Der Fischbecker Wandteppich* (1955). Other plays: *Lilofee* (1936, folk ballad); *Hafenbar* (1954, realistic Christian drama);

Aufruhr in der Marktkirche (1957, Mystery play); *Die Zauberin von Buxtehude* (1959, celebrates the 1000th anniversary of the founding of the town of Buxtehude).

HAY, Julius, b. 1900, Hungarian dramatist. Produced plays with Communistic tendencies in Berlin after World War I. *The New Paradise,* (1932, socialists in America); *God, Emperor and Farmer* (1932, Hussite drama); *Property* (1938, 1954, conditions in a Hungarian village, where there is a wave of poisonings caused by avarice); *Judgment Day* (1951); *Bridge of Life* (1951); *The Dam on the Theiss* (1953); *Three Difficult Days* (1953); *Gaspar Varro's Right* (1955). Among the writers of the Hungarian rebellion in 1956.

HECHT, Ben, b. 1893, American journalist and dramatist. *The Front Page* (1928, with Charles MacArthur); *Twentieth Century* (1932, with MacArthur); *The Great Magoo* (1912, with Gene Fowler); *Jumbo* (1935, musical, with MacArthur and Richard Rodgers and Lorenz Hart); *To Quito and Back* (1937); *Winkelberg* (1958); and others.

HEDBERG, Tor, 1862-1931, Swedish dramatist. *Johan Ulfstjerns* (1907); *The National Monument* (1924, a "spiritual comedy"), and others.

HEIBERG, Gunnar, 1857-1929, Norwegian dramatist. Social criticism in *Aunt Ulrikke* (1884); *King Midas* (1890); *The Balcony* (1894, translated); *The Jackpot* (1895); *The Tragedy of Love* (1904, translated); and others.

HEIJERMANS, Herman, 1864-1924, Dutch novelist and dramatist. Realistic plays with occasional romantic and symbolic tendency. Most important representative of Dutch realism on the stage. *Dora Kremer* (1893); *Ghetto* (1899); *The Seventh Commandment* (1900, comedy of manners); *The Good Hope* (1901, translated, internationally popular sea play); *The Armor* (1902, romantic military play); *Children* (1903); *All Souls' Day* (1905); *Theater-Studies* (1904-05, in four parts); *The Great Flight* (1908); *Rusk with Candy* (1911); *Good Luck!* (1911, play about miners); *The Rising Sun* (1911); *The Wise Tomcat* (1919), a wicked fairy tale); *Eva Bonheur* (1919); *The Flying Dutchman, or the Big Wager* (1920); *Dawn* (1920); *"The Morning Star" of Old* (1924), and others.

HEISELER, Bernt von, b. 1907, German dramatist of the Christian school. *Das laute Geheimnis* (1931, comedy based on Calderon); *Des Königs Schatten* (1936, comedy); *Cäsar* (1941, tragedy); *Der Bettler unter der Treppe* (1942); *Was des Kaisers ist* (1939-45, Hohenstaufen trilogy); *Semiramis* (1943, based on Calderón); *Das Stephanus-Spiel* (1947); *Ländliche Winterkomödie* (1948, topical comedy); *Das Haus der Angst oder der goldene Schlüssel* (1950, mystery play); *Das Haller Spiel von der Passion* (1954), and others.

HELLMAN, Lillian, b. 1905, American dramatist, a critic of society and an expert craftsman, best known through her drama of social criticism, *The Little Foxes* (1939, vicious entrepreneurs in the American South of 1900). Other plays: *The Children's Hour* (1934, an American family learns from an anti-Nazi); *The Searching Wind* (1944); *Another Part of the Forest* (1946, the family of *The Little Foxes* 20 years earlier); *Montserrat* (1949, adapted from Emmanuel Roblès); *The Autumn Garden* (1950); *The Lark* (1955, adapted from Anouilh); *Candide* (1956, musical from Voltaire, with Richard Wilbur, John Latouche, and Dorothy Parker; score by Leonard Bernstein); *Toys in the Attic* (1960, a man tries to free himself from his family); *My Mother, My Father and Me* (1963, from Burt Blechman's novel *How Much?*).

HEMINGWAY, Ernest, 1899-1961, American novelist. Wrote one play, *The Fifth Column* (Written 1937, the Spanish Civil War).

HENSEN, Herwig, b. 1917, Flemish dramatist. Wrote *Lady Godiva; Queen Christina; Agamemnon; Alcestis; Polycrates; The Other Joan* (Joan of Arc), and others.

HERRMANN, Klaus, b. 1903, East German novelist and dramatist. *Die Prüfungen Hiobs* (1931, comedy); *Vorstadttragödie* (1932); *Augustus Potter* (1936); *Im Himmel und auf Erden* (1940, comedy); *Salto mortale* (1946); *Die Götterwitwe* (1947); *Die tote Zeit* (1958).

HERTOG, Ary den, 1889-1958, Dutch novelist and dramatist. *Jap, the Flapper* (1927); *Living Dead* (1928); *Soldier's Honor* (1928); *The Private Secretary* (1932, later given the title *Atalanta*); *Quiet Strength* (1932, takes place in Indonesia); *Ex-King Peter* (1933); *The Devil's Prayerbook* (1937); *The Laughter of the Gods* (1938); *Operation Excellent* (1941, comedy); *Opened by Censor* (1948, comedy); *The Wonderful Hour* (1948, open-air play to celebrate the 700th anniversary of The Hague); *The Face of the Clock* (1951); *Circus Europa* (1952); *Sybrec Willemsdochter* (1956, historical drama).

HERZBERG, Abel J., b. 1898, Dutch novelist and dramatist. *Fatherland* (1934); *Herodes* (1955); *Saul's Death* (1958).

HEY, Richard, b. 1926, German dramatist of the post-World War II generation. Wrote *Revolutionäre* (1954, satiric farce); *Thymian und Drachentod* (1955. The drama of a refugee from the East who does not fit into the West and dies in No Man's Land. Abstract figures: the king, the premier, the agent.); *Lysiane* (1956, comedy); *Der Fisch mit dem goldenen Dolch* (1957, comedy); *Margaret oder das wahre Leben* (1958, one-act); *Jeden Abend ammermusik* (1959); *Weh dem, der nicht lügt* (1962); *Lysiane* (written 1955, performed 1963).

HEYWARD, DuBose, 1885-1940, American writer. *Porgy* (1927. With Dorothy Heyward, from his novel. Basis of musical, *Porgy and Bess*); *Brass Ankle* (1931); *Mamba's Daughters* (1939, with Dorothy Heyward, from his novel).

HIKMET, Nazim, 1902-1963, Turkish poet, in exile after 1951. World Peace Prize, Moscow, 1950. Dramas, comedies, farces, folk plays. *House of a Dead Person* (1932); *The Skull* (1932); *Forgotten by All* (1935); *Yusuf Prekrasinyi* (1948); *Legend of Love* (1948, Joseph's conflict with Pharaoh treated as a workers' strike); *Was It Given by Ivan Ivanovich?* (1956, surrealistic cabaret farce on the destruction of the cult of personality); *A Comical Man* (1959).

HILDESHEIMER, Wolfgang, b. 1916, German author of the post-World War II generation. Has written radio plays, one of which, *Der Drachenthron* (1955, Turandot story), has also been put on the stage. Also wrote *Die Herren der Welt* (1957); *Pastorale* (1958, one-act. Subtitle, "Time for Cocoa"); *Landschaft mit Figuren* (1959); *Die Uhren* (1959); *Der* *schiefe Turm von Pisa* (1959, one act); *Das Opfer Helena* (1960, one act); *Rivalen* (1961, after Sheridan's *The Rivals*); *Die Verspätung* (1961); *Nachtstück* (1963, one act). Tendency to Theater of the Absurd.

HIRCHE, Peter, b. 1923, German dramatist of the post-World War II generation. *Triumph in tausend Jahren* (1955, war play); *Die Söhne des Herrn Proteus* (1962).

HOCHHUTH, ROLF., b. 1931, German dramatist. *Der Stellvertreter* (1963, *The Representative*. Gerhart Hauptmann Prize). This play has the effect of dispelling the doubts expressed by Dürrenmatt as to whether the modern world can be exhibited on stage in representative figures, for here Pope Pius XII (modelled somewhat on Schiller's Philip II) is shown as a Pilate figure washing his hands over the persecution of the Jews during World War II. The bad Pope is offset by a good priest (suggested by a real person, Father Maximilian Kolbe) who puts on the star of David, gets himself sent to Auschwitz and, while resisting one of the Nazi monsters, is killed. (American title, *The Deputy;* British title, *The Representative.*)

HOCHWÄLDER, Fritz, b. 1911, Austrian dramatist. Self-willed personality, separate from all current styles. Effective historical plays. International success with *Das heilige Experiment* (1943, performed 1947, translated as *The Strong Are Lonely*. The tragic destruction of the communistic holy state of the Jesuits in Paraguay); *Hotel de commerce* (1945, comedy, based on de Maupassant's *Boule de suif*); *Der Flüchtling* (1945. Three-character play based on an idea by Georg Kaiser; revised in 1955. A parable of humanity: the fugitive, the border guard, and his wife); *Meier Heimbrecht* (1946. Story of the farmer's son who becomes a bandit. Takes place in the early Middle Ages); *Die verschleierte Frau* (1946. Comedy); *Der öffentliche Ankläger* (1948, performed 1949, Reign of Terror in the French Revolution); *Der Unschuldige* (1949, 1956. Comedy); *Donadieu* (1953. Episode from the Huguenot Wars: a Huguenot nobleman, whose wife has been killed, finds the murderer in his power; the latter, however, is a king's messenger entrusted with the task of bringing the edict of mercy from Nîmes. If the Huguenot takes his revenge, thousands of people will die; he refrains.); *Die Her-*

berge (1957. Parable play: A usurer is robbed of his gold in an inn. There is an investigation. The inn becomes a scene of universal human experience); *Donnerstag* (1959, modern Mystery play for the Salzburg Festival); *Schicksalskomödie* (1960); *Der verschwundene Mond* (1960).

HOFMANNSTHAL, Hugo von, 1874-1929, German poet and playwright, one of the representatives of the poetic theater of the first half of the century. Very individualistic progress from early aestheticism (a more profound aestheticism, however, than that of d'Annunzio and Maeterlinck) to communication, proclamation, symbolism, and mysticism. From the beginning he allied himself with the Hispano-Austrian baroque tradition, which he used in his comedies with or without music, as well as the Renaissance adaptations of the mediaeval drama and the *Theatrum mundi.* Early plays: *Gestern* (impressionistic-naturalistic play written when Hofmannstahl was seventeen); *Der Tod des Tizian* (1892, *The Death of Titian*); *Der Tor und der Tod* (1893, *Death and the Fool.* The Fool, lost in a dream world, recognizes the meaning of his life in his mother, his friend, and the woman he loves); *Die Frau im Fenster* (1897, *Madonna Dianora*); *Der weisse Fächer* (1897, The White Fan); *Der Kaiser und die Hexe* (1897, *The Emperor and the Witch*); *Das kleine Welttheater* (1897, *The Little Theatre of the World*); *Das Bergewerk zu Falun* (1899); *The Mine at Falun,* from E. T. A. Hoffman); *Die Hochzeit der Sobeide* (1899, *The Marriage of Zobeide*); *Der Abenteurer und die Sängerin* (1899, *The Adventurer and the Singer,* Venice).— Descriptive remarks about this early period: "The poet has come from that most elevated of all worlds, where Death is the messenger." Reproduction of this world in reality in means of magic, introversion, i.e., mysticism, elevation, purity, sacrifice. From "pre-existence" to existence. The unity of all life: "the sweetness of confession" (*Ad me ipsum*).— Second phase: Classical materials. Made an *Alcestis* adaptation as early as 1893. *Elektra* (1903, *Electra,* music by Richard Strauss); *Ödipus und die Sphinx* (1906); *König Ödipus* (1910). Also wrote *Das gerettete Venedig* (1905), an adaptation of Thomas Otway's *Venice Preserv'd* (translated as *Venice Preserved*).—Third phase: the comedies with or without music, the Renaissance adaptations—*Cristinas Heimreise* (versions 1908, 1910, *Cristina's*

Journey Home, suggested by the *Memoirs of Casanova;* Venetian comedy); *Ariadne auf Naxos* (1910, *Ariadne on Naxos.* Uses Molière's *Le bourgeois Gentilhomme* as a basis, music by Richard Strauss); *Der Rosenkavalier* (1911, *The Cavalier of the Rose.* Music by Richard Strauss); *Jedermann* (1911, *The Play of Everyman.* Based on the mediaeval English morality play, *Everyman*); *Die Frau ohne Schatten* (1919, music by Richard Strauss; symbolic fairy tale); *Der Schwierige* (1921, *The Difficult Man.* Picture of Viennese upper-class society with a typically Austrian character, the fastidious man with a horror of his own feelings and of decisions.); *Dame Kobold* (1920, new adaptation of Calderón's play, *La dame duende*); *Der Unbestechliche* (1922. A comedy of Austrian pre-war society seen through one of the manservants, who represents the old world with its strict standards); *Das Salzburger Grosse Welttheater* (1922, *The Salzburg Great Theatre of the World,* from Calderón's *El gran teatro del mundo.* *Theatrum mundi* with allegorical figures: Curiosity, Death, The Adversary, The King, Beauty, Disembodied Souls, Wisdom, Beggars).—Last phase: *Der Turm* (Several versions, stage version in 1927, *The Tower.* Based on themes from Calderon's *La vida es sueño.* The great parable play of the failure and possible ultimate victory of those who are pure and decent. Prince Sigismund, seemingly feeble-minded and imprisoned in the tower of the title, is released but then sentenced to death by his father. The projected excution unchains the rebellion which—here begins Hofmannstahl's prophetic extension of the old theme—is led by the terrorist Olivier. Sigismund is called upon to be the King of the Poor, but is reluctant to serve as a figurehead for Olivier's dictatorship. Olivier: "I and a few others have offered ourselves up to the people in order to take the burden of making decisions away from them, so that they might not become dizzy from weakness." Sigismund's scruples lead to his liquidation. Sigismund to the tyrant: "I know that the Here and Now will enslave many. But not me, for I am here and yet not here! You have nothing to entice me with!" Sigismund's last words: "Give witness I was here, though no one knew me." Hofmannstahl himself: "The Tower represents the pitilessness of our existence, into which the soul has strayed, as out of a dark, mythic sphere." *Die Ögyptische Helena* (1928, music by Richard Strauss). *Arabella* (published 1933, trans-lated, music by Richard Strauss). E. R. Curtius: "Everything that Hofmannstahl wrote from 1917 to his death in 1929 is shot through with this dreadful knowledge of suffering and at the same time with the secret renewal of strength. He was thus completely divorced from everything that had to do with contemporary affairs. 'We conceal the terror of the times,' he wrote once, 'with other-earthly terrors: the present becomes more and more veiled to us as we sense the presence of a higher reality.' "). —Important posthumous fragments: *Semiramis* (based on Calderon) and *Xenodoxus* (based on the baroque drama of Bidermann).

HÖIJER, Björn-Erik, b. 1907, Swedish dramatist. *A Light in the Cottage* (1950); *Isaak Juntti Has Many Sons* (1954), and others.

HOLM, John Cecil, b. 1906, American dramatist. *Three Men on a Horse* (1935, with George Abbott); *Best Foot Forward* (1941); *Gramercy Ghost* (1951); *The Southwest Corner* (1955); and others.

HOLT, Hans, b. 1909, Austrian actor and dramatist. Achieved success with the comedy *Der Herzspezialist* (1957). Previously wrote *Es wird einmal* (1948) and *Der Zaun* (1951). Most recent play *Die Rabenmutter* (1959).

HOLZ, Arno, 1863-1929, German dramatist and theorist of Naturalism; wrote the naturalistic model play, *Die Familie Selicke* (1890) in collaboration with Johannes Schlaf. Also wrote *Sozialaristokraten* (1896, with Paul Ernst); *Traumulus* (1904, with Oskar Jerschke).

HÖMBERG, Hans, b. 1903, German comedy author. *Kirschen für Rom* (1904, *Lucullus* theme); *Napoleon auf Korsika* (1945); *Der Tapfere Herr S.* (1942, Socrates theme); *Die chinesische Witwe* (1955), and others.

HOME, William Douglas, b. 1912, English dramatist, social comedies with political overtones. *Now Barrabas* (1947); *The Chiltern Hundreds* (1947); *Master of Arts* (1949); *The Thistle and the Rose* (1949); *The Bad Samaritan* (1952); *The Manor of Northstead* (1954); *The Reluctant Debutante* (1955); *The Iron Duchess* (1957); *The Bad Soldier Smith* (1961); *The Reluctant Peer* (1964); and others.

HONOLD, Rolf, b. 1919, German dramatist of the post-World War II generation. *Die Spinne* (1950); *Der Stoss nach Ssogrebitsche* (1952); *Geschwader Fledermaus* (1955); *Der Fall Zikade* (1956); *Der grosse Traum* (1959); *. . . und morgen die ganze Welt* (1961).

HOORNIK, Ed., b. 1910, Dutch dramatist. *The Seeker* (1952); *The Sea Wolf* (1955); *The Sin of Cain* (1955); *The Water* (1957).

HORVATH, Ödön von, 1901-1938, Hungarian dramatist of the post-World War I period. Wrote in German. Naturalistic reporting in a bitter tone with non-realistic tendencies. *Revolte auf Côte 3018* (1927, later re-titled *Die Bergbahn*. Folk play. Building of a mountain railroad); *Sladek, der schwarze Reichswehrmann* (1928, history); *Rund um den Kongress* (1929); *Zur schönen Aussicht* (1930); *Italienische Nacht* (1930, folk play); *Geschichten aus dem Wienerwald* (1931, folk play. Kleist Prize. Exposé of the Viennese petit bourgeois); *Kasimir und Karoline* (1932); *Glaube, Liebe, Hoffnung* (sub-titled "A Small Dance of Death" 1932); *Die Unbekannte aus der Seine* (1933); *Hin und Her* (1933, farce. Scene is a bridge between two border posts); *Ein Dorf ohne Männer* (1934, historical comedy based on Mikszáth); *Himmelwärts* (1937); *Figaro lässt sich scheiden* (1934, comedy); *Der Jüngste Tag* (1938, tragedy of a railroad man); *Don Juan kommt aus dem Krieg* (1938); *Pompeii* (1938, sub-titled "An Earthquake Comedy").

HOUGHTON, Stanley, 1881-1913, English dramatist. Pioneer of the modern realistic drama, belonging to the Manchester School of dramatists. *The Dear Departed* (1908); *Independent Means* (1909); *The Younger Generation* (1910); *The Master of the House* (1910); *Hindle Wakes* (1912, frank treatment of the double standard of morality), and others.

HOUSMAN, Laurence, 1865-1959. English writer and dramatist. *Bethlehem* (1902); *The Chinese Lantern* (1908); *The Land of the Harvest* (1910); *A Likely Story* (1910); *Bird in Hand* (1918); *The Little Plays of St. Francis* (1922); *Mr. Gladstone's Comforter* (1929); *Victoria Regina* (1935, a considerable popular success); *Jacob* (1942); *The Family Honor* (1950), and others.

HOWARD, Sidney, 1891-1939, American dramatist. *Swords* (1921); *They Knew What They Wanted* (1924); *Lucky Sam McCarver* (1925); *Ned McCobb's Daughter* (1926); *The Silver Cord* (1926); *Salvation* (1928, with Charles MacArthur); *Half Gods* (1929); *Alien Corn* (1933); *Yellow Jack* (1934, with Paul De Kruif); *The Ghost of Yankee Doodle* (1937); *Madam, Will You Walk?* (performed posthumously). Adaptations: *Marseilles* (1930, from Marcel Pagnol); *The Late Christopher Bean* (1932, from René Fauchois); *Dodsworth* (1934, from Sinclair Lewis); *Paths of Glory* (1935, from Humphrey Cobb's novel), and others.

HRASTNIK, Franz, b. 1904, Austrian painter and dramatist. *Vincent* (1945, Van Gogh); *Therese Krones* (1956); *Das Fräulein vom Kahlenberg* (1958), and others.

HUBALEK, Claus, b. 1926, German dramatist of the post-World War II generation. *Der Hauptmann und sein Held* (1954, war play); *Keine Fallen für die Füchse* (1957, divided Berlin); *Die Festung* (1958. The drama of the German officer. First act: June 30, 1934; second act: July 20, 1944; third act: April 7, 1945); *Die Stunde der Antigone* (1960, the ancient story adapted to the last days of the Third Reich); *Stalingrad* (1961, after Theodor Plievier).

HUCHEL, Peter, b. 1903, German lyric poet and dramatist, editor-in-chief of the East Berlin journal, *Sinn und Form.* Plays: *Doktor Faustens Teufelspakt und Höllenfahrt* (1934); *Die Magd und das Kind* (1935).

HUGHES, Hatcher, 1881-1945, American dramatist. *Wake Up, Jonathan* (1920, with Elmer Rice); *Hell Bent fer Heaven* (1924, Pulitzer Prize); *Ruint* (1925); *Honeymooning* (1927); *It's a Grand Life* (1930, with Alan Williams); *The Lord Blesses the Bishop* (1934); and others.

HUGHES, Langston, b. 1902, American dramatist of Negro life. *Scottsboro Limited* (1931); *Mulatto* (1935); *Little Ham* (1936); *Troubled Island* (1936); *Joy to My Soul* (1937); *Front Porch* (1938); *Simply Heavenly* (1958, musical, score by David Martin); *Tambourines to Glory* (1963); others.

HUNTER, N. C., b. 1908, English dramatist. *All Rights Reserved* (1935); *Ladies and Gentlemen* (1937); *Party for Christmas* (1938); *Grouse in June* (1939); *Smith in Arcady* (1947); *Picture of Autumn* (1950); *Waters of the Moon* (1951); *Adam's Apple* (1951); *A Day by the Sea* (1953); *A Touch of the Sun* (1958); *A Piece of Silver* (1960); *The Tulip Tree* (1962); and others.

HUXLEY, Aldous, 1894-1963, English novelist, essayist. *The World of Light* (1931); *The Gioconda Smile* (1949); *The Genius and the Goddess* (1958, dramatization of the novel).

IBSEN, Henrik, 1828-1906, Norwegian dramatist who best embodies the social drama and the self-criticism of the late 19th century. His favorite theme is the unmasking of the life-lie in act-divided plays which become constantly stricter in form. A master of dramatic structure. The body of his work belongs to the 19th century, but with the dramas of his second phase he lays down the basic pattern of modern drama and then anticipates subsequent departures. His early plays reflect a romantic concern with history, both Roman and Scandinavian, and with legend. With the later plays, we come to the drama of ideas and of social comment, but his primary concern is with character; the development of each of the late plays is a strategy for revealing the submerged, unacknowledged reality of character.—First phase: *Catiline* (1850); *The Warrior's Barrow* (1850); *St. John's Night* (1853); *Lady Inger of Östråt* (1855); *The Feast at Solhaug* (1856); *The Vikings at Olaf Liljekrans* (1857); *The Vikings at Helgeland* (1858); *Love's Comedy* (1862, an ironic comedy of marriage); *The Pretenders* (1863, two rivals for a primitive throne); *Brand* (1866, episodic tragedy of an ascetic); *Peer Gynt* (1867, episodic drama of an egoist); *The League of Youth* (1869, politics in a small town— the play that inaugurates Ibsen's realistic period and the modern realistic drama); *Emperor and Galilean* 1873).—Second phase: *Pillars of Society* (1877); *A Doll's House* (1879, a pampered wife rebels); *Ghosts* (1881. Shocked prudes the world over. A "progressive" woman learns her late husband had syphilis and her son inherited the tragic burden. Many critics choose to be reminded of Greek tragedy); *An Enemy of the People* (1882. In the story of a physician who discovers that the baths are polluted, Ibsen defends himself against the attacks on *Ghosts*); *The Wild Duck* (1884, carrying a heavier load of symbolism, Ibsen establishes the necessity of illusion); *Rosmersholm* (1866, an idealist has a painful collision with reality); *The Lady from the Sea* (1888, a mysterious stranger beckons to a married woman); *Hedda Gabler* (1890, a destructive woman—and a favorite role); *The Master Builder* (1892, an aging man faces the challenge of youth in its various forms); *Little Eyolf* (1894, the death of a child forces the reassessment of a marriage); *John Gabriel Borkman* (1896, two sisters and the man they both loved demand the younger generation compensate them for their disappointments); *When We Dead Awaken* (1899, art intrudes between an artist and life).

ILLYÉS, Gyula, b. 1902, Hungarian lyric poet, novelist, and dramatist. Historical plays dealing with the Revolution of 1848-1849.

ILYENKOV, Vassily, b. 1897, Russian dramatist. *The Square of Flowers* (1944; translated. German invaders in Russia).

INGE, William, b. 1913, American dramatist. After writing his first play, *Farther Off from Heaven* (1947, rewritten as *The Dark at the Top of the Stairs*), he achieved international success with *Come Back, Little Sheba* (1950). Also wrote *Picnic* (1953, Pulitzer Prize); *Bus Stop* (1955); *The Dark at the Top of the Stairs* (1957); *A Loss of Roses* (1959); *Natural Affection* (1963). Inge: "I have never sought to write plays that primarily tell a story; nor have I sought deliberately to create new forms. I have been most concerned with dramatizing something of the dynamism I myself find in human motivations and behavior. I regard a play as a composition rather than a story, as a distillation of life rather than a narration of it. It is only in this way that I feel myself a real contemporary."

IONESCO, Eugène, b. 1912, Parisian dramatist of Rumanian origin. Chief representative of the surrealistic avant-garde. Break-through of reality into a grotesquely fantastic world, usually from a starting point in ordinary middle-class surroundings. People destroy or change their identities under the stress of particular situations; ideas become real and take on corporeal form. The most radical form of unreality, always proceeding, however, from logical necessity out of an ordinary situation. The form is that of modern farce. *La Cantatrice chauve* (1950. *The Bald Soprano*. Subtitled "An Anti-play in one act." Satire on the emptiness of conversation); *La Leçon* (1951, *The Lesson*. "Comic drama." A professor, his maid, and a pupil. The professor becomes carried away by a completely meaningless lecture that he gives on linguistic and arithmetical problems and finally, with an imaginary knife, stabs the pupil, who has been suffering from an ever increasing toothache. With the help of his maid, who informs us that this is already the fortieth such occurrence that day, he hides the body. The bell rings again; the next pupil.); *Les Chaises* (1951. *The Chairs*. "Tragic farce," Pantomimic theater. An ancient couple receives imaginary guests and set out chairs for them. None of the guests really appears: they are seen only in the gestures which the old couple make to them. The old couple become more and more excited as their fantasy progresses; finally they announce that the Emperor has arrived. The guests have been invited to hear the old man's message to the world. The message is to be delivered by a professional orator. As the play ends the old couple jump out of the window, and the orator turns out to be incapable of speech.); *Victimes du devoir* (1953, *Victims of Duty*. "Pseudodrama." The search for a person named Mallot. A detective who does his duty investigates a man and his wife. Descent into the abyss. The poet Nicholas d'Eu berates the detective and stabs him but the search for Mallot goes on.); *Jacques ou la soumission* (1953, *Jack, or The Submission*. "Naturalistic comedy." One act); *Le Salon de l'automobile* (performed on radio 1951, published 1953). *Amédée ou Comment s'en débarrasser* (1954, *Amédée, or How to Get Rid of It*. Comedy in three acts. The scene is a middle-class living room in which mushrooms are growing. The occupants of the apartment, a playwright and his wife, are constantly peeping into the next room where a dead body is growing larger. Two huge dead feet advance through the door. Amédée: "There's nothing that can be done. He's suffering from geometric progression, the incurable disease of the dead." In the second act one half of the stage is completely filled with the dead man's legs and feet. Huge mushrooms grow. The feet keep advancing with sporadic leaps and bounds. The stage grows darker. The dead man keeps on growing. Amédée and his wife determine to get the body out through the window. Amédée: "I'm sorry to have to part from him.... One who gets used to such things. The house will be empty without him. He was the silent witness of our past, which, naturally, was not always very pleasant." A cold, bright light from outside floods the stage. The mushrooms turn silver. The beautiful is contrasted with the horrible. Amédée: "Look, Madeleine.... All the acacias are gleaming. Their blossoms are opening. The moon is unfolding in the middle of heaven. . . . The light is like silk. I had never touched it before. Blooming flowers made of snow, trees in the sky, gardens, willows. Vaults, arches, pillars, temples. He can't see any of it any more. And space, space, endless space." Hurriedly they shove the body through the window. Everything is upset; clouds of dust rise; but finally they get him out. She: "We will have to get new furniture in order to fill up all the empty space." Several versions of the third act exist. Amédée and the dead man vanish forever.); *Le Tableau* (1955, subtitled, "Guignolade." A clown farce, ending in a transformation scene); *L'Impromptu de l'Alma* (1956, *Improvisation*); *Le nouveau Locataire* (1957, *The New Tenant*, one-act); *L'Avenir est dans les oeufs* (1957, *The Future Is in Eggs*); *Tueur sans gages* (1959, *The Killer*. Pseudo-detective play in three acts. *Le Rhinocéros* (1960. *Rhinoceros*. A rhinoceros suddenly appears in the peaceful streets of a little town. Pretty soon there are two of them, then three, four, and more and more. This in intended to symbolize the attractive powers of a "movement"—in this case, distinctly a reference to the Nazi movement—which, like "rhinoceritis," spreads like an epidemic. In the third scene we see the transformation of an average citizen into a rhinoceros: "one has to move with the times." In the last scene practically everyone has become a rhinoceros. Only the eternal individualist, the Bohemian and nonconformist, still refuses to join the trend. An advocate of the opportunistic attitude that is rampant in the town says: "One must at least show neutrality and open-mindedness. . . . Perhaps this is an experience which we ought to undergo. . . . One must always try to understand and understanding means justifying." The last surviving anti-rhinoceros cries out, "I am the last human being and I will remain a human being to the end. I will not capitulate!"). *Le Roi se meurt* (1962, *Exit the*

King); Le Piéton de l'air (1962, *A Stroll in the Air*); contributed to *Chemises de nuit* (1962; his contribution translated as *Bedlam Galore, for Two or More*).

IORGA, Nicolae, 1871-1940, Rumanian politician and historian, and author. Wrote historical dramas, e.g., *Tudor Vladimirescu* (1922); *Dante's Death* (1922); *Molière Avenges Himself* (1922); *Cleopatra* (1928).

ISHERWOOD, Christopher, b. 1904, English novelist. Wrote plays with W. H. Auden, q.v.

IVANOV, Vsevolod, b. 1895, Russian revolutionary dramatist. Known through *Armored Train 14-69* (1927. Capture of a White Russian armored train by Red partisans); *The Blockade* (1929, the Kronstadt rebellion); *Doves of Peace* (1938).

IWASKIEWICZ, Jaroslav, b. 1894, Polish dramatist. *Kwidam* (1921); *Dionizje* (1921); *The Lovers of Verona* (1927); *A Summer in Nohant* (1936, Chopin drama); *Masquerade* (1938, about Pushkin); *Gospodarstwo* (1941); *Balzac's Wedding* (1950).

JAHNN, Hans Henny, 1894-1959, German writer and dramatist. Developed from Expressionism to a personal form of unreality. Main theme: Life confused by erotic drives. *Pastor Ephraim Magnus* (1919); *Die Krönung Richards III* (1921); *Der Arzt, sein Weib, sein Sohn* (1923); *Der gestohlene Gott* (1925); *Medea* (1925); *Strassenecke* (1931); *Neuer Lübecker Totentanz* (1930); *Armut, Reichtum, Mensch und Tier* (1948, Peasant tragedy with mystic overtones); *Spur des dunklen Engels* (1952); *Thomas Chatterton* (1956. The short life of the English prodigy, who committed suicide at eighteen after being accused of dishonesty because he had invented an imaginary identity. He communes with the other world. After he dies by poison, the angel snuffs the candle at his bedside and steps on to the apron: "When an eighteen-year-old, touched by genius, dies neglected and hungry, someone is guilty. The poor, who possess nothing, are guiltless. The rulers, the possessors, the lords, who have their mouths stuffed full, however, may be asked: Do you expect the powerless angel who guards the chosen one to bargain, steal, rob, deceive, get the better of you in order to obtain a better life? The angel has other duties. But it is the duty of men to remain guiltless towards those who are the best.").—Other plays: *Hier ist ein Neger zu lynchen; Der staubige Regenbogen* (1961, tragedy of an atomic physicist).

JAMES, HENRY, 1843-1916, American novelist. Wrote several plays, none of them successful. *Pyramus and Thisbe* (1869, one-act); *Still Waters* (1871, one-act); *A Change of Heart* (1872, one-act); *Daisy Miller* (published 1883, dramatization of the novel); *The American* (1891, dramatization of the novel); *Tenants* (published 1894); *Disengaged* (published 1894, performed 1909); *The Album* (published 1895); *The Reprobate* (published 1895); *Guy Domville* (1895. A psychological study of religious conflict); *Summersoft* (1895, one-act); *The High Bid* (1907); *The Saloon* (1908, one-act); *The Other House* (1908, influenced by Ibsen, with a heroine recalling Rebecca West); *The Outcry* (1909); *The Saloon* (1911, from the story "Owen Wingrave"). Many novels subsequently adapted, the most successful being *Washington Square*, dramatized as *The Heiress* by Ruth and Augustus Goetz (1947).

JAMIAQUE, Yves, b. 1922, French dramatist. *Negro Spiritual* (1954); *Habeas Corpus* (1954, one act); *Lingots du Havre* (1956); *La Queue du diable* (1958, *A Murderer Among Us*); *Les Cochons d'Inde* (1959, comedy).

JARDIEL PONCELA, Enrique, 1901-1952, Spanish novelist and dramatist, influenced by Pirandello. His plays are in a form somewhere between satire and farce. Most important play was *Eloisa esta debajo de un almendro* (1943). Other plays: *Las ladrones sonos gente honrada; Los fantasmas de la casa deshabitada; Usted tiene ojos de mujer fatal.*

JARRY, Alfred, 1873-1907, French dramatist, especially well-known because of his anti-naturalistic play, *Ubu Roi* (*King Turd*, first performed in 1888 with marionettes and in 1896 with actors, theater scandal). Other *Ubu*-plays: *Les Minutes de sable mémorial*, published 1894); *Ubu enchaîné* (1900, *King Turd Enslaved*); *Ubu cocu* (published 1944, *King Turd Cuckolded*); *Ubu sur la Butte* (1901). *César-Antéchrist* (published 1895, mystery play). *Par la taille* (published 1906); *Les Silènes* (published 1901); *Pantagruel* (1911); *L'Objet aimé* (possibly published 1906); *Le Moutardier du Pope* (possibly published 1906).

JEFFERS, Robinson, 1887-1962, American poet. Dramatization of his long poem, *The Tower Beyond Tragedy.* (Modern *Oresteia*); *Medea* (1946, from Euripides); *The Cretan Woman* (1954, from Euripides' *Hippolytus*).

JOHN, Errol, young West Indian dramatist. *Moon on a Rainbow Shawl* (1958, set in Trinidad, winner of the *London Observer* playwriting competition).

JOHNSTON, Denis, b. 1901, Irish poetic and expressionistic dramatist. *The Old Lady Says "No!"* (1929, expressionistic play about Robert Emmet and Irish freedom); *The Moon in the Yellow River* (1931, comic critique of Irish life); *A Bride for the Unicorn* (1933); *Storm Song* (1934); *Blind Man's Buff* (1936, adapted from Ernst Toller); *The Golden Cuckoo* (1938); *The Dreaming Dust* (1940, also known as *Weep for the Cyclops*. Experimental play about Jonathan Swift); *Strange Occurrence on Ireland's Eye* (1956); *The Scythe and the Sunset* (1958, a reply, in a fashion, to O'Casey's *The Plough and the Stars*).

JOHST, Hanns, b. 1890, German dramatist of the post-World War I period. Nazi. Expressionistic dramas: *Der Einsame* (1917, about Christian Grabbe); *Der König* (1920, *The King*); *Propheten* (1922, Luther); *Die frohliche Stadt* (1925); *Thomas Paine* (1927); *Schlageter* (1932); and others.

JOSEPHSON, Ragnar, b. 1891, Swedish dramatist. *Perhaps a Poet* (1932, translated). *Leopold the Tightropewalker* (1934); *Dangerous Innocence* (1939); *The Last Leap* (1945).

JOYCE, James, 1882-1941, Irish writer, revolutionized the modern novel wtih his stream-of-consciousness method, which has had some influence on the non-illusionistic theater. Only play: *Exiles* (1918, problem play in late Ibsen style).— Dramatization of his novel *Ulysses* as *Ulysses in Nighttown* (1958) by Marjorie Barkentin and *Bloomsday* by Allen McClelland (1958).

KAFKA, Franz, 1883-1924, German writer, born in Czechoslovakia. His works have had great influence on the breakdown of reality in the modern theater. His only dramatic work was a fragment, *Der Gruftwächter* (posth., *The Warder of the Tomb*). Dramatization of his three novels: *Der Prozess* (1947, *The Trial* by André Gide and Jean-Louis Barrault); *Das Schloss* (1953, by Max Brod); *Amerika* (1957, by Max Brod).

KAISER, Georg, 1878-1945, German dramatist. Expressionist. All his plays are written like scenarios, referring back to the pure skeleton structure. The speech is similarly reduced, in his expressionist plays, to a skeletal form. This practice was later abandoned, but the emphasis on the structural aspects instead of the human and dramatic aspects remained, even in the last verse dramas. *Die judische Witwe* (written 1904, published 1921); *Rektor Kleist* (written 1905, performed 1918); *Die Bürger von Calais* (written 1912-13, performed 1917; based on Rodin); *Von morgens bis mitternachts* (written 1912, performed 1917. *From Morn to Midnight.* Excesses of a bank-teller who wants to "live just once"); *Die Koralle* (1917, *The Coral*); *Das Frauenopfer* (1918); *Hölle, Weg, Erde* (1919); *Gas I* (1918, translated) and *Gas II* (1920, translated. Vision of annihilation. The workers, slaves of the gas, refuse to be liberated: they have become robots); *Brand im Opernhaus* (1918, *Fire in the Opera House.* 1763 fire at the Paris Opera House); *Der gerettete Alkibiades* (1920, *Alkibiades Saved*); *Kanzlist Krehler* (1922); *Noli me tangere* (published 1922); *Gilles und Jeanne* (1923); *Die Flucht nach Venedig* (1923); *Nebeneinander* (1923); *Koltportage* (1924. Parody of pulp novels); *Der mutige Seefahrer* (1925); *Gats* (1925); *Zweimal Oliver* (1926); *Papiermühle* (1926); *Der Präsident* (1928); *Oktobertag* (1928; *The Phantom Lover,* drama of occult love); *Die Lederköpfe* (1928); *Hellseherei* (1929), *Mississippi* (1930); *Der Silbersee* (1933, with Kurt Weill); *Adrienne Ambrossat* (1935); *Agnete* (written 1935, performed 1949); *Das Los des Ossian Balvesen* (1936); *Vincent verkauft ein Bild* (1937, unperformed); *Napoleon in New Orleans* (written 1938; performed 1950); *Der Gärtner von Toulouse* (published 1938, performed 1945); *Der Schuss in die Offentlichkeit* (written 1938, performed 1949); *Alain und Elise* (published 1940, performed 1954); *Der Soldat*

Tanaka (1940); *Rosamunde Floris* (published 1940, performed 1953); *Klawitter* (written 1940, performed 1949); *Der englische Sender* (written 1940, performed 1947); *Die Spieldose* (written 1942, performed 1945); *Das Floss der Medusa* (completed 1943, performed 1945); *Zweimal Amphitryon* (1944, verse drama); *Pygmalion* (written 1944, performed 1953. Verse drama); *Bellerophon* (written 1944, performed 1953. Verse drama); *Das gordische Ei* (Fragment, completed in 1958 by Robert Schnorr); and others.

KANIN, Garson, b. 1912, American dramatist. *Born Yesterday* (1946); *Smile of the World* (1949); *The Rat Race* (1949); *The Live Wire,* 1950), book of musical comedy *Do Re Mi* (1961); *A Gift of Time* (1962); *Come on Strong* (1962).

KÄSTNER, Erich, b. 1899, German novelist and lyric poet. Dramatizations of his juvenile novels, *Emil und die Detektive, Pünktchen und Anton, Das doppelte Lottchen;* also comedies such as *Zu treuen Händen* (written in 1949 under the pseudonym of Melchior Kurtz); the parable-satire *Die Schule der Diktatoren* (1957) and the one-act play, *Das Haus der Erinnerung* (1958). Most recent play, *Emil und die drei Zwillinge* (1961).

KATAEV, Valentin, b. 1897, Russian story teller and dramatist. International success with *Squaring the Circle* (1928, translated. Comedy-satire on love and the housing shortage in the Soviet Union); also wrote *The Embezzlers* (1928, from his novel); *The Department Store* (1929); *The Vanguard* (1929); *A Million Torments* (1931); *Time, Forward!* (1932, from his novel); *Path of Flowers* (1934, performed by the Federal Theater in America); *Under the Big Top* (1934, musical, with Ilf and Petrov); *A Lonely White Sail Gleams* (1937); *I, Son of the Working People* (1938); *The Blue Kerchief* (1943); *The Son of the Regiment* (1949); *The Parental Home* (1945); *World Record in Three Acts* (1959).

KAUFMAN, George S., 1889-1961, American dramatist and man of the theater. Wrote most of his plays in collaboration with other authors. Cf. under Moss Hart and Marc Connelly for plays written in collaboration with these authors. Other plays: *Someone in the House* (1918. With Larry Evans

and Walter Percival); *Minick* (1924, with Edna Ferber); *The Butter and Egg Man* (1925); *The Cocoanuts* (1925, with music by Irving Berlin); *The Good Fellow* (1926, with Herman Mankiewicz); *The Royal Family* (1927, with Edna Ferber. Also known as *Theatre Royal*); *Animal Crackers* (1928, with Morrie Ryskind); *The Channel Road* (1929, with Alexander Woollcott, from "Boule de Suif"); *June Moon* (1929, with Ring Lardner); *Strike Up the Band* (1930, musical with Morrie Ryskind, score by George Gershwin); *The Band Wagon* (1931, musical, with Howard Dietz); *Of Thee I Sing* (1931, musical with Morrie Ryskind, score by George Gershwin); *Dinner at Eight* (1932, with Edna Ferber); *Let 'Em Eat Cake* (1933, musical, with Morrie Ryskind, score by George Gershwin); *The Dark Tower* (1933, with Alexander Woollcott); *First Lady* (1935, with Katherine Dayton); *Stage Door* (1936, with Edna Ferber); *The Land Is Bright* (1941, with Edna Ferber); *The Late George Apley* (1944, with J. P. Marquand, from Marquand's novel); *Park Avenue* (1946, musical, with Nunnally Johnson); *Bravo!* (1948, with Edna Ferber); *The Small Hours* (1951, with Leueen MacGrath); *Fancy Meeting You Again* (1952, with Leueen MacGrath); *The Solid Gold Cadillac* (1953, with Howard Teichmann); *Silk Stockings* (1955, musical, with Leueen MacGrath).

KAZANTZAKIS, Nikos, 1883-1957, Greek epic poet and dramatist. Visionary and ecstatic dramas. *Odysseus* (1927); *Christus* (1928); *Prometheus* (trilogy); *Julian the Apostate* (1945); *Constantine Paleologus; Nicephorus Phocas* (1927); *Kapodistrias; Melissa; Yang-tse; The Golden Apple; Fire Over Sodom* (1950); *The Greek Passion* (1953, dramatization of his own novel); *Christopher Columbus* (1954), and others.

KELLY, George, b. 1887, American dramatist. Skillfully constructed social satires. *Poor Aubrey* (published 1925, with other one-act plays; later expanded into *The Show-Off*); *The Torchbearers* (1922); *The Show-Off* (1924); *Craig's Wife* (1925, Pulitzer Prize); *Daisy Mayme* (1926); *Behold the Bridegroom* (1927); *Maggie the Magnificent* (1929); *Philip Goes Forth* (1931); *Reflected Glory* (1936); *The Deep Mrs. Sykes* (1945); *The Fatal Weakness* (1946); and others.

KINGSLEY, Sidney, b. 1906, American dramatist. *Men in White* (1933, Pulitzer Prize); *Dead End* (1935, slums of New York. Gassner: "Idealistic naturalism"); *Ten Million Ghosts* (1936, war play); *The World We Make* (1939, dramatization of a novel by Millen Brand); *The Patriots* (1943); *Detective Story* (1949); *Darkness at Noon* (1951, from Arthur Koestler's novel); *Lunatics and Lovers* (1954); *Night Life* (1962).

KINOSHITA, Junji, Japanese dramatist. *Seasons in the Textile Mill; Twilight of the Cranes; The Ascension of a Frog.*

KIPPHARDT, Heinar, b. 1922, German dramatist. *Entscheidungen* (1952); *Shakespeare dringend gesucht* (1953, comedy); *Der staunenswerte Aufstieg und Fall des Alois Piontek* (1956, satiric comedy); *Esel schreien im Dunkeln* (1958, comedy); *Die Stühle des Herrn Szmil* (1961, satirical comedy based on a Russian novel); *Der Hund des Generals* (1961, a brutal general who loves animals).

KIRKLAND, Jack, b. 1901, American journalist and playwright. *Frankie and Johnnie* (1928); *Tobacco Road* (1933, adapted from Erskine Caldwell. Original production ran until 1939); *Tortilla Flat* (1938, adapted from John Steinbeck); *I Must Love Someone* (1939, with Leyla Georgie); *Suds in Your Eye* (1944); *Georgia Boy* (1945, from Erskine Caldwell's novel); *Mr. Adam* (1949); *The Man with the Golden Arm* (1956, from Nelson Algren's novel); and others.

KIRSHON, Vladimir, b. 1902, Russian dramatist. *Red Rust* (1927, with A. Ouspensky, translated. The problem of adjusting to the Revolution); *The Rails Hum* (1928); *City of Winds* (1929); *Bread* (1930, translated; the farm problem); *The Trial* (1933, political conflict in Germany); and others.

KLABUND (Alfred Henschke), 1890-1928, German poet of the post-World War I generation. Adaptation of a Chinese play, *Der Kreidekreis* (1924, *The Circle of Chalk*); the triangle-comedy, *XYZ* (1927). Also wrote *Die Nachtwandler* (1920); *Brennende Erde* (1926); *Der Teufelspakt* (1925).

KLINGER, Kurt, b. 1928, Austrian poet and dramatist of the post-World War II generation. *Hans Christian Andersen* (1952); *Der goldene Käfig* (1952); *Odysseus muss wieder reisen* (1954); *Das kleine Weltkabarett* (1958); *Sera* (1960, one-act); *Wer die Wahl hat* (1960, comedy); *Die Neue Wohnung* (1960, after Goldoni).

KNAUTH, Joachim, b. 1931, East German dramatist. *Heinrich VIII oder der Ketzerkönig* (historical comedy); *Der Tambour und sein Herr König* (historical comedy); *Bedenweiler Abgesang* (1960); *Die sterblichen Götter* (1960, one-act).

KOKOSCHKA, Oskar, b. 1886, German painter and writer of expressionistic plays. *Sphinx und Strohmann* (1907); *Mörder, Hoffnung der Frauen* (1907, one act, *Murderer the Woman's Hope*); *Der brennende Dornbusch* (1911); *Hiob* (1917, *Job*); *Orpheus und Eurydike* (1918); *Der gefesselte Kolumbus* (1921).

KOLAR, Slavko, b. 1891, Croatian dramatist. Realist with humor. *The People are Patient* (1947); *Seven Men in a Cellar* (1948); *Uncle Laszy* (1949).

KOMMERELL, Max, 1902-1944, German literary historian and poet. *Das kaiserliche Blut* (1938, drama in Baroque style); *Kasperlespiele für Erwachsene* (posth.); *Die Gefangenen* (posth.).

KOPIT, Arthur, b. 1938, American dramatist. *Oh Dad, Poor Dad, Mamma's Hung You in the Closet and I'm Feelin' So Sad* (performed in London 1961; in New York, with more success, 1962; subtitled: "A Pseudoclassical Tragifarce in a Bastard French Tradition").

KOPS, Bernard, b. 1926, English dramatist. Attained success with *The Hamlet of Stepney Green* (1956, fantasy of lower-class London Jewish life, with some echoes of *Hamlet*). Other plays: *Goodbye, World* (1958); *The Dream of Peter Mann* (1960, expressionistic fantasy); *Change for the Angel* (1960); *Enter Solly Gold* (1962).

KORNEICHUK, Alexander, b. 1905, Ukrainian dramatist, member of the Central Committee of the Communist Party. *The Sinking of the Squadron* (1934, scuttling the Russian Black Sea Fleet, 1918); *Platon Krechet* (1935, translated); *The Banker* (1936); *Truth* (1937); *Bogdan Khmelnit-*

ski (1938, the Ukrainian rebellion against the Poles, 1648); *The Front* (1942, translated); *On the Ukrainian Steppes* (1941); *Guerrillas of the Ukrainian Steppes* (1942, translated; sequel to previous play); *Mr. Perkins' Mission to the Land of the Bolsheviks* (1944, skit about an imaginary Chicago sausage-king's visit to the Soviet Union); *Come to Zvonkoe!* (1945); *Wings* (1953, translated); *Why Do the Stars Smile?* (1956, comedy); *The Surgeon.*

KORNFELD, Paul, 1889-1942, German dramatist, Expressionist. Murdered by the Nazis. *Die Verführung* (1913); *Himmel und Hölle* (1919); *Der ewige Traum* (1922, comedy); *Palme oder der Gekränkte* (1924, comedy); *Kilian oder die gelbe Rose* (1926, comedy); *Jud Süss* (1930, tragedy). Adaptation of Kalidasa's *Shakuntala* (1925).

KOSOR, Josip, 1871-1961, Croatian dramatist. *Passion's Furnace* (1910); *The Reconciliation* (1914); *At the Café du Dome* (1922); *The Rotunda and Humanity* (1925); and others.

KRAMM, Joseph, b. 1907, American dramatist. *The Shrike* (1952, Pulitzer Prize).

KRAUS, Karl, 1875-1936, Viennese social critic. Wrote the tragic satire, *Die Letzten Tage der Menschheit* (written 1915-1918. An indictment of the ruling classes and the society of the pre-war and war years, using documented evidence. The printed text runs to nearly 800 pages). Also: *Wolkenkuckucksheim* (1923; after Aristophanes' *The Birds*); *Traumtheater* (1924, curtain-raiser); and others.

KRLEZA, Miroslav, b. 1893, celebrated Croatian poet; pacifist and Marxist. Most successful play was *The Glembays* (1928); also wrote *Christopher Columbus* (1917); *Michelangelo Buonarroti* (1918); *Galicia* (1920); *Golgotha* (1922); *Werewolf* (1923); *Agony* (1927); *Leda* (1923); *Areteos* (1959, ancient and modern parallels, attack on dictatorship).

KROG, Helge, 1889-1962, Norwegian dramatist. *The Big We* (1919, newspaper melodrama); *The House of Jarl* (1923); *On Life's Sunny Side* (1927, translated); *The Copy* (1928); *The Sounding Shell* (1929, translated); *On the Way* (1931, translated); *Triad* (1933); *Break-up* (1936, translated).

KRUCZKOWSKI, Leon, 1900-1962. Polish novelist and dramatist. *The First Day of Freedom* (1959, Polish soldiers at the end of the war.); *The Death of the Governor* (1960, after a story by Andreyev); and others.

KUBA, Kurth Barthel, b. 1914, East German writer. National Prize winner. Wrote the dramatic ballad, *Störtebeker* (1959).

KUHN, Fritz, b. 1919, East German dramatist. Won success with the drama, *Venezianisches Glas* (1958). Also wrote *Kredit bei Nibelungen* (1960).

KÜHNELT, Hans Friedrich, b. 1918, Austrian dramatist. *Spass muss sein* (1947, comedy); *Der Steinbruch* (1950); *Der Schauspieler* (1952); *Bevor der Zug kommt* (1953); *Es ist später als du denkst* (1958); *Ein Tag mit Edward* (1958, comedy); *Geliebtes schwarzes Schaf* (1956, comedy); *Eusebius und die Nachtigall* (1959); *Der Boden unter den Füssen* (1960).

LACOUR, José André, b. 1919, Belgian dramatist. Success with *L'Année du bac* (1958). Other plays: *Notre Peau* (1950); *Le Temps nous a* (1952); *Oh, mes Aieux* (1953).

LAGERKVIST, Pär, b. 1891, Swedish poet and novelist. Nobel Prize. On the stage with *The Last Man* (1917, vision of the dying of the earth); *The Secret of Heaven* (1919); *The Invisible Man* (1923); *He Who Lived His Life Over Again* (1928); *The King* (1932); *The Hangman* (1934, from his novel); *The Man without a Soul* (1936, from his novel); *Victory in the Dark* (1939); *Midsummer Dream in the Workhouse* (1941, translated); *Let Man Live* (1949, translated. One-act play—the characters: Judas, Giordano Bruno, Socrates, Joan of Arc, Paolo and Francesca, a lynched Negro, martyrs, a witch, victims of dictatorship, etc.), and others. Has also dramatized his novel, *Barrabas* (1953. Tragedy of a man who cannot believe until, under Nero, he meets the same death as Christ).

LAMPEL, Peter Martin, 1894-1962, German dramatist of the post-World War I generation. Wrote topical indictments of society in a naturalistic style. *Revolte im Erziehungshaus* (1928); *Verschwörer* (1929); *Giftgas über Berlin* (1929. Rebellion of factory workers who are secretly being forced to manufacture poison gas by the government); *Putsch* (1929); *Pennäler* (1929); *Wir sind Kameraden* (1930); *Vaterland* (1931); *Alarm im Arbeitslager* (1932); *Flucht vor uns selber* (1951); *Vier aus dem Bunker* (1951); *Billy* (1951); *Kampf um Helgoland* (1952); *Die Möwe ist wieder da* (1956); *Heinrich Geratewohls Söhne* (1956); *Aber wir wollen nicht tot sein* (1956).

LANGENBECK, Curt, 1906-1953, German dramatist. Became prominent under Hitler with the tragedies, *Alexander* (1934); *Heinrich VI* (1936); *Der Hochverräter* (1938); *Das Schwert* (1940).

LANGER, Frantisek, b. 1888, Czech dramatist, *Periphery.* (1925, naturalistic drama of the Prague suburbs); *The Camel through the Needle's Eye* (1923, translated, comedy); *The Conversion of Ferdys Pistora* (1929); and others.

LANGNER, Ilse, b. 1899, German novelist and dramatist. *Die Heilige aus USA* (1931); *Klytemnestra* (1947); *Iphigenie kehrt heim* (1948); *Heimkehr* (1949); *Sylphide und der Polizist* (1950); *Métro* (1950); *Das Wunder von Amerika* (1951); *Der venezianische spiegel* (1952); *Ich überlebe meine Hinrichtung* (1952); *Rettet Saint Julien le Pauvre* (1954); *Cornelia Kungström* (1955); *Die grosse Zauberin* (1955); and others.

LASKER-SCHÜLER, Else, 1876-1945, German poetess. *Die Wupper* (1909, Kleist Prize) and *Arthur Anonymus und seine Väter* (1932). Lasker-Schüler: "I consider the art of the drama to be a developing lyricism."

LAUCKNER, Rolf, 1887-1954, German dramatist. Expressionist. *Der Umweg zum Tod* (1915, five short dramas and five conversations); *Der Sturz des Apostels Paulus* (1918); *Predigt in Litauen* (1919); *Wahnschaffe* (1920); *Die Riese gegen Gott* (1923, Gauguin). Historical plays: *Herzog Theodor von Gothland* (1932); *Bernhard von Weimar* (1933); *Der letzte Preusse* (1937), and many others. Comedy: *Der Hakim weiss es* (1936).

LAURENTS, Arthur, b. 1920, American dramatist. A psychological emphasis. *Home of the Brave* (1945, soldiers facing prejudice.); *Heartsong* (1947); *The*

Bird Cage (1950); *The Time of the Cuckoo* (1952, a repressed spinister visits Venice); *A Clearing in the Woods* (1956); *West Side Story* (1957, musical, lyrics by Stephen Sondheim, score by Leonard Bernstein, directed by Jerome Robbins. Romeo and Juliet transferred to the streets of New York.); *Gypsy* (1959, musical, lyrics by Stephen Sondheim, score by Jule Styne; from the memoirs of Gypsy Rose Lee. An aggressive mother and her two daughters in show business).

LAVEDAN, Henri, 1859-1940, French dramatist. Superficial social comedies. *Le Prince d'Aurec* (1892, translated as *Prince d'Aurec.* An aristocrat in conflict with a Jewish banker.); *Les deux Noblesses* (1894, a sequel); *Viveurs* (1895); and others.

LAVERY, Emmet, b. 1902, American dramatist. *The First Legion* (1934, internal differences among the Jesuits.); *Monsignor's Great Hour* (1935, one-act); *The Magnificent Yankee* (1946); *Song at the Scaffold* (1949, from Gertrud von Le Fort); *Fenelon* (1956); *The Indispensable Man* (1956, comedy); & others.

LAVRENEV, Boris, 1892-1959, Soviet dramatist. *For Those At Sea; The Break* (1928, the battle of the cruiser "Aurora" during the October Revolution); *The Song of the Black Sea Sailors* (1943); *The Voice of America* (1949, Stalin Prize; against the American "warmongers"); *Lermontov* (1952); *The Last Shot* (1961; with Bratko Kraft).

LAWLER, Ray, b. 1922, Australian dramatist. Realist. *The Summer of the Seventeenth Doll* (1957, characters are Australian sugar-cane cutters and barmaids); *The Piccadilly Bushman* (1961).

LAWRENCE, David Herbert, 1885-1930, English novelist. *A Collier's Friday Night* (written 1906-07, published 1934); *The Widowing of Mrs. Holroyd* (published 1914, performed 1920. The death of a miner.); *Touch and Go* (written 1919, published 1920. Miners on strike.); *David* (published 1926, performed 1927. The biblical story.); *My Son's My Son* (unfinished play, completed by Walter Greenwood, performed 1936). Plays published posthumously: *Altitude* (1938); *The Married Man* (1940); *Merry-Go-Round* (1941). Also, *The Fight for Barbara* (apparently unpublished). A story,

"You Touched Me," freely dramatized by Tennessee Williams and Donald Windham (1945), under its own title.

LAWSON, John Howard, b. 1895, American dramatist, Marxist. Won fame in 1920's with a series of plays of social criticism in a variety of experimental styles (expressionism, living newspaper, cabaret, etc.). Wrote many film scripts, blacklisted in 1948. *Standards* (1914); *Servant-Master-Lover* (1917); *Roger Bloomer* (1923); *Processional* (1925); *Nirvana* (1926); *Loud Speaker* (1927); *The International* (1928); *Success Story* (1932); *The Pure in Heart* (1934); *Gentlewoman* (1934); *Marching Song* (1937); *Parlor Magic* (1962).

LENGYEL, Melchior, b. 1880, Hungarian dramatist. Wrote thrillers like *Typhoon* (1910, English adaptations performed); actors' vehicles like *The Czarina* (1917, also performed in English, Catherine the Great); comedies like *Antonia* (1922); the farce, *Battle of Waterloo* (1924); International success with the film *Ninotchka* (1939); more recently, the play *The Quiet House* (1957).

LENORMAND, Henri René, 1882-1951, French dramatist, influenced by Einstein and Freud. *La Folie blanche* (1906); *Les Possédés* (1909); *Le Temps est un songe* (1919, Time Is a Dream); *Les Ratés* (1920, The Failures); *Le Simoun* (1920); *Le Mangeur de rêves* (1922, The Dream Doctor); *A l'Ombre du mal* (1924); *L'Homme et ses fantômes* (1924, Man and His Phantoms); *Le Lâche* (1925, The Coward); *L'Amour magicien* (1926, spiritualism); *Asie* (1931); *Sortilèges* (1932, Grand-Guignol); *La Folle du ciel* (1936); *Terre de Satan* (1942); and others.

LEONOV, Leonid, b. 1899, Russian writer and dramatist. *The Badgers* (1927; from his novel about Partisans); *Untilovsk* (1928); *Skutarevski* (1934); *The Orchards of Polovchansk* (1938); *Invasion* (1941, concerns the German invasion. Sacrificial death of a forced laborer); *Lenushka* (1943); *An Ordinary Man* (1945); *The Golden Coach* (1946); *The Russian Forest* (1959, from his novel); and others.

LERNET-HOLENIA, Alexander, b. 1897, Austrian novelist, lyric poet, and dramatist. Dramas written in strict form; *Demetrius* (1926); Saul (1944); *Alkestis* (1945); *Lepanto* (1946).—Austrian comedies: *Ollapotrida* (1926); *Österreichische Komödie* (1927); *Parforce* (1928); *Glastüren* (1937).—Other plays: *Die Frau des Potiphar* (1934); *Spanische Komödie* (1947); *Die Lützowschen Jäger* (1956); *Radetzky* (1956); *Finanzamt* (1957).

LESSING, Doris, b. 1919, British novelist and dramatist. Born in Rhodesia. *Mr. Dolinger* (1958); *Each His Own Wilderness* (1958); *The Truth about Billy Newton* (1960); *Play with a Tiger* (1962).

LEVI, Paolo, b. 1919, Italian dramatist of the post-World War II generation. *Anna e il telefono* (1951); *Legittima difesa* (1952); *Il Caso Pinedus* (1954, The Pinedus Affair); *Come per scherzo* (1955); *I nemici* (1955); *Gli dei di pietra* (1957. Levi: "My new play is not about war, although it takes place during the partisan fighting. The war atmosphere was solely to give me the opportunity to put my religious theme forward. Partisan fighters of the second World War meet once more after several years at the scene of one of their battles. The leading character is David, a Jew, the clear-sighted leader of the group. In his capacity as leader he had, during the confusion of the last days of the war ten years before, been responsible for the death of a comrade, 'under circumstances,' as he confesses to God in his despairing search for judgment, 'which would prevent any earthly jury from judging me.' His present happy life is also the direct result of this crime. This is the substance of the conflict . . ."); *Il gioco e fatto* (1957); *L'astrico d'inferno* (1958); *Fra una mese, fra un anno* (1960, from a novel by Françoise Sagan); *Indirizzo sconosciuto* (1963).

LEVIN, Meyer, b. 1905, American novelist. *Compulsion* (1957, from his novel about a murder of the 1920's; published in author's original version, 1959).

LEVY, Benn W., b. 1900, English dramatist. Light comedies and farces. *This Woman Business* (1925); *Mrs. Moonlight* (1928); *Art and Mrs. Bottle* (1929); *The Devil* (1930); *Topaze* (1930, adaptation); *Evergreen* (1930); *Springtime for Henry* (1931); *Hollywood Holiday* (1931, with John van

Druten); *The Jealous God* (1939); *Clutterbuck* (1946); *Return to Tyassi* (1950); *Cupid and Psyche* (1953); *The Rape of the Belt* (1957); *The Tumbler* (1960); and others.

LEWIS, Sinclair, 1885-1951, American novelist. *Dodsworth* (1934, adapted from his novel, with Sidney Howard.); *Jayhawker* (1934, with Lloyd Lewis. Historical play about Kansas.); *It Can't Happen Here* (1936, adapted from his novel, with John C. Moffitt).

LINDSAY, Howard, b. 1889, and **Russel CROUSE,** b. 1893, American dramatists. *Red, Hot and Blue* 1936, musical); *Hooray for What* (1937); *Life With Father* (1939, from Clarence Day; ran more than seven years); *Strip for Action* (1942); *State of the Union* (1945, Pulitzer Prize); *Life With Mother* (1948, from Clarence Day); *Call Me Madam* (1950, musical, with Irving Berlin); *Remains To Be Seen* (1951); *The Prescott Proposals* (1953); *The Great Sebastians* (1956); *Happy Hunting* (musical); *Tall Story* (1958, from a novel by Howard Nemerov); *The Sound of Music* (1959, musical, with Richard Rodgers and Oscar Hammerstein); *Mr. President* (1962, musical, with Irving Berlin).

LINKLATER, Eric. b. 1899, Scottish novelist and dramatist. *Crisis in Heaven* (1944); *Breakspear in Gascony* (1959).

LOGUE, Christopher, b. 1926, English dramatist. Radical social criticism; some inspiration from Brecht, emphatic didacticism. *Cob and Leach* (1959); *The Lily-White Boys* (1960, musical); *Antigone* (1960, performed with *Cob and Leach* as *Trials by Logue*).

LONSDALE, Frederick, 1881-1954, English dramatist. Society comedies. International success with *The Last of Mrs. Cheney* (1925). *Also Spring Cleaning* (1923); *On Approval* (1927); and others.

LORCA, Federico Garcia, 1899-1936, Spanish dramatist. Renewer of the lyric theater, employing the elements of the Spanish folk ballad and folk play. Was director of the student theater, "La Barraca." *El maleficio de la mariposa* (1920, *The But-*

terfly's Evil Spell, insect comedy); *Mariana Pineda* (1927, translated, freedom fighters of Granada); *La zapatera prodigiosa* (1930, *The Shoemaker's Prodigious Wife.* Farce in Commedia dell'arte style. A husband runs away from his nagging wife and comes back disguised as a traveling player. He lectures his wife in a ballad he sings to her. She tells him that she loves only her husband. But when he reveals himself she instantly begins all over again: "Gallows-bird, rascal!" Director's note: "The director must be sure to hit any actor who overplays this part over the head with a stick. Nobody may overact. The farce must always be acted with naturalness. . . . Simplicity!").—*Amor de Don Perlimplín, con Belisa en su jardín* (1931, *The Love of Don Perlimplín and Belisa in the Garden.* Subtitled, "Four scenes of an erotic picture-book in the style of a chamber play." *Así que pasen cinco años* (1931, *If Five Years Pass.* Subtitled, "A Legend of the Times." Type characters: Youth, Old Age, Father, Friend, Harlequin. The dead child with the cat. The mannequin in the wedding dress, gray face with gold lips and eyebrows: "I sing the death which I never felt." Transcendence of various levels of reality. Forest scene in baroque style with Harlequin, the Girl, Pagliaccio. A huge ace of hearts appears, impaled with an arrow. The Youth dies, saying, "There are no human beings here."). *Bodas de Sangre* (1933, *Blood Wedding.* Subtitled, "A lyric tragedy." An ancient Andalusian country family with ancient passions and rules of honor. A bride is abducted by her childhood lover and flees with him to the ghost forest. Darkness, pursuit. The moon speaks. The beggar woman. The fleeing couple. She: "It is right that I should die here, / with my feet in the water and thorns / on my head. Weep for me, O you leaves! Cast out wife and virgin." He: "And if they part us now / They part us over my dead body." The rivals kill each other. Last scene: The mother of the bride alone. The bride comes back. The mother knocks her to the ground. The bride restrains the neighbor who would assist her: "Let her alone. I came back to be killed by her." Wake for the dead.). *Yerma* (1934, translated same title. Subtitled, "A tragic poem." The childless wife strangles her husband because he is neither able nor willing to give her love.); *Doña Rosita la soltera* (1935), *Dona Rosita the Spinster.* Subtitled, "A poem of Granada around the year 1910, taking places in various gardens, with song and dance." Year after year Rosita waits for her lover, who has gone to America. Only his letters, on which she bases all her hopes, sustain her. Finally we learn that he has married another woman in America. But it is too late: Rosita can no longer rid herself of her love, which has spun a web around her. The action is so handled that it appears sometimes poetic, sometimes ethereal, sometimes extremely realistic.). *La casa de Bernarda Alba* (Completed in 1936, first performance in Buenos Aires 1945, *The House of Bernarda Alba*. Subtitled, "A tragedy of the women of the Spanish villages." The tyranny of a puritanically strict mother over her five daughters. The attempts of the youngest to break away. She loves the fiancé of the oldest sister. The hump-backed sister spies on the two in the stable. A picture of the man is found in the bed of another sister. The hate of the sisters for each other becomes more and more threatening. One night the youngest sister, despite all warnings and threats, goes once more to a rendezvous in the stable. The other sisters call the mother who shoots at the man, although she is unable to see him. The hump-backed sister tells the youngest that the mother's shot found its mark. The youngest sister hangs herself. The mother, having learned nothing from the experience, tells her other daughters, "Take her down! My daughter died a virgin! Take her to her room and dress her as a virgin. None of you say a word about this! She died untouched. See that the bells are tolled twice at break of day. No lamentation. One must be able to look death in the face. Quiet! Silence, I say!").

LOVINESCU, Horia, b. 1917, Rumanian dramatist. Conversion from critical to socialist realism. Principal success with *The Destroyed Fortress* (1955) and *The Boga Sisters* (1959). Also: *The Light in Ulmi* (1954); *The Inn at the Crossroads* (1957); *The Death of an Artist* (1960).

LUCKE, Hans, b. 1927, East German actor and dramatist. *Fanal* (1953; on Ernest Thälmann); *Taillenweite 68* (1953, farce); *Glatteis* (1956. Rogues' comedy); *Der Keller* (1957, war play); *Kaution* (1958); *Der Siebzehnte* (1959); *Untersuchungshaft* (1960); *Satanische Komödie* (1961).

LUNACHARSKI, Anatoli, 1875-1931, Russian Commissar of Education and dramatist. Protector of such theatrical experimenters as Meyerhold, Taïrov, and Vachtangov. Gave a Soviet reinterpretation to past history and literature. *The Magi* (1918, translated); *Vasilisa the Wise* (1918, translated); *Oliver Cromwell* (1920); *Faust and the City* (1920, translated); and others.

LÜTZKENDORF, Felix, b. 1906, German dramatist. *Die Grenze* (1932); *Opfergang* (1934); *Liebesbriefe* (1939); *Das Jahr 1000* (1940); *Friedrich der Zweite* (1944); *Fuge in Moll* (1947); *Cyprische Antigone* (1957); *Die Eisscholle* (1959, comedy).

MACKAYE, Percy, 1875-1956, American poet and dramatist. Son of the pioneer American theater man, Steele MacKaye. Poetic plays and patriotic masques. *The Canterbury Pilgrims* (published 1903, performed 1909); *Fenris the Wolf* (1905); *Jeanne d'Arc* (1906); *Sappho and Phaon* (1907); *Mater* (1908); *The Scarecrow* (Published 1908; from Hawthorne's story "Feathertop." Legend of a scarecrow that is turned into a human being through love); *Anti-Matrimony* (1910); *A Masque of Labor* (1912); *Tomorrow* (1912); *Sanctuary, A Bird Masque* (1913); *One Thousand Years Ago* (1913); *The Immigrants* (1915); *Caliban, A Community Masque* (1916); *Sinbad the Sailor* (1917); *Rip Van Winkle* (1919); *This Fine-Pretty World* (1923); *The Mystery of Hamlet* (1949); and others.

MACKEN, Walter, b. 1915, Irish actor and playwright. *Mungo's Mansion* (1946, Irish rural life); *Vacant Possession* (1948); *Home is the Hero* (1953); *Twilight of a Warrior* (1958); *Look in the Looking Glass* (1958).

MACLEISH, Archibald, b. 1892, American poet. *Nobodaddy* (1926, verse play not for staging); *Panic* (1935); *This Music Crept by Me upon the Waters* (1953); *J. B.* (1958. Scene is the corner of a circus tent. Time: the present. Two comedians play God and Satan. Two levels of action on which the tragedy of a modern Job [Everyman] is played.); has also written radio plays, e.g., *The Fall of the City* (1937) and *Air Raid* (1938).

MACLIAMMOIR, Micheál, b. 1899, Irish actor, producer, and dramatist. Co-founder of the Dublin Gate Theater with Hilton Edwards. Irish fantasies and farces in the 19th century style. *Where Stars Walk* (1940); *Dancing Shadows* (1941); *Ill Met by Moonlight* (1946); *Portrait of Miriam* (1947); *The Mountains Look Different* (1948); *Home for Christmas* (1950); *A Slipper for the Moon* (1954), and others. Autobiography. *All for Hecuba* (1946).

MACNAMARA, Brinsley (A. E. Weldon), b. 1890, Irish dramatist. Plays about the Irish rebellion and Irish peasant life. *The Rebellion in Ballycullen* (1919); *The Land for the People* (1920); *The Glorious Uncertainty* (1923); *Look at the Heffernans* (1926); *The Master* (1928); *Margaret Gillan* (1933); *The Grand House in the City* (1936); *The Three Thimbles* (1941); *Marks and Mabel* (1945).

MACNEICE, Louis, 1907-1963. English poet. *Out of the Picture* (1937); *Christopher Columbus* (1944). Radio plays, including *The Dark Tower* (1946). Translations of the *Agamemnon* of Aeschylus and Goethe's *Faust*.

MAETERLINCK, Maurice, 1862-1949, Belgian poet, chief representative of symbolism and aestheticism at the turn of the century. Nobel Prize. *La Princesse Maleine* (1889); *L'Intruse* (1890, *The Intruder*); *Les Aveugles* (1890, *The Blind*); *Pelléas et Mélisande* (1892, set to music by Debussy); *Monna Vanna* (1902, trans. same title); *L'Oiseau bleu* (1908, *The Bluebird*. Celebrated production by Stanislavski); and many others.

MALAPARTE, Curzio, 1898-1957, Italian author. Aggressively realistic. *Du côté de chez Proust* (1949, one-act); *Das Kapital* (1949, Marx in London); *Anche la donne hanno perso la guerra* (1952, *The Women Lost the War Too*, takes place in Vienna in 1945).

MALRAUX, André, b. 1901, important French novelist, journalist, politician, and aesthetician. Dramatization of his novel, *La Condition humaine* (1954, with Thierry Maulnier. China at the beginning of the Civil War).

MALTZ, Albert, b. 1908, American dramatist. Marxist social protest. *Black Pit* (1935, coal-mining play), *Private Hicks* (1936, one-act). Plays written in collaboration with George Sklar (q.v.).

MARCEAU, Félicien, b. 1913, Belgian novelist. International success with *L'Oeuf* (1956, *The Egg*. Satire against conformity, "the world of the others, which is as smooth, unbroken, and windowless as the surface of an egg, and which one has to join if one wants to make anything of oneself." Play within a play in farce style: the protagonist comments upon himself). *L'École des moroses* (1953); *Catarina* (1954). Also: *La bonne Soupe* (1958, *The Good Soup*); *L'Étouffe-chrétien* (1960, about Nero); *Les Cailloux* (1962).

MARCEL, Gabriel, b. 1887, French Christian Existentialist philosopher, critic and dramatist. Socratic theater: appeal through questions to make existence "sacred" once again. *La Grâce* (1911); *Le Palais de sable* (1914); *Le Coeur des autres* (1920); *Le Regard neuf* (1922); *L'Iconoclaste* (1923); *La Chapelle ardente* (1925, *The Funeral Pyre*); *Le Fanal* (1936); *Le Chemin de Crête* (1936, translated as *Ariadne*); *Le Dard* (1938); *L'Horizon* (1945); *Un Homme de Dieu* (1949, *A Man of God*); *Rome n'est plus dans Rome* (1951. Drama of ideologies: a "premature refugee" flees to Brazil because he fears the coming of Communism. In Brazil, however, he finds that a fanatical clergy is threatening the academic freedom which, as a university professor, he is committed to defend. He finds the way to the true church after he has appealed, via radio, to his countrymen to hold out in the fight against Communism.); *Les Coeurs avides* (1952); *La Dimension Florestan* (1953); *Mon Temps n'est pas le votre* (1955); *Croissez et multipliez* (1958); and others.

MARINETTI, Filippo, 1876-1944, Italian author, founder of Futurism. *Le Roi Bombance* (1909, written in French); *Anti-neutralità* (1912, *Anti-neutrality*, one-act.); *Simultaneità* (1912, *Simultaneity*, one-act.); and others, including later plays written in accordance with Futurist theory.

MARTÍNEZ SIERRA, Gregorio, 1881-1947, Spanish dramatist. *Vida y dulzura* (1908, with Santiago Rusiñol); *El ama de la casa* (1910); *Canción de cuna* (1911, *The Cradle Song*); *Lirio entre espinas* (1911, *A Lily among Thorns*); *Los pastores* (1913, *The Two Shepherds*); *La mujer del héroe* (1914); *El reino de Dios* (1915, *The Kingdom of God*); *Sueño de una noche de agosto* (1918, *The Roman-*

tic Young Lady). *Don Juan de España* (1921); *Triángulo* (1930); others.

MARTYN, Edward, 1859-1923, Irish dramatist. Briefly associated with the Abbey Theater. *The Heather Field* (1899); *Maeve* (1900); *An Enchanted Sea* (1902); *The Tale of a Town* (1902); *Grangecolman* (1912); *The Dream Physician* (1918); and others.

MASEFIELD, John, b. 1878. English poet. Principally verse dramas and history plays, e.g., *Pompey the Great* (1910); *Philip the King* (1914, in rhyme); *The Faithful* (1915); *Tristan and Isolt* (1927); *A King's Daughter* (1928); Religious dramas: *The Trial of Jesus* (1916); *Good Friday* (1917); *The Empress of Rome* (1937, adaptation of French miracle play). Psychological dramas: *The Campden Wonder* (1907); *The Tragedy of Nan* (1908, bourgeois tragedy in manner of Ibsen, but in verse); *The Witch* (1910); and others.

MAUGHAM, W. Somerset, b. 1874, English novelist and dramatist. English society dramas with exotic coloring and tendency to cater to public taste. *A Man of Honour* (1903); *Lady Frederick* (1907, comedy in manner of Wilde); *Jack Straw* (1908, an Archduke pretends to be a waiter who pretends to be an Archduke); *Our Betters* (1917, Anglo-American social relations); *The Circle* (1921, romantic history repeats); *East of Suez* (1922); *The Constant Wife* (1926, a wife's revenge upon the double standard); *The Letter* (1927, a wife has murdered her lover); *The Sacred Flame* (1928, a theme from Ibsen—the mercy-killing of a son by his mother); *For Services Rendered* (1932); and others.

MAURIAC, François, b. 1885, French novelist and dramatist. Nobel Prize. Christian theater in Ibsen style: *Asmodée* (1937, translated under original title. A demonic tutor poisons the family life of a young widow on a country estate. Mother and daughter love the same man. The mother gives him up.); *Les mal aimés* (1945. A domineering father destroys his daughter's life); *Passage de malin* (1947); *Le Feu sur la terre* (1951. Destruction of a marriage through perverted sibling love).

MAYAKOVSKI, Vladimir, 1893-1930, Russian lyric poet. On the stage with the revolutionary drama, *Mystery Bouffe* (1918, translated, symbolic-sur-realistic Mystery play); *The Bedbug* (1929, translated. Satire. Takes place in 1979: the hero awakes after a fifty-year hibernation and sees a society which has developed to the "highest ideal"); *The Bathhouse* (1930, translated. "Magical drama with circus and fireworks").

MAYER, Edwin Justus, 1897-1960, American dramatist. *The Firebrand* (1924); *Children of Darkness* (1930, about Jonathan Wild); *Sunrise in My Pocket! or, The Last Days of Davy Crockett, an American Saga* (published 1941), and others.

McCULLERS, Carson, b. 1917, American story writer. On the stage with the internationally successful *Member of the Wedding* (1950. Dramatization of her novel of the same name). Also *The Square Root of Wonderful* (1957). Her story "The Ballad of the Sad Cafe" dramatized by Edward Albee.

MEANO, Cesare, 1906-1958, Italian dramatist. Most successful plays were *Nascità di Salome* (1937); *Spettacolo fuori programma* (1940); and *Melisandra per me* (1940). Other plays: *Venti-quattro ore felici* (1947); *Diana non vuole amore* (1953); *Fondarono una città* (1954); *Bella* (1955); *Chiara nell'ombra* (1957).

MEHRING, Walter, b. 1896, German writer of the post-World War I generation. *Der Kaufmann von Berlin* (1929, an Eastern Jew in capitalistic Berlin. Produced by Piscator).

MEIER, Herbert, b. 1928, Swiss dramatist of the post-World War II generation. First attracted notice with his symbolic poetic play, *Die Barke von Gawdos* (1950, based on a novel, *Iorgu Koruga*). Also wrote *Kalondji* (1948, African comedy); *Kaiser Jovian* (1951, Roman comedy); *Herodias tanzt moch* (1956); *Die weissen Stühle* (1957); *Jonas und der Nerz* (1959); *Die Guitarre* (1961).

MELAS, Spyros, b. 1883, Greek dramatist. *The King and the Dog* (1953, comedy about Diogenes); *Papaflessas* (1962); *Rigas Vestimlis* (1963).

MELL, Max, b. 1882, Austrian poet. Began to revive the anti-illusionistic Christian theater on the basis of the old miracle and morality play forms, together with Hofmannsthal. From the beginning he was thus committed to a transcendence of reality on the stage, as in *Das Wiener Kripperl von 1919* (1921), in which the despairing and oppressed, wood-gatherers, working women, citizens, officers, commuters, street-car conductors, street-sweepers, and children experience a mystic transformation at a street-car terminal on a winter evening: in the fog the street-car becomes a phantom vehicle and the terminal waiting-room becomes the manger of Bethlehem. —From *Das Schutzengelspiel* (1923), Mell went to the frequently played *Das Apostelspiel.* (1923, *Apostle Play.* Two dissolute characters break into a lonely mountain-hut on a winter's night. The children's belief transforms them into apostles), *Das Nachfolge-Christi-Spiel* (1927) raises this theme to a universal level: a Styrian castle is captured by a band of deserters and incendiaries during the Turkish wars. The lord of the castle is nailed to a cross, where he is found by Imperial troops who have routed the deserters. He is revived, and he, "who has seen the world from above," pleads for mercy for his torturers. His death which he has begged as a "miracle," supplies the Christian ending.—*Die Sieben gegen Theben* (1932) seems like an exercise in the strict form of tragedy. Mell insists on the Aristotelian unities of time, space, and action for the sake of purity of form. Thus he comes by way of the *Spiel von den deutschen Ahnen* (1935) to the dramatization of the Nibelung Saga in two parts: *Die Nibelunge Not* (1944-1951. Turns the saga into a myth in an attempt to recover its "real" content. Purity enters the world in the person of Siegfried, is stained, and must be cleansed. In this sense all mythical material is tragic and all tragic material must become mythical. The path away from guilt is the Christian one: sacrifice. Siegfried gives up his sword and thus gains greater strength. Thus, the return home becomes a return to the ultimate source, and departure becomes a quest for eternity. The play, which seems to have been written for the future, is written in a peculiar verse form, the speech being of the strictest simplicity. In his last work, *Jeanne d'Arc* (1956), Mell applies his principle of strict form to this frequently used plot. The action is concentrated on the last phases of the trial at Rouen—on Jeanne's recantation and on the recantation of her recantation. By inventing two characters who are merely hinted at in the documents, an English lawyer and a French lady, who both consider Jeanne innocent at first, Mell for the first time makes a Christian interpretation possible: these two characters experience the process of sanctification (for Jeanne is Purity come into the world, which must return to its original source): "This world, into which we have been put, is terrible. One consolation is that it cannot prevent saints from growing on it." Mell's theater is anti-illusionistic in that it favors the greatest possible strictness of form. The contra-reality which he presents is for him the true reality itself.

MICHAEL, Friedrich, b. 1892, German novelist and dramatist. Wrote the delicate comedies *Der blaue Strohhut* (1942); *Grosse Welt* (1943); *Ausflug mit Damen* (1946, Continuation of the Amphitryon theme. Jupiter, accompanied by Juno and Iris, visits the widow Alkmene on the 20th birthday of Hercules).

MICHALKOV, Sergei, b. 1913, Russian dramatist. Soviet Academy. "In his plays are the aphoristic character of his fables, a gay humor, and angry, sharp satire." *I Want To Go Home* (1949); *Ilya Golovin* (1949, a "formalist" composer repents); *Sombrero* (1956).

MICINSKI, Tadeusz, 1873-1919, Polish lyric poet and dramatist. Poetic theater: *Count Potemkin; Queen Teofanu.*

MILLAY, Edna St. Vincent, 1892-1950, American poet and dramatist. *The Princess Marries the Page* (1918, one-act); *Aria da Capo* (1919, one-act); *The Lamp and the Bell* (1921); *Launzi* (1923, from Ferenc Molnar); *The King's Henchman* (1927, opera libretto with music by Deems Taylor).

MILLER, Arthur, b. 1915, American dramatist of the post-World War II generation. Chief representative of American realism, has attempted departures from realism. Themes of social criticism raised to a universal human level. Early drama: *The Man Who Had All the Luck* (1944). First international success: *All My Sons* (1947. Family drama in manner of Ibsen with widespread ramifications. The father, an armaments manufacturer in the second World War, has caused the death of many pilots by delivering faulty goods. He shoots himself when he learns that one of his sons, a flyer, has deliberately crashed his machine on hearing of his father's crime.). *Death of a Salesman* (1949. Subtitled, "Certain Private Conversations in Two Acts and a Requiem": the tragedy of an American travelling salesman who, although discharged from his job because of old age and lack of sales, attempts to maintain his family life with illusions. He has two sons whom he has brought up to believe in the dream world he has created for himself. Neither has turned out to be any good at anything. Nothing that they or their father attempt to do succeeds. The salesman decides to choose the one last way out: he will die "accidentally" and the family will collect the $20,000 life insurance. The Requiem: at the grave the dead man's neighbor speaks of the dream of the travelling salesman, who rides "on a smile and a shoeshine." His wife speaks the shatteringly ambiguous words, "We're free . . . We're free . . ." over the grave. Anti-illusionistic technique with flashbacks, dream scenes, hallucinations, supernatural insertions into reality, and revelation of reality as seeming.); *The Crucible* (1952. The historical persecution of the "witches of Salem" who escaped from the oppressiveness of Puritanical society by conducting nocturnal orgies. Together with many innocent people they are persecuted with horrible vindictiveness by the Puritans. The plot revolves around a wife who is accused and sentenced as a witch and her husband who "confesses" in order to die with her. Miller: "The witch hunt was a perverse manifestation of the panic which set in among all classes when the balance began to turn toward greater individual freedom." Thereupon he goes on to draw the natural parallel with witch hunts of our own day. "When one rises above the individual villainy displayed, one can only pity them all, just as we shall be pitied someday. It is still impossible for man to organize his social life without repressions, and the balance has yet to be struck between order and freedom." The application of these remarks to the facts of present intolerance is obvious.); *A View from the Bridge* (1955, revised 1957. Tragedy set among New York dock workers and illegal immigrants. A model of a theoretically based social drama written in the Greek manner. An attorney who "views from the

bridge" is used as a commentator on the action in the manner of a Greek chorus. Miller said he could have written a play in which he interpreted the "hero's antecedent life forces—his relationships to his parents, his uncles, his grandmother, and the incident in his life which, when revealed toward the end of the second act, is clearly what drove him inevitably to his disaster. But as many times as I have been led backward into Eddie's life, 'deeper' into the subjective forces that made him what he evidently is, a counter-impulse drew me back. It was a sense of form, the shape of this work. . . . What struck me first about this tale when I heard it one night in my neighborhood was how directly, with what breathtaking simplicity, it did evolve. It seemed to me, finally, that its very bareness, its absolutely unswerving path, its exposed skeleton, so to speak, was its wisdom and even its charm and must not be tampered with. . . . When I heard this tale first it seemed to me that I had heard it before, very long ago. After a time I thought that it must be some re-enactment of a Greek myth which was ringing a long-buried bell in my own subconscious mind. . . . The thought has often occurred to me that the two 'submarines,' the immigrants who come to Eddie from Italy, set out, as it were, two thousand years ago."); *A Memory of Two Mondays* (1955. Miller: ". . . a pathetic comedy; a boy works among people for a couple of years, shares their troubles, their victories, their hopes, and when it is time for him to be on his way he expects some memorable moment, some sign from them that he has been among them, that he has touched them and been touched by them. In the sea of routine that swells around them they barely note his departure. It is a kind of letter to that sub-culture where the sinews of economy are rooted, that darkest Africa of our society from whose interior only the sketchiest messages ever reach our literature or our stage. . . . After all, from this endless, timeless, will-less environment, a boy emerges who will not accept defeat or its mood as final, and literally takes himself off on a quest for a higher gratification. I suppose we simply do not want to see how empty the lives of so many of us are. . . . The play speaks not of obsession but of rent and hunger and the need for a little poetry in life and is entirely out of date in those respects— so much so that many took it for granted it had been written a long time ago and exhumed.").

Script for the film *The Misfits* (1960); *After the Fall* (1964).

MILNE, A. A., 1882-1956, English novelist and dramatist. Whimsical comedies. *Wurzel Flummery* (1917); *Belinda* (1918); *The Boy Comes Home* (1918); *Make-Believe* (1918); *The Camberley Triangle* (1919); *Mr. Pim Passes By* (1919); *The Romantic Age* (1920); *The Truth About Blayds* (1921); *The Dover Road* (1922); *The Lucky One* (1922); *The Great Broxopp* (1923); *Success* (1923); *To Have the Honour* (1924); *Ariadne* (1925); *Portrait of a Gentleman in Slippers* (1926); *The Ivory Door* (1927); *Miss Marlow at Play* (1927); *The Fourth Wall* (1928); *Michael and Mary* (1929); *Toad of Toad Hall* (1930, adaptation); *Other People's Lives* (1932); *Miss Elizabeth Bennet* (1936); *Sarah Simple* (1937); *Gentleman Unknown* (1938).

MIRBEAU, Octave, 1848-1917, French novelist and dramatist. Satirical critic of bourgeois life. *L'Epidémie* (1897, *The Epidemic*, one-act. A political gathering in a provincial town.); *Les mauvais Bergers* (1897, labor vs. capital.); *Les Affaires sont les affaires* (1903, *Business is Business*. Portrait of a business man); *Le Foyer* (1908, with Thadée Natanson. Attack on professional philanthropists).

MISHIMA, Yukio, b. 1925, Japanese dramatist. Has attained international success with the modern Noh-plays, *The 1000 Nights; The Dream Cushion;* and the five such plays (1950-55) which have been translated: *Sotoba Komachi, The Damask Drum; Kantan; The Lady Aoi; Honja.* Also *Azaleas in the Morning Sun* (1957).

MITCHELL, Langdon, 1862-1935, American dramatist. Early attempt at realistic portrayal of society. *The New York Idea* (1906); and others.

MLADENOVIC, Ranko, 1893-1947, Serbian dramatist. Wrote plays of social criticism, e.g., *Fear of Truth* (1937).

MOBERG, Vilhelm, b. 1898, Swedish novelist and dramatist. His plays deal with current problems; also wrote folk comedies. *The Wife* (1929); *Violence* (1933); *Widower Jarl* (1940); *Man's Woman* (1941, based on his novel and translated as *Fulfillment*); *Our Unborn Son* (1946); *Ride This Night* (1946, from his novel); *The Judge* (1957, tragicomedy); *The Night Waiter* (1961); *The Fairytale Prince* (1961).

MOERS, Hermann, b. 1930, German dramatist. *Zur Zeit der Distelblüte* (1959. Kafkaesque play about prison life); *Im Haus der Riesen* (1961); *Beginn der Badesaison* (1961. Comedy); *Der Klinkenputzer* (1963).

MOLNAR, Ferenc, 1878-1952, Hungarian comedy writer. His plays possess all aspects of the boulevard play, but every so often his poetic inspiration (mostly of an ironic nature) enables the plays to break out of the routine path. The allegorical play, *The Devil* (1907, translated), was followed in 1909 with the world famous *Liliom* (translated, basis of Rodgers' and Hammerstein's musical *Carousel*. Fairground milieu with Liliom as a carnival employee and friend of a jealous carousel owner. He falls in love with a housemaid, loses his job, and then falls in love with the maid when she leaves her job for his sake despite his warnings. He marries Julie and turns over a new leaf. They live in a hut, but when Liliom finds himself unable to get work he begins to mistreat his wife in his fury at his own ineffectiveness. The "Prater," or fairground, calls to him again. Julie tells him she is pregnant. He is happy at the news, but feels the necessity of earning money more than ever. During an unsuccessful attempt at robbery, Liliom and an accomplice are surprised by the police. The accomplice escapes, but Liliom stabs himself to avoid capture. He dies, after a farewell scene with Julie. At his trial in Heaven, Liliom is sentenced to 16 years purgatorial fire. Once he has expiated he will be permitted to spend one more day on earth. When the day comes around he behaves as impossibly as ever: his wife and sixteen-year-old daughter throw him out and the Heavenly Police come and take him away again.); *The Guardsman* (1910, translated. Typically erotic piquancy: an actor disguises himself as a guardsman in order to seduce his wife and wonders whether she has recognized him); *The Tale of the Wolf* (1912, translated, dream play: a wife, who is constantly nagged by a pedantic husband suffering from a jealousy mania, falls asleep and dreams of four men, four idols, with whom she has affairs. At the end there is a return to reality, seen through the newly acquired perspective of the dream's irony.); *The Swan* (1914; translated. About royalty); *Fashions for Men* (1915; translated); *Carnival* (1917; translated); *The Glass Slipper* (1925; translated); *One, Two, Three* (1926, also translated as *President;* one act. For Max Pallenberg); *The Play's the Thing* (1926; translated. An actor is overheard making love to a girl while they are both guests at a castle. Two comedy writers hastily set about saving him by writing a play which contains such a scene: the overheard scene becomes thus merely an innocent rehearsal. The irony lies in the two-edged joke: first, the scene, performed and repeated, has an endlessly banal effect; second, the piece begins precisely according to the rules for writing a successful play and follows through in the same manner throughout.); *Riviera* (1927, translated); *Olympia* (1928, translated. A comedy of royalty); *The Good Fairy* (1930, translated); *Arthur* (1931, translated); *Waxworks* (1944, translated); and others.

MONTHERLANT, Henry de, b. 1896, French poet, novelist, and dramatist. One of the last adherents of the strict style in drama. Aristocractic pessimism, extreme severity, heroism based on contempt for the world. *L'Exil* (1929); *Pasiphae* (1936); *La Reine morte* (1942; *Queen after Death*. Subtitled *How to Kill Women*. King Ferrante has the morganatic wife of his son murdered. Why? For reasons of state or for the preservation of the purity of the blood-line? No. The motivation is neither idealistic nor ideological. The king's motives are to be found in the depths of the unconscious. Lenormand: "His soul seems to sink into the peacefulness of the mire. It is full of corruption, but satiated."); *Fils de personne* (1943, *No Man's Son*); *Un Incompris* (1943); *Malatesta* (1946, translated, same title. Renaissance tragedy about Cesare Borgia); *Le Maître de Santiago* (1947, *The Master of Santiago*. The asceticism of a Spanish grandee who forces his daughter to give up her engagement and enter a convent in order to guard her purity from the corruption of the world); *Demain il fera jour* (1949; *Tomorrow the Dawn*, sequel to *Fils de personne*); *Celles qu'on prend dans ses bras* (1950. Topical play; five characters; the tribulations of love); *La Ville dont le prince est un enfant* (1951); *Port Royal* (1954; translated, same title. The famous convent which was a victim of the struggle over Jansenisim. Under the leadership of Mother Angelique, the nuns, motivated by faith, take upon themselves the persecution which runs through church and state. As always, Montherlant is not interested here in the conflicting arguments, with the pro and con of the Church's problems, but with the readiness of certain persons to behave in the heroic manner.); *Brocéliande* (1956); *Don Juan* (1958); *La Cardinal d'Espagne* (1960).

MORAVIA, Alberto, b. 1907, Italian novelist. Dramatization of his novel, *La Mascherata* (1954. Tragicomedy about the dictator of an imaginary republic, from the novel *The Fancy-Dress Ball*); Renaissance tragedy, *Beatrice Cenci* (1957. Tragedy of boredom as the new ground for Francesco Cenci's crimes: he rapes his daughter out of *ennui*); *Il Provino* (1955, one-act).

MORGAN, Charles, 1894-1958, English novelist, dramatist, and drama critic. Wrote topical plays: *The Flashing Stream* (1938. In a secret naval laboratory the entrance of the commander's wife into the world of men causes confusion.); *The River Line* (1952. Drama of the French Resistance); *The Burning Glass* (1954. The burning glass is a monstrous invention; the play asks whether such a discovery should be handed over to the politicians.).

MORTIMER, John, b. 1923, English novelist and dramatist. *The Dock Brief* (1957, one-act); *What Shall We Tell Caroline?* (1958, one-act); *The Wrong Side of the Park* (1960); *Lunch Hour* (1960, one-act); *Two Stars for Comfort* (1962); and others.

MOSTAR, Gerhart Hermann, b. 1901, German journalist and dramatist. *Der Zimmerherr* (1945); *Bis der Schnee schmilzt* (1947); *Putsch in Paris* (1948); *Die Geburt* (1948, mystery play); *Meier Helmbrecht* (1949).

MÜLLER, Artur, b. 1909, German dramatist. *Oliver Cromwell* (1936); *Didos Tod* (1937); *Demetrius* (1938); *Fessel und Schwinge* (1939); *Im Namen der Freiheit* (1949); *Wacht auf, Verdammte dieser Erde* (1950); *Admiral Canaris* (1952); *Francois Cenodoxus, Doktor von Paris* (1950); *Die letzte Patrouille* (1958).

MÜLLER, Heiner, b. 1928, East German dramatist. Together with Inge Müller he wrote two plays which are considered models of Socialist Realism: *Der Lohndrücker* and *Die Korrektur* (1958). *Also* wrote *Spartakus* (1959), *Klettwitzer Bericht* (1959); *Die lustigen Weiber von Sternberg* (1960); *Die Umsiedlerin* (1960).

MUNK, Kai, 1898-1944 (shot by the Gestapo), Danish clergyman and dramatist. Wrote plays of a Christian-humanist cast. *An Idealist* (1928, translated as *Herod the King*); *In the Breakers* (1929); *Cant* (1931, translated; about Henry VIII); *The Word* (1932, translated. Folk play about a miracle which increases belief); *Victory* (1937, Mussolini in Ethiopia); *He Sits at the Melting-Pot* (1938, translated; against anti-Semitism); *Niels Ebbesen* (1942, play about national freedom in historical guise); *Before Cannae* (1945, translated, one-act); and others.

MUNRO, C. K., b. 1889, English dramatist. *Wanderers* (1915); *The Rumour* (1922); *At Mrs. Beam's* (1923); *Progress* (1924); *Storm* (1924); *The Mountain* (1926); *Cocks and Hens* (1927); *Veronica* (1928); *Mr. Eno* (1930); *Bluestone Quarry* (1931); *Bletheroe* (1931); *The True Woman* (1932); *Ding & Co.* (1934); *Coronation at Mrs. Beam's* (1938).

MURRAY, T. C., 1873-1959, Irish dramatist. Realistic studies of Irish peasant life. *The Wheel of Fortune* (1909, revised as *Sovereign Love*, 1913); *Birthright* (1910); *Maurice Harte* (1912); *Spring* (1918); *Aftermath* (1922); *Autumn Fire* (1924); *The Pipe in the Fields* (1927); *The Blind Wolf* (1928); *A Flutter of Wings* (1930); *Michaelmas Eve* (1932); *A Spot in the Sun* (1938); *Illumination* (1939), and others.

MUSIL, Robert, 1880-1942, Austrian writer, famous through his novel, *Der Mann ohne Eigenschaften*. In 1921 he wrote the play *Die Schwärmer* (problems of marriage among intellectuals with different psychologies) and in 1923 the farce *Vincenz und die Freundin bedeutender Männer*.

NALKOWSKA, Zofia, 1885-1954, Polish novelist. *House of Women* (1930, marriage drama); *The Day of His Return* (1931); *Rensata Sluczanska* (1935, dramatization of a novel).

NASH, N. Richard, b. 1916, American dramatist. Early plays: *Second Best Bed* (1946); *The Young and Fair* (1948); *See the Jaguar* (1952). International success with *The Rainmaker* (1954, a "romantic comedy"). Also wrote *Girls of Summer* (1956, comedy); *Handful of Fire* (1958), *Wildcat* (1960, musical).

NEUMANN, Alfred, 1895-1952, German novelist and dramatist of the post-World War I generation. *Der Patriot* (1926. Count Pahlen kills the insane Czar Paul I and then commits suicide because he was unable to keep his promise to the Czarevitch not to kill the Czar); *Königsmaske* (1928); *Frauenschuh* (1929); *Haus Danieli* (1930); *Viele heissen Kain* (1944).

NEVEUX, Georges, b. 1900, French dramatist. Surrealist. *Juliette* (1929); *Le Bureau central des rêves* (1930); *Zamore* (1934); *Plainte contre inconnu* (1946); *Le Système deux* (1955); *Le Chien du jardinier* (1955, from Lope de Vega); *La Voleuse de Londres* (1960).

NICOLAI, Aldo, b. 1920, Italian dramatist. *Teresina e il cantastoria* (1954); *Ciao Albergo!* (1955); *La ballata del soldato Piccio* (1955); *Avventura di cronaca* (1956); *Ricci di mare* (1956); *La stagione delle albicocche* (1959).

NIJHOFF, Martinus, 1894-1953, Dutch dramatist. *Pierrot at the Lantern* (1916); *The Flying Dutchman* (1930, festival play for marine production); *An Idyll, Protesilaos and Laodamia* (1940); *The Holy Wood* (1940-43. Three plays for Christmas, Easter, and Whitsuntide). Has translated Euripides, Shakespeare, Eliot, Ramuz.

NIKOLAIEVIC, Dusan, 1885-1961, Serbian dramatist. Plays of social criticism, e.g., *Volga, Volga* (1935).

NOAK, Christian, b. 1927, German dramatist of the post-World War II generation: *Marie Antoinette* (1953); *Hafen der Dämmerung* (1954); *Rauch über den Gärten* (1956, burlesque).

NOSSACK, Hans Erich, b. 1901, German novelist and dramatist. *Die Rotte Kain* (1949); *Die Hauptprobe* (1956, burlesque).

NOWACZYNSKI, Adolf, 1876-1944, Polish journalist and dramatist. *Czar Dmitri* (1908); *The Great Frederick* (1910); *War for War* (1928); *Spring of Nations* (1929); *Caesar and Man* (1937, Cesare Borgia and Copernicus).

NUGENT, Elliott, b. 1900, American actor and dramatist. Collaborated with his father, J. C. Nugent, on *Kempy* (1922); *The Poor Nut* (1925); and other plays. *The Male Animal* (1940, with James Thurber); *A Place of Our Own* (1945).

OBEY, André, b. 1892, French dramatist. Known especially for his biblical drama *Noé* (1931, Noah; poetic theater) and his play about Iphigenia, *Une Fille pour du vent* (1952). Also wrote *La Viol de Lucrèce* (1931, adapted by Wilder as *Lucrece*); *La Bataille de la Marne* (1931); *Venus et Adonis* (1933); *Revenu de l'étoile* (1939); *Maria* (1946); *Oedipe* (1948); *Lazare* (1951); *Les trois Coups de minuit* (1958); and others. Adapted Reginald Rose's *Twelve Angry Men* as *Douze Hommes en colère* (1958).

OBOLER, Arch, b. 1907, American dramatist. *Night of the Auk* (1955); and others. Prolific writer of radio plays.

O'CASEY, Sean, b. 1884, Irish dramatist. Began his career with sensational tragi-comic dramas about Anglo-Irish strife, which were as critical of the Irish as of the English. Later turned to pro-Communist drama and still later to criticisms of social conventionality. *The Robe of Rosheen* (published 1918, one-act); *The Shadow of a Gunman* (1923); *Cathleen Listens In* (1923; one-act); Juno and the Paycock (1924, tragicomedy of the Irish rebellion); *Nannie's Night Out* (1924, one-act); *The Plough and the Stars* (1926); *The Silver Tassie* (published 1928, performed 1929. Anti-war satire, partly in expressionistic style); *Within the Gates* (1934); two one-act plays published in *Windfalls* (1934): *The End of the Beginning* and *A Pound On Demand; The Star Turns Red* (1940); *Purple Dust* (published 1940, performed 1945); *Red Roses for Me* (published 1942, acted 1943) *Oak Leaves and*

Lavender (published 1946, performed 1947); *Cock-a-doodle Dandy* (performed 1949); *The Hall of Healing* (1951, one-act); *Bedtime Story* (1951, one-act); *Time To Go* (1951, one-act); *The Bishop's Bonfire* (1955); *The Drums of Father Ned* (1959); three one-act plays published in 1961: *Behind the Green Curtains, Figuro in the Night, The Moon Shines on Kylinamoe.*

O'CONNOR, Frank, b. 1903, Irish short story writer and dramatist. Contributed four plays to the Abbey Theatre of Dublin, of which he was a director: *In the Train* (1937, from his short story. One-act.); *The Invincibles* (1937, with Hugh Hunt); *Moses' Rock* (1938, with Hugh Hunt); *Time's Pocket* (1938).

ODETS, Clifford, 1906-1963, American dramatist. Social critic, strongly aggressive, but with tendencies towards the poetizing of realism. *Awake and Sing!* (1935. Jewish middle-class family in New York; its unsuccessful attempt to overcome its miseries); *Waiting for Lefty* (1935. Left-wing one-act play about the New York taxi strike); *Till the Day I Die* (1935, anti-Nazi play); *Paradise Lost* (1935); *Golden Boy* (1937. Bitter attack on the American worship of success. A violinist is ruined when he becomes a successful boxer.); *Rocket to the Moon* (1938); *Night Music* (1940); *Clash by Night* (1941); *The Big Knife* (1949, attack on Hollywood, based on Odets' own experiences); *The Country Girl* (1950. International success. A wife rehabilitates her alcoholic husband, a famous actor. Retitled *Winter Journey* in England); *The Flowering Peach* (1954. Poetic realism; Noah's fate presented in the life of a Jewish family. Religious elements).

OELSCHLEGEL, Gerd, b. 1926, German author of the post-World War II generation. Realism. *Zum guten Nachbarn* (1954); *Romeo und Julia 1953 in Berlin* (1954); *Die Tödliche Lüge* (1956); *Staub auf dem Paradies* (1957). Advocates "objective theater," theater "in which we re-discover Man, his troubles, his needs, his loneliness, his anxiety, his love, his lies—everything except one thing: his answer."

OGRIZOVIC, Milan, 1877-1923, Croatian dramatist. Wrote the symbolic drama, *The Wish* (1901).

Other plays: *The Decline of the Croatian Kings* (1905); *Years of Love* (1906); *The Curse* (1906); *Hassan Aga's Wife* (1909); *The Death of Czar Diocletian* (1913); *The Zrinjski-Frangepan Tragedy* (1921).

O'HARA, John, b. 1905, American novelist. *Pal Joey* (1940, based on his short stories. Musical, lyrics by Lorenz Hart, music by Richard Rodgers); five plays never professionally produced, published together in 1961: *The Farmers Hotel* (based on his novel); *The Searching Sun; The Champagne Pool; Veronique; The Way It Was.*

OLESHA, Yuri, 1899-1960, Soviet novelist and dramatist. Known especially for *Conspiracy of Feelings* (1927, from his novel, *Envy*). Other plays: *The List of Assets* (1931, translated, drama about an actress); *The Severe Youth* (1932); *The Three Fat Men.* Purged in 1932.

O'NEIL, George, 1898-1940, American poet and dramatist. *American Dream* (1933, panoramic criticism of the American way of life); *Mother Lode* (1934, with Dan Totheroh).

O'NEILL, Eugene, 1888-1954, America's greatest dramatist. One of the revolutionaries of 1910, American pioneer, follower of Strindberg. Nobel Prize. Elevation of social criticism to general criticism of humanity. Attack on American Puritanism, by which, however, he was himself influenced in that he was greatly concerned with the problem of guilt. This problem brought him to the classical tragedies and a consequent attempt to adapt classical themes to modern times.—Experimental efforts: formal disintegration of reality with tricks, e.g., the use of masks or soliloquies. The work of his old age, composed in absolute solitude because he suffered from a rare ailment resembling Parkinson's disease, is a personal synthesis of all his philosophical and spiritual experiences. Deep pessimism together with a deep belief in the power of human opposition to fate.—Early period: Sea plays (collected as *S.S. Glencairn*); *The Web* (written 1913, published 1914); *Bound East for Cardiff* (written 1914, performed 1916); *The Moon of the Caribbees* (performed 1918. Drunken, frustrated sailors in the tropical night).—Second (Strindberg) period: *Beyond the Horizon* (1920. A woman between two

brothers; all three ruin their lives); *Exorcism* (1920, one-act); *Diff'rent* (1920); *The Straw* (1921); *Gold* (1921); *Anna Christie* (1921, first produced the previous year as *Chris Christopherson*. A decayed sea captain meets his daughter, with whom he has not concerned himself for years. She has meanwhile, as the audience learns, become a whore. Unaware of this, he takes her aboard his coal barge, where a stoker, a primitive but honest man, falls in love with her. When he proposes marriage to her, she tells him about her past. The father blames everything on "dat ole davil sea," by which, however, he himself is completely enslaved. For Anna Christie men in general are to blame, especially her father, though her lover is not excepted either. Both of them try to talk themselves out of their share of the guilt, but they have a dream of a better life, and it is with this that O'Neill leaves them to find the way.); *The First Man* (1922); *Welded* (1924).—Third (experimental) period: *The Emperor Jones* (1920, expressionistic play. The monologue of a Negro during his flight through the jungle. He is a former Pullman porter who has made himself emperor of an island. The sounds of the forest drive him into a state of hysterical anxiety. He sees visions.); *The Hairy Ape* (1922. A primitive, barbaric stoker on a ship feels himself insulted by a representative of the "better people" and tries to revenge himself. He frees a gorilla from the zoo in order to unite with him, but is instead crushed by the animal. Expressionistic.); *Desire under the Elms* (1924, rural tragedy. Love vs. the lust for possession); *All God's Chillun Got Wings* (1924. Doomed love and marriage between a Negro and a white woman.); *The Fountain* (1925); *The Great God Brown* (1926, drama with masks. Reflects the falsity of our existence. When the characters put on their masks, their fellows love and honor them, but as soon as they take them off, they become rejected. O'Neill contrasts two extreme types: the artist and the businessman. The latter is envious of the artist's success with women. After the artist's death the businessman puts on his mask and lives a double life with the wife and mistress of the dead man. Finally the police shoot him.); *Marco Millions* (1928, history. Prologue: A glass coffin is brought in. It contains the body of an extremely beautiful woman, who, we are told, has been deeply injured by a Venetian: it is the

Queen of Persia who is being taken back to the kingdom of her father Kublai Khan. The various stages of Marco Polo's journey to China in 1271 follow. Kublai Khan, at whose court the warrior has almost nothing to say and the scholar speaks instead of the priest, shows favor to the young man. Marco, however, behaves like an American boy, worshipping the ideals of conformity—business, prudery, and "keep smiling!" What is happiness? Self-justification, self-satisfaction! Marco does not notice that the princess is in love with him. She stabs herself: "I implored an ox to see my soul! I no longer can endure the shame of living." Marco Polo: "I never believed people—some people—ever seriously tried" to commit suicide. So the princess dies. As the lights go up in the auditorium, O'Neill has a man get up from the front row of seats, yawning noisily: it is Marco Polo. For a moment he was "not a little irritated. . . . His face begins to clear of all disturbing memories of what had happened on the stage. The noise, the lights of the streets, recall him at once to himself. Impatiently he waits for his car, casting a glance here and there at faces in the groups around him, his eyes impersonally speculative, his bearing stolid with the dignity of one who is sure of his place in the world. . . . Marco Polo, with a satisfied sigh at the sheer comfort of it all, resumes his life."); *Strange Interlude* (1928. A woman torn between several men. The impermanence of emotions. Experiment: the characters speak their thoughts in soliloquies.); *Lazarus Laughed* (1928, revival of Mystery play); *Dynamo* (1929. God is dead; the dynamo is God); *Mourning Becomes Electra* (1931. Adaptation of the *Oresteia* to fit an American family of the Civil War. Three parts in the manner of the classical trilogy. 1. "Homecoming," 4 acts: General Mannon/Agamemnon returns home from the war and learns that his wife, Christine/Clytemnestra, loves Capt. Brant/Aegisthus. Lavinia/Electra hates her mother; but her moral accusations are caused only by suppressed jealousy. Christine poisons her husband. Lavinia swears revenge. 2. "The Hunted," 5 acts: Orin Mannon/Orestes comes home from the war and learns from Lavinia what has happened. His love for his mother is turned to hate: he kills the captain and forces his mother to kill herself. 3. "The Haunted," 4 acts: Lavinia's transformation. The curse of guilt. The son kills himself, but Lavinia

determines to do penance: she will wear mourning all her life. She has the windows sealed and retires into the accursed house in order to be alone with the ghosts of her guilt.); *Ah, Wilderness!* (1933, A comedy of youth); *Days Without End* (1934, two actors play the two souls of one man.).—Last (illness) period: *Long Day's Journey into Night* (Written 1940-41, posthumously produced, 1956. Autobiographical. Takes place in the country house of an actor whose wife has only recently been released from a mental institution. She has been a drug addict and is about to become one again because she cannot cope with the conditions of her life. The long day's journey into night is the revelation of the past. It is the husband's fault: he is pathologically miserly. The lives of his two sons are also completely ruined. One of them, a drunkard and good-for-nothing, lives off his father. The other, a poet and sailor, is, as we soon learn, incurably sick with tuberculosis. In the last scene the father and the sons pass judgment on each other and on themselves. They attack each other and then become reconciled. One of them says the important thing is the tiny margin of love above the mass of hate. The mother, who has become sick again, has reverted to childhood in her flight from reality. Here again realism is raised to the philosophical level by the Puritan question of guilt. The particular case stands for all our lives and hopelessness.); *The Iceman Cometh* (Written 1939, performed 1946. A waterfront saloon, reminiscent of Gorki's "lower depths," in which down-and-outs gather. Their desires and illusions have been stimulated by a "prophet" who turns out to be a murderer. A parable of Man's hopeless struggle.); *A Moon for the Misbegotten* (Written 1943, performed 1947, Romeo and Juliet in the bitterness of modern times. A small farm, an alcoholic father, his daughter, and a young man who is courting her. Once, one night—Act II—the moon shines for the misbegotten; once, one night, they speak all their dreams—purity, blessedness, Elysium—and when it is all over, the next morning, when they have to go back to work and everyday life, it still remains as some illusion that once was.); *A Touch of the Poet* (Written approximately 1947; first performed in Stockholm, 1957. Like all of O'Neill's later dramas, this is a variation on the theme of real and dream life. The play is about the attempt of Cornelius Melody, a poor Irish innkeeper near Boston in 1828, to live the dream life of an officer and gentleman, hero of the Battle of Talavera, in the face of reality and the mockery of his family and friends, who consider him either insane or ridiculous. Melody's frustration seems to end comically: he ends up in the tavern where he will "jine the Democrats, and I'll vote for Andy Jackson, the friend of the common men like me." A terrible testament could be hidden here: what is all poetry, the old, lonely, sick poet complains, if it is not like Con Melody's dream—swagger, madness, idiocy, nonsense? That is what it is—measured against reality, which we can endure only if we are like everyone else, if we submit ourselves to a dictatorship of Everyman and substitute the norm for the dream. Unlike Ibsen and Shaw, O'Neill draws no conclusions. He says only that men will always have some among them who will have their dreams and who will then come to grief because of their dreams.); *Hughie* (Written 1941, one-act. First performed, Stockholm, 1958. A two-character play, in which only one person really speaks: Erie, a poor hanger-on who considers himself a man of the world. Every night when he came home to his shabby Broadway hotel he used to tell stories of his imaginary adventures and successes to Hughie, the night desk clerk. Now Hughie is dead and has been replaced by a new desk clerk. Will he listen to Erie as Hughie did? He will. Hard of hearing and dead for sleep he "listens" to Erie's vaporings. Erie has found a new Hughie. Illusions are the last resort in the tragic lives of the lonely down-and-outs.). The director of the Swedish State Theater in Stockholm, K. R. Gierow, who has been permitted to examine O'Neill's posthumous works by his widow, has the following to say about them: *The Iceman Cometh, A Moon for the Misbegotten,* and *Long Day's Journey into Night* are parts of an autobiographical cycle. *A Touch of the Poet* belongs to a historical cycle designed to show 150 years of American history; a large fragment of this cycle, entitled *More Stately Mansions* (performed in Stockholm 1962), also exists. A scenario for a long drama has the American automobile industry as its theme; another gives the plan of a Mystery play about Christ and the Devil. According to O'Neill's widow, a number of manuscripts were destroyed at the request of the dramatist.

OSBORN, Paul, b. 1901, American dramatist. *Hotbed* (1928); *A Ledge* (1929); *The Vinegar Tree* (1930); *Oliver Oliver* (1934); *On Borrowed Time* (1938, from a novel by Lawrence Watkins. Death is up in an apple tree and cannot come down. Realistic fairy tale.); *Morning's at Seven* (1939); *The Innocent Voyage* (1943, from Richard Hughes' novel); *A Bell for Adano* (1944, from John Hersey's novel); *Point of No Return* (1951, from J. P. Marquand's novel); *Maiden Voyage* (1957); *The World of Suzie Wong* (1958, based on a novel by Richard Mason).

OSBORNE, John, b. 1929, English dramatist of the post-World War II generation. International success with *Look Back in Anger* (1956). Earlier plays: *The Devil Inside Him* (1950, with Stella Linden, performed outside London); *Personal Enemy* (1955, with Anthony Creighton, performed outside London); *Epitaph for George Dillon* (written before *Look Back in Anger* with Creighton, but not performed until 1958. A preliminary study of an angry young man possibly of an autobiographical nature—the protagonist is an actor and dramatist. Thanks to the motherly feelings of a secretary in an office where he had worked briefly he is introduced into a typical London middle-class family circle. Although he has a clear insight into the drabness of this family's life, he imposes upon them mercilessly. After his return from a stay in a tuberculosis sanitarium he finally achieves success. The family holds a celebration for him, but he is more alone than ever, for what he wrote was a betrayal, and the daughter of the family, whom he must marry, is in fact a worse choice than the wife who has left him, a Communist intellectual who saw through him.). *Look Back in Anger* is typical of the non-conformity and the contradictory attitude of the younger generation. The hero, however, is in no way idealized—quite the contrary. He revenges himself on the bourgeoisie by marrying one of their women and tormenting her. Even though the author clearly favors his opinions, this hero is extremely unpleasant. When his wife becomes pregnant she goes back to her family, where she loses the child. Meanwhile the young man consoles himself with his wife's friend, who takes her "place at the ironing board" and her place elsewhere as well but leaves him when the wife comes back. The play, which appears to owe much to Ibsen's technique, is raised to the symbolic level by the device of repeating the events of the first two acts in the third act. In *The Entertainer* (1957) the hero is again at the same time negative and tragic: a third-class music-hall star who attempts to conceal the failure of his professional and family life with false joviality and alcohol. Even more than in the previous play the author tries to achieve a form which will emphasize his intentions. He used the music-hall conventions in order to eliminate the restrictions of the naturalistic theater. *The World of Paul Slickey* (1959, musical satire against the sensational press.); *Luther* (1961, Brechtian historical drama about Martin Luther); *Plays for England* (1962, two one-act plays critical of English life—*The Blood of the Bambergs* and *Under Plain Cover*).

OULD, Herman, 1886-1951, English dramatist. *Between Sunset and Dawn* (1913); *Christmas Eve* (1919); *The Black Virgin* (1922, moral corruption in Germany after World War I), and others.

PAGNOL, Marcel, b. 1895, French dramatist. Satires and folk plays. Began with verse dramas, e.g., *Catulle* (1922); then wrote topical satires: *Les Marchands de gloire* (1925, with Paul Nivoix, *Merchants of Glory*); *Monsieur Topaze* (1928, *Topaze*. An international success. The rise of a young teacher who is used as a front man by corrupt elements but finally beats them with their own weapons); *Jazz* (1926). These plays were followed by the poetic folk trilogy *Marius*, which made him world famous: *Marius* (1929, adapted as *Sea Fever* by John van Druten and Auriol Lee and as *Marseilles* by Sidney Howard. Father and son in a Marseilles waterfront saloon. Marius' wanderlust represses his love for his childhood sweetheart Fanny, but, out of jealousy, she makes him declare himself. Fanny's horrified mother demands that they marry after she learns that they have had an affair. With a heavy heart Marius gives up his ship, but Fanny, perceiving that he is sacrificing himself, aids his escape after all.); *Fanny* (1930, translated, same title. Marius' father and Fanny wait for news of Marius. Now that Marius is away, a former admirer of Fanny's is courting her again; she accepts him only after she has confessed to him that she is bearing Marius' child. Marius' father, Cesar,

however, insists on the right of his son, who is expected back in two years, to marry Fanny, but out of regard for the child he gives in. Marius returns when the child is ten months old, and Fanny tells him what has happened. He insists that she return to him. The child becomes sick, and in the general confusion Marius leaves again.); *César* (1936. Fanny's husband is dying, Marius' son is now a student, and the parish priest presses the mother to tell him who his real father is. The son tracks Marius down and finds him operating a garage in Toulon. After many obstacles, chief of which is Fanny's money, which Marius does not want, the play ends happily for the child's sake.). Other plays: *Angèle* (1934); *Toni* (1936); *Regain* (1936); *Madame Aurélie* (1938); *La fille du puisatier* (1940); *Judas* (1944, produced 1955); *La Belle meunière* (1948); *Le Rosier de Madame Husson* (1949); *Manon des sources* (1952), and others.

PAQUET, Alfons, 1881-1944, German dramatist of the post-World War I generation. *Fahnen* (1922, subtitled "Epic drama." A series of scenes dealing with Anarchists in Chicago in 1886. Documentary reporting, called the "first Marxist drama" by Piscator); *Markolph* (1924); *Sturmflut* (1926, utopian drama of the Russian Revolution; allegorical); *William Penn* (1929); *Eleonora Duse* (1929); *Stinchen von der Krone* (1932); *Stein* (1933).

PASO, Alfonso, b. 1926, Spanish dramatist. *El cielo dentro de casa* (1957, *Blue Heaven*); *Catalina no es formal* (1958); *Receta para un crimes* (*Recipe for a Crime*); *Vernaneando* (1963); and others.

PASSEUR, Stève, b. 1899, French dramatist. *Un Bout de fil coupé en deux* (1925); *Traversée de Paris à la nage* (1926); *Pas encore* (1927, directed by Dullin); *A quoi penses-tu?* (1928); *Suzanne* (1929); *L'Acheteuse* (1930); *La Chaîne* (1931); *Les Tricheurs* (1932); *Une vilaine Femme* (1932); *L'Amour gai* (1934); *La Bête noire* (1934); *Je vivrai un grand amour* (1935); *Le Témoin* (1935); *Suzanne* (1936); *Le Normand* (1936); *Le Folle du ciel* (1936); *Le Château de cartes* (1937); *Pacifique* (1937); *Vin du souvenir* (1946), and others.

PATRICK, John, b. 1902, American dramatist. Wrote the war play *The Hasty Heart* (1945. Conflict between friendship, pride, and pity in a jungle army hospital) and the internationally successful comedy *The Teahouse of the August Moon* (1953, from Vern Sneider's novel. The relations between the inhabitants of a Pacific island and the American occupation troops). Other plays: *The Willow and I* (1942); *The Story of Mary Surratt* (1947); *The Curious Savage* (1950); *Lo and Behold* (1951).

PENZOLDT, Ernst, 1892-1955, German story writer and dramatist. Wrote the comedies *Die portugalesische Schlacht* (1931); *Sand* (1931); *So war Herr Brummel* (1933); *Graf Schlabrendorf oder Die verlorenen Schuhe* (1946); *Der gläserne Storch oder Es hat alles sein Gutes* (1950, magic comedy); *Squirrel oder Der Ernst des Lebens* (1953).

PERETZ, Isaac Loeb, 1852-1915, Yiddish short story writer and dramatist. *The Golden Chain* (Performed 1906, published 1907); *A Night in the Old Market* (Published 1907, symbolic drama).

PÉREZ GALDÓS, Benito, 1843-1920, Spanish novelist and dramatist. Realist, with a novelist's special attention to character. *Realidad* (1892, from his novel); *La loca de la casa* (1893); *La de San Quintín* (1894, *The Duchess of San Quentin*); *Doña Perfecta* (1896, from his novel); *Electra* (1901, translated under its original name. A girl's doubts about convent life.); *El abuelo* (1904, *The Grandfather*).

PERZYNSKI, Wodzimierz, 1878-1930, Polish novelist and author of comedies. Achieved his greatest success with *The Prodigal Sister* (1904) and *The Luck of Poor Frank* (1909). Also, *The Ashantee* (1906).

PINGET, Robert, b. 1920, French dramatist. *Lettre morte* (1960, *Dead Letter*); *Ici ou ailleurs* (published 1961, *Clope*); *L'Hypothèse* (published 1961); *La Manivelle* (1962, adapted by Beckett as *The Old Tune*); Architruc (1962).

PINSKI, David, b. 1872, Yiddish novelist, journalist and dramatist. *Isaac Sheftel* (1899); *The Treasure* (1910, directed by Reinhardt in Berlin. Translated. The effects of greed.); *King David and His Wives* (1913-16, a series of short plays, translated.); and others.

PINTER, Harold, b. 1932, English dramatist. Influence of Beckett but in a realistic milieu. *The Birthday Party* (1958); *The Room* (1960, one-act); *The Dumb Waiter* (1960, one-act); *The Caretaker* (1960, an international success); *A Night Out* (1960, television play); *A Slight Ache* (1961, one-act); *The Collection* (1962; one act); and others.

PIRANDELLO, Luigi, 1867-1936, Italian dramatist. Nobel Prize. Representative of the modern Italian theater, revolutionized the presentation of human character on the stage with his more and more complete fusion of appearance and reality. The theme of his great trilogy, which begins with *Six Characters in Search of an Author* and ends with *Tonight We Improvise,* is that what is "played" enters into real life and becomes real action. Anouilh sees in Pirandello the founder of the modern theater; he is in fact the most important inventor of stage characters who have lost their proper qualities and consequently cannot represent any definite personage with precisely describable characteristics. As an anti-illusionist he is less a creator of new scenes than an analyst. Human beings and their milieu have lost the ground beneath their feet in his plays, but the stage world itself is usually held together in the strict form of the act-divided play. Chief themes of Pirandello's middle period: how Man appears to others and above all to himself in an indifferent world; the impossibility of attaining any agreement as to what this or that person is and what *I* am; the depths of the abyss within us in which we are left hanging in this remarkable manner, without knowledge of what we must do—and the consequent impossibility of understanding each other. Pirandello's largely clinical and seemingly "individual" cases are examples of the greater and more general truth that Man does not possess any definite personality based on environment and upbringing nor any static, unchangeable structure, but is rather an indefinite being with blurred edges instead of definite characteristics and a combination of various hardly fathomable possibilities instead of a precise structure. Pirandello's technique in this period is individualistic; it departs from realism because of his concern with the universal elements in his analyses of humanity without bothering himself with the world, the society, or the historical background in which humanity lives.—Pirandello employed the theatrical parable for his theme (appearance and reality) in his trilogy (*Six Characters in Search of an Author, Each in His Own Way, Tonight We Improvise*), thereby attempting to rise into the realm of universals.—The later Pirandello discovered in addition the device of *il mito*—the myth. The social myth: *La nuova colonia;* the religious myth: *Lazzaro;* the myth of motherhood: *La favola del figlio bambiato* (1934); and finally the high point: *I giganti della montagna.*—The most important plays (with dates of first performance): *La morsa* (1910, *The Vise.* One-act.); *Lumíe di Sicilia* (1910, *Sicilian Limes.* One-act.); *Il dovere del medico* (1913, *The Doctor's Duty.* One-act.); *Liolà* (1916, translated, same title); *Così è (se vi pare)* (1917, *Right You Are, If You Think So.* A problem in knowledge but also a lesson in kindness.); *Il berretto a sonagli* (1917); *La giara* (1917, *The Jar.* One-act); *Il piacere dell'onestà* (1917, *The Pleasure of Honesty*); *Ma non è una cosa seria* (1918); *Il gioco delle parti* (1918, *The Rules of the Game*); *L'uomo, la bestia e la virtù* (1919, *Man, Beast, and Virtue,* also called *Say It with Flowers*); *Tutto per bene* (1920); *Come prima, meglio di prima* (1920); *La Signora Morli, una e due* (1920); *Sei personaggi in cerca d'autore* (1921, *Six Characters in Search of an Author.* Fantasy that comments on the art of the theater and the irrationality of human behavior.); *Enrico IV* (1922, *Henry IV.* A man in flight from reality.); *Vestire gli ignudi* (1922, *Naked* or *To Clothe the Naked*); *L'uomo dal fiore in bocca* (1923, *The Man with the Flower in His Mouth.* One-act.); *La vita che ti diedi* (1923, *The Life I Gave You*); *Ciascuno a suo modo* (1924, *Each in His Own Way*); *Diana e la Tuda* (1927, *Diana and Tuda*); *L'amica delle mogli* (1927, *The Wives' Friend*); *La nuova colonia* (1928, *The New Colony*); *O di uno o di nessuno* (1929); *Lazzaro* (1929, *Lazarus*); *Come tu mi vuoi* (1930, *As You Desire Me*); *Questa sera si recita a soggetto* (1930, *Tonight We Improvise*); *Trovarsi* (1932, *To Find Oneself*); *Quando si è qualcuno* (1933, *When Someone Is Somebody*); *La favola del figlio cambiato* (1934); *Non si sa come* (1935, *No One Knows How*); *I giganti della montagna* (1937, *The Mountain Giants.* Two-act fragment. The last act has been staged by Giorgio Strehler in Milan on the basis of Pirandello's account to his son. The first two acts tell the story of the meeting between a down-and-out troupe of travelling players and the inhabitants of a mysterious house at the foot of a mountain. These people are known as "birds of ill omen": they are people who are considered insane by the world and consequently invent supernatural apparitions in order to keep other people away. Led by a "magician," they live in a world made up of their own fantasies and dreams. In the second act the players, who have acted the "legend of the lost son" without success "down there in the world," are drawn into the fantastic and supernatural world of the mountain people. Ilsa, the star actress, is asked to perform the "legend" for the inhabitants of the villa, but she is reluctant to do so. She wants to go still higher to the "giants of the mountain," the third level of the symbolic action. The giants are the mighty ones of the world, the conquerors of the earth, the powerful realists to whom Beauty means nothing. The plays are unable to win Ilsa back to Beauty, and she is killed by the giants. "But," according to the account given by Pirandello's son, "this does not mean a rejection of poetry; only the poor, fanatical servants of life, to whom the spirit does not speak—though it may speak to them one day—have crushed the servants of Art in their blind rage. These servants of Art are not understood by the masses because they have turned their backs on the life of reality.").

PLIEVIER, Theodor, 1892-1955, German writer of the post-World War I generation. Wrote the revolutionary plays *Des Kaisers Kulis* (1930, mutiny in Kiel) and *Haifische* (1930).

POGODIN, Nikolai, 1900-1962. Soviet dramatist. Wrote many revolutionary dramas and plays of Soviet everyday life. *Tempo* (1930, translated); *The Poem of the Ax* (1931); *My Friend* (1932); *Snow* (1932); *After the Ball* (1934); *The Aristocrats* (1934, translated. Comedy. Forced laborers are rehabilitated and won back to the Party during the building of the White Sea-Baltic Sea Canal. Called a modern Mystery play by Van Gyseghem); *The Man with the Gun* (1937, Lenin in October, 1917; *Gioconda* (1938); *The Silver Ravine* (1939); *The Moth* (1939); *The Chimes of the Kremlin* (1940, translated); *Moscow Nights* (1942); *The Boat Woman* (1943); *A Sentimental Acquaintance*

(1945); *The Creation of the World* (1945); *The Missouri Waltz* (1949, anti-American play); *The Petrarchan Sonnet* (1956); *The Little Student Girl* (1958); *The Third Pathétique* (1958, the last years of Lenin); *Albert Einstein* (1961); and others.

PORTO-RICHE, Georges de, 1849-1930, French dramatist. Analyst of sexual passion. *La Chance de Françoise* (1888, *Francoise' Luck,* one-act.); *L'Amoureuse* (1891, *A Loving Wife*); and others.

POUND, Ezra, b. 1885, American expatriate poet. *The Classic Noh Theatre of Japan* (1916, with Ernest Fenellosa. Essay and translations.); modern version of Sophocles' *Women of Trachis* (1956).

PRIESTLEY, John Boynton, b. 1894, English novelist, journalist, and dramatist. Topical social criticism, symbolic comedies, experiments with the use of time. *Dangerous Corner* (1932); *Laburnum Grove* (1933); *Eden End* (1934); *Time and the Conways* (1937); *I Have Been Here Before* (1937); *Music at Night* (1938); *Johnson over Jordan* (1939); *The Long Mirror* (1940); *They Came to a City* (1943); *Desert Highway* (1943); *An Inspector Calls* (1945); *The Linden Tree* (1947); *A Severed Head* (1963, with Iris Murdoch, from Miss Murdoch's novel); and others.

PRZYBYSZEWSKI, Stanislaus, 1868-1927, founder of Polish modernism. *For Happiness* (1902); *The Golden Fleece* (1902); *The Mother* (1902); *Snow* (1903); and others.

PUGET, Claude-André, b. 1905, French dramatist. Poetic theater. *La Ligne de coeur* (1931); *Les Jours heureux* (1938, adapted as *Happy Days* by Zoë Akins); *Le Coeur volant* (1957); and others.

QUINTERO, Serafín Alvarez, 1871-1938, and Joaquin Alvarez, 1873-1944, authors of about 200 Spanish folk plays, mostly of Andalusian character. Wrote *zarzuelas* (Spanish song plays). Characteristic examples are *Las flores* (1901); *El patio* (1900); *El amor que pasa* (1904, *Love Passes by*); *Mañana de sol* (1905, *A Bright Morning*); *Las de Cain* (1908); *Papa Juan: Centenario* (1909, *A Hundred Years Old*); *Doña Clarines* (1909, translated same title); *Malvaloca* (1912, translated with same title); *Pueblo de las mujeres* (1912, *The Women Have Their Way*); *Fortunato* (1912, trans-

lated same title); *La consuela* (1914, *A Lady from Alfaqueque*). *Concha la limpia* (1924); and others.

RATTIGAN, Terence, b. 1911, English stage writer, comedies, problem plays. *First Episode* (1934); *French without Tears* (1936); *After the Dance* (1939); *Flare Path* (1942); *While the Sun Shines* (1943); *Love in Idleness* (1944, called *O Mistress Mine* in U. S.); *The Winslow Boy* (1946); *Playbill* (*The Browning Version* and *Harlequinade,* 1948); *Adventure Story* (1949); *Who is Sylvia?* (1950); *The Deep Blue Sea* (1952, international success. Concerns a woman who has run away from her husband and now attempts suicide because her lover, an alcoholic flier, misuses her. The second attempt never takes place because a doctor who has been in prison talks her out of it. The scene is a drab apartment in London.); *The Sleeping Prince* (1953); *Separate Tables* (1954, two one-act plays); *Variation on a Theme* (1958); *Ross* (1960, T. E. Lawrence); *Man and Boy* (1963).

RAYNAL, Paul, b. 1890, French dramatist of the post-World War I period. His best known play is *Le Tombeau sous l'Arc de Triomphe* (1924, *The Unknown Warrior.* The experiences of a frontline soldier who has obtained a furlough by volunteering for a certain-death mission). Other plays: *Le Maître de son coeur* (1920); *La Francerie* (1933); *La Matérial humain* (1935, criticism of the stubbornness of the military mind); *Napoléon unique* (1936, comedy about Napoleon and Josephine); *A souffert sous Ponce Pilate* (1939, Judas theme).

REHBERG, Hans, 1901-1963, German dramatist of the post-World War I generation. Frequently produced under Hitler although he does not fill his plays with Nazi propaganda. Sought to create a modern, impersonal historical style. *Cecil Rhodes* (1932) and *Johannes Kepler* (1933) were followed by the Prussian dramas *Der Grosse Kurfürst* (1934); *Friedrich I* (1934); *Friedrich Wilhelm I* (1935); *Kaiser und König* (1936); *Königin Isabella* (1938); *Der Siebenjährige Krieg* (1941); *Heinrich und Anna* (1942); *Karl V* (1943); *Die Wölfe* (1944); *Heinrich VII* (1947); *Cäsar* (1949); *Wallenstein* (1950); *Maria und Elisabeth* (1952); the Atrides dramas, *Der Opfertod* (1953), *Der Gattenmord* (1953), and *Der Muttermord* (1953); *Rembrandt* (1956); *Kleist* (1958); and others.

REHFISCH, Hans José, 1891-1960, German dramatist of the post-World War I period. Scenic reporting and topical criticism. *Heimkehr* (1918, return from the war); *Wer weint um Juckenack* (1924, tragicomedy of the little man); *Nickel und die 36 Gerechten* (1925); *Duell am Lido* (1926); *Der Frauenarzt* (1927); *Die Affäre Dreyfus* (1929, with W. Herzog); *Brest-Litovsk* (1930); *Sprung über Sieben* (1931); *Wasser für Canitoga* (1937, with Egon Eis); *Das ewig Weibliche* (1951); *Lysistrates Hochzeit* (1952); *Der Kassenarzt* (1954); *Oberst Chabert* (1955); *Jenseits der Angst* (1958); *Bumerang* (1960); *Verrat in Rom* (performed 1961); *Jenseits der Angst* (1962). Also: *Apostel der Hexen; Doctor Semmelweis.*

RENARD, Jules, 1864-1910, French novelist and dramatist. *Le Plaisir de rompre* (1897, one-act. The end of a love affair.); *Le Pain de ménage* (1898, one-act); *Poil de carotte* (1900, from his story. One act. Autobiographical: a little boy mistreated by his mother.); *Monsieur Vernet* (1903); *La Bigote* (1909, the family of *Poil de Carotte* again); and others.

RICE, Elmer, b. 1892, American dramatist. Wrote the expressionistic social drama, *The Adding Machine* (1923. In the second part the executed bookkeeper Mr. Zero is seen in a pessimistically conceived "Beyond" where he must always go downwards). Other plays: *On Trial* (1914); *The Subway* (1929); *Street Scene* (1929, Pulitzer Prize); *See Naples and Die* (1929); *The Left Bank* (1931); *Counsellor-at-law* (1931); *We, the People* (1933); *Judgment Day* (1934, the trial following the burning of the Reichstag); *American Landscape* (1938); *Two on an Island* (1940); *Flight to the West* (1940); *A New Life* (1943); *Dream Girl* (1945, international success. Dream world of a young American girl who is not satisfied with the drabness of her real life, but finally manages to contract a realistic marriage); *The Grand Tour* (1951); *Cue for Passion* (1958); *Love among the Ruins* (1963); and others.

RICHARDSON, Jack, b. 1935, American dramatist. *The Prodigal* (1960, reworking of the story of Orestes); *Gallows Humor* (1961, two sardonic, closely connected one-act plays); *Lorenzo* (1963).

RIGGS, Lynn, 1899-1954, American dramatist. Regional dramas of the American Southwest. *Big Lake* (1927); *Two Oklahoma Plays* (*A Lantern to See by; Sump'n Like Wings,* published 1928); *Roadside* (1930); *Green Grow the Lilacs* (1931, basis of the musical *Oklahoma*); *Russet Mantle* (1936); *The Cherokee Night* (Published 1936); *The Lonesome West* (1936); *Four Plays* (*The Year of Pilàr; A World Elsewhere; The Cream in the Well; Dark Encounter,* published 1947).

RITTNER, Tadeusz, 1873-1921, important Polish dramatist, wrote 17 plays, among them *In a Little House* (1904); *Foolish James* (1909); *The Man in the Prompter's Box* (1913); *Wolves in the Night* (1916).

RIVEMALE, Alexandre, b. 1918, French dramatist. International success with the comedy, *L'Elephant dans la maison* (1952, with Henri Colpi). Also wrote *Azouk* (1953); *Nemo* (1958); and others.

ROBINSON, Lennox, 1886-1958, Irish dramatist. General manager of the Irish National Theater Society. Most of his plays produced at the Abbey. *The Clancy Name* (1908, one-act); *The Cross Roads* (1909); *Patriots* (1912); *The Dreamers* (1915); *The Whiteheaded Boy* (1916); *The Lost Leader* (1918); *The Round Table* (1922); *Crabbed Youth and Age* (1922, one-act); *Never the Time and the Place* (1924); *Portrait* (1925); *The White Blackbird* (1926); *The Big House* (1926); *The Far-Off Hills* (1928); *Church Street* (1934); *Killycreggs in Twilight* (1937); *Bird's Nest* (1938).

ROBLÈS, Emmanuel, b. 1913, French novelist and dramatist. Principally known for *Montserrat* (1948, adapted by Lillian Hellman under the same title. Venezuela in 1812. A lieutenant of the Spanish occupation forces betrays his cause—he cannot bring himself to reveal the hiding-place of the resistance leader whom he has helped to escape. Six natives picked at random are shot before his eyes.). Other plays: *La Vérité est morte* (1953); *L'Horloge* (1958); *Porfirio* (1958, burlesque); *Carlotta* (1960).

ROLAND-HOLST, Henriette, 1869-1952, Dutch dramatist. Wrote, among others, *The Rebels* (1910); *Thomas More* (1912); *Michael* (1916); *Children of This Time* (1931); *The Mother* (1932).

ROLLAND, Romain, 1866-1944, French writer, pacifist, and fighter for justice. Nobel Prize. From 1890 on he wrote a series of symbolic-idealistic dramas such as *Empedocles, Niobe, Caligula, Orsino, Saint Louis* (1897), *Aërt* (1898). In 1903 he issued a pamphlet attacking the boulevard theater and proposing a "Theater of the People." Wrote a dramatic cycle dealing with the French Revolution: *Les Loups* (1898, *The Wolves*); *Le Triomphe de la raison* (1899, the Girondists die for their ideas); *Danton* (1900, translated under the same title; the idealist Danton against the cold dogmatist, Robespierre); *Le 14 juillet* (1902, *The Fourteenth of July*, pageant); *Les trois Amourneuses* (1906). Later plays: *Le Jeu de l'amour et de la mort* (1925, *The Game of Love and Death*, drama of idealism in the worst days of the French Revolution); *Paques fleuris* (1927, *Palm Sunday*); *Les Leonides* (1928. Revolutionary emigres settle their factional differences in order to combine against the tyranny of Napoleon). Various others, including the anti-war play *Le Temps viendra* (1903) and *Robespierre* (1938), a partial vindication of the revolutionary.

ROMAINS, Jules, b. 1885, French novelist, comedies and topical satires, particularly the international success, *Knock; ou, Le Triomphe de la médecine* (1923, *Doctor Knock*), in which a country doctor turns his small practice into a gigantic industry though advertising. Other plays: *L'Armée dans la ville* (1911); *Cromedeyre le vieil* (1920, celebrated production by Copeau); *M. Le Trouhadec saisa par le débouche* (1923); *Le Mariage de M. Le Trouhadec* (1925); *Démétrios* (1925); *Le dictateur* (1926); *Musse; ou, L'école de l'hypocrisie* (1930); *Donogoo Tonka; ou, Les Miracles de la science* (1930, *Donogoo*. Second comedy of the triumph of bluff. Donogoo Tonka is an imaginary country); *Le Roi masqué* (1931); *Grâce encore pour la terre* (1942); *L'An mil* (1949); and others.

ROSSMANN, Hermann, b. 1902, German dramatist. Wrote a popular prisoner-of-war play, *Fünf Mann —ein Brot* (1952); *Titanen* (1954); *Mann im Mond* (1955); *Testflug B 29* (1957, about Hiroshima); *Der Dreizehnte* (1958). Has also written a series of plays for amateurs.

ROSTAND, Edmond, 1869-1918, French dramatist. Became world-famous with the romantic verse drama, *Cyrano de Bergerac* (1897, trans. same title. An actor's play in the grand manner); and with *L'Aiglon* (1900, *The Eaglet*. The fate of Napoleon's son). Other plays: *La Princesse lointaine* (1895, *The Faraway Princess*); *La Samaritaine* (1897, *The Woman of Samaria*); *Les Romanesques* (1900, *The Romantics*); *Chantecler* (1910, *Chanticleer*); *La dernière Nuit de Don Juan* (Published 1921, *The Last Night of Don Juan*); and others.

ROSTAND, Maurice, b. 1891, French dramatist, author of verse dramas in the style of his father, Edmond. *L'Homme que j'ai tué* (1924). A French soldier seeks the relatives of the Germans he has killed in the war). Other plays: *La Gloire* (1921); *Le Phénix* (1923); *Napoleon IV* (1928); *Le Procès d'Oscar Wilde* (1935); and others.

ROSTWOROWSKI, Karol Hubert, 1877-1938, Polish dramatist. Anti-naturalist. For a "monumental theater." *Judas Iscariot* (1913); *Caligula* (1917); *Charity* (1920); the trilogy *The Surprise* (1928); *The Way Up* (1930); *At the Goal* (1932).

ROUSSIN, André, b. 1911, French author of comedies in the erotic boulevard style. *La sainte Famille* (1946); *La petite Hutte* (1947, *The Little Hut*); *Les Oeufs de l'autruche* (1948); *Nina* (1949); *Bobosse* (1950); *L'Amour fou* (1955); *La Mamma* (1957); *Les Glorieuses* (1960, in verse); *L'École des autres* (1962); and others.

ROZOV, Victor, b. 1913, Russian dramatist. *Good Luck* (1955); *The Immortal Ones* (1958); *Unequal Combat* (1960); *ABCDE* (1961); *Before Supper* (1962).

RUDORF, Günther, b. 1921, German dramatist of the post-World War II generation. *Die Stunde der Unschuldigen* (1955); *Der einsame Wolf; Königsallee* (1959).

RYDEL, Lucjan, 1870-1918, Polish lyric poet and dramatist. *The Enchanted Circle* (1899); *A Polish Bethlehem* (1905); *Zygmunt August* (1913).

SALACROU, Armand, b. 1899, French dramatist. Historical plays in a non-realistic style and conversation comedies. *Tour à terre* (1925); *Le Pont de l'Europe* (1927); *Patchouli* (1930); *Atlas-Hôtel* (1931); *Les Frénétiques* (1934); *Une Femme* libre (1934); *L'Inconnue d'Arras* (1935. The events of the protagonist's life take place in the second in which he commits suicide); *Un Homme comme les autres* (1936, character farce); *La Terre est ronde* (1938, Savonarola drama on modern dictatorship); *Histoire de rire* (1939, dialogue on the subterfuges of marriage); *Les Nuits de la colère* (1946); *L'Archipel Lenoir* (1947); *Une Femme trop honnête* (1956); *Boulevard Durand* (1960, story of a forgotten trial in 1910).

SANCHEZ, Ramon Diaz, b. 1903, Spanish-writing dramatist in Venezuela. *La casa* (1955).

SAN-GIORGIU, Ion, 1893-1950, Rumanian dramatist. *The Mask of the Two-Souled Woman* (1925); *Madame Sevastita* (1936).

SAN SECONDO, Rosso di, 1887-1956, Italian dramatist. Began with the anti-illusionistic grotesque theater (à la Chiarelli, Pirandello). *Marionette, che passione!* (1918. Three people meet at the post-office on a Sunday afternoon and suddenly break out into pitiful self-confessions: they are marionettes of fate—the lady in the blue fox, the man in mourning, and the man in gray); *La bella addormentata* (1919); *La roccia e i monumenti* (1923); *L'avventura terrestre* (1924, comedy. Two people, a Sicilian and a Russian emigrée, fight for self-knowledge in love—are we as we see ourselves? The attempt to avoid the terror of loneliness; life on earth seen as a shadow which only reflects the real life.) Other plays: *Per fare l'alba* (1919); *Amara* (1919); *Primavera* (1920); *L'Ospite desiderato* (1921); *Peccati di gioventù* (1922); *Lazzarina fra i coltelli* (1923); *La danza su un piede* (1923); *Una cosa di carne* (1924); *Il delirio dell'oste Bassà* (1925); *La scala* (1925, *The Stairs*); *Musica di foglie morte* (1925); *L'illusione dei giorni e delle notti* (1926); *Tra vestiti che ballano* (1927); *Canicola* (1929); *La signora Falkenstein* (1931); *Lo spirito della morte* (1941); *Finestre* (1954), and others.

SARAUW, Paul, b. 1883, Danish dramatist, known mainly for his comedy, *The Rational Man* (1936).

SARMENT, Jean, b. 1897, French dramatist. Parallels with Pirandello, at least in his characters' quest for alternatives to reality. *La Couronne de carton* (1920); *Le pêcheur d'ombres* (1921, *Rude Awakening*); *Le Mariage d'Hamlet* (1922); *Je suis trop grand pour moi* (1924); and others.

SAROYAN, William, b. 1908, American story writer and dramatist. Romantic-lyric realism. His most successful plays: *My Heart's in the Highlands* (1939. An old Shakespearian actor who is an expert trumpet player brings joy to the home of an unsuccessful poet with his friendship for the latter's nine-year-old son.); *The Time of Your Life* (1939. A San Francisco bar filled with various hangers-about and down-and-outs who bring their fates on the stage: A vagabond with his friend, a truck driver, a prostitute, a dancer, etc.); *The Beautiful People* (1941). Other plays: *Love's Old Sweet Song* (1940); *Across the Board on Tomorrow Morning* (1941); *Jim Dandy* (1941); *Hello Out There* (1942, one-act); *Get Away Old Man* (1943); *Don't Go Away Mad* (published 1949); *Sam Ego's House* (published 1949); *A Decent Birth, A Happy Funeral* (published 1949); *The Cave Dwellers* (1957); *The Paris Comedy* (1960); *Settled Out of Court* (1960, adaptation of Henry Cecil's novel); *Sam, the Highest Jumper of All* (1960).

SARTRE, Jean Paul, b. 1905, French philosopher, novelist, and dramatist. Drama, in which his existentialist philosophy is embodied on the stage. Thesis plays closely allied to French theatrical tradition. Although the action is worked out with the most exact logic and dialectic, the Existentialist concept of freedom (freedom and lack of restraint are one and the same thing; Man is constantly obliged to make decisions without reference to any "morality") often brings the themes of the plays to the border of the absurd. The socio-political program is derived from the protest against false obligations—"Nobody can be free if all others are not free as well" (Hegel). Surrealistic tendencies are never signs of fantasy but rather clarifications of the theses. Sartre is more formal than conservative and he is a master of the technique of the classic act-divided play. *Les Mouches* (1941, *The Flies*. New version of the *Oresteia*. Orestes returns to a city which is ruled by a dictator, Aegistheus, by means of religious terror. Millions of flies, which make life unbearable, have been interpreted as a god-sent punishment for the murder of Agamemnon, for which the people as a whole must suffer rather than only the guilty. Zeus, disguised as a merchant, tries to persuade Orestes to leave the town, but Orestes witnesses a quarrel between Clytemnestra and Electra, who has been commanded by Aegistheus to appear in mourning at the funeral ceremonies on the day of public repentance. Electra dances instead in festive clothes before the people and before the king, who banishes her from the country. Orestes and his sister now meet each other and plan revenge. Aegistheus refuses to resist so that Orestes will have to bear the curse of murder. Orestes orders his sister to kill their mother. Electra, who shrinks from the prospect in horror, calls on Zeus for help, but Orestes asserts the rightness of his deed. Zeus speaks the key sentence of the play: "Once freedom lights its beacon in a man's heart, the gods are powerless against him." At the end Orestes refuses the throne in order to draw the Furies out of the city once and for all. He leaves alone, followed by the howling chorus.); *Huis-clos* (1944, *No Exit*. An Empire-style room in a rundown hotel—which is in reality Hell. The walls have the symbolic character of a cage in which three people, i.e., three dead souls, are locked up, inseparable, without hope of flight. They do not even, as we learn later, have the hope of killing themselves since they are dead already. The action is an unmasking process, stripping bare the innermost depths of character. Each one is the other's devil. The moral is that Hell is not metaphysical—it is the world, *our* world.); *Morts sans sépulture* (1946, *The Victors*. Resistance fighters in the hands of collaborators. Human steadfastness and honor in the face of death and torture.); *La Putain respectueuse* (1946, *The Respectful Prostitute*. Racial corruption in the American South. The prostitute has to protect a Senator's son from the law by accusing an innocent man, who is a Negro.); *Les Mains sales* (1948, *Dirty Hands,* also presented as *Red Gloves* and *Crime Passionel.* The individual enmeshed in the Communist Party. An intellectual is ordered—in the last phases of an East European partisan war—to liquidate a partisan leader who is working against the Party. Since he is a weak man, the intellectual finds the courage to do the deed only through personal emotion: he kills the man out of jealousy. When he is released from prison and looks up his old comrades he finds that policy has changed—the murdered man has now been re-

habilitated and consequently his murderer must now be liquidated.); *Le Diable et le bon dieu* (1951, *The Devil and the Good Lord.* Sartre's *Faust.* Takes place in the world of the German Reformation during the Peasant Wars of 1524-25. Nietzsche's "God is dead" is demonstrated by showing Man's vain and helpless wrestling between good and evil. The peasant leader Götz begins as a brutal terrorist and amoralist. After giving assurances of safety, he orders the massacre of Worms. This betrayal fills him with diabolical pleasure. Suddenly, in an unexpected and unmotivated turnabout, he becomes the "Commander of the Good" and wants to found a "City of Light" as leader of the poor. In order to create this city of love and goodness he presses the war of the peasants against the nobles. The peasants break into the neutral land of the City of Light, burn it down, and kill its inhabitants. Götz recognizes the fact of sin in all men and becomes a penitent. In a long dialectical scene between the penitent and the recreant priest Heinrich, the absurd reaches its climax: each acknowledges the opposite of what he has always believed. Götz kills Heinrich and takes over the command of the rebelling peasants, for good and evil are inextricably intertwined.); *Kean* (1953, translated with the same title. Based on the play by Dumas. Witty comment on the old theme of theater as opposed to real life. The famous actor Kean explains that real life is only an inferior imitation of art. The hero wavers between two women, who reveal themselves to be the opposite of what he had thought them to be. This happens during the spectacular fourth act, in which the last act of *Othello* is given on the stage within the stage until Kean-Othello breaks out of his role.); *Nekrassov* (1955, trans. same title. Satiric farce directed against a certain type of anti-Communism. A swindler saves himself from the police by pretending to be the defecting Soviet foreign minister. He saves a bankrupt newspaper with his "revelations," is praised to the skies, and is finally exposed. When he offers his revelations about "How I Became Nekrassov" to the Soviets, the other side falls into the trap again. Now it is, "Nekrassov abducted by the Soviets."); *Les Séquestrés d'Altona* (1959, *The Condemned of Altona.* Tragedy of guilt. A shipbuilder in Altona wishes to make his will because he is suffering from cancer. His house is full of ghosts of the past. The father has suffered; his older son, who stays in his room in order to hide from the world, has suffered and not suffered: dressed in his lieutenant's uniform, he is cared for by his incestuously involved sister and he spends his time throwing oyster shells at a mildewed picture of Hitler. He is persuaded to come down from his room and once more face his father and the world. When he sees the "Wonderland" which he has supposed to be filled with misery and want, he determines to "become a part of his times." He takes his father for a ride in the car and drives into the Elbe at 100 m.p.h.—The play, complicated by flashbacks and murky symbolism, exemplifies the main theses of Sartre's philosophy in the style of the act-divided drama. c.f. Ibsen's *John Gabriel Borkman*). Also, motion-picture scenarios: *Les Jeux sont faits* (published 1947, *The Chips Are Down*) and *L'Engrenage* (published 1948, *In the Mesh*).

SASTRE, Alfonso, b. 1926, important Spanish dramatist of the younger generation. Four one-act plays published 1949: *Ha sonado la muerte* (with Medardo Fraile); *Comedia sonambula* (with Medardo Fraile); *Cargamento de suenos; Uranio 235. Escuadra hacia la muerte* (1953, *The Condemned Squad*); *La mordaza* (1954); *La sangre de Dios* (1955); *El pan de todos* (1957); *El cuervo* (1957); *La cornado* (1960); *Anna Kleiber* (1961; translated, same title); *En la red* (1961, set in North Africa.)

SAUVAJON, Marc Gilbert, b. 1909, French author of comedies. Most successful play has been *Les Enfants d'Edouard.*

SAVORY, Gerald, b. 1909, English dramatist. Comedies: *George and Margaret* (1937); *A Likely Tale* (1956); *A Month of Sundays* (1957); *Come Rain, Come Shine* (1958); and others.

SAYERS, Dorothy L., 1893-1957, English author of detective novels and of plays. *Busman's Honeymoon* (1936, from her detective novel); *The Zeal of Thy House* (1937, religious play); *The Devil to Pay* (1939, religious play).

SCHÄFER, Walter Erich, b. 1901, German dramatist of the post-World War I generation. *Richter Feuerbach* (1930); *Der 18. Oktober* (1932); *Schwarzmann und die Magd* (1933); *Die Reise nach Paris* (1936); *Theres und die Hoheit* (1938); *Der Leutnant Vary* (1940); *Claudia* (1942); *Die Verschw
rung* (1949. The July 20, 1944, attempt on Hitler's life); *Zwischen Abend und Morgen* (1952, Friedrich Wilhelm I).

SCHAIK-WILLING, Jeanne van, b. 1895, Dutch novelist and dramatist. *The Portrait* (1948); *Odysseus Weeps* (1953); *Free People* (1945, one act of the Dutch Freedom Play).

SCHEHADÉ, Georges, b. 1906, French dramatist from Lebanon. Poetic surrealism. *Monsieur Bob'le* (1951); *La Soirée des proverbes* (1954); *Histoire de Vasco* (1956, *Vasco*. One of the important plays of the contemporary French drama. The scene is a forest in which we see the caravan of a vagabond pair, father and daughter. The father is a "scholar" who understands the language of the birds, the daughter, young and beautiful, seeks her love and her bridegroom in her dreams since nothing ever happens to her in real life. The two dream inside their caravan, which glows like a hell-mouth. As they begin quite unromantically to snore, the Black Lieutenant comes along through the forest searching for a certain Vasco. While the father is showing the lieutenant a number of puppies, from the sale of which he lives, cannon fire is heard and the red flare of a battle flickers in the distant sky—it is war. In the last scene the mad "scholar" puts the question, "Why are all battles red? Couldn't that be changed? A green battle, ah, Lieutenant! how beautiful that would be!" Lieutenant: "But that would be the spring then." But who is Vasco? It turns out that he is a young barber who possesses all the qualities which do *not* make a hero. For this reason he is being forced to become one. The general of one of the armies needs him to take dispatches through the enemy lines. Vasco, however, is about as suitable for such a mission as a rabbit who runs over all the mines and explodes them. In the last scene his body lies in the forest in which the action began. The girl is watching over him, imagining him to be the lover she has always dreamed of, and the Black Lieutenant looks long and slowly at the dead man, after calling out the word "Victoire." The play is a parable of the powerless nonconformist, the man without an ideology and with contempt for uniforms.); *Les Violettes* (1960); *Le Voyage* (1961).

SCHICKELE, René, 1883-1940, German-Alsatian Expressionistic author. *Hans im Schnakenloch* (1916) and *Am Glockenturm* (1919).

SCHLAF, Johannes, 1862-1941, German dramatist. Naturalism. *Papa Hamlet* (1889 and *Familie Selicke* (1890, both with Arno Holz); *Meister Oelze* (published 1892).

SCHMIDTBONN, Wilhelm, 1876-1952, German dramatist. Began writing in the pre-World War I period with neo-romantic historical plays. *Mutter Landstrasse* (1904); *Der Graf von Gleichen* (1908); *Der Zorn des Achilles* (1909); *Die Stadt der Besessenen* (1915). Later, parable plays: *Passion* (1919); *Der verlorene Sohn* (1912); *Bruder Dietrich* (1929). Also wrote the aviation drama, *Der Geschlagene* (1920) and the tragicomedy *Hilfe! Ein Kind ist vom Himmel gefallen* (1910).

SCHNEIDER, Reinhold, 1903-1958, German writer of Christian tendency. *Las Casas vor Karl V* (1938); *Der Kronprinz* (1948); *Belsazar* (1949); *Der grosse Verzicht* (1950, the quarrel between Pope Celestin V and Pope Boniface VIII); *Tarnkappe* (1951); *Traum des Eroberers* (1952); *Zar Alexander* (1952); *Innozenz und Franziskus* (1953).

SCHNITZLER, Arthur, 1862-1931, Austrian dramatist, novelist, and physician. One of the representatives of the "modern" writers of the '90's, who are too narrowly designated as "naturalists." First appearance of Freudian psychoanalysis on the stage. Schnitzler's main interest is the "thousand souls" which each person has within himself. Hence his treatment of eroticism and his belief that morbid, sick, or compulsive love can be represented just as well as pure love. Social factors intrude into this treatment of love as well: morbidity in love is usually attributed to the upper classes, while simple love is possible only for ordinary people. The lasciviousness of which his contemporaries accused him actually existed in the lives of these same contemporaries, and it is in his re-creation of it on the stage that Schnitzler is a member of the naturalistic movement. The scandal caused by the publication of *Reigen* (1900), led Schnitzler to prohibit productions of the work. With the exception of the Berlin production of 1920, which caused a renewal of the scandal, and several foreign productions, the work has so far been performed only on film. In Schnitzler's works the elements of charm and melancholy are at the same time personal and Viennese characteristics; they are bound up with a subtle art of implication, nuance, and atmosphere. The succession of scenes, which is the form in which *Anatol* and *Reigen* are written, is a symptom of the decline of the act-divided play rather than a preliminary example of the epic drama. It may be taken as an unconscious reversion to the medieval station play ("Dance of Death" type), especially in the case of *Reigen;* the theme of this most significant of Schnitzler's plays is the modern dance of death of love. *Anatol* (1893, translated with the same title. Seven scenes from the love life of a spoiled, very Viennese melancholic: "Questioning Fate," "Christmas Shopping," "Episode," "Memorials," "Farewell Supper," "Agony," "Anatol's Wedding Morning." In place of the last scene Schnitzler has recommended "Anatol's Megalomania" for stage production. The scenes are concerned with Anatol's affairs with ladies, cocottes, actresses, ballerinas, milliners.); *Das Märchen* (1894, *The Fairy-Tale*); *Liebelei* (1895, *Light-o'-Love*. The affair between a well-born young man and Christine, the daughter of an orchestra violinist. When Christine learns that the man whom she loves above everything has been shot in a duel over a married woman, she kills herself: "And I—what am I, after all?"—Hofmannsthal had already sensed a disguised rococo style—comedy as life—in *Anatol,* and here Schnitzler's instinct for form becomes clearer with his introduction of a second pair of lovers, a parallel buffoon pair.). *Der grüne Kakadu* (1899, *The Green Cockatoo*) is an even more distinct forerunner of the Pirandello style. In this one-act play, which Schnitzler called "grotesque" (the Italian theater revolutionaries of 1910 also spoke of "grotesque theater"), we see an inn which has been arranged to look like a thieves' den by the host in order to attract society people who wish to enjoy the sensation without running the danger. Suddenly the pretence becomes reality. The time is the day on which the French Revolution began. The problem plays, *Freiwild* and *Das Vermächtnis,* were followed by *Reigen* (1900, *Hands Around,* also known as *La Ronde.* Consists of the "stations," "The Prostitute and the Soldier," "The Soldier and the Housemaid," "The Housemaid and the Young Gentleman," "The Young

Gentleman and the Young Wife," "The Young Wife and the Husband," "The Husband and the Sweet Young Girl," "The Sweet Young Girl and the Poet," "The Poet and the Actress," "The Actress and the Count," "The Count and the Prostitute."). The titles of the scenes themselves are sufficient to demonstrate Schnitzler's intention: the round dance of love can exist only with the help of conditions which we associate with infidelity. This amorality is typical of the real life of the city and of the times. Schnitzler makes no judgments, only revelations. At the same time he is looking for a climactic moment in the gradual upward trend of the social spheres. This occurs in the middle scene and is retained from then on, for the poet is already quite high in the social sphere—his room is furnished "with comfortable taste." It is retained till the end, when the highest social level (the Count) is connected with the lowest level and at the same time with the beginning of the circle (the Prostitute)—an almost musical symmetry. Later works: the one-act plays, *Lebendige Stunden* (1901, *Living Hours*) and *Literatur* (1901, *Literature*); the drama, *Der Schleier der Beatrice* (1900); the marriage dramas, *Der einsame Weg* (1903, *The Lonely Way*) and *Das weite Land* (1911, *The Vast Domain*); *Der junge Medardus* (1909, historical panorama); the comedy, *Komtesse Mizzi* (1907, *Countess Mizzi*); *Professor Bernhardi* (1912, translated with same title. Problem play about a Jewish physician); *Grosse Szene* (1915, *The Big Scene*, one-act); *Die Schwestern oder Casanova in Spa* (1919, verse comedy); *Komödie der Verführung* (1924); *Spiel im Morgengrauen* (1927); *Der Gang zum Weiher* (1926); *Im Spiel der Sommerlüfte* (1930); *Sterben* (1931), and others.

SCHOLZ, Wilhelm von, b. 1874, German dramatist. Began with neo-classicism (in the manner of Paul Ernst). *Der Jude von Konstanz* (1905); *Meroë* (1906); *Vertauschte Seelen* (1910); *Das Herzwunder* (1918); followed with the occult problem plays, *Der Wettlauf mit dem Schatten* (1922) and *Die gläserne Frau* (1924). Also wrote *Die Frankfurter Weihnacht* (1938); *Claudia Colonna* (1941); *Ayatari* (1944); *Ewige Jugend* (1949); *Das Säckinger Trompetenspiel* (1955). Adaptation of Hölderlin's *Empedokles* (1915). Adaptations from Calderon: *Über allen Zauber Liebe* (1931); *Das Leben ein Traum* (1933); *Der Richter von Zala-*

mea (1937); *Das Deutsche Grosse Welttheater* (1941).

SCHÖNHERR, Karl, 1867-1943, Austrian dramatist. Naturalism in localized dramas. *Der Judas von Tirol* (1897, Andreas Hofer theme); *Die Bildschnitzer* (1900); *Sonnwendtag* (1902); *Karrnerleut'* (1904); *Erde* (1907); *Das Königreich* (1908, folk fairy tale). His two biggest successes: *Glaube und Heimat* (1910, *Faith and Fireside*. Folk tragedy set in the time of the Counter-Reformation) and *Der Weibsteufel* (1914. Three characters: the Man, his Wife, a young Border Guard. Place: a Tyrol mountain hut. Brutally erotic thriller). Other plays: *Volk in Not* (1915, patriotic dramatization of the Tyrolese freedom fight of 1809); *Frau Suitner* (1916); *Narrenspiel des Lebens* (1918); *Kindertragödie* (1919); *Es* (1923); *Der Armendoktor* (1927); *Haben Sie zu essen, Herr Doktor?* (1930, topical satire on the poverty of young doctors); *Passionspiel* (1933); *Die Fahne weht* (1936), and others.

SCHREYVOGL, Friedrich, b. 1899, Austrian dramatist. *Die Flucht des Columbus* (1926); *Johann Orth* (1928); *Habsburgerlegende* (1933); *Der Gott im Kreml* (1937, Demetrius); *Das Liebespaar* (1940); *Die Kluge Wienerin* (1941, comedy set in the Vienna of Roman times); *Die weisse Dame* (1942); *Titania* (1943); *Der Liebhaber* (1951); *Die Nacht liegt hinter uns* (1953); *Der weisse Mantel* (1953); *Die Versuchung des Tasso* (1955); *Eine Stunde vor Tag* (1956, play of theater life); *Ton und Licht* (1960, Maximilian and Carlotta of Mexico); *Der Gott darf nicht sterben* (1961); *Ich liebe eine Göttin* (1961).

SCHWARZ, Yevgeni, 1896-1958, Russian dramatist. Fairy-tale plays: *The Shadow* (1933, translated); *Little Red Riding Hood* (1937); *The Snow Queen* (1938); *The Dragon* (1943, translated); *Cinderella* (1947); *The First-Class Girl* (1947); *The Story of an Early Marriage* (1955); *An Ordinary Wonder* (1956).

SCHWEIKART, Hans, b. 1895, German. The popular comedies, *Lauter Lügen* (1937) and *Ich brauche dich* (1941); the detective play, *Nebel;* and the dramatization, with Gerhard Menzel, of Pushkin's *The Postmaster.*

SCHWIEFERT, Fritz, b. 1890, German writer. Biggest success with the comedy, *Marguerite: 3* (1930). Other plays: *Frackkomödie* (1939); *Das Leben fängt mit vierzig an* (1952); *Weisst du, wieviel Sternlein stehen* (1954); and many others.

SHAFFER, Peter, b. 1926, English dramatist. International success with *Five Finger Exercise* (1958). Program of one-act plays (1962, *The Private Ear; The Public Eye*).

SHAW, George Bernard, 1856-1950, most important English dramatist since Shakespeare, contributor of the most extensive and comprehensive body of drama to the repertoire of the world theater since Molière. Nobel Prize. On his own testimony he never wrote a line "for art's sake." He belonged to the movement which believed it possible to change the world by means of the theater. For Shaw the most important thing was his tenacious and uncompromising fight for social justice and again superannuated conventions, prejudices, and prerogatives. His weapons in his struggle for a world of truth, in whose triumph he believed all the more because he set science above metaphysics (he was a biologist, positivist, and monist), were the stage and his wit. The realization of the good seemed to him a matter of the attainment of reason. Consequently he considered all of his plays to be, on a more profound level, didactic pieces. They were the lectures of a schoolmaster who did not shrink from the employment of any and all tricks in order to aid the victory of reason. What he did not openly confess was the indisputable fact that the use of these tricks gave him the greatest pleasure: he wrote his plays under the stimulation of a desire to be amusing in the theater. In saying that on the stage truth is the greatest joke of all he put himself on the same ground as Aristophanes and a theatrical tradition which is as ancient as it is new: that of the author who maintains his right to the jester's freedom of expression. He tells the world's powerful and powerless the truth, and above all he loves the type of laughter which has a touch of the morbid in it. From writing plays for their amusement value to himself, Shaw instinctively came to a point where he broke through the illusionism of the stage world. The most notable example of this is the epilogue of *Saint Joan,* but there are plenty of other examples—to mention only a few, the "Don Juan" inter-

mezzo in *Man and Superman* or the "metabiological pentateuch" of the five parts of *Back to Methusalah,* which has a time span from Adam and Eve to 31290 A.D. Shaw's place in world theater is not as a propagandist of world change but rather as the greatest representative of satiric comedy since Aristophanes. Chronology of plays: *Widowers' Houses* (1892); *The Philanderer* (written 1893, performed 1905); *Mrs. Warren's Profession* (written 1893, performed 1902); *Arms and the Man* (1894); *Candida* (1895); *The Man of Destiny* (written 1895, performed 1897); *You Never Can Tell* (written 1895, performed 1899); *The Devil's Disciple* (written 1896-7, performed 1897); *Caesar and Cleopatra* (copyright performance 1899, 1907); *Captain Brassbound's Conversion* (1900); *The Admirable Bashville* (written 1900, from Shaw's novel *Cashel Byron's Profession*); *Man and Superman* (written 1901-3, performed 1905); *John Bull's Other Island* (1904); *How He Lied to Her Husband* (1904); *Passion, Poison and Petrifaction; or The Fatal Gazogene* (1905); *Major Barbara* (1905); *The Doctor's Dilemma* (1906); *Getting Married* (1908); *Press Cuttings* (1909); *The Shewing-up of Blanco Posnet* (1909); *The Glimpse of Reality* (written 1909, performed 1927); *The Fortunate Foundling* (written 1909, performed 1928); *Misalliance* (1910); *The Dark Lady of the Sonnets* (1910); *Fanny's First Play* (1911); *Androcles and the Lion* (1912); *Overruled* (1912); *Pygmalion* (1913); *The Great Catherine* (1913); *The Music Cure* (1914); *O'Flaherty, V.C.* (written 1915, performed 1920); *The Inca of Perusalem* (1916); *Augustus Does His Bit* (1917); *Annajanska, the Bolshevik Empress* (1918); *Heartbreak House* (1920); *Back to Methuselah* (1922); *Saint Joan* (1923); *Jitta's Atonement* (1923, free translation of a play by Trebitsch); *The Apple Cart* (1929); *Too True to Be Good* (1932); *Village Wooing* (written 1933, performed 1934); *On the Rocks* (1933); *The Simpleton of the Unexpected Isles* (written 1934, performed 1935); *The Six of Calais* (1934); *The Millionairess* (1936); *Geneva* (1938); *In Good King Charles's Golden Days* (1939); *Cymbeline Refinished* (written 1945); *Buoyant Billions* (1948); *Shakes versus Shav* (1949); *Farfetched Fables* (1950).

SHAW, Irwin, b. 1913, American dramatist. Topical, critical problem plays. *Bury the Dead* (1936); *Siege*

(1937); *Quiet City* (1939); *The Gentle People* (1939); *Retreat to Pleasure* (1940); *Sons and Soldiers* (1943); *The Assassin* (1945); *Children from Their Games* (1963).

SHELDON, Edward, 1886-1946, American dramatist. Among the earliest American exponents of modern realism. *Salvation Nell* (1908); *The Nigger* (1910); *The Boss* (1911); *Romance* (1913); *The Song of Songs* (1914, from Sudermann's *Das hohe Lied*); *The Garden of Paradise* (1914); *Lulu Belle* (1926, with Charles MacArthur); and others.

SHERRIFF, Robert Cedric, b. 1896, English dramatist. Became internationally known with the war play, *Journey's End* (1928). *Badger's Green* (1930); *Windfall* (1933); *St. Helena* (1935, with Jeanne de Casalis); *Miss Mabel* (1948); *Home at Seven* (1950); *The White Carnation* (1953); *The Long Sunset* (1955); *The Telescope* (1957); *A Shred of Evidence* (1960).

SHERWOOD, Robert Emmet, 1896-1955, American dramatist. Critical realism with symbolic tendencies. Pessimism followed by hopefulness. History plays. *The Road to Rome* (1927, Hannibal); *The Love Nest* (1927, from a story by Ring Lardner); *The Queen's Husband* (1928); *Waterloo Bridge* (1930); *This Is New York* (1930); *Reunion in Vienna* (1931); *Acropolis* (1933); *The Petrified Forest* (1935. "A burned-out intellectual who takes no pride in his kind and understands the uselessness of his capacities. Young as he is, he has lived beyond his time; nature is taking revenge for his intellectual arrogance." [Brooks Atkinson]); *Idiot's Delight* (1936, Pulitzer Prize. Ironic comedy taking place on the eve of war in a hotel in the Italian Alps); *Abe Lincoln in Illinois* (1938, Pulitzer Prize); *There Shall Be No Night* (1940, Pulitzer Prize); *The Rugged Path* (1945); *Small War on Murray Hill* (Produced 1959, comedy set in the American War of Independence).

SHOLEM ALEICHEM, pseudonym of Sholem Rabinowitz, 1859-1916, Yiddish short story writer and dramatist. *Two Hundred Thousand* (1915); *Hard to Be a Jew* (Published 1914, performed 1919); and others. One of his stories was adapted by Arnold Perl in *The World of Sholem Aleichem* (1953); Perl used others for *Tevya and His Daughters* (1957).

SIFTON, Paul, b. 1898, American dramatist. Left-wing social criticism. *The Belt* (1927); *Midnight* (1930, with Claire Sifton. Also known as *The Age of Plenty*); *Blood on the Moon* (1933, with Claire Sifton).

SILONE, Ignazio, b. 1900, Italian novelist. *Ed egli si nascose* (1945, *And He Hid Himself*, dramatization of *Bread and Wine*).

SIMONOV, Konstantin, b. 1915, Russian writer and lyric poet. *Bearskin* (1940); *A Fellow from Our Town* (1940, Stalin Prize); *The Russian People* (1942, translated), *Wait for Me* (1942); *And so It Will Be* (1943, translated as *The Whole World Over*); *The Russian Question* (1946); *Under the Chestnut Trees of Prague* (1947); *The Fourth* (1961, translated), and others.

SMITH, Winchell, 1871-1933, American dramatist. One of the longest running plays of the American stage: *Lightnin'* (1918, with Frank Bacon. Homey comedy about a lovable loafer. 1291 performances). Also *The Fortune Hunter* (1909); and others.

SODERBERG, Hjalmar, 1869-1941, Swedish dramatist. Impressionism. Best known for *Gertrud* (1906).

SOFRONOV, Anatol, b. 1911, Soviet dramatist. *In a City* (1945); *The Moscow Character* (1947); *Beketov's Career* (1949); *Money* (1955); *The Cook* (1959); and others.

SOLOGUB, Fyodor, pseudonym of Fyodor Teternikov, 1863-1927, Russian poet, novelist, and dramatist. Fantasy, symbolism. *The Triumph of Death* (1907, translated); *Vanka the Butler and Jean the Page* (1909, contrasts between French and Russian life); *Hostages of Life* (1913); and others.

SORGE, Reinhard Johannes, 1892-1916, German dramatist whose drama, *Der Bettler* (Written 1912, performed 1917, *The Beggar*) is an early example of Expressionism (ecstatic subjectivism with dream visions). Later he turned to Christian themes. *Guntwar, die Schule eines Propheten* (1914); *Metanolite* (1915, three mysteries); *König David* (1916); *Gericht über Zarathustra* (1921); *Mystische Zwiesprache* (1922); *Der Sieg des Christos* (1924).

SOTELO, Joaquin Calvo, b. 1905, Spanish dramatist. *La murala* (1954); *La herencia* (1957). National Prize for *La visita que no tocó el timbre* (1950) and *Criminal de guerra* (1951). Another prize for *Lá carcel infinita* (1945).

SOYA, Carl Erik, b. 1896, popular Danish dramatist. Satiric comedies. *The Parasite* (1929); *Who Am I?* (1932); *Chas* (1938); *My Top Hat* (1939); *Fragments of a Pattern* (1940); *Two Threads* (1941); *Thirty Years' Delay* (1944); *Free Choice* (1948); *The Late Mr. Jonsen* (1957).

SPENDER, Stephen, b. 1909, English lyric poet, story writer, and critic. *Trial of a Judge* (1938); *To the Island* (1951, verse drama on the Spanish Civil War).

SPEWACK, Samuel, b. 1899, American journalist and stage writer. Collaborated with his wife, Bella, on the book for the musical *Kiss Me Kate* (1956, based on Shakespeare's *The Taming of the Shrew*, music by Cole Porter.). Collaborated with his wife on: *The Solitaire Man* (1926); *Poppa* (1928); *The War Song* (1928); *Clear All Wires* (1932); *Spring Song* (1934); *Boy Meets Girl* (1935. Hollywood satire); and other plays. Sole author of *Two Blind Mice* (1949); *The Golden State* (1950); *Under the Sycamore Tree* (1952).

SQUARZINA, Luigi, b. 1922, Italian dramatist. *Gli indifferenti* (1948, with Alberto Moravia); *Tre quarti di luna* (1953); *La sua parte di storia* (1954. Murder in a Sardinian village, involving a young American woman physician who has been sent by a foundation to battle an epidemic); *Romagnola* (1959, Premio Marzotto).

STANGE, Claude Richard, b. 1913, Swiss dramatist. *Lionel der Löwe* (1955, comedy); *Abschied von Sodom* (1956).

STEFFEN, Albert, 1884-1963, Swiss dramatist and anthroposophist. *Der Auszug aus Ägypten* (1916); *Die Manichäer* (1916); *Das Viergetier* (1920); *Der Chef des Generalstabs* (1927); *Der Sturz des Antichrist* (1928); *Friedenstragödie* (1936, about Woodrow Wilson), *Fahrt ins andere Land* (1938); *Pestalozzi* (1939); *Märtyrer* (1942); *Barrabas* (1949); *Alexanders Wandlung* (1953); and many others.

STEHLIK, Miroslav, b. 1916, Czech dramatist. *The Village of Mlada* (1949); *The Fatal Ravine* (1949, village drama of the time of Nazism); *Spring Thunderstorm* (1952); *The High Summer Sky* (1955); *Love among the Farmers* (1955, tragicomedy); *When the Steel Was Tempered* (1955, after Ovstrovsky); *Flags on the Tower* (1956); *The Tiger Skin* (1960); *Love and Palms* (1961).

STEIN, Alexander, b. 1906, Soviet dramatist. *Talent* (1934); *The Code of Honor* (1948); *A Personal Case* (1954); *Prologue* (1955, about Stalin's youth); *Hotel Astoria* (1956); *A Twisted Knot* (1957); and others.

STEIN, Gertrude, 1874-1946, American writer. Originator of the term, "The Lost Generation." Had great influence on many literary rebels—Cummings, Dos Passos, Hemingway. Wrote the dadaistic-surrealistic piece, *Four Saints in Three Acts* (Written 1927, performed 1934. Music by Virgil Thomson); *Doctor Faustus Lights the Lights* (Written 1938); *The Mother of Us All* (Written 1946, performed 1947); and others.

STEINBECK, John, b. 1902, American novelist. Nobel Prize 1962. Dramatization of his novel *Of Mice and Men* (1937. Tragedy of a cretin who becomes a murderer and of his vagabond-friend, who tries in vain to save him) and with the dramatization of his novel *The Moon Is Down* (1942, partisans in Norway); also *Burning Bright* (1950).

STERNHEIM, Carl, 1878-1942, German dramatist, one of the chief representatives of Expressionism, to which he contributed his own abrupt and twisted dialogue style. After beginning with less characteristic plays, *Der Heiland* (1898, comedy); *Das eiserne Kreuz* (1901); *Judas Ischariot* (1901); *Don Juan* (written 1910, acted 1912, translated); and others, he wrote the "comedies of middle-class heroes," satiric parodies directed against the bourgeois in all his manifestations; *Die Hose* (1911, *The Underpants*); *Die Kassette* (1912, *The Strongbox*); *Bürger Schippel* (1913. The rise of the first tenor of a glee club in a small town); *Der Snob* (1914, *The Snob*. Sequel to *Die Hose*, in which the bourgeois' son becomes a reactionary industrialist and marries a noblewoman); *1913* (written 1913-14, published 1915, performed 1919.); *Napoleon* (1915); *Meta*

(1916); *Tabula rasa* (written 1916, performed 1919); *Der Stänker* (1916); *Die Marquise von Arcis* (1919; *The Mask of Virtue,* from Diderot's *Jacques le fataliste*); *Das leidende Weib* (1919); *Der entfesselte Zeitgenosse* (1920); *Manon Lescaut* (1921); *Der Nebbich* (1922); *Das Fossil* (1923. A Prussian cavalry general and the children he has brought up to be like himself. The wife of his son is a member of the bourgeois family on which the "snob" plays were written. This is the last play in the "middle-class hero" cycle. Example of Sternheim's use of dialogue: "Ago: Is feudal Germany still so strict? —Otto: Even the Marxist part, all boxing match and command! Only we in the middle become part, flow with it.—Ago: Why d'you call the old man a fossil, not a radical?—Sofie: Because he puts become above becoming.—Ago: What's happened has to be reformed; but not in the aristocratic mold with plus and minus signs.—Otto: For him you're a minus.—Sofie: Far less than zero.—Ago: That would be an idiocy which I couldn't believe of him. As his enemy I must mean something to him.— Otto: How did you become that?"); *Oscar Wilde, sein Drama* (1925); *Die Schule von Uznach* (1926).

STRINDBERG, August, 1849-1912, Swedish dramatist. The first great dramatic anti-illusionist. Was only temporarily part of the optimism of the socially conscious theater. Suffered from congenital pessimism and psychic complexes which led him to hatred of women, to mystical visions, and finally from the unmasking of society to the unmasking of all humanity. His protest and opposition were thus lifted out of a topical concern into the basic, universal issues. His protest against the state of the world and of the human race helped him to a reappraisal of reality which enabled him, after his "Inferno" period and his conversion, to achieve new theatrical forms: apparitions, ghosts, mysterious visions, symbolism carried to the borders of surrealism. His most important dramas are his chamber plays. The history plays are mostly sketchy in character, but logical progression could hardly have been expected in view of Strindberg's disturbed character.—Early plays: *Master Olof* (Written in prose 1871-72, performed 1881. Written in verse 1876, performed 1890, translated. Swedish reformer seen by the poet in various guises); *The Secret of the Guild* (1880); *Lucky Pehr* (Written 1881-82, performed 1883, translated. Fairy tale play); *Ritter Bengt's Wife* (1882); *Marauders* (1886, revised as *Comrades,* published 1888, performed 1910, translated. First influence of Zola and Antoine, and Strindberg's first example of the battle of the sexes as a theme).—The new style (smaller number of characters and concentration on erotic psychology): *The Father* (1887, translated); *Miss Julie* (1888, translated, "naturalistic tragedy"); *Creditors* (1890, translated); and the allegorical drama, *The Keys of the Kingdom* (published 1892). The turn towards anti-illusionism: *To Damascus,* Parts I & II (published 1898, Part I performed 1900, both parts translated); *There Are Crimes and Crimes* (1900, translated); the historical plays, *The Saga of the Folkungs* (Written 1899, performed 1901, translated); *Gustavus Vasa* (1899, translated); *Erik XIV* (1899, translated); *Gustav Adolf* (Written 1899-1900, performed 1912, translated); *Engelbrekt* (1901, translated); *Charles XII* (1902, translated); *Queen Christina* (Written 1901, performed 1908, translated); *Gustav III* (Written 1902, performed 1916, translated). The first "season" plays: *Advent* (Written 1898, translated); *Midsummer* (1901); *Easter* (1901, translated). Fairytale plays: *The Bridal Crown* (Written 1901, performed 1907, translated); *Swanwhite* (Written 1901, produced 1908, translated). The marriage play, *Dance of Death* (Written 1901-2, performed 1907). Further historical plays: *The Nightingale in Wittenberg* (Written 1903); *The Last of the Knights* (1909, translated); Part III of *To Damascus* (Written 1900-04, translated). The later plays. Chamber plays: *The Thunderstorm* (1907, translated); *After the Fire* (1907, translated); *The Ghost Sonata* (Published 1907, performed 1908, translated); *The Pelican* (1907, translated). The later historical plays: *Earl Birger of Balbo* (1909, translated); *The Regent* (Written 1908, performed 1911, translated). Last play: *The Great Highway* (Written 1909, performed 1910, translated. Seven stations of a journey; the hero, a hunter, retires at the end into the purity of the Alpine snows. Verse).

STRINDBERG, Axel, b. 1910, Swedish dramatist. Greatnephew of August Strindberg. Expressionistic, surrealistic dream plays and problem plays. *Club of Neutrals* (1945); *Hours of Grace* (1946); *The Son of the Caliph* (1947); *The Festival Is almost Over* (1950); and others.

STRITTMATTER, Erwin, b. 1912, East German dramatist. National Prize. Rural comedy, *Katzgraben* (1950, re-written in verse by Brecht); *Die Holländerbraut.* (1960).

SUDERMANN, Hermann, 1857-1928, German dramatist of the naturalistic school. International success with *Die Ehre* (1889, *Honor*). Further success with *Heimat* (1893, *Magda*). Other plays: *Sodoms Ende* (1891, *A Man and His Picture*); *Schmetterlingsschlacht* (1894); *Glück im Winkel* (1895, *The Vale of Content*); *Johannisfeuer* (1900, *St. John's Fire*); *Stein unter Steinen* (1905); *Blumenboot* (1906); *Der Bettler von Syrakus* (1911); *Die Lobgesänge des Claudian* (1914); *Die Raschhoffs* (1919); *Das deutsche Schicksal* (1921); *Der Hasenfellhändler* (1927); and others.

SUPERVIELLE, Jules, b. 1884, French lyric poet. *La Belle au bois* (1932); *Bolivar* (1936); *La première Famille* (1936, farce); *Scheherezade* (1948); *Robinson* (1949); and the dramatization of his popular novels, *Le Voleur d'enfants* (1948) and *Le Survivant* (1948).

SUROV, Anatol, Soviet dramatist. *Free Trip* (1948); *The Unhappy Hardware Dealer* (1949, satiric comedy); *Decent People* (1949).

SYLVANUS, Erwin, b. 1917, German dramatist. Began writing with plays for amateurs: *Das Soester Friedensspiel* (1952); *Das St.-Barbara-Spiel der Bergleute* (1956); *Das Graf-Gottfried-Spiel* (1956). Frequently performed: *Dr. Korczak und die Kinder* (1957. A series of scenes about the battle of the Warsaw Ghetto. Korczak was a great Polish-Jewish teacher who went voluntarily to the gas ovens with his pupils); *Zwei Worte töten* (1959); *Unter dem Sternbild der Waage* (1960); *Der rote Buddha* (1961. Victims and executioners in six parts from Paris 1767 to Hiroshima 1945); *Ein Pfeiler, der die Welt tragt* (1961); *Der 50. Geburtstag* (1962).

SYNGE, John Millington, 1871-1909, Irish dramatist. Wrote folk plays whose demonic power broke through the conventional rural naturalism. There is a Celtic pagan element in his characters, who speak the speech of the fishermen of the Aran Islands (where Synge lived several years). Barbaric fury and eternal human dreams. *The Tinker's Wed-* *ding* (Written 1902, published 1908, comedy); *In the Shadow of the Glen* (1903); *Riders to the Sea* (1904. A fisherman's wife who has already lost her husband and three sons to the sea waits for news of her missing fourth son and finally learns she must give him up too); *The Well of the Saints* (1905); *The Playboy of the Western World* (1907. A young man appears in an Irish country inn and confesses that he has killed his drunken father. The guests are so enraptured by his account that they drive him to ever greater elaborations of his story. The daughter of the innkeeper falls in love with him and he becomes "the playboy of the western world." Suddenly his father, head bandaged, appears. Despairingly attempting to affirm the truth of his story, the playboy strikes his father a second time but again fails to kill him. Even the innkeeper's daughter forsakes the playboy, and father and son depart together from the village.); *Deirdre of the Sorrows* (1910, unfinished tragedy).

SZANIAWSKI, Jerzy, b. 1886, Polish dramatist. National Prize, 1958. *The Bird* (1924. The hero lets an exotic bird loose in order to bring joy to the stuffy atmosphere of a small town); *The Sailor* (1925); *The Bridge* (1927, between daydreams and reality); *The Girl from the Forest* (1929); *Two Theaters* (1945), and others.

TAGORE, Rabindranath, 1861-1941, Indian lyric poet, and dramatist. Attempted to create a modern, lyrico-romantic, semi-Western theater out of the old Indian tradition. Nobel Prize. *Sacrifice* (Published in Bengali 1890, in English 1917); *Vaikuntha's Manuscript* (Published 1891, comedy); *Chitrangada* (Published 1893); *Karna and Kunti* (Written 1899); *The King of the Dark Chamber* (English version published 1910); *The Post Office* (Published 1912, performed 1914).

TAMÁSI, Aron, b. 1897, Hungarian writer. *The Singing Bird* (1934); *Jeremy the Magnificent* (1936); *Brave Soul* (1941); and others.

TARDIEU, Jean, b. 1903, French avant-garde dramatist. Writes *études* for an experimental theater. *Chamber Theater* (1945-55, published 1955, one-act plays, including *Qui est là?; La Politesse inutile; La Sonate; Le Guichet; Société Apollon; Le Meuble; Faust et Yorick; Il y avait foule au manoir; Un* geste pour un autre; Conversation Sinfonietta; Oswald et Zenaide; Ce que parler veut dire; Eux seuls le savent). Tardieu on his theater: "The problem is not deciding for or against realistic theater in the future but rather the creation of new forms to express the material and the unremitting search for new means of expression. Since no amount of theorizing can be more effective than practical application, I have written a number of 'Etudes' for the theater. These make partial use of the traditional means of expression, but also attempt to push forward into hitherto unexplored territory . . . I hope to follow with other pieces in order to create an experimental theater along the lines of the 'Well-tempered Clavichord.'" Poèmes à jouer (published 1960) include L'A.B.C. de notre vie, Une Voix sans personne, Les Amants du Métro and other short plays.

TEIRLINCK, Herman, b. 1879, important Flemish writer. Under the influence of Gordon Craig and the German Expressionists he has given the priority to the word and the author rather than to the actor and the plot in his plays. *Slow Motion Picture* (1922. Danced, sung, and spoken drama); *I Serve* (1923); *The Play of the Attack on the Tower* (1923); *The Man without a Body* (1925); *The A to Z Play* (1925); *The Lame and Blind* (1926); *Ave* (1928); *The Magpie on the Gallows* (1937); *Oresteia* (1946); *Taco* (1958). Advocates "monumental theater" in his book, *Wijding voor een derde Geborrte* (1956, *Dedication for a Third Birth*).

THIESS, Frank, b. 1890, German novelist. *Der ewige Taugenichts* (1935); *Die Herzogin von Langeais* (1935, based on Balzac); *Zar Iwan* (1945); *Zarin Marina* (1948); *Tödlicher Karneval* (1948); *Stimme des Toten* (1949); *Theater ohne Rampe* (1956, chamber theater). Also: *Perspectiven* (drama); *Der heilige Dämon* (dramatic ballad); *Der Mann ohne Namen* (tragedy).

THOMA, Ludwig, 1867-1921, German (Bavarian) dramatist and story writer. Powerful, partially satiric, comedies. Drastic realism. *Die Medaille* (1901); *Die Lokalbahn* (1902); *Moral* (1909, translated under its own title and as *Morality*. Satiric small town comedy about the confusion caused by revelations from a brothel in the town); *Magdalena* (1912, Strindberg in the Bavarian villages; tragedy of a fallen woman); *Lottchens Geburtstag* (1911, comedy); *Witwen* (produced in 1958 for the first time).

THOMAS, Dylan, 1914-1953, Welsh lyric poet. Extraordinarily powerful speech and fantasy. Wrote a radio "play for voices" based on his story, "Quite Early One Morning," on which he worked for ten years and which was finally titled *Under Milk Wood*. Public reading in New York, 1953. Revised and performed in 1956 in Edinburgh and then in London and New York; represents a landmark in the poetic-realistic theater. The action takes place at night in a Welsh village. The characters pass before us like ghosts, each full of fate and truth. Everyday occurrences are transferred into the realm of dreams, though the play never becomes characterized by a dull and thin romanticism: Thomas's visions have depth and point. Scenario of a film, *The Doctor and the Devils* (published 1953) dealing with the case—previously dramatized by James Bridie—of the Edinburgh physician, Dr. Knox (Dr. Rock in the play), who hired two Irish laborers to supply him with bodies for his anatomical experiments. Thomas's life was the subject of a play, *Dylan,* by Sidney Michaels (1964).

TOLLER, Ernst, 1893-1939, German dramatist. One of the chief representatives of radical Expressionism. Subjectivism, love of humanity, visionary station plays or symbolic reality. After the rise of the Nazis he came to America in 1936; later committed suicide. *Die Wandlung* (1919, *Transfiguration*. Autobiographical play; an artist who has returned from the war with decorations changes his love for his fatherland to a love for humanity. We see him with a prostitute, as a preacher in a hospital, as a worker. In the last role he experiences the misery of humanity and undergoes an inner transformation into a revolutionary. Key statement: "He who wishes to go unto men must first find the Man within himself."); *Masse Mensch* (1921, *Man and the Masses*. Alfred Kerr: "A martyr play. The sacrifice of Sonia, leader of a rebellion, arrested by the police of the old, papal-militaristic state after the suppression of the rebellion. Sonia can be freed if a warder is killed. She declines because she refuses to use force. The violent acts in which she has unwillingly taken part cause her to feel remorse. She is shot, and the example she sets is intended to symbolize the peaceful improvement of the world in the future. . . . Occasionally the play approaches pure allegory."); *Maschinenstürmer* (1922; *The Machine-Wreckers*. Takes place in England in 1815 and concerns the anti-capitalistic destruction of the new weaving machines); *Der deutsche Hinkemann* (1923, translated as *Hinkemann* and as *Brokenbrow*. Tragedy of a man wounded in the war); *Der entfesselte Wotan* (1923); *Hoppla, wir leben* (1927, *Hoppla! Such is Life!*); *Feuer aus den Kesseln* (1930, *Draw the Fires*. The mutiny at Kiel); *Wunder in Amerika* (1931, with Hermann Kesten, *Miracle in America*, also known as *Mary Baker Eddy*); *No More Peace* (1937); *Blind Man's Buff* (1938, new version, with Denis Johnston, of *Blinde Göttin*); *Pastor Hall* (1939, published only in English translation.).

TOLSTOY, Alexei, 1883-1945, Russian novelist, supporter of the revolution. Wrote the patriotic drama, *On the Rock* (1929, about Peter the Great. Revised 1935, as *Peter I*, revised again 1939) and two plays about Ivan the Terrible, *The Eagle and His Mate* (1944) and *Difficult Years* (1946). Other plays: *Love Is a Golden Book* (1923, comedy); *The Empress's Conspiracy* (1924); *The Factory of Youth* (1927); *The Road to Victory* (1939); *The Devil's Bridge* (1939); *The Evil Forces* (1942), and others.

TOLSTOY, Leo Nikolayevitch, 1828-1910, Russian novelist, dramatist. Wrote several dramas which employed both the dialogue technique of the society drama and the methods of the then new naturalistic drama. Considered by the Naturalists to be a member of their movement but actually he broke through the framework of the dramatic axioms, both formally and philosophically, in each of his plays for the sake of a great personal concept of confession, penitence, and abnegation. *The Power of Darkness* (written 1886, performed in Paris 1888, in St. Petersburg 1895. Peasant milieu); *The Fruits of Enlightenment* (1891); *The Living Corpse* (Written 1900, performed 1911, also known as *Redemption*. Bourgeois milieu); *And Light Shines in Darkness* (Unfinished. Aristocratic milieu); and one-act plays. All these plays have been translated.

TOTHEROH, Dan, b. 1898, American poet and playwright. *Wild Birds* (1925); *Distant Drums* (1932); *Moor Born* (1934, the Brontës); *Mother Lode*

(1934, with George O'Neil); *Searching for the Sun* (1936); and others.

TREADWELL, Sophie, American dramatist. Experimental social protest plays. *Gringo* (1922); *Oh, Nightingale* (1925); *Machinal* (1928, expressionistic play about a famous murder case); *Ladies Leave* (1929); *Lone Valley* (1932); *Plumes in the Dust* (1936. Edgar Allan Poe): *Hope for a Harvest* (1941).

TRENYOV, Konstantin, 1884-1945, Russian dramatist. *Ljubov Yarovaya* (1926, revised 1937. Psychological drama set in the Russian Civil War).

TRETYAKOV, Sergei, 1892-1937, Russian dramatist, known mainly through the revolutionary play, produced by Meyerhold, *Roar China!* (1926, translated. The persecution of Chinese coolies by white colonialists); also wrote the revolutionary play, *The Earth Rises Up* (October Revolution); *Gas Masks* (1924, mutiny of German workers in a poison gas factory); *I Want a Child*.

TRIESTE, Leopoldo, b. 1919, Italian dramatist. *La fronticia* (1946); *Cronaca* (1946); *Trio a solo* (1946); *N.N.* (1947).

TUCIĆ, Srdan, 1873-1940, Croatian dramatist. At first influenced by Tolstoy and Sudermann; later turned to symbolism. *Return to Home* (1898); *The End* (1899); *Storm* (1905); *Golgotha* (1913); *The Liberators* (1913).

TURNER, W. J., 1889-1946, English literary critic. Wrote the experimental drama, *The Man Who Ate the Popomack* (1922).

UNAMUNO, Miguel de, 1864-1936, Spanish philosopher and poet. *La esfingo* (Written ca. 1900, staged 1909); *El pasado que vuelve* (Written 1910); *Fedra* (Written 1910, staged 1918. Legend of Phaedra); *Soledad* (Written 1921, staged 1953); *Raquel encadenada* (Written 1921); *Sombras de sueño* (Written 1926, staged 1930); *El otro* (Written 1926, staged 1932); *El hermano Juan o El mundo es teatro* (Written 1929. Legend of Don Juan); *Medea* (Adapted from Seneca and staged 1933).

UNRUH, Fritz von, b. 1885, German dramatist. One of the foremost Expressionists. Subjective ecstaticism. Later attempted to achieve a more regular form. *Offiziere* (1912); *Louis Ferdinand, Prinz von Preussen* (Written 1913, performed 1921. Kleist-type drama about the higher duty to disobey military commands; the hero a typical expressionistic representative of youth); *Vor der Entscheidung* (Written 1914, published 1919. Dramatic poem; anti-war play); *Ein Geschlecht* (1916. A mother's complaint against war; brotherhood of lovers against "the barracks of might"); *Platz* (1920, sequel to *Ein Geschlecht*); *Stürme* (1922); *Rosengarten* (1923); *Heinrich von Andernach* (1925, pageant play); *Bonaparte* (1926, translated); *Phäa* (1930, comedy set in the film world); *Zero* (1932, comedy); *Charlotte Corday* (1936); *Hauptmann Werner* (1936, composed in the USA); *Der Befreiungsminister* (1948, comedy); *Wilhelmus, Prinz von Oranien* (1953); *Duell an der Havel* (1954); *Bismarck oder Warum steht der Soldat da?* (1955, comedy. Takes place 1859, in St. Petersburg, where Bismarck was an envoy); and others.

USTINOV, Peter Alexander, b. 1921, English dramatist and actor. International success with *The Love of Four Colonels* (1951. Political tensions transferred into an almost surrealistic fairy tale allegory. The point of departure is highly realistic: four colonels of the occupation forces in a small German town. The good and bad fairies call on them and lead them to the castle where the German Sleeping Beauty lies. All four have to play a scene with the Princess, but none of them can conquer her); *Romanoff and Juliet* (1956. A second attempt to deal with the East-West problem through an old theatrical plot.). Other plays: *House of Regrets* (1942); *Blow Your Own Trumpet* (1943); *The Banbury Nose* (1944); *The Tragedy of Good Intentions* (1945); *The Indifferent Shepherd* (1948); *The Moment of Truth* (1951); *No Signs of the Dove* (1953); *The Empty Chair* (1956); *Paris Not So Gay* (1958, Paris and Helen); *Photo Finish* (1962); and others.

VAILLAND, Roger, b. 1907, French novelist. Theatrical success with the Don Juan comedy, *Monsieur Jean* (1959). Earlier: *Heloïse et Abelard* (1949); *Colonel Foster plaidera coupable* (1952, anti-American).

VALÉRY, Paul, 1871-1945, French lyric poet and thinker. Dramatic poem, *Mon Faust* (1945, *My Faust*. Part I: "Luste, or the Crystal Girl," a comedy; Part II: "The Only One, or the Curses of the Cosmos." The metaphysical element is completely set aside, and the figures are modernized—Faust becomes a writer and philosopher, Miss Luste is his secretary, and Mephisto a conjurer. Valéry's thought is allied with the element of opposition in modern drama through the denial and negation that run throughout the play.). Also poems in dramatic form, including *Amphion* (1931, translated with same title); *Semiramis* (1934, trans. same title); *Cantate du Narcisse* (1944, *The Narcissus Cantata*); and many dialogues.

VAN DRUTEN, John, 1901-1957, English dramatist. Wrote the comedy, *The Voice of the Turtle* (1943, a GI on furlough spends a week-end with a girl in a New York apartment). Other plays: *Young Woodley* (1925); *Diversion* (1928); *London Wall* (1931); *There's Always Juliet* (1931); *Behold, We Live* (1932); *The Distaff Side* (1933); *Old Acquaintance* (1940); *I Remember Mama* (1944, from Kathryn Forbes' *Mama's Bank Account*); *Bell, Book and Candle* (1950); *I Am a Camera* (1951), from Christopher Isherwood's *Berlin Stories*); and others.

VARNLUND, Rudolf, 1900-1945, Swedish dramatist. Politico-social plays on contemporary problems. *The Holy Family* (1932); *Singers* (1933, folk comedy); *The Teacher* (1935); *The Way to Canaan* (1935); *U 39* (1939).

VAUTHIER, Jean, b. 1910, French dramatist of the avant-garde. *L'Impromptu d'Arras* (1951); *Capitaine Bada* (1952); *La nouvelle Mandragore* (1952); *Le Personnage combattant ou Fortissimo* (1956. The end of a writer's life. In order to write his great novel, an author returns to a hotel room which holds memories for him. He reads extracts from his first work, which he also wrote in this hotel room, and recognizes that what he has gained in virtuosity he has lost in integrity. Three persons speak in the person of the one important character in this monodrama: the young writer of the past, the established author of today, and the man who has come to see the vanity of his life. The only other character to appear is the waiter, but we also hear voices from the neighboring room: the professor, a mezzo-soprano, a man, a woman. The hero loses his struggle for the recovery of his youthful idealism: he destroys his manuscripts, throws his money out of the window, and is dragged out by the waiter.); *Les Prodiges* (1957); *Le Rêveur* (published 1960). Contributed to *Chemises de nuit* (1962).

VERNEUIL, Louis, 1893-1952, French comedy writer. Boulevard pieces with predominantly erotic themes. Examples: *Mlle. ma mère* (1920); *Le Mariage de maman* (1925). Later plays with semi-political themes: *Affairs of State* (1950).

VIDAL, Gore, b. 1925, American novelist and dramatist. *Visit to a Small Planet* (1957, farce about a visitor from another world); *The Best Man* (1960, comedy of presidential politics); *Romulus* (1962, adaptation of Dürrenmatt's *Romulus der Grosse*); television plays.

VILDRAC, Charles, b. 1882, French dramatist. Plays set in the middle-class milieu, e.g., *Le Paquebot Tenacity* (1920, *S.S. Tenacity*); *Madame Béliard* (1925); *La Brouille* (1930); *Le Jardinier de Samos* (1932); *L'Air du temps* (1938).

VISHNEVSKI, Vsevolod, 1901-1951, Russian dramatist. Wrote the revolutionary play, *First Cavalry Regiment* (1930) and *The Optimistic Tragedy* (1932, translated. One of the most popular and most discussed plays in the Communist countries. Hans Meyer: "Anarchists have taken over a warship of the former Imperial Russian Fleet during the Revolution. The leader of this anarchistic group, a former anti-Czarist fighter who has long ago divorced himself from all true revolutionary principles, is basically a cynical, misanthropic, and power-mad individual who cares nothing for other human lives as long as they contribute to the maintenance of his power ... His trusted right-hand man is the 'Croaker,' a criminal character, rotted both in mind and body. Together with a small group of fellow-spirits, all of them also basically cowardly and unprincipled, these two exercise a tyranny thinly disguised as revolutionary ardor over the slack, undecided mass of the sailors, who are tired alike of war and of discipline. The conflict begins when the Soviet government sends a military commissar to take over the ship. This commissar is a woman. Which will win—the temporary anarchistic misuse of power, or the principles of the new Soviet order? The fact that the sailors want peace

and are tired of fighting favors the present balance of power, i.e., the anarchist leader; the new commissar and the party of Lenin, on the other hand, are obliged to ask these men to fight against the foreign interventionists who are threatening the revolution, to swear allegiance to a new military order, to obey the orders of experienced officers, even if these are former Czarist officers." In the first act there is a sort of truce between the anarchists and the commissar. In the second, the bestiality of the anarchists is revealed by their murder of two wounded officers. This enables the commissar to disarm the anarchist leader and have him killed. Under the command of a former officer the "first marine regiment of the newly created Red Army" is created. The third act shows the testing of the new order in military action. At the end the mortally wounded commissar cries, "Hold high our flag, the flag of our Idea."). Other plays: *Endless Stretches the Sea* (1942); *Before the Walls of Leningrad* (1944); *Unforgettable 1919* (1949, translated. With Stalin as hero); and others.

VOJNOVIC, Ivo, 1857-1929, Croatian dramatist, symbolist. Most important work: *A Trilogy of Dubrovnik* (1901-02, translated); folk themes in *The Death of the Jugovich Mother* (1906) and *The Resurrection of Lazarus* (1913, translated).

VOLLMER, Lula, d. 1955, American dramatist. Regional dramas of the Carolina mountains. *Sun-Up* (1923); *The Shame Woman* (1923); *The Dunce Boy* (1925); *Trigger* (1927); *Moonshine and Honeysuckle* (1933); *The Hill Between* (1938); and others.

VOLLMOELLER, Karl, 1878-1948, German dramatist. Aestheticism of the Maeterlinck type. *Catherina, Gräfin von Armagnac, und ihre beiden Liebhaber* (1903, baroque drama); *Assüs; Fitme und Sumurud* (1904, oriental); *Giulia* (1905); *Der deutsche Graf* (1906); *Wieland* (1911); *Das Mirakel* (1912, *The Miracle*, mystery-pantomime made famous by Reinhardt); *Die Schiessbude* (pantomime—tragedy of a puppeteer); *Cocktail* (1930).

VOSKOVEC, Jiri, Czech dramatist, actor, manager of the ABC Theater in Prague. Particularly successful with *Ragged Ballads* (1935, with Jan Werich). Now, as George Voskovec, active as an actor in Hollywood and New York.

WALSER, Martin, born 1927, German novelist and dramatist. *Der Abstecher* (1961, *The Detour*, farcical treatment of a love triangle); *Eiche und Angora* (1962, *The Rabbit Race*, realistic satire on the fellow-travellers of Nazism); *Überlebensgross Herr Krett* (1963).

WANGENHEIM, Gustav von, b. 1895, East German dramatist. East German National Prize. *Die Mausefalle* (1931); *Hier liegt der Hund begraben* (1932); *Wer ist der Dümmste?* (1933); *Das Urteil* (1933); *Die Maus in der Falle* (1946); *Du bist der Richtige* (1950); *Wir sind schon weiter* (1951); *Auch in Amerika* (1951); *Die fromme Marta* (1953); *Das ängstliche Mariechen* (1956); *Studentenkomödie* (1959); *Die vertauschten Brüder* (1960).

WANNER, Paul, b. 1896, German dramatist. Wrote the prisoner of war play, *PG* (*Prisonnier de Guerre,* 1931) and a series of open-air plays, e.g., *Baumeister Gottes; Bettler vor dem Kreuz; Die Weiber von Schorndorf; Der Schneider von Ulm; Das Kaiserspiel;* and others. Recent plays; *Der Leonberger Landtag* (1957) *and Der Geiger von Gmünd* (1960).

WARREN, Robert Penn, b. 1905, American poet, novelist, and dramatist. *All the King's Men* (1948, directed by Erwin Piscator, revised 1959. "Epic" drama, adapted from Warren's novel of the same name, about a Southern politician who resembles Huey Long); *Brother to Dragons* (published 1953, "a tale in verse and voices").

WEDEKIND, Frank, 1864-1918, German dramatist. Saw the theater as a moral institution with drama as a distorted reflection of human treachery, lying, pretended piety, horror, cynicism, and weakness. Used anti-illusionistic devices for the purpose of strengthening the illusion—demonic exaggeration of the driving force in mankind, over-emphasis of elements to the point of the ridiculous, condensation through rejection of nuance and values, caricature, grotesquerie, cabaret elements. (Wedekind was one of the representatives of the literary cabaret style). As destroyer of the conventional act-divided play and as a sworn enemy of aestheticism he was chosen by the Expressionists as the prophet of their revolution. The pandemonium of the *Lulu* dramas points in another direction, however: Nietzsche's innocence of the flesh is here objectified in the relations of a group of ethereal characters—in a sort of modern morality play. Chief works: *Frühlings Erwachen* (Written 1890-91, published 1891, staged by Reinhardt, 1906. A tragedy of youth); *Der Liebestrank* (1891-92, farce); *Erdgeist* (Written 1892-94; published 1895; performed 1898. *Earth Spirit.* Part I of *Lulu*); *Die Büchse der Pandora* (Written 1892-1901, published 1904, performed 1905. *Pandora's Box.* Part II of *Lulu;* both parts are designated as tragedies. Basis of opera by Alban Berg.); *Der Kammersänger* (1899, *The Tenor,* three scenes); *Der Marquis von Keith* (1900, *The Marquis of Keith*); *König Nicolo oder So ist das Leben* (1901, *King Nicolo, or Such Is Life*); *Hidalla oder Karl Hetmann, der Zwergriese* (1903); *Tod und Teufel* (1905, also known as *Totentanz* and translated as *Death and Devil* and as *Damnation.* Three scenes); *Musik* (1906, subtitled "A Picture of Morals in Four Scenes"); *Die Zensur* (1907, subtitled "A Theodicy in One Act"); *Oaha, die Satire der Satire* (1908, later titled *Till Eulenspiegel,* comedy); *Schloss Wetterstein* (1910, *Castle Wetterstein*); *Franziska* (1911, Subtitled "A Modern Mystery Play." Prose, verse, choruses); *Simson oder Scham und Eifersucht* (1913, dramatic poem); *Bismarck* (1916); *Herakles* (1917, dramatic poem). Also wrote *Die Kaiserin von Neufundland* (1897, pantomime).

WEIGEL, Hans, b. 1880, Austrian journalist and dramatist. Wrote *Barrabas* (1946); *Wartesaal* (1949); also *Der eingebildete Doktor; Das wissen die Götter,* and others. Has adapted Nestroy.

WEISENBORN, Günther, b. 1902, German dramatist. Wrote the anti-war play, *U-Boot S4,* in living newspaper style in 1928. Other plays: *SOS* (1929); *Die Arbeiter von Jersey* (1931); *Die Neuberin* (1935, written under the pseudonym Eberhard Förster-Munk); *Die guten Feinde* (1936, about Robert Koch); *Babel* (1945, written in prison); *Die Illegalen* (1945); *Die Ballade vom Eulenspiegel, vom Federle und der dicken Pompanne* (1949); *Das Spiel vom Thomaskantor* (1950); *Die spanische Hochzeit* (1951); *Drei ehrenwerte Herren* (1951); *Zwei Engel steigen aus* (1954); *Lofter oder Das verlorene Gesicht* (1956); *Die Familie von Nevada* (1958, atom bomb tests); *15 Schnüre Geld* (1958, based on the old Chinese play by Chu-Su-Chen). *Göttinger Kantate* (1958, anti-atom bomb oratorio). Weisenborn: "The theater is a place where humanity can talk with itself—here it reproaches itself, despairs, or becomes either confused or delighted. In contrast to the parliament, the theater is the inner voice of the people. The dream becomes realized in costume, the personal longing in dialogue, the personal hope in the plot. The uninterrupted flow of characters over the stage that has gone on for centuries has changed our people, be they the Cid, Hamlet, Lulu or Galileo. The theater can be an operating room, a tree nursery, a flower garden, or a laughing cabinet; but it is always a place of change."

WELK, Ehm, (Thomas Trimm), b. 1884, East German journalist, novelist, and dramatist. East German National Prize. *Gewitter über Gotland* (1926, produced by Piscator); *Kreuzabnahme* (1929); *Michael Kobbe* (1931, comedy); *Schwarzbrot* (1932).

WELTI, Albert J., b. 1894, Swiss painter and writer. First wrote dialect plays and pageant plays. His straight plays consist of *Maroto und sein König* (1926); *Der Vertrag mit dem Teufel; Ramon Lull; Hiob der Sieger* (1955, deals with Kepler's intervention on behalf of his mother who is on trial as a witch); and others.

WENDLER, Otto Bernhard, 1895-1957, East German dramatist. *Theater eines Gesichts* (1925); *Liebe, Mord und Alkohol* (1931); *Ein Schauspieler geht durch die Politik* (1932); *Pygmalia* (1943); *Die Glut in der Asche* (1950, tragicomedy); *Eine Handvoll Männer* (1956); and others.

WENDT, Stephan, b. 1909, German dramatist. Lives in London. *Hôtel de la Liberté* (1955); *Politik und Liebe* (1956).

WERFEL, Franz, 1890-1945, Austrian lyric poet, story writer, and dramatist. Began as an Expressionist with *Troerinnen* (1915, based on Euripides); *Bockgesang* (1921, *Goat Song*); *Spiegelmensch* (1920, "magical trilogy." Symbolic drama of a man with two personalities, the real one and the apparent one in the apparent world.); *Schweiger* (1922. Psychoanalysis and politics: A man's past is revealed—he has committed a murder but has been relieved of the memory of the crime by psy-

choanalysis and now lives as a harmless watchmaker. He is exposed when the Socialists take him as the prototype of the happy man.). After he left Expressionism, Werfel wrote historical plays which became more and more religious in theme: *Juarez und Maximilian* (1924, *Juarez and Maximilian*); *Paulus unter den Juden* (1926, *Paul among the Jews*); *Das Reich Gottes in Böhmen* (1930, Hussite drama); *Der Weg der Verheissung* (Published 1935, staged in New York by Reinhardt, 1936 as *The Eternal Road*. Biblical play.); *In einer Nacht* (1937). While in exile he wrote the popular comedy, *Jakobowski und der Oberst* (1944, *Jacobowsky and the Colonel*. A Jewish civilian and a Polish officer as refugees in France in 1940).

WERICH, Jan, Czech man of the theater. See Voskovec, Jiri.

WESKER, Arnold, b. 1932, English dramatist. Socialist critic of society. Triology of (mainly Jewish) life in England: *Chicken Soup with Barley* (1958); *Roots* (1959); and *I'm Talking with Jerusalem* (1960). Also, *The Kitchen* (1959, as a one-act play; 1961, as a full-length play); *Chips with Everything* (1962, about the R.A.F.).

WEXLEY, John, b. 1907, American dramatist. *The Last Mile* (1930, prison drama); *Steel* (1931); *They Shall Not Die* (1934, Scottsboro case); *Running Dogs* (1936, communism in China).

WEYMANN, Gert, b. 1919, German dramatist of the post World War II generation. Wrote *Generationen* (1954. Written in the strict technique of the Ibsen play without theses. Deals with an external conflict in modern times); *Eh die Brücken verbrennen* (1958).

WHITING, John, 1917-1963, English dramatist of the post-World War II generation. Symbolic realism and comedy. Wrote *Saints' Day* (1951, a savage character tragedy); *A Penny for a Song* (1951, comedy); *Marching Song* (1954. Mixture of a modern abstract play and contemporary circumstances: an imaginary defeated country; the representative of the former ruling class, a general, is released from prison and returns to the villa of his former mistress. The Chancellor of the new ruling class visits him in order to persuade him to poison himself. He wants to prevent the general's trial. The general's mistress, however, makes him want to live. But only for a moment: the decision has already been dictated by conscience, for the general has been obliged to shoot a child during the war. He takes the poison.); *The Gates of Summer* (1956); *The Devils* (1961, based on Aldous Huxley's *The Devils of Loudun*. A witch-hunt in the 17th century).

WIED, Gustav, 1858-1914, Danish comedy writer. *Dancing Mice* (1905); *2 times 2 equals 5* (1907); and many others.

WILDE, Oscar, 1854-1900, English essayist, poet, novelist, dramatist. Raised the 19th century drawing-room drama to the level of art. *Vera, or the Nihilists* (Written 1881); *The Duchess of Padua* (Written 1883, performed 1891); *Lady Windermere's Fan* (1892. Satire of drawing-room melodrama); *Salome* (Published 1893, one act, in French); *A Woman of No Importance* (1893); *An Ideal Husband* (1895); *The Importance of Being Earnest* (1895, one of the greatest comedies in the English language. Satirizes the devices of 19th-century comedy); *A Florentine Tragedy* (Published posthumously. In blank verse; unfinished); *Courtisane, or The Woman Covered with Jewels* (Published posthumously; unfinished).

WILDER, Thornton, b. 1897, American writer, novelist and dramatist. Anti-illusionistic theater. Breakdown of reality in form and in religion. Theme: the border between life and death and the overlapping of both spheres. Christian in the sense that temporal life has meaning only insofar as it can receive the light from the life beyond. Few writers are as familiar as Wilder is with the forms and other possibilities of dramatic creation. He has stated that he found the source for the pantomimic-dialogue experiment which he uses most effectively in the one-act *Happy Journey* in the Chinese drama by way of Meyerhold and Taïrov. But he has also been influenced by the Mystery plays, the Moralities, Nestroy, the Greeks, and the Spaniards. Accordingly, he employs the most varied forms and often combines them for new dramatic significance. The form of his latest play, *The Alcestiad,* only gives the appearance of being based on the Attic trilogy and satyr play; in reality the succession of acts in the inner form constitutes a change of style. Early plays: *The Trumpet Shall Sound* (Pub-lished 1919-20, performed 1926). The "Three-Minute Plays" (collected in 1928 under the title *The Angel That Troubled the Waters*. These plays appear to be exercises in style, but the wide ramifications of the subject matter can be seen in their titles: "Nascuntur Poetae," "Proserpina and the Devil," "Fanny Otcott," "Brother Fire," "The Penny That Beauty Spent," "The Angel on the Ship," "The Message and Jehanne," "Childe Roland to the Dark Tower Came," "Centaurs," "Leviathan," "And the Sea Shall Give Up Its Dead," "Now the Servant's Name Was Malchus," "Mozart and the Gray Steward," "Hast Thou Considered My Servant Job?" "The Flight Into Egypt," "The Angel That Troubled the Waters." Actually these are all plays for three characters. Wilder has credited Herbert Eulenberg's *Schattenbilder* with providing him with inspiration.). One-act plays: *The Long Christmas Dinner* (takes place over ninety years); *Queens of France* (A young Frenchwoman is told that she is the legitimate heir to the throne of the Bourbons. The time is 1869); *The Happy Journey to Trenton and Camden* ("No scenery is required for this play. . . . The Stage Manager not only moves forward and withdraws the few properties that are required, but he reads from a typescript the lines of all the minor characters." The play concerns an average family's departure on an auto journey and the journey itself—the automobile is represented by chairs.); *Love and How to Cure It* (takes place on the stage of the London Tivoli in 1895—soubrettes, dancers, comedians, student. An unhappy lover, resolved on suicide, is healed by a new love); *Pullman Car Hiawatha* (again with a stage manager and no set; monologues of nine people in their Pullman berths). The one-act plays appeared in 1931 under the title, *The Long Christmas Dinner.—Our Town* (1938. No props and very little set; stage manager. Place: a small town in America; time: May 7, 1901. Right and left, the houses—only vaguely indicated—of the doctor and the newspaper editor. Everyday scenes between the couples and their children—breakfast, school, cooking, feeding the chickens, getting the milk and the newspapers, etc. The second act takes place three years later. Stage Manager: "The First Act was called Daily Life. This act is called Love and Marriage. There's another act coming after this: I reckon you can guess what that's about." This third act, nine years later, takes place on a "beautiful spot" with "lots of sky, lots of clouds—often lots of sun and moon and stars"; it is the cemetery. The attendant explains the gravestones to a visitor. The bride of the second act has died giving birth to her second child. She is about to be buried. The dead sit on the stage, and the coffin is brought in, followed by the mourners. The dead speak in chorus. The newcomer wishes to live through one happy day once more—her twelfth birthday. As she lives through the day again, she learns, "That's all human beings are! Just blind people...That's what it was to be alive. To move about in a cloud of ignorance."); *The Skin of Our Teeth* (1942. Family play as world theater. The family: Mr. Antrobus—Adam, Mrs. Antrobus—Eve, Henry, their son—Cain, Sabina the maid—Lilith. In each act the family escapes a universal catastrophe by the skin of its teeth: the Ice Age, the Flood, and war. Within these times other times are joined, e.g., two saurians crawl about as house pets during the first act; Moses and Homer are neighbors, but the family is dressed in modern clothes. In the last act the wise men of all ages appear to give their views. The play concerns eternal Man.); *The Matchmaker* (1954, previously *The Merchant of Yonkers,* 1938. Americanization of Nestroy's farce, *Einen Jux will er sich machen*); *Alcestiad* (1955, originally *A Life in the Sun,* new version, 1957. The Alcestis story in the second act: Alcestis' sacrifice for her husband, Admetus and her rescue from Hades by Hercules. The first act takes place twelve years previously, when Alcestis is a young bride afraid of her husband. She wishes to go to Delphi to consult Apollo and learn the meaning of life from him. This is the basic theme—knowledge, understanding, for "the greatest evil is ignorance." The prophet Tiresias appears and says that Apollo wishes to serve incognito at the court of Admetus. He is one of the four shepherds that have just arrived, but nobody knows which one. Alcestis takes this as a sign and agrees to marry Admetus, saying that she will live for him as if she were ready at any moment to die for him. The last act takes place twelve years later. Terrible things have happened—the barbarians have overrun the country, epidemics rage, the king and all his servants are dead—all except a long-lost son and Alcestis, who draws water like a slave. When the daughter of the barbarian-king dies of the epidemic and the long-lost son comes home as Orestes did—seeking revenge, Alcestis applies her new wisdom. She decrees that the son must forgive and the barbarian-king must go, for the epidemic and the slaughter were signs that something had changed and that there is now a bridge between life and death, between the present and the beyond, the gods and men. A ray of light has pierced the darkness: "Love," says Alcestis, "is not the meaning. It is only one of the signs that there *is* a meaning." A satyr play follows —"The Drunken Sisters." This shows Apollo making the Parthians drunk and winning the life of Admetus from them by asking them a riddle. Wilder's purpose was undoubtedly the elevation of the Alcestis story out of the everyday—the bride's fear—into the mythic and the Christian.); *The Emporium* (Unfinished). *Plays for Bleecker Street* (1962, three one-act plays, *Infancy, Childhood, Lust*).

WILDGANS, Anton, 1881-1932, Austrian dramatist. Stands between Naturalism and Expressionism. *In Ewigkeit Amen* (1913); *Armut* (1914); *Liebe* (1916); *Dies irae* (1918); *Kain* (1920).

WILLEMS, Paul, b. 1912, Flemish dramatist of the post-World War II generation. Plays of folk life and fairy tale plays. *Le bon Vin de Monsieur Nuche* (1948, comedy); *Peau d'ours* (1950); *Off et la lune* (1954. Chief character is a dog, played by an actor); *Un Merle n'est pas un merle* (1957); *Il pleut dans ma Maison* (1958); *Phébus ou la plage aux anguilles.* Willems: "The theater is properly the place where the irrational reveals itself. Tenderness or harshness, belief or doubt, tragedy or comedy, it is life itself that is put on the stage and speaks the language of poetry . . . The theater offers no examples, it reveals ourselves."

WILLIAMS, Emlyn, b. 1905, English actor and dramatist. International success with *Night Must Fall* (1935), *He Was Born Gay* (1937); and *The Corn Is Green* (1938). Other plays: *The Light of Heart* (1940); *Spring 1600* (1945); *Accolade* (1950); *Someone Waiting* (1953); *Beth* (1958).

WILLIAMS, Jesse Lynch, 1871-1929, American dramatist. Popular society drama. *The Stolen Story* (1906); *Why Marry?* (1917); *Why Not?* (1922); *Lovely Lady* (1925).

WILLLIAMS, Tennessee, b. 1914, American dramatist. Together with Anouilh and Miller one of the most successful of the present-day playwrights. His success is due to his proficiency with the technique of the conventionally constructed play which is robust when it has to be and delicate when it has to be, and to a plot line mixed of equal parts of brutality and sophistication. The plots are almost exclusively concerned with problems in psychology. Williams is the chief representative of the psychoanalytic drama, for which he considers himself to have a mission. One would think that the desire to live on illusions was a prerogative of the middle classes, but it is probable that the women whom Williams shows us in their "nylonized" doll's houses represent a common American type. Williams knows how to individualize their stories, but the decisive stroke which is directed against them is almost always referred to a type of situation carried to an extreme in order to shock. The shock has the function of making us afraid that it could happen to us if we keep withdrawing from the real world. The extreme situation is regulated strictly according to Freud in that greater and greater waves of frustration are created as a person becomes more and more entangled in the world of illusion. Thus, sophisticated women throw themselves helplessly into the arms of he-men in these extreme situations. Williams usually equates the world of illusion with poetry and romanticism, while the brutal driving forces are equated with the "true" world. Since this "truth" is only vaguely intended to be socially critical, it is difficult to say what Williams thinks of the relation of people to people, particularly with regard to the sexes. His opinions seem to be primarily negative. He puts himself on the side of opposition, but he seems to believe that clarification is all that is needed to free men from their spiritual problems. In *Camino Real,* where he attempts to break through reality, his clarification has no other choice than to become mystical (under the influence of Jung). Early plays: *American Blues* (Published 1948, five one-acters: *Moony's Kid Don't Cry, The Dark Room, The Case of the Crushed Petunias, The Long Stay Cut Short, or, The Unsatisfactory Supper, Ten Blocks on the Camino Real*); *Battle of Angels* (1940, reworked as *Orpheus Descending* in 1957. Orpheus as a Southern guitar player; Eurydice as the wife of a cancer-ridden man she does not love, who catches her with the guitarist and shoots her. The guitarist is hunted by the sheriff's hounds); *Stairs to the Roof* (1941); *You Touched Me* (1945, with Donald Windham, from a story by D. H. Lawrence); *I Rise in Flames, Cried the Phoenix* (Published 1951, one-act, about D. H. Lawrence). First hit: *The Glass Menagerie* (1945. The glass menagerie is a collection of glass animals which are loved by a lame, illusion-bound girl. Her mother is lost in her memories and fantasies but is trying to get a husband for her daughter. The son, who is the chorus of the play, finally flees this bizarre milieu, as his father did before him. But first he brings a friend who wants an evening's amusement. The friend helps the daughter cast off her inhibitions to the extent of letting herself be kissed, but then he leaves in order to go to his fiancée. The disappointed women are finally deserted.); *A Streetcar Named Desire* (1947. His second big success. "If I can be said to have a home, it is in New Orleans where I've lived on and off since 1938 and which has provided me with more material than any other part of the country. I live near the main street of the Quarter which is named Royal. Down this street, running on the same tracks, are two street-cars, one named Desire and the other named Cemetery. Their indiscourageable progress up and down Royal struck me as having some symbolic bearing of a broad nature on the life in the Vieux Carré—and everywhere else for that matter." These same street-cars are heard in this play. A young couple is bound together by sexual desire. The wife's sister, Blanche, a delicate, hysterical schoolteacher with exaggerated airs, enters and is courted by a friend of the husband's. The husband himself is filled with an animal-like longing for her. He discovers certain facts about Blanche's past, discourages her boy friend, and rapes her after telling her some brutal truths. In the last scene Blanche is taken away to a madhouse.); *Summer and Smoke* (1948); *The Rose Tattoo* (1951. A Sicilian woman in New Orleans is so absorbed in mourning her dead husband that she lives completely in a dream world into which she tries to draw her daughter. She is healed after she meets a man who seems to have a rose tattooed on his chest just like her husband.).—*Camino Real* (1953. Sixteen stations of a Mystery play. The scene is a place where all sorts meet—criminals and fugitives, actors and beggars, spies and vagabonds. Others who appear include Casanova and the Lady of the Camelias, Proust's Baron de Charlus, Lord Byron, Don Quixote and Sancho Panza. The chief character is Kilroy, a red-blooded American boy and former boxing champion. As soon as he appears someone steals his money, leaving him with nothing at all since he has given up smoking, drinking, and sex for reasons of health. He now has three problems: "One: I'm hungry. Two: I'm lonely. Three: I'm in a place where I don't know what it is or how I got here." He becomes a clown, and with the others he seeks the way out of the Camino Real. A gypsy tries to trap him with her daughter, he is beaten up, and finally he joins forces with Don Quixote. The play consists of revue-type scenes, and the thin line of the Morality play action is bolstered by literary and allegorical allusions, interrupted by theatrical "thriller" effects such as chases, airplane motor sound effects, etc.) *Cat on a Hot Tin Roof* (1955); *Garden District* (1958, two one-act plays: *Something Unspoken*, a dialogue between two old women who have lived together for fifteen years and now feel something coming between them. *Suddenly Last Summer*. "Two women fight for spiritual possession of a dead man: an old and rigid woman who considers her son her property, despite his death, and Catherine, a young girl who witnessed his brutal murder. . . . In her statement, which is made in the presence of the family under the influence of truth serum, she reconstructs his death. . . . The shattering of the dream by means of the word—that is the theme and content of this work. Just as Blanche in *Streetcar* is stifled by the unspoken and suppressed word and just as Brick frees himself from the things that burden him in his conversation with Big Daddy in *Cat on a Hot Tin Roof* by expressing them, so Catherine is the only one who has the courage to speak the truth . . . in the face of the family's opposition." [Hans Sahl]); *Sweet Bird of Youth* (1959); *Period of Adjustment* (1960. Comedy); *The Night of the Iguana* (1961); *The Milk Train Doesn't Stop Here Anymore* (1962, Spoleto; 1963, New York). Other one-act plays, among them *27 Wagons Full of Cotton* (1946, later adapted and filmed under the title *Baby Doll*).

WILLIAMS, William Carlos, 1883-1963, American poet, novelist, dramatist, and physician. *The First President* (Published 1936, libretto for an opera about George Washington.); *Many Loves* (Written 1940, published 1942, professionally performed 1959. Three kinds of love examined in three connected one-act plays.); *A Dream of Love* (Published 1948, performed 1949); *Tituba's Children* (Completed 1950, published 1961. About the Salem witch-hunt.); *The Cure* (Completed 1960, published 1962).

WILLINGHAM, Calder, b. 1922, American novelist and dramatist. Known principally for *End as a Man* (1951, dramatization of the novel of the same name. Power madness in a military school). Other plays: *The Automobile Man* (1956, comedy); *The Pink House* (comedy).

WILSON, Edmund, b. 1895, American literary critic. *The Crime in the Whistler Room* (1924); *This Room and This Gin and These Sandwiches* (Published 1937, formerly titled *A Winter in Beech Street*); *Beppo and Beth* (Published 1937); *The Little Blue Light* (1951. Liberalism, power politics and some elements of fantasy); *Cyprian's Prayer* (Published 1954, fantasy).

WIRTA, Nikolai, b. 1906, Russian dramatist and story writer. *The Land* (1937); *The Great Days* (1947, Stalingrad); *Our Daily Bread* (1947); *The Renunciation of the Damned* (1948); *Three Pillars of Belief* (1960, Lenin on the eve of the revolution of 1905); and others.

WITKIEWICZ, Stanislav Ignacy, 1885-1939, Polish painter and poet. Theoretician of "pure form." Experimental plays, partly surrealistic. *Metaphysics of a Calf With Two Heads* (1921); *The Pragmatists* (1922); *The Nun and the Madman* (1923); *Beelzebub's Sonata* (1925); *The Cobblers* (1927-1934, revolutionary play).

WITTLINGER, Karl, b. 1922, German dramatist of the post-World War II generation. Wrote the comedies, *Der Himmel der Besiegten; Junge Liebe auf Besuch;* the popular two-character piece, *Kennen Sie die Milchstrasse?* (1955, *Do You Know the Milky Way?* Cabaret-style Utopian play); *Kinder des Schattens* (1957, comedy); *Lazarus* (1958); *Zwei rechts, zwei links* (1960); *Seelenwanderung* (1963); *Zum Frühstück zwei Männer* (1963).

WOLF, Friedrich, 1888-1953, German dramatist of the post-World War I generation, physician, active Communist, East German diplomat. *Das bist du* (1918); *Der Unbedingte* (1919); *Die schwarze Sonne* (1919); *Mohammed* (1919); *Tamar* (1921); *Der arme Konrad* (1923, Peasants' Revolt); *Kolonne Hund* (1926); *Cyankali* (1929); *Die Matrosen von Cattaro* (1930; *The Sailors of Cattaro*, mutiny of the Austrian fleet); *Tai Yang erwacht* (1931, rebellion against the capitalists in Shanghai led by a working-girl); *Professor Mamlock* (1933, translated with same title, tragedy of a Jewish surgeon); *Floridsdorf* (1935, translated with same title, rebellion of the Viennese workers in 1934); *Das trojanische Pferd* (1937); *Beaumarchais* (1940, the tragic end of freedom's champion of 1789); *Patrioten* (1943, French Resistance fighters); *Dr. Lilli Wanner* (1944); *Was der Mensch säet* (1945); *Die letzte Probe* (1946); *Bürgermeister Anna* (1949, comedy); *Thomas Münzer* (1953); *Das Schiff auf der Donau* (1955, posthumous).

WOLFE, Thomas, 1900-1938, American epic novelist. *The Return of Buck Gavin* (1924) and *Mannerhouse* (Written in 1925. Chief characters: the general and his amiable son who is rebelling against the old order. The son loses his property to a *parvenu* businessman and supports himself). Also, *Welcome to Our City*. His novel *Look Homeword, Angel* dramatized by Ketti Frings (1957).

WOUK, Herman, b. 1915, American novelist and dramatist. International success with the dramatization of part of his novel, *The Caine Mutiny* as *The Caine Mutiny Court-Martial* (1954. Deals with the court-martial of a mutineer who deposed his captain on grounds of insanity. He is acquitted, but he and his friends are accused by his lawyer in an epilogue). Other plays: *The Traitor* (1949, atom spies); *Nature's Way* (1957).

WYSPIANSKI, Stanislav, 1869-1907, important Polish painter and dramatist. Praised by Gordon Craig as an example of the struggle for "pure theater." Not performed in Poland after the war until the "Polish October." *Legend* (1898); *The Maid of Warsaw* (1898; *Meleager* (1898); *Protesilaos and Laodamia* (1899); *Legion* (1899); *The Curse* (1899); *The Wedding* (1901, his most important

work); *Liberation* (1903); *Acropolis* (1904); *The Judges* (1907, modern drama in the style of the Greek tragedies).

YEATS, Jack B., 1871-1957, Irish painter and dramatist, brother of W. B. Yeats. *La La Noo* (1942); and other plays.

YEATS, William Butler, 1865-1939, Irish poet. Nobel Prize winner. Representative of the anti-illusionistic poetic drama, co-founder of the Abbey Theater, a distinctive force in the modern stage. Used mythical and mystical material, as well as the medieval forms. Finally came *Plays for Dancers* which go back to the Japanese Noh Theater. *The Countess Cathleen* (Published 1892, performed 1899. Legend of the Countess who sells her soul in order to save her country from starvation); *The Land of Heart's Desire* (1894, fairy tale); *The Shadowy Waters* (Published 1900, revised and staged 1904, revised again 1911. Symbolic drama); *Cathleen ni Houlihan* (1902, a beggar woman sends a young man from his wedding out to fight for his country); *The Pot of Broth* (1902, one act in prose); *The Hour-Glass* (1903, morality); *The King's Threshold* (1903); *On Baile's Strand* (1904); *Deirdre* (1906, the Irish Helen, also used by Synge); *The Unicorn from the Stars* (1907, with Lady Gregory); *The Golden Helmet* (1908, later revised as *The Green Helmet*. Heroic farce); *Four Plays for Dancers* (Published 1921): *At the Hawk's Well* (1917), *The Only Jealousy of Emer* (1919), *The Dreaming of the Bones* (1919), *Calvary* (1920); *The Player Queen* (1922, grotesque); *The Cat and the Moon* (1926); *Fighting the Waves* (1929, a variant of *The Only Jealousy of Emer*); *The Words Upon the Window Pane* (1930); *Purgatory* (1938).

ZAMYATIN, Yevgeni, 1884-1937, Russian story writer and dramatist. Supporter of the Russian Revolution. Left Russia in 1937 and died in Paris. Wrote *The Fires of St. Dominic* (1923); *The Flea* (1925, Commedia dell'arte piece based on Leskov); *Honorary Bell-Ringers* (1926, dramatized novel); *Attila* (1928, tragedy discovered after his death).

ZAPOLSKA, Gabriela, 1860-1921, important Polish dramatist and actress. *The Other One* (1896, melodrama); *In Dabrowa Gornicza* (1897, proletarian life); *Malka Szwarcenkopf* (1897, Jewish life); *The Morality of Mrs. Dulska* (1907, comedy of manners. Satiric depiction of the spiritual and moral atmosphere of a middle-class house. "Kulska" became a synonym for bourgeois types); *Miss Meliczewska* (1910, theater milieu).

ZARDI, Federicao, b. 1912, Italian dramatist. Comedies with satirico-critical tendencies. History in epic style. *E chi lo sa?* (1938); *La Livrea* (1951); *Emma* (1952); *I Giacobini* (1955, thirty scenes of the French Revolution, 1789-1794. Four parts based on the historical development of the Revolution: Constitutional Assembly, Gironde, Terror, Thermidor. Vindication of Robespierre, "the Incorruptible," who tried to protect the Revolution from corruption through terror and paid for it with his life. In a dialogue with St. Just, the eternal accuser, whom Lamartine has called the "archangel of death," Robespierre recognizes that he will not live to see the beginning of a purer and freer world; he is lonely; the uselessness of everything oppresses him; and yet the hope that the future may bring what the past could not produce leaves him the hope that his work may not have been entirely in vain. Zardi's idea is that a man grows out of himself for the sake of an idea and perishes because of it. Zardi thus sets himself against Brecht's view of history. Uses original documents and sources); *I tromboni* (1956, comedy about the Montesi scandal); *Serata di Gala* (1958).

ZAVATTINI, Cesare, b. 1903, Italian dramatist and film writer. *Come nasce un soggetto cinematografico* (1959).

ZEROMSKI, Stefan, 1864-1925, important Polish novelist and dramatist. *The Rose* (1909, dramatic treatment of the revolutionary events of 1905); *Sulkowski* (1910, historical drama about one of Napoleon's adjutants); *I Will Be Whiter than the Snow* (1919, social problems); *My Little Quail Has Fled* (1924, comedy); *The Sin* (Written 1897, published posthumously with a new ending by novelist Kruczkowski).

ZILAHY, Lajos, b. 1891, Hungarian novelist and dramatist. Has lived in the United States since 1947. *The Soul in Torment* (1922); *Bright Sunshine*

(1924); *Musical Clowns* (1925); *The White Stag* (1927); *The General* (1928); *The Night of the 17th of April* (1932); *The Virgin and the Kid* (1937); *A Girl of Good Family* (1937); *The Return Home* (1946); *The Wooden Towers* (1948); and others.

ZINNER, Hedda, b. 1907, German dramatist. Wrote history plays which are popular in East Germany: *Teufelskreis* (1953, burning of the Reichstag in living newspaper style); *Die Lützower* (1955, patriotic play in verse); *General Landt* (1957. Based on a novel by Martha Dodd and opposed to Zuckmayer's *Des Teufels General:* the non-political officer who is drawn more and more into Nazism through greed, honors, and fear—"The general's insignia nullify all human emotions.") Other plays: *Caféhaus Payer* (1945); *Spiel ins Leben* (1951); *Der Mann mit dem Vogel* (1952); *Was wäre wenn?* (1959, comedy); *Die Fischer von Niezow* (1960); *Leistungskontrolle* (1960); *Ravensbrücker Ballade* (1961).

ZOFF, Otto, b. 1890, Austrian dramatist, now living in the USA. Particularly successful with his new version of *Freier* (1923, after Eichendorff) and *König Hirsch* (1957, after Gozzi). Other plays: *Kerker und Erlösung* (1917); *Der Schneesturm* (1919); *Die zwei Abenteurer* (1926); *Rosen und Vergissmeinnicht* (1933); *Caesars Traum* (1942); *Die Glocken von London* (1958, after Dickens); *Brother and Sister Erskine* (1962).

ZUCKMAYER, Carl, b. 1896, German writer, most popular living German dramatist. Representative of a poetic theater in which the theatrical is emphasized almost more than the poetic. Zuckmayer turned to anti-programmatic drama when he left Expressionism in order to open up new channels of communication with the audience. He raised the style of scenic reporting, which was very popular at the time, to a literary level with *Hauptmann von Köpenick*. He successfully brought folk elements back into comedy and had the courage to show non-bourgeois heroes romantically (that is, he had the courage not to criticize them). There is a good deal of youthful high spirits mixed into this pattern, but he writes with much theatrical power and understanding of human nature. He uses forms which are adapted rather than newly created but always superbly controlled—in his use of forms Zuckmayer is no less an exponent of the renaissance of forms than Brecht or Anouilh. Zuckmayer's work, of which several pieces already belong to the classic repertory of the German-speaking theater, can be divided into three periods, of which the middle one is the best. First period, expressionistic: *Kreuzweg* (1920); *Die Wiedertäufer* (1921, unfinished); Adaptation of Terence's *Eunuch* (1923, caused theatrical scandal in Kiel); *Pankraz erwacht oder die Hinterwäldler* (1925, a play of the Far West). Second period: *Der fröliche Weinberg* (1925, comedy. About a vineyard owner who requires his daughter to marry a man who will give her a child.); *Schinderhannes* (1927. Play about the outlaw chief Johann Bückler in the days of Napoleon. Schinderhannes-Bückler attacks only the rich. The poor are on his side. He takes up with the ballad-singer Julchen and takes her with him. They are pursued by the gendarmes, who have set a price of 1000 gold pieces on Hannes' head. Hannes reads the reward offer to his band, but no one dares to betray him. They prepare to ambush a detachment of French soldiers by night. Time passes, and Julchen leaves Hannes because he has struck her in anger. His luck has left him too, for the people are no longer on his side. He has the opportunity to escape to the other side of the Rhine, but his only thought is to find Julchen again. He finds her in a cornfield where she is having birth pangs, but he is betrayed and captured. The execution is to take place in Mainz. He is permitted to spend his last night with Julchen. In the morning he is executed before 15,000 onlookers.); *Katharina Knie* (1929. Play about rope dancers. A small circus is not doing well—they cannot even buy fodder for the animals. Father Knie, the owner, is shattered when his daughter confesses that she has stolen fodder for the donkey, and he orders his daughter to return it to the farmer. The farmer, however, has fallen in love with her and wants to marry her. Father Knie cannot understand how anyone could want to leave the circus and settle down. In the second act Katharina has determined to marry but is hardly able to make up her mind to break the news to her father. During their conversation the father dies. Katharina gives up her lover and takes over the circus—the show must go on.); *Kakadukakada* (1929, children's play); *Der Hauptmann von Köpenick* (1931, *The

Captain from Köpernick*. Subtitled, "A German Fairy Tale in Three Acts and 21 Scenes." The famous story of Voigt, the shoemaker, who fools half of Berlin by putting on a captain's uniform, which he does simply in order to obtain a passport so that he can earn his living honestly. Precisely described milieu of Imperial Germany. Militarism and bureaucracy as objects of satire. Scenic reporting raised to the level of the parable or exemplum); *Der Schelm von Bergen* (1934. Based on a Rhineland folk story about the hangman's son and the emperor's daughter who love each other without knowing who they are.); *Bellman* (1938, revised as *Ulla Winblad* in 1953. Eight scenes about the loves of the 18th century Swedish poet and vagabond Carl Michael Bellman. Bellman's mistress, Ulla Winblad, marries a baron, while Bellman becomes court poet to Gustav III. The baron leads a conspiracy to murder the king. He succeeds and Bellman loses his protector. Baroness Ulla leaves the baron but finds Bellman dying. He ends his dissolute and glorious life in her arms. Many songs.). Third period—exile and return; *Des Teufels General* (1945, *The Devil's General*. The tragedy of the aviator Udet in the strict form of the act-divided play. Luftwaffe General Harras in the midst of his comrades, women, friends, and the state functionaries, and his downfall.); *Barbara Blomberg* (1949. Panoramic history play about a beautiful woman against the background of the Dutch struggle for freedom. Barbara Blomberg was the mistress of the Emperor Charles V in Regensburg. Her child became Don Juan of Austria, and she is living comfortably in Brussels as the widow of a ruined army major. She captivates Alba but is unable to save her friend, the English agent Rathcliff, from being arrested. Don Juan of Austria is named ruler of the Netherlands. In a grand *scène à faire* mother and son meet for the first time since he was taken away from her as a child. Barbara has sufficient generosity to see that she can only harm her son as a Belgian lady of influence and none too pure reputation. So she goes to Spain after she has obtained Rathcliff's release in order to end her days with Don Juan's foster parents.); *Der Gesang im Feuerofen* (1950, an attempt to give a poetic account of the anti-Nazi resistance. The place is the Swiss border. One of the chief characters is a young Frenchman who becomes a traitor. The SS sets fire to a castle in which the resistance fighters have taken refuge. They sing the "Te Deum Laudamus" which becomes the "song in the furnace." Mythical figures also take part in the drama.); *Das kalte Licht* (1955, play about atomic espionage based on the Klaus Fuchs case. The betrayal is begun on idealistic grounds, but in the last discussion between the hero, Wolters, and the British investigator there is a sort of reversal of conscience. The play is in the form of a station play. Zuckmayer: "The picture form is now my form; I do not want to become too dialectical. It is possible to write in a strict prose style and still pour forth a whole cornucopia of life. I believe that I can say that this is my special gift. And if one enjoys doing a thing so much, why shouldn't one?"). *Die Uhr Schlägt eins* (1961).

ZUPANCIĆ, Oton, 1878-1949, Slovenian poet. *Veronika Desemška* (1924). Well-known translator of Shakespeare.

ZUSANEK, Harald, b. 1922, popular Austrian dramatist of the post-World War II generation. Wrote *Warum gräbst du, Centurio?* (1949); *Die Strasse nach Cavarcere* (1952); *Jean von der Tonne* (1954); *Schloss in Europa* (1960); *Piazza* (1960).

ZWEIG, Arnold, b. 1887, German novelist and dramatist. East German National Prize. Wrote *Das Spiel vom Sergeanten Grischa* in 1921 which later, as a novel, became a world-wide success (translated as *The Case of Sergeant Grischa*). Other plays: *Abigail und Nabal* (1913); *Ritualmord in Ungarn* (1914); *Die Umkehr* (1927); *Bonaparte in Jaffa* (1939); *Soldatenspiele* (1956).

ZWEIG, Stefan, 1881-1942, Austrian writer. On the stage with the early drama, *Tersites* (1907); *Das Haus am Meer* (1911); *Der verwandelte Komödiant* (1912); *Jeremias* (1917; *Jeremiah*); *Legende eines Lebens* (1919); *Das Lamm des Armen* (1939); *Die schweigsame Frau* (1939, comic opera based on Ben Jonson's *Epicoene*, with score by Richard Strauss). Particularly successful with his adaptation of Ben Jonson's *Volpone* (1927).

CHRONOLOGY OF FIRST PERFORMANCES

1 9 0 0

Hauptmann	*Michael Kramer*	Berlin
Rolland	*Danton*	Paris
Rostand	*L'Aiglon* (with Bernhardt)	Paris
Strindberg	*Gustav Adolf*	Stockholm

1 9 0 1

Wedekind	*Marquis von Keith*	Berlin
Strindberg	*Easter*	Frankfurt
Shaw	*Caesar and Cleopatra*	London
D'Annunzio	*Francesca da Rimini* (with Duse)	Rome
Chekhov	*Three Sisters* (Stanislavski)	Moscow
Wyspianski	*The Wedding*	Warsaw
Strindberg	*Dance of Death*	Stockholm

1 9 0 2

Wedekind	*König Nicolo*	Munich
Thoma	*Moral*	Munich
Maeterlinck	*Monna Vanna*	Paris
Rolland	*July 14*	Paris
Shaw	*Mrs. Warren's Profession*	London
Yeats	*Cathleen ni Houlihan*	Dublin
Strindberg	*Charles XII*	Stockholm
Gorki	*The Lower Depths* (Stanislavski)	Moscow
Barrie	*The Admirable Crichton*	Edinburgh
Fitch	*The Girl With the Green Eyes*	New York

1 9 0 3

Hauptmann	*Rose Bernd*	Berlin
Halbe	*Der Strom*	Berlin
Schnitzler	*The Lonely Way*	Vienna
Wedekind	*Pandora's Box*	Nuremberg

1 9 0 4

Wedekind	*The Tenor*	Berlin
Barrie	*Peter Pan*	London
Synge	*Riders to the Sea* (Abbey Theater)	Dublin
Chekhov	*The Cherry Orchard* (Stanislavski)	Moscow

1 9 0 5

Shaw	*Man and Superman*	London

1 9 0 6

Hauptmann	*And Pippa Dances*	Berlin
Gorki	*Enemies* (Reinhardt)	Berlin
Wedekind	*Spring's Awakening* (Reinhardt)	Berlin
Shaw	*The Doctor's Dilemma*	London
Andreyev	*The Life of Man* (Meyerhold)	Moscow
Blok	*The Puppet Show* (Meyerhold)	Moscow

1 9 0 7

Strindberg	*The Dream Play*	Stockholm
Synge	*The Playboy of the Western World* (Abbey Theater)	Dublin
Zapolska	*Madame Dulska's Moral Code*	Warsaw

1 9 0 8

Strindberg	*The Ghost Sonata*	Stockholm
Maeterlinck	*The Bluebird* (Stanislavski)	Moscow

1 9 0 9

Bahr	*The Concert*	Vienna
Molnar	*Liliom*	Budapest
Fitch	*The City*	New York

1 9 1 0

Kokoschka	*Der brennende Dornbusch*	Berlin
Schnitzler	*Das weite Land*	Vienna
Schönherr	*Glaube und Heimat*	Vienna
Hamsun	*In the Grip of Life*	Oslo
Sheldon	*The Nigger*	New York

1 9 1 1

Hauptmann	*The Rats*	Berlin
Hofmannsthal	*Everyman* (Reinhardt)	Berlin
Sternheim	*The Underpants* (Reinhardt)	Berlin
Tolstoy	*The Living Corpse* (Stanislavski)	Moscow
Sheldon	*The Boss*	New York

1 9 1 2

Tolstoy	*The Light Shines in Darkness* (Reinhardt)	Berlin
Thoma	*Magdalena*	Berlin
Schnitzler	*Professor Bernhardi*	Vienna
Claudel	*The Tidings Brought to Mary* (Copeau)	Paris

1 9 1 3

Sternheim	*Bürger Schippel* (Reinhardt)	Berlin
Shaw	*Pygmalion*	Vienna
Claudel	*The Tidings Brought to Mary* (Dalcroze-Appia)	Hellerau
Sheldon	*Romance*	New York

1 9 1 4

Sternheim	*The Snob* (with Bassermann)	Berlin
Wildgans	*Armut*	Vienna

1 9 1 5

Schönherr	*Der Weibsteufel*	Vienna
Wildgans	*Liebe*	Vienna

1 9 1 6

Hasenclever	*Der Sohn*	Dresden
Chiarelli	*The Mask and the Face*	Rome
Galsworthy	*Justice* (with John Barrymore)	New York
O'Neill	*Bound East for Cardiff*	Provincetown

1 9 1 7

Sorge	*Der Bettler* (Reinhardt)	Berlin
Kornfeld	*Die Verführung*	Frankfurt
Kaiser	*Die Bürger von Calais*	Frankfurt
Kaiser	*From Morn to Midnight*	Munich
Apollinaire	*Les Mamelles de Tirésias*	Paris

1 9 1 8

Kaiser	*Gas*	Frankfurt
Unruh	*Ein Geschlecht* (Hartung)	Frankfurt
Rossi di San Secondo	*Marionette, che passione!*	Rome
Mayakovski	*Mystery Bouffe* (Meyerhold)	Moscow

1 9 1 9

Toller	*Transfiguration* (with Kortner)	Berlin
Goering	*Seeschlacht* (Reinhardt)	Berlin
Sternheim	*Tabula rasa*	Berlin
Sternheim	*1913* (Hartung)	Frankfurt

1 9 2 0

Schnitzler	*La Ronde*	Berlin
O'Neill	*The Emperor Jones* (Provincetown)	New York
Cohan and Gannt	*The Tavern*	New York
Capek	*RUR*	Prague

1 9 2 1

Toller	*Men and the Masses* (Fehling)	Berlin
Unruh	*Louis Ferdinand* (Hartung)	Darmstadt
Hofmannstahl	*Der Schwierige* (Stieler, with Waldau, Bergner)	Munich
Hasek	*Schweik* (Cabaret)	Prague
Pirandello	*Six Characters in Search of an Author*	Rome
O'Neill	*Anna Christie*	New York
Kaufman & Connelly	*Dulcy*	New York

1 9 2 2

Hofmannsthal	*Das Salzburger Grosse Welttheater* (Reinhardt)	Salzburg
Pirandello	*Six Characters . . .* (Pitoëff)	Paris
Cocteau	*Antigone* (Picasso scenery)	Paris
Pirandello	*Henry IV*	Rome
Capek	*The Insect Comedy*	Prague
Galsworthy	*Loyalties*	London
O'Neill	*The Hairy Ape*	New York
Shaw	*Back to Methuselah*	New York
Ansky	*The Dybbuk* (Vachtangov)	Moscow
Brecht	*Trommeln in die Nacht*	Munich

1 9 2 3

Brecht	*In the Jungle of Cities* (Engel)	Munich
Brecht	*Baal*	Leipzig
Romains	*Dr. Knock* (Jouvet)	Paris
Pirandello	*Naked*	Rome
Shaw	*Saint Joan*	New York
Rice	*The Adding Machine*	New York

1 9 2 4

Rehfisch	*Wer weint um Juckenack?*	Berlin
_juet	*Fahnen* (Piscator)	Berlin
Brecht	*Edward II* (Brecht)	Munich
Barlach	*Die Sündflut*	Stuttgart
Mell	*Apostelspiel*	Graz
Raynal	*Le Tombeau sous l'Arc de Triomphe*	Paris
M. Rostand	*L'Homme que j'ai tué*	Paris
O'Casey	*Juno and the Paycock*	Dublin
Szaniawski	*The Bird*	Warsaw
O'Neill	*Desire Under the Elms*	New York
Kelly	*The Show-off*	New York
Howard	*They Knew What They Wanted*	New York
Kaufman & Connelly	*Beggar on Horseback*	New York

1 9 2 5

Zuckmayer	*Der fröhliche Weinberg*	Berlin
Werfel	*Juarez and Maximilian*	Magdeburg
Rolland	*Le Jeu de l'amour et de la mort*	Paris
Langer	*Periphery*	Prague
Bergman	*The Nobel Prize*	Stockholm
Kaufman	*The Butter and Egg Man*	New York

1 9 2 6

Barlach	*Der blaue Boll* (Fehling/George)	Berlin
Brecht	*A Man's a Man*	Darmstadt
Bruckner	*Krankheit der Jugend*	Hamburg

1 9 2 6

Hauptmann	*Dorothea Angermann* (Reinhardt)	Vienna
Cocteau	*Orphée* (Pitoëff)	Paris
Romains	*Le Dictateur* (Jouvet)	Paris
O'Casey	*The Plough and the Stars*	Dublin
Howard	*The Silver Cord*	New York
O'Neill	*The Great God Brown*	New York
Kelly	*Craig's Wife*	New York
Tretyakov	*Roar, China!*	Moscow
Bulgakov	*The Days of the Turbins*	Moscow

1 9 2 7

Zuckmayer	*Schinderhannes* (with Klopfer/Dorsch)	Berlin
Maugham	*The Constant Wife*	London
Ivanov	*Armored Train 14-69*	Moscow
Toller	*Hoppla, Such Is Life!* (Piscator)	Berlin
Green	*In Abraham's Bosom*	New York
Behrman	*The Second Man*	New York

1 9 2 8

Zuckmayer	*Katharine Knie* (with Bassermann)	Berlin
Brecht	*The Threepenny Opera* (Engel)	Berlin
Bruckner	*Die Verbrecher* (Hilpert)	Berlin
Hasek (Brod/Reimann)	*Schwejk* (Piscator/Brecht/Pallenberg)	Berlin
Weisenborn	*U-Boat S4*	Berlin
Hofmannstahl	*Der Turm* (Falckenberg)	Munich
O'Neill	*Strange Interlude*	New York
Pagnol	*Topaze*	Paris
Giraudoux	*Siegfried* (Jouvet)	Paris

1 9 2 9

Kaiser	*Zwei Kravatten* (with Albers and Marlene Dietrich)	Berlin
Fr. Wolf	*Zyankali*	Berlin
Lampel	*Revolte im Erziehungshaus*	Berlin
Mehring	*Der Kaufmann von Berlin* (Piscator)	Berlin
Rehfisch-Herzog	*Die Affäre Dreyfus*	Berlin
Giraudoux	*Amphitryon 38* (Jouvet)	Paris
Pagnol	*Marius* (with Raimu)	Paris
O'Casey	*The Silver Tassie*	London
Sherriff	*Journey's End*	London
Shaw	*The Apple Cart*	Warsaw
Rice	*Street Scene*	New York
Behrman	*Holiday*	New York
Katayev	*Squaring the Circle*	Moscow

1 9 3 0

Bruckner	*Elizabeth of England* (Hilpert)	Berlin
Pirandello	*Tonight We Improvise* (Reinhardt)	Berlin

1 9 3 0

Plievier	*Des Kaisers Kulis*	Berlin
Brecht-Weill	*Mahagonny*	Leipzig
Cocteau	*The Human Voice*	Paris
Connelly	*The Green Pastures*	New York
Barry	*Hotel Universe*	New York
Riggs	*Green Grow the Lilacs*	New York
Anderson	*Elizabeth the Queen*	New York
Kaufman and Hart	*Once in a Lifetime*	New York

1 9 3 1

Zuckmayer	*The Captain from Koepenick* (Hilpert/Werner Krauss)	Berlin
Wolf	*Tai Yang erwacht* (Piscator)	Berlin
Unruh	*Phäa* (Buch)	Frankfurt
Giraudoux	*Judith* (Jouvet)	Paris
Obey	*Noah*	Paris
O'Neill	*Mourning Becomes Electra*	New York
Kaufman & Ryskind	*Of Thee I Sing*	New York
Gorki	*Somov and Others*	Moscow
Johnston	*The Moon in the Yellow River*	Dublin

1 9 3 2

Hauptmann	*Before Sundown* (Krauss)	Berlin
Goetz	*Dr. med. Hiob Prätorius*	Berlin
W. E. Schäfer	*Der 18. Oktober*	Munich
Anouilh	*The Ermine*	Paris
Pirandello	*To Find Oneself*	Rome
Gorki	*Yegor Bulychov and the Others*	Moscow
Vishnievski	*The Optimistic Tragedy*	Moscow

1 9 3 3

Hauptmann	*The Golden Harps* (Falckenberg)	Munich
Wolf	*Professor Mannheim* (later *Professor Mamlock*)	Zürich
Giraudoux	*Intermezzo* (Jouvet)	Paris
Lorca	*Blood Wedding*	Madrid
Kingsley	*Men in White*	New York

1 9 3 4

Lorca	*Yerma*	Madrid
Cocteau	*The Infernal Machine* (Jouvet)	Paris
O'Casey	*Within the Gates*	London
Gertrude Stein	*Four Saints in Three Acts*	New York
Hellman	*The Children's Hour*	New York

1 9 3 5

Giraudoux	*Tiger at the Gates*	Paris
Salacrou	*L'Inconnue d'Arras*	Paris
Eliot	*Murder in the Cathedral*	Canterbury Cathedral

1 9 3 5

Heyward & Gershwin	*Porgy and Bess*	New York
Sherwood	*The Petrified Forest*	New York
Odets	*Waiting for Lefty*	New York
Odets	*Awake and Sing*	New York
Anderson	*Winterset*	New York

1 9 3 6

Lorca	*The House of Bernarda Alba*	Madrid
Salacrou	*Un Homme comme les autres*	Paris
Kingsley	*Dead End*	New York

1 9 3 7

Lernet-Holenia	*Glastüren*	Vienna
Giraudoux	*Electra* (Jouvet)	Paris
Anouilh	*Traveler Without Luggage*	Paris
Priestley	*Time and the Conways*	London
Odets	*Golden Boy*	New York
Steinbeck	*Of Mice and Men*	New York
Alexey Tolstoy	*Ivan the Terrible*	Moscow
Mauriac	*Asmodée* (Copeau)	Paris

1 9 3 8

Cocteau	*Intimate Relations*	Paris
Anouilh	*Restless Heart* (Pitoëff)	Paris
Anouilh	*Thieves' Carnival* (Barsacq)	Paris
Salacrou	*La Terre est ronde* (Dullin/Barrault)	Paris
Spender	*Trial of a Judge*	London
Emlyn Williams	*The Corn Is Green*	London
Wilder	*Our Town* (Jed Harris)	New York
Sherwood	*Abe Lincoln in Illinois*	New York

1 9 3 9

Hauptmann	*Die Tochter der Kathedrale*	Berlin
Hauptmann	*Ulrich von Lichtenstein* (Müthel)	Vienna
Giraudoux	*Ondine* (Jouvet)	Paris
Eliot	*The Family Reunion*	London
Saroyan	*My Heart's in the Highlands*	New York
Saroyan	*The Time of Your Life*	New York
Lindsay & Crouse	*Life With Father*	New York
Hellman	*The Little Foxes*	New York
Kaufman and Hart	*The Man Who Came to Dinner*	New York

1 9 4 0

Kaiser	*Der Soldat Tanaka*	Zürich
Anouilh	*Time Remembered*	Paris
Thurber and Nugent	*The Male Animal*	New York

1 9 4 1

Hauptmann	*Iphigenie in Delphi*	Berlin
Rehberg	*Der Siebenjährige Krieg*	Berlin
Brecht	*Mother Courage* (Lindtberg)	Zürich
Pogodin	*The Chimes of the Kremlin*	Moscow
Cocteau	*The Typewriter*	Paris
Anouilh	*Eurydice*	Paris

1 9 4 2

Montherlant	*Queen After Death*	Paris
Wilder	*The Skin of Our Teeth* (Kazan)	New York
Steinbeck	*The Moon is Down*	New York

1 9 4 3

Brecht	*The Good Woman of Setzuan* (Steckel/Maria Becker)	Zürich
Brecht	*Galileo* (Steckel)	Zürich
Hochwalder	*The Strong Are Lonely*	Biel-Solothurn
Claudel	*The Satin Slipper* (Barrault)	Paris
Sartre	*The Flies* (Dullin)	Paris
Giraudoux	*Sodom et Gomorrah*	Paris
Rodgers and Hammerstein	*Oklahoma*	New York

1 9 4 4

Sartre	*No Exit*	Paris
Anouilh	*Antigone*	Paris
Camus	*The Misunderstanding*	Paris
Werfel & Behrman	*Jacobowsky and the Colonel*	New York

1 9 4 5

Frisch	*Nun singen sie wieder*	Zürich
Giraudoux	*The Madwoman of Chaillot* (Jouvet)	Paris
Camus	*Caligula* (with Gérard Philipe)	Paris
Williams	*The Glass Menagerie*	New York
Lorca	*The House of Bernarda Alba*	Buenos Aires
Leonov	*Invasion*	Moscow

1 9 4 6

Weisenborn	*Die Illegalen*	Berlin
Zuckmayer	*The Devil's General* (Hilpert/Knuth)	Zürich
Frisch	*Santa Cruz* (Hilpert)	Zürich
Frisch	*The Chinese Wall*	Zürich
Sartre	*The Victors*	Paris
Sartre	*The Respectful Prostitute*	Paris
Audiberti	*Quoat-Quoat*	Paris
de Filippo	*Questi fantasmi*	Naples
Priestley	*An Inspector Calls*	London

1 9 4 6

Rattigan	*The Winslow Boy*	London
O'Neill	*The Iceman Cometh*	New York
Rice	*Dream Girl*	New York
Hellman	*Another Part of the Forest*	New York
Kanin	*Born Yesterday*	New York
Zuckmayer	*The Devil's General*	New York
Simonov	*The Russian Question*	Moscow

1 9 4 7

Borchert	*The Man Outside*	Hamburg
Anouilh	*Romeo et Jeannette*	Paris
Anouilh	*Ring 'Round the Moon*	Paris
Audiberti	*Le Mal court*	Paris
Genet	*The Maids* (Jouvet)	Paris
Pirandello	*The Mountain Giants* (Strehler)	Milan
O'Neill	*A Moon for the Misbegotten*	New York
Williams	*A Streetcar Named Desire* (Kazan)	New York
Miller	*All My Sons* (Kazan)	New York
Brecht	*Galileo* (2nd version, with Charles Laughton)	Hollywood

1 9 4 8

Sartre	*Dirty Hands*	Paris
Camus	*State of Siege* (Barrault)	Paris
Anouilh	*Ardèle*	Paris
Anouilh	*Medea*	Paris
Roblès	*Montserrat*	Paris
Fry	*The Lady's Not For Burning*	London
Brecht	*The Caucasian Chalk Circle* (Carleton College Theater)	Northfield, Minnesota
Brecht	*Herr Puntila und sein Knecht* (Hirschfeld/Steckel)	Zürich

1 9 4 9

Frisch	*Als der Krieg zu Ende war*	Zürich
Camus	*The Just Assassins*	Paris
Betti	*Corruzione al Palazzo di Giustizia*	Rome
Eliot	*The Cocktail Party*	Edinburgh
Miller	*Death of a Salesman* (Kazan)	New York
Jeffers	*Medea* (with Judith Anderson)	New York

1 9 5 0

Strittmatter	*Katzgraben* (Brecht)	Berlin
Andres	*Gottes Utopia*	Düsseldorf
Zuckmayer	*Gesang im Feuerofen* (Hilpert)	Göttingen
Anouilh	*The Rehearsal* (Barrault)	Paris
Adamov	*L'Invasion*	Paris
Kafka-Barrault-Gide	*The Trial*	Paris
Ionesco	*The Bald Soprano*	Paris

1 9 5 0

De Filippo	*Napoli millionaria*	Naples
Fry	*Venus Observed*	London
Odets	*The Country Girl*	New York
Inge	*Come Back Little Sheba*	New York

1 9 5 1

Brecht-Dessau	*The Trial of Lucullus*	Berlin
Barlach	*Der Graf von Ratzeburg*	Darmstadt
Bernanos	*Les Dialogues des Carmélites* (Wälterlin)	Zürich
Sartre	*The Devil and the Good Lord* (Jouvet)	Paris
Anouilh	*Mademoiselle Colombe*	Paris
Cocteau	*Bacchus* (Barrault)	Paris
Marcel	*Rome n'est plus dans Rome*	Paris
Ionesco	*The Lesson*	Paris
Ustinov	*The Love of Four Colonels*	London
Williams	*The Rose Tattoo* (Kazan)	New York

1 9 5 2

Dürrenmatt	*Die Ehe des Herrn Mississippi* (Schweikart)	Munich
Rattigan	*The Deep Blue Sea*	London
Willems	*Bärenhäuter*	Amsterdam
Ionesco	*The Chairs*	Paris
O'Neill	*A Moon for the Misbegotten*	Columbus, Ohio

1 9 5 3

Kafka-Brod	*The Castle* (Noelte)	Berlin
Zuckmayer	*Ulla Winblad* (Hilpert)	Göttingen
Frisch	*Don Juan*	Zürich
Giraudoux	*Battle of Angels*	Paris
Sartre	*Kean* (Brasseur)	Paris
Anouilh	*The Lark*	Paris
Beckett	*Waiting for Godot* (Blin)	Paris
Ionesco	*Victims of Duty*	Paris
Eliot	*The Confidential Clerk*	Edinburgh
Whiting	*Marching Song*	London
Patrick	*The Teahouse of the August Moon*	New York/ London
Lagerkvist	*Barrabas*	Stockholm
Miller	*The Crucible*	New York
Williams	*Camino Real*	New York
Inge	*Picnic*	New York
R. Anderson	*Tea and Sympathy*	New York
Sastre	*Escuadria hacie la muerte*	Madrid

1 9 5 4

Hubalek	*Der Hauptmann und sein Held*	Berlin
Dürrenmatt	*Ein Engel kommt nach Babylon* (Schweikart/Ponto)	Munich

1 9 5 4

Montherlant	Port Royal	Paris
Fry	The Dark Is Light Enough (Peter Brook)	London
Wouk	The Caine Mutiny Court-Martial	New York

1 9 5 5

Zuckmayer	Das kalte Licht (Gründgens)	Hamburg
Weymann	Generationen	Berlin
Hey	Thymian und Drachentod (Hering)	Stuttgart
Faulkner	Requiem for a Nun (Lindtberg)	Zürich
Anouilh	Ornifle (with Pierre Brasseur)	Paris
Sartre	Nekrassov (Jean Meyer)	Paris
Adamov	Ping-Pong (Mauclair)	Paris
Wilder	Alcestiad	Edinburgh
Zardi	I Giacobini (Strehler)	Milan
Williams	Cat on a Hot Tin Roof (Kazan)	New York
Miller	A View From the Bridge	New York
Wilder	The Matchmaker (Guthrie)	New York

1 9 5 6

Hauptmann	Magnus Garbe (Stroux)	Düsseldorf
Ahlsen	Philemon und Baukis	Munich
Hacks	Die Eröffnung des indischen Zeitalters (Schweikart)	Munich
Jahnn	Thomas Chatterton	Hamburg
Mell	Jeanne d'Arc (Gielen)	Bregenz
Brecht	Die Tage der Kommune	Karl-Mark-Stadt
Dürrenmatt	The Visit (Wälterlin)	Zürich
Schehadé	L'Histoire de Vasco (Barrault)	Paris
Anouilh	Pauvre Bitos	Paris
Ionesco	The Chairs (Mauclair)	Paris
Marceau	The Egg	Paris
Vauthier	Fortissimo (Barrault)	Paris
O'Casey	Purple Dust	London
Osborne	Look Back in Anger	London
Behan	The Quare Fellow (Littlewood)	London
Ustinov	Romanoff and Juliet	London
Thomas	Under Milk Wood	Edinburgh
O'Neill	Long Day's Journey Into Night	Stockholm
Lerner & Loewe	My Fair Lady	New York

1 9 5 7

Brecht	Die Gesichte des Simone Machard (Buckwitz)	Frankfurt
Bruckner	Das irdene Wägelchen	Mannheim/Essen
Hochwälder	Die Herberge (Gielen)	Vienna
Wilder	Alcestiad (Lindtberg/Becker)	Zürich
Kafka-Brod	Amerika (Steckel)	Zürich

1 9 5 7

Beckett	*Endgame* (Blin)	London
Genet	*The Balcony*	London
Osborne	*The Entertainer* (with Olivier)	London
Williams	*Orpheus Descending* (Clurman)	New York
Saroyan	*The Cave Dwellers*	New York
O'Neill	*A Moon for the Misbegotten*	New York
Adamov	*Paolo Paoli*	Paris
O'Neill	*A Touch of the Poet*	Stockholm

1 9 5 8

Brecht	*Der aufhaltsame Aufstieg des Arturo Ui* (Palitzsch)	Stuttgart
Frisch	*The Firebugs* (Wälterlin)	Zürich
Ionesco	*The Killer* (Sellner)	Darmstadt
Marceau	*The Good Soup*	Paris
Beckett	*Krapp's Last Tape*	London
Behan	*The Hostage* (Littlewood)	London
Osborne & Creighton	*Epitaph for George Dillon*	London
Simpson	*The Hole*	London
Wesker	*Chicken Soup with Barley*	London
MacLeish	*J. B.* (Yale University)	New Haven, Conn.
	(Oskar Fritz Schuh)	Salzburg
Williams	*Garden District*	New York
Gibson	*Two for the Seesaw*	New York
O'Neill	*Hughie* (Gierow)	Stockholm
Eliot	*The Elder Statesman*	Edinburgh
Mrozek	*The Police*	Warsaw

1 9 5 9

Brecht	*Saint Joan of the Stockyards* (Gründgens)	Hamburg
Dürrenmatt	*Frank V* (Wälterlin)	Zürich
Genet	*The Balcony*	Berlin
Albee	*The Zoo Story*	Berlin
Ionesco	*Rhinoceros*	Dusseldorf
Camus	*The Possessed*	Paris
Anouilh	*The Fighting Cock*	Paris
Anouilh	*Becket*	Paris
Sartre	*The Condemned of Altona*	Paris
Delaney	*A Taste of Honey*	London
Arden	*Serjeant Musgrave's Dance*	London
Wesker	*Roots*	London
O'Casey	*Cock-a-Doodle Dandy*	Edinburgh
Williams	*Sweet Bird of Youth*	New York
Gelber	*The Connection* (Living Theater)	New York
Arbusov	*It Happened in Irkutsk*	Moscow

1 9 6 0

Schehadé	*Les Violettes* (Schalla)	Bochum
Saroyan	*Paris Comedy* (Steinboeck)	Vienna
Montherlant	*Le Cardinal d'Espagne* (with Ernst Deutsch)	Vienna
Ionesco	*Rhinoceros* (Barrault)	Paris
Pinter	*The Caretaker*	London
Wesker	*I'm Talking about Jerusalem*	London
Rattigan	*Ross* (with Alec Guinness)	London
Hellman	*Toys in the Attic*	New York
Williams	*Period of Adjustment*	New York
Richardson	*The Prodigal*	New York
De Filippo	*Pulcinella*	Milan

1 9 6 1

Genet	*The Screens*	Berlin
Frisch	*Andorra*	Zürich
Schehadé	*Le Voyage* (Barrault)	Paris
Osborne	*Luther*	Paris/London
Whiting	*The Devils* (Hall)	London
Kopit	*Oh Dad, Poor Dad*	London
Fry	*Curtmantle*	Tilburg/Holland
Williams	*The Night of the Iguana*	New York
Albee	*The American Dream*	New York

1 9 6 2

Dürrenmatt	*The Physicists*	Zürich
Hauptmann	*Die Atriden*	Berlin
Ionesco	*Le Piéton de l'air*	Dusseldorf
Valéry	*Mon Faust*	Paris
Audiberti	*La Fourmi dans le corps* (Comédie Française)	Paris
Ionesco	*Le Roi se meurt*	Paris
Wesker	*Chips with Everything*	London
Osborne	*Plays for England*	London
Wilder	*Plays for Bleecker Street*	New York
Albee	*Who's Afraid of Virginia Woolf?*	New York
Williams	*The Milk Train Doesn't Stop Here Anymore*	Spoleto

1 9 6 3

Ionesco	*Le Piéton de l'air* (Barrault)	Paris
Dürrenmatt	*Herkules und der Stall des Augias*	Zürich
Hochhuth	*The Deputy* (Piscator)	Berlin
Beckett	*Play*	Ulm

1 9 6 4

Miller	*After the Fall* (Kazan)	New York

BIBLIOGRAPHY

INTERNATIONAL MODERN DRAMA

General Studies:

Lionel Abel, *Metatheatre* (New York, 1953).

Eric Bentley, *In Search of Theater* (New York, 1953).

—— *The Playwright as Thinker* (New York, 1946).

Frank W. Chandler, *Modern Continental Playwrights* (New York, 1931).

Barrett H. Clark, *A Study of Modern Drama* (New York, 1938).

—— and George Freedley, eds., *A History of Modern Drama* (New York, 1947).

Toby Cole, ed., *Playwrights on Playwriting* (New York, 1960).

Robert Corrigan, ed., *Theatre in the Twentieth Century* (New York, 1963).

Thomas H. Dickinson, ed., *The Theatre in a Changing Europe* (New York, 1937).

Margret Dietrich, *Das moderne Drama* (Stuttgart, 1961).

Martin Esslin, *The Theatre of the Absurd* (New York, 1961).

Francis Fergusson, *The Human Image in Dramatic Literature* (New York, 1957).

Bamber Gascoigne, *Twentieth Century Drama* (London, 1962).

John Gassner, *Form and Idea in Modern Theatre* (New York, 1956).

—— *The Theatre in Our Times* (New York, 1954).

Rosamond Gilder, Hermione Rich Isaacs, Robert H. MacGregor, Edward Reed, eds., *Theatre Arts Anthology* (New York, 1950).

Isaac Goldberg, *The Drama of Transition* (Cincinnati, 1922).

Randolph Goodman, *Drama on Stage* (New York, 1961).

Mordecai Gorelik, *New Theatres for Old* (New York, 1940).

David I. Grossvogel, *Four Playwrights and a Postscript* (Ithaca, 1962).

James Huneker, *Egoists: A Book of Supermen* (London, 1909).

—— *Iconoclasts: A Book of Dramatists* (London, 1905).

Jean Jacquot, ed., *Le Théâtre moderne: hommes et tendances* (Paris, 1958).

Walter Kerr, *How Not to Write a Play* (New York, 1955).

Joseph Wood Krutch, *"Modernism" in Modern Drama* (Ithaca, 1953).

Martin Lamm, *Modern Drama* (Oxford, 1952).

Allan Lewis, *The Contemporary Theatre* (New York, 1962).

Ludwig Lewisohn, *The Modern Drama* (New York, 1915).

Frederick Lumley, *Trends in Twentieth Century Drama* (London, 1956; revised, 1961).

Siegfried Melchinger, *Theater der Gegenwart* (Frankfurt, 1956).

John Palmer, *Studies in the Contemporary Theatre* (Boston, 1927).

Ronald Peacock, *The Poet in the Theatre* (New York, 1946; revised, 1960).

George Oppenheimer, ed., *The Passionate Playgoer* (New York, 1958).

Elmer Rice, *The Living Theatre* (New York, 1959).

Peter Szondi, *Theorie des Modernen Dramas* (Frankfurt, 1959).

Raymond Williams, *Drama from Ibsen to Eliot* (London, 1952).

MODERN AMERICAN DRAMA

General Studies:

Harold Clurman, *The Fervent Years* (New York, 1945).

Alan Downer, *Fifty Years of American Drama 1900-1950* (Chicago, 1951).

—— *Recent American Drama* (Minneapolis, 1961).

Hallie Flanagan, *Arena* (New York, 1940).

John Gassner, *Theatre at the Crossroads* (New York, 1960).

Morgan Y. Himelstein, *Drama Was a Weapon: The Left-Wing Theatre in New York, 1929-1941* (New Brunswick, 1963).

Joseph Wood Krutch, *The American Drama since 1918* (New York, 1939; revised 1957).

Jordan Y. Miller, ed., *American Dramatic Literature* (New York, 1961).

Frank H. O'Hara, *Today in American Drama* (Chicago, 1939).

Arthur Hobson Quinn, *A History of American Drama from the Civil War to the Present Day* (New York, 1937).

Gerald Weales, *American Drama since World War II* (New York, 1962).

Collections of play reviews:

Brooks Atkinson, *Broadway Scrapbook* (New York, 1947).

Eric Bentley, *The Dramatic Event* (New York, 1954).

—— *What is Theatre?* (Boston, 1956).

John Mason Brown, *Broadway in Review* (New York, 1940).

—— *Seeing Things* (New York, 1946).

—— *The Modern Theatre in Revolt* (New York, 1929).

—— *Two on the Aisle* (New York, 1938).

—— *Dramatis Personae* (New York, 1963).

Harold Clurman, *Lies Like Truth* (New York, 1938).

Walter Kerr, *Pieces at Eight* (New York, 1957).

—— *The Theatre in Spite of Itself* (New York, 1963).

Ludwig Lewisohn, *The Drama and the Stage* (New York, 1922).

Mary McCarthy, *Sights and Spectacles* (New York, 1957).

George Jean Nathan, *Another Book on the Theatre* (New York, 1915).
—— *The Theatre in the Fifties* (New York, 1953).
—— *The Theatre Book of the Year, 1942-43* (New York, 1943). (This series continues through 1950-51).
Alexander Woollcott, *Enchanted Aisles* (New York, 1924).
—— *Going to Pieces* (New York, 1928).
—— *Shouts and Murmurs* (New York, 1922).
Stark Young, *The Flower in Drama* (New York, 1923).
—— *Immortal Shadows* (New York, 1948).

Individual authors:

Mabel Driscoll Bailey, *Maxwell Anderson: The Playwright as Prophet* (New York, 1957).
D. E. Jones, *The Plays of T. S. Eliot* (London, 1960).
Carol H. Smith, *T. S. Eliot's Dramatic Theory and Practice* (Princeton, 1963).
William Gibson, *The Seesaw Log* (New York, 1959).
Dennis Welland, *Arthur Miller* (Edinburgh, 1961).
Oscar Cargill, N. B. Fagin, and William J. Fisher, eds., *O'Neill and His Plays* (New York, 1961).
Barrett H. Clark, *Eugene O'Neill, The Man and His Plays* (New York, 1947).
Edwin Engel, *The Haunted Heroes of Eugene O'Neill* (Cambridge, Mass., 1953).
Arthur and Barbara Gelb, *O'Neill* (New York, 1962).
Clifford Leech, *Eugene O'Neill* (Edinburgh, 1963).
Sophus Keith Winther, *Eugene O'Neill* (New York, 1934; revised 1961).
Elmer Rice, *Minority Report* (New York, 1963).
Rex Burbank, *Thornton Wilder* (New York, 1961).
Signi Falk, *Tennessee Williams* (New York, 1961).
Benjamin Nelson, *Tennessee Williams: His Life and Work* (New York, 1961).
Nancy M. Tischler, *Tennessee Williams: Rebellious Puritan* (New York, 1961).

MODERN BRITISH DRAMA

General Studies:

W. A. Armstrong, ed., *Experimental Drama* (London, 1963).
John Russell Brown and Russell Harris, eds., *Contemporary Theatre* (London, 1962).
Denis Donoghue, *The Third Voice: Modern British and American Verse Drama* (Princeton, 1959).
Laurence Kitchin, *Mid-Century Drama* (London, 1960).
Sean O'Casey, *The Green Crow* (New York, 1956).
Ernest Reynolds, *Modern English Drama* (London, 1949).
George Bernard Shaw, *Shaw on Theatre* (New York, 1958).
John Russell Taylor, *Anger and After: A Guide to the New British Drama* (London, 1962).
J. C. Trewin, *Dramatists of Today* (London, 1954).
Glynne Wickham, *Drama in a World of Science* (London, 1962).

Collections of play reviews:

James Agate, *Buzz Buzz* (London, 1918), *An Anthology* (London, 1961), and many other volumes.
Max Beerbohm, *Around Theatres* (London, 1953).
Nigel Dennis, *Dramatic Essays* (London, 1962).
Desmond MacCarthy, *Theatre* (London, 1954).
George Bernard Shaw, *Our Theatres in the Nineties*, 3 volumes (London, 1932).
Kenneth Tynan, *Curtains* (New York, 1961).
T. C. Worsley, *The Fugitive Art* (London, 1952).

IRISH THEATER

Una Ellis-Fermor, *The Irish Dramatic Movement* (London, 1939; revised, 1954).
Lady Augusta Gregory, *Our Irish Theatre* (London, 1913).
Peter Kavanagh, *The Irish Theatre* (New York, 1950).
A. E. Malone, *The Irish Drama* (London, 1929).
Lennox Robinson, *Ireland's Abbey Theatre* (London, 1951).
—— ed., *The Irish Theatre* (London, 1939).
Alan Simpson, *Beckett and Behan and a Theatre in Dublin* (London, 1962).
W. B. Yeats, *Plays and Controversies* (London, 1923).

INDIVIDUAL AUTHORS

W. A. Darlington, *J. M. Barrie* (New York, 1938).
Robert Greacen, *The Art of Noel Coward* (Aldington, 1953).
V. Dupont, *John Galsworthy: The Dramatic Artist* (Toulouse, n. d.).
Leon Schalit, *John Galsworthy, a Survey* (London, 1929).
C. B. Purdom, *Harley Granville Barker* (London, 1955).
Elizabeth Coxhead, *Lady Gregory: A Literary Portrait* (New York, 1961).
Robert Hogan, *The Experiments of Sean O'Casey* (New York, 1960).
David Krause, *Sean O'Casey: The Man and His Work* (London, 1960).
Eric Bentley, *Bernard Shaw* (Norfolk, Conn., 1947; revised, New York, 1957).
G. K. Chesterton, *George Bernard Shaw* (London, 1909).
St. John Ervine, *Bernard Shaw* (New York, 1956).
Archibald Henderson, *George Bernard Shaw: Man of the Century* (New York, 1956).
Louis Kronenberger, ed., *Shaw: A Critical Survey* (Cleveland, 1953).
Desmond MacCarthy, *Shaw* (London, 1951).
Arthur N. Nethercot, *Men and Supermen: The Shavian Portrait Gallery* (Cambridge, Mass., 1954).
Hesketh Pearson, *G. B. S.: A Full Length Portrait* (New York, 1942).
—— *G. B. S.: A Postscript* (New York, 1950).
R. F. Rattray, *Bernard Shaw: A Chronicle* (New York, 1951).

David H. Greene and Edward M. Stephens, *J. M. Synge* (New York, 1959).

Hesketh Pearson, *Oscar Wilde: His Life and Wit* (New York, 1946).

Oscar Wilde, *The Letters,* edited by Rupert Hart-Davis (New York, 1962).

Peter Ure, *Yeats the Playwright* (London, 1963).

Helen Hennessy Vendler, *Yeats's VISION and the Later Plays* (Cambridge, Mass., 1963).

F. A. C. Wilson, *W. B. Yeats and Tradition* (New York, 1958).

—— *Yeats's Iconography* (1960).

MODERN FRENCH DRAMA

General Studies:

Marc Beigbeder, *Le Théâtre en France depuis la Liberation.* (Paris, 1959).

Joseph Chiari, *The Contemporary French Theatre: The Flight from Naturalism* (London, 1958).

Frank W. Chandler, *The Contemporary Drama of France* (Boston, 1920).

Barrett H. Clark, *Contemporary French Dramatists* (Cincinnati, 1915).

Wallace Fowlie, *Dionysus in France: A Guide to Contemporary French Theater* (New York, 1960).

David I. Grossvogel, *The Self-Conscious Stage in Modern French Drama* (New York, 1958). (Reprinted 1961, as *20th Century French Drama.*)

Leonard Cabell Pronko, *Avant-Garde: The Experimental Theater in France* (Berkeley, 1962).

Jacques Guicharnaud (with June Beckelman), *Modern French Theatre from Giraudoux to Beckett* (New Haven, 1961).

Pierre-Henri Simon, *Théâtre-Destin* (Paris, 1959).

H. A. Smith, *Main Currents of Modern French Drama* (New York, 1925).

Special issues of *Yale French Studies* (Nos. V, XIV, XXIX) and *L'Esprit Créateur* (Winter, 1962).

Collections of play reviews:

Jacques Copeau, *Critiques d'un autre temps* (Paris, 1923).

Jean-Jacques Gautier, *Paris-sur-Scene* (Paris, 1951).

—— *Deux Fauteuils d'orchestre* (Paris, 1962).

Robert Kemp, *La Vie du théâtre* (Paris, 1956).

Gabriel Marcel, *L'Heure théâtrale* (Paris, 1960).

Studies of individual authors:

Leonard Cabell Pronko, *The World of Jean Anouilh* (Berkeley, 1961).

Ruby Cohn, *Samuel Beckett: The Comic Gamut* (New Brunswick, 1962).

Frederick J. Hoffman, *Samuel Beckett: The Language of Self* (Carbondale, 1962).

Hugh Kenner, *Samuel Beckett* (New York, 1961).

Paul Blanchart, *Henry Becque* (Paris, 1930).

Germaine Brée, *Camus* (New Brunswick, 1959).

John Cruickshank, *Albert Camus and the Literature of Revolt* (London, 1959).

Joseph Chiari, *The Poetic Drama of Paul Claudel* (London, 1954).

Neal Oxenhandler, *Scandal and Parade: The Theatre of Jean Cocteau* (New Brunswick, 1957).

Joseph H. McMahon, *The Imagination of Jean Genet* (New Haven, 1963).

James C. McLaren, *The Theatre of André Gide* (Baltimore, 1953).

Donald Inskip, *Jean Giraudoux: The Making of a Dramatist* (London, 1958).

Laurent LeSage, *Jean Giraudoux: His Life and Works* (Pennsylvania State University, 1959).

Richard N. Coe, *Eugene Ionesco* (Edinburgh, 1961).

Maurice Cranston, *Jean-Paul Sartre* (Edinburgh, 1962).

Edith Kern, ed., *Sartre* (Englewood Cliffs, 1962).

Iris Murdoch, *Sartre* (New Haven, 1953).

Philip Thody, *Jean-Paul Sartre* (London, 1960).

MODERN GERMAN DRAMA

General Studies:

Julius Bab, *Das Theater der Gegenwart* (Leipzig, 1928).

Bernard Diebold, *Anarchie im Drama* (Frankfurt, 1921).

H. F. Garten, *Modern German Drama* (London, 1959).

Walter H. Sokel, ed., *An Anthology of German Expressionist Drama* (New York, 1963).

—— *The Writer in Extremis: Expressionism in Twentieth Century German Literature* (Stanford, 1959).

Benno von Wiese, ed., *Das Deutsche Dràma,* Volume II (Dusseldorf, 1958).

Collections of play reviews:

Julius Bab, *Über den Tag Hinaus* (Heidelberg, 1960).

Herbert Jhering, *Von Reinhardt bis Brecht,* 3 volumes (Berlin, 1961).

Alfred Kerr, *Die Welt in Drama* (Cologne, 1954).

Studies of individual authors:

Bernard Dort, *Lecture de Brecht* (Paris, 1960).

Martin Esslin, *Brecht* (New York, 1960).

Ronald Gray, *Bertolt Brecht* (Edinburgh, 1961).

Werner Hecht, *Brechts Weg zum epischen Theater* (Berlin, 1962).

Herbert Lüthy, *Von armen Bert Brecht* (Frankfurt, 1952).

Hans Mayer, *Bertolt Brecht und die Tradition* (Pfullingen, 1961).

John Willett, *The Theatre of Bertolt Brecht* (London, 1959).

Hans Bänziger, *Frisch und Dürrenmatt* (Berne, 1960).

Elisabeth Brock-Sulzer, *Dürrenmatt* (Zurich, 1960).

Eduard Stäuble, *Max Frisch* (Amriswil, 1960).

C. F. W. Behl, *Wege zu Gerhart Hauptmann* (Goslar, 1948).

H. F. Garten, *Gerhart Hauptmann* (Cambridge, Eng., 1954).

Margaret Sinden, *Gerhart Hauptmann: The Prose Plays* (Toronto, 1957).

B. J. Kenworthy, *Georg Kaiser* (Oxford, 1957).

Sol Liptzin, *Arthur Schnitzler* (New York, 1932).

MODERN ITALIAN DRAMA

Nicola Chiaramonte, *La situazione drammatica* (Milan, 1960).

Lander MacClintock, *The Age of Pirandello* (Bloomington, 1951).

Thomas Bishop, *Pirandello and the French Theatre* (New York, 1960).

Walter Starkie, *Luigi Pirandello* (New York, 1937).

Domenico Vittorini, *The Drama of Luigi Pirandello* (Philadelphia, 1935).

MODERN SPANISH DRAMA

Jean-Paul Borel, *Théâtre de l'impossible* (Neufchatel, 1963).

Walter Starkie, *Jacinto Benavente* (London, 1924).

Arturo Barea, *Lorca, the Poet and his People* (New York, 1949).

Roy Campbell, *Lorca: An Appreciation of His Poetry* (New Haven, 1952).

Manuel Duran, ed., *Lorca* (Englewood Cliffs, 1962).

Edwin Honig, *Garcia Lorca* (Norfolk, Conn., 1944).

Robert Lima, *The Theatre of Garcia Lorca* (New York, 1963).

MODERN SCANDINAVIAN DRAMA

Muriel C. Bradbrook, *Ibsen the Norwegian* (London, 1946).

Brian W. Downs, *A Study of Six Plays by Ibsen* (Cambridge, Eng., 1950).

—— *Ibsen: The Intellectual Background* (Cambridge, Eng., 1946).

Angel Flores, ed., *Ibsen* (New York, 1937).

Halvdan Koht, *The Life of Ibsen* (New York, 1931).

F. L. Lucas, *Ibsen and Strindberg* (London, 1962).

James W. McFarlane, *Ibsen and the Temper of Norwegian Literature* (London, 1960).

John Northam, *Ibsen's Dramatic Method* (London, 1953).

George Bernard Shaw, *The Quintessence of Ibsenism* (London, 1891).

P. F. D. Tennant, *Ibsen's Dramatic Technique* (Cambridge, Eng., 1948).

Hermann J. Weigand, *The Modern Ibsen* (New York, 1925).

Adolph E. Zucker, *Ibsen, the Master Builder* (London, 1929).

Alrik Gustafson, *A History of Swedish Literature* (Minneapolis, 1961).

Arthur Adamov, *Strindberg dramaturge* (Paris, 1955).

Carl E. W. L. Dahlström, *Strindberg's Dramatic Expressionism* (Ann Arbor, 1930).

Walter Johnson, *Strindberg and the Historical Drama* (Seattle, 1963).

B. G. Madsen, *Strindberg's Naturalistic Theatre* (Seattle, 1962).

Brita M. E. Mortensen and Brian W. Downs, *Strindberg: An Introduction to His Life and Works* (Cambridge, Eng., 1949).

Elizabeth Sprigge, *The Strange Life of August Strindberg* (New York, 1949).

P. M. Mitchell, *A History of Danish Literature* (New York, 1958).

MODERN RUSSIAN DRAMA

General Studies:

Alexander Bakshy, *The Path of the Modern Russian Stage* (Boston, 1918).

Faubion Bowers, *Broadway, U. S. S. R.* (New York, 1959).

Ben W. Brown, *Theatre at the Left* (Providence, 1938).

Huntly Carter, *The New Spirit in the Russian Theatre, 1917-1928* (London, 1929).

H. W. L. Dana, *Drama in Wartime Russia* (New York, 1943).

—— *A Handbook on Soviet Drama* (New York, 1938).

Rëné Fülöp-Miller and Joseph Gregor, *The Russian Theatre* (Philadelphia, 1930).

Nikolai A. Gorchakov, *The Theatre in Soviet Russia* (New York, 1957).

Norris Houghton, *Moscow Rehearsals* (New York, 1936).

—— *Return Engagement* (New York, 1962).

Joseph Macleod, *Actors Cross the Volga* (London, 1946).

—— *The New Soviet Theatre* (London, 1943).

Vsevolod Meyerhold, *Le Théâtre théâtral* (Paris, 1963).

Vladimir Nemirovich-Danchenko, *My Life in the Russian Theatre* (London, 1937).

Oliver M. Sayler, *Inside the Moscow Art Theatre* (New York, 1925).

—— *The Russian Theatre* (New York, 1920, 1922, 1923).

Marc Slonim, *Russian Theater: From the Empire to the Soviets* (New York, 1961).

Konstantin Stanislavsky, *My Life in Art* (Boston, 1924).

Andre Van Gyseghem, *Theatre in Soviet Russia* (London, 1943).

Leo Wiener, *The Contemporary Drama of Russia* (Boston, 1924).

Peter Yershov, *Comedy in the Soviet Theater* (New York, 1956).

Individual authors:

W. H. Bruford, *Chekhov* (London, 1957).

—— *Chekhov and His Russia* (London, 1947).

William Gerhardi, *Anton Chekhov* (New York, 1923).

Ronald Hingley, *Chekhov* (London, 1950).

S. S. Koteliansky, ed., *Anton Tchekhov: Literary and Theatrical Reminiscences* (London, 1927).

—— and P. Tomlinson, *Life and Letters of Anton Tchekhov* (New York, 1925).

David Magarschack, *Chekhov: A Life* (New York, 1953).

—— *Chekhov the Dramatist* (London, 1952).

Ernest Simmons, *Chekhov: A Biography* (Boston, 1962).

Vladimir Yermilov, *A. P. Chekhov* (Moscow, n. d.).

Nina Gourfinkel, *Gorky* (New York, 1960).

Alexander Kaun, *Maxim Gorki and His Russia* (New York, 1931).

The additional entries below list playwrights whose claims on our attention have recently become too great to be overlooked, whether because of new writings, new productions or new editions of their works, which appeared after the main body of this book went to press.

CLARKE, Austin, b. 1896, Irish poet and dramatist. *The Son of Learning* (1927, comedy); *The Flame* (1932, one act); *Sister Eucharia* (1939); *Black Fast* (1942, a "poetic farce," one act); *The Kiss* (1942, one-act comedy, from French of Theodore de Banville); *As the Crow Flies* (1942, radio play); *The Plot is Ready* (1943); *The Viscount of Blarney* (1944); *The Second Kiss* (1946, one-act comedy); *The Plot Succeeds* (1950, "a poetic pantomime"); *The Moment Next to Nothing* (1958).

DENKER, Henry, b. 1912, American dramatist. *Time Limit* (1956, with Ralph Berkey, brainwashing and collaboration in the Korean War); *A Far Country* (1961, Sigmund Freud's first case); *Venus at Large* (1962, about a film star who resembles Marilyn Monroe); *A Case of Libel* (1963).

DORST, Tankred, b. 1925. German dramatist. *Gesellschaft im Herbst* (1959); *Die Kurve* (1960, one act); *Freiheit für Clemens* (1960, one-act farce); *Grosse Schmährede an der Stadtmauer* (1961, one act); *Der tote Oberst* (1961, comedy).

DUBILLARD, Roland, young French dramatist. *Naïves Hirondelles* (1961); *La Maison d'os* (1962).

DURAS, Marguerite, b. 1914 in Indo-China, French novelist and dramatist, wrote script of film *Hiroshima mon amour*. *Le Square* (1956, two-person play); *Barrage contre la Pacifique* (1959, adapted from her novel); *Les Viaducs de la Seine-et-Oise* (1960); *La Bête dans la jungle* (1963, from the story by Henry James).

GATTI, Armand, b. 1924, French dramatist. *Le Poisson noir* (published 1958, Chinese setting); *Le Crapaud-buffle* (1959, a Latin American dictator and an Inca legend; directed by Jean Vilar); *L'Enfant-rat* (published 1960); *Le Voyage du grand'Tchou* (published 1960); *Le Quetzal* (published 1960); *La Vie imaginaire de l'éboueur Auguste G.* (1962, directed by Planchon); *Chroniques d'une planète provisoire* (1962), *La deuxième Existence du camp de Tatenberg* (1962).

HANLEY, James, b. 1901, Dublin. Novelist, short story writer and dramatist. *Say Nothing* (1962. Adapted from his novel of the same title. A young man takes up lodgings in a house in the North of England and becomes deeply involved with a curious family united by tragedy); *The Inner Journey* (1963).

HANLEY, William, b. 1931. American dramatist. Off-Broadway success with program of one-act plays: *Mrs. Dally Has a Lover* and *Whisper into My Good Ear* (1962); *Today Is Independence Day* (published 1963, one act).

HANSBERRY, Lorraine, b. 1930, American dramatist. *A Raisin in the Sun* (1959, middle-class Negro life in Chicago); *The Sign in Sidney Brustein's Window* (1964).

KENAN, Amos, b. 1927, Israeli dramatist, living in Paris, writing in French. *Le Lion* (*The Lion*); *Le Ballon; Un Froid de chien* (one act); *Voilà l'homme* (three one-act plays).

LENZ, Siegfried, b. 1926, German novelist and dramatist. *Die Zeit der Schuldlosen* (1962; some prisoners have to find and surrender the guilty among them. Thesis: in a time of injustice, no one is without guilt. Only one has murdered, but could have done it).

LIVINGS, Henry, b. 1930, English dramatist. *Jack's Horrible Luck* (television play, written 1958, produced 1961); *The Arson Squad* (television play); *The Rise and Fall of a Nignog* (unproduced television play); *Jim All Alone* (television play); *The Quick and the Dead Quick* (privately performed 1961, about François Villon); *Stop It, Whoever You Are* (1961, a comedy, the suffering and death of an old lavatory attendant); *Big Soft Nelly* (1962); *Nil Carborundum* (1962); *Kelly's Eye* (1963, drama of a killer); and other television plays.

MICHAELS, Sidney, b. 1927, American dramatist. Adapted Billetdoux's *Tchin-Tchin* for Broadway (1962); *Dylan* (1964, about Dylan Thomas).

MICHELSEN, Hans Günther, b. 1920, German dramatist. *Stienz* (1963); *Lappschiess* (1963); *Feierabend 1 und 2* (1963).

MROZEK, Slavomir, b. 1930, Polish dramatist. Best known for his satire *The Police* (1958, translated). *The Martyrdom of Peter Ohey* (1959, tragic farce); *The Elephant* (one act, translated); *The Turkey-cock* (1960, satire); *Striptease* (1961, satire); *Karol* (1961, satire); *On the High Seas* (1963).

OBALDIA, René de, b. 1918, French novelist and dramatist. His "impromptus" (one-act plays) include *Le Grand Vizir* (1956); *Le Défunt* (1957); *Le Sacrifice du bourreau* (1957); *L'Azote* (1960); *Les Jumeaux étincelants* (1960); *Édouard et Agrippine* (published 1961, *Edward and Agrippina*); *Poivre de Cayenne* (1961); Other plays: *Génousie* (1960); *Le Satyre de la villette.*

PLANCHON, Roger, b. 1931, French director, actor, and dramatist. *La Remise* (1962, realistic drama of the life of French peasants); *O M'man Chicago* (1963, musical about Al Capone).

SCHISGAL, Murray, b. 1929, American dramatist. *Ducks and Lovers* (1961); *The Typists* and *The Tiger* (1963, off-Broadway program of one-act plays, produced in London in earlier version); *Luv* (1963).

SIMPSON, Norman Frederick, b. 1919, English dramatist. Plays suggestive of Ionesco and Lewis Carroll. *A Resounding Tinkle* (1957. Performed in two-act and one-act versions); *The Hole* (1957, one act); *One Way Pendulum* (1959, "A Farce in a New Dimension"); *The Form* (1961, one act); revue sketches.

VALLE-INCLÁN, Ramón, 1866-1936, Spanish poet, novelist, and dramatist. (The first date given for each play is that of publication.) *Tragedia de ensueño* (1903, one act); *Comedia de ensueño* (1903, *The Dream Comedy,* one act); *El Marqués de Bradomín* (1907, "romantic colloquies"); *Aguila de blasón* (1907, performed 1960, first of a series of "barbaric comedies," about a *hidalgo* and his sons); *Romance de lobos* (1908, "barbaric comedy"); *El yermo de las almas* (1908, "episodes of intimate life"); *Cuento de abril* (1910, performed 1910, "rhymed scenes in an extravagant manner"); *Voces de gesta* (1911, performed 1912, "pastoral tragedy" in verse); *La Marquesa Rosalinda* (1913, performed 1912, "sentimental and grotesque farce"); *El embrujado* (1913, "tragedy of the land of Salnes"); *Farsa infantil de la cabeza del dragón* (1914, performed 1910, *The Dragon's Head*); *Farsa italiana de la enamorada del rey* (1920); *Farsa y licencia de la reina castiza* (1920); *Divinas palabras* (1920, performed 1933, performed by Barrault and his company in Paris, 1963; "tragicomedy of village life"); *Los cuernos de don Friolera* (1921, the first *esperpento*—"something grotesque"); *Cara de plata* (1922, "barbaric comedy"); *Luces de bohemia* (1924, performed 1963, by Jean Vilar's company in Paris, *esperpento*); *La rosa de papel* (1924, "melodrama for marionettes"); *La cabeza del Bautista* (1924, performed 1924, "melodrama for marionettes"); *Ligazón* (1927, "*auto* for silhouettes"); *Sacrilegio* (1927, "*auto* for silhouettes"); *Las galas del difunto* (1930, *esperpento*); *La hija del capitán* (1930, *esperpento*).

VIAN, Boris, 1920-1959, French dramatist. *L'Équarrissage pour tous* (1950), *Les Batisseurs d'empire ou le Schmurz* (1959, *The Empire Builders.* According to Vian, this experimental work can be played "as farce, but also as national tragedy, as realistic drama, or as allegory"; it "should embarrass the spectator."); *Le Dernier des métiers* and *Le Goûter des généraux.*